Kodai School Classes of 55 & 56

Paul Heusinkveld

Kodai School
Classes of 55 & 56

Missionary Kids Growing up in India

Paul Heusinkveld

Mindscapes Press

© 2024 Paul Heusinkveld
All rights reserved

Mindscapes Books
1462 Stoney Lake Dr.
Holland, MI 49424
United States of America

MindscapesBooks@gmail.com

Printed in the United States of America

ISBN: 978-0-9908901-7-1

Author and General Editor
Paul A. Heusinkveld

Project Editor
Mary Coleman Lowry

Layout and Cover Design
Paul A. Heusinkveld

Artwork
David Wiebe and Bruce Peck

Cover: Painting of Kodaikanal by Grace Hiebert Zapata who attended Kodai School from 1938 to 1942 when she was forced to leave India because of WWII (she would have graduated in 1947).

Mindscapes Press

To the parents of the Kodai School classes of '55 and '56, who gave their children countless adventures, showing them how magnificent the world can be.

Maps

Contents

Also by Paul Heusinkveld

3-D Space Mazes
Elephant Baseball, A Missionary Kid's Tale
Margaret's Mission
Mindscapes, Escher's Challenge
Kodai School Class of 1968
Returning to Kodai School
From Polio to Arabia (pending)
A Call for Dutch Immigration (pending)

Preface

Kodai is an idyllic village in the mountains of South India. At 7,000 feet, its pristine air and magnificent views overlooking the plains below come as close to Shangri-La as anyplace on Earth. For most kids at Kodai School, Kodai was a little bit of heaven, for some it was a little bit of that other place. For me it was mostly the former.

P. A. Heuser

My formative years were spent in a boarding school on a mountain top in South India.[1] That period of adolescence formed my mindset, personality, and world view.

I shared the experience with hundreds of "Kodai kids" and maintain a close relationship with many of them—who are not unlike brothers and sisters—and I believe this book speaks for all of us.

Although Kodai School was mostly for missionary children, a good cross-section of the student body was not. It might be assumed that we missionary kids felt very different from those who came from the diplomatic, business and non-government organization (NGO) families, but—thank goodness—that was not the case. For the most part we felt the common bond of humanity and were close friends no matter who our parents were and what background—cultural, religious, linguistic, national—we came from. None of these attributes dictated who our friends were, who we chose as roommates, who we sat with in the dining room, who we identified with, etc.

The student body at Kodai School was a surprisingly—and pleasantly—egalitarian community where diversity reigned supreme and was thoroughly

---

[1] South India, also known as Dakshina Bharata or Peninsular India, consists of the Indian States Andhra Pradesh, Karnataka, Kerala, Tamil Nadu, and Telangana, as well as the union territories of Lakshadweep and Puducherry.

enjoyed. And this was done without consciously striving for it or even thinking about such matters.

For the most part, we students at Kodai School had unique backgrounds. We grew up in a culture vastly different from that of our home citizenship and language. We were bilingual, lived in multiple cultures, ate all kinds of different cuisines, witnessed our fellow humans living in abject poverty or sumptuous wealth, traveled extensively, witnessed a vast swath of human experience, and knew at a gut-level that there was no one normal—or even correct—way to live or view life. Our broad experiences afforded us a view of the greater human experience. We saw how broken the world can be, as well as much reason for believing in a bright future for humanity.

At a visceral level, we had no doubt there was no single approach to life, to understanding what is good and what is not, what is valuable and what isn't.

We were quite different.

We were not only different from the local population, but even—and significantly so—from our parents, as well as the teaching staff at the school who had grown up in the western world.

A consequence of this expansive experience—and probably coupled with the missionary zeal that pervaded life at Kodai School—is that many of us now sense a moral obligation to share the insights, perspectives, and lessons that came from such a childhood.

How to achieve that is the challenge.

Hopefully, this book may, in part, achieve that goal. Herein is a collection of stories about ourselves, our school, and the environment we grew up in. There are insights into history, other cultures and life in general—some humorous, some sad, some dramatic, and all real. I'm pleased that I was able to save these amazing stories and document them for others.

Also herein, is a collection of paintings by David Wiebe and etchings by Bruce Peck to help us along this journey. Many thanks to David and Bruce for sharing their India artwork. Their artwork catches the essence of India in a way that speaks to heart and soul.

In many ways, this book is a commonly shared quest for all alumni of Kodai School to come to terms with our exotic, cross-culture roots. There are probably hundreds of stories like this, but few are written and the vast majority will be lost from memory—the adventures forgotten, the lessons learned but not passed on, the documenting of the human spirit that is lost, and thus not there to inspire in a time when such stories are sorely needed.

As with most cross-culture kids, we developed a broad and open mindset. This was necessary for us to come to grips with the seemingly conflicting realities and truths inherent with each of the different cultures, languages, and nations we lived in and traveled to and from. We learned to cope and to accommodate to the vast changes. There are almost certainly some valuable insights worth sharing.

Paul Heusinkveld
Hope College, Holland, Michigan
August 2024

Perumal mountain viewed from Kodai. (D. Wiebe)

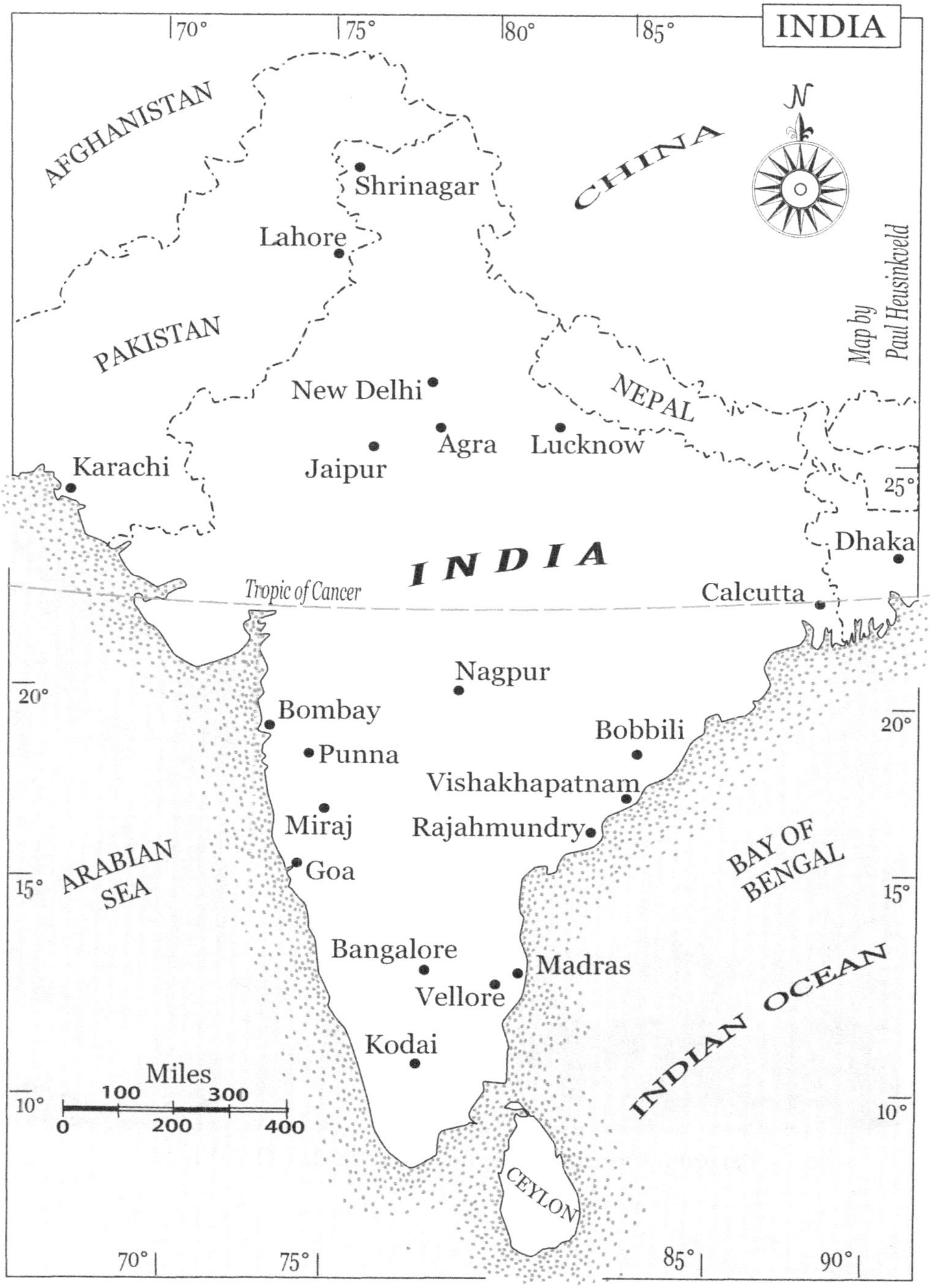

INDIA
70°
75°
80°
85°
90°
25°
20°
15°
10°
AFGHANISTAN
CHINA
PAKISTAN
NEPAL
INDIA
Shrinagar
Lahore
New Delhi
Agra
Lucknow
Jaipur
Karachi
Dhaka
Calcutta
Tropic of Cancer
Nagpur
Bombay
Punna
Bobbili
Vishakhapatnam
Miraj
Rajahmundry
Goa
ARABIAN SEA
BAY OF BENGAL
Bangalore
Madras
Vellore
Kodai
INDIAN OCEAN
CEYLON
Miles
0
100
200
300
400
N
Map by Paul Heusinkveld

CHAPTER 1

Introduction

"The answer to the question, 'Who am I?' can only be given if we ask, 'What is my story?' and that can only be answered if there is an answer to the further question, 'What is the whole story of which my story is a part?'"

Lesslie Newbigin[2]

When the wind blows away the mists there's perhaps no fairer scene than that from Coaker's Walk—a narrow footpath meandering atop a steep mountain escarpment,[3] overlooking the vast plains of Southern India six thousand feet below. Distant patterned landscapes of rice paddies, wending rivers, and thatched-roof villages and hamlets are ever-changing under the moving shadows of massive clouds drifting overhead. It's a majestic view one can watch for hours and never tire of. On a clear day, you can see about 150 miles to the distant eastern horizon where the Indian Ocean's waters shimmer under the equatorial sunshine. There's a sensation of magic in the air wafting up from the grassy slopes and tree-lined valleys below.

Next to Coaker's Walk lies the village of Kodaikanal where views of the surrounding mountains are only slightly less dramatic, though still awe-inspiring.

---

[2] Lesslie Newbigin (1909-1998) was a theologian who spent much of his life as a missionary in South India. His children attended Kodai School.

[3] The escarpment is part of the Western Ghats—also called The Great Escarpment of India—which stretch for 990 miles along the west coast of the Indian peninsula. UNESCO has designated the area as one of the eight biodiversity hotspots in the world. The Western Ghats are older than the Himalayas and influence India's monsoon weather patterns by intercepting the rain-laden monsoon winds. The average elevation is about 4,000 feet and the highest peak is 8,842 feet. (Wikipedia)

Within the village stand the granite-stone buildings that form the campus of Kodai School. The roofs of the buildings—of orange-red, terracotta shingles—contrast sharply against the lush green jungle surrounding the village. Once beheld, these views reside in one's soul forever.

Spending our formative years in Kodai left our impressionable minds with a sense of awe and wonder at how magnificent the world can be. This is where the classes of '55 and '56 grew up and formed their world view, forever coloring their thoughts, dreams, and aspirations.

* * *

Kodai School was founded as a missionary boarding school and most of the students were children drawn from a variety of missionary church denominations in India.

To better understand what life was like for the students and the families they came from, some background on the missionary movement is helpful.

During the Great Missionary Movement from the early 1800s to the 1970s, tens of thousands of Christian missionaries from America and Europe left their homelands to live austere lives of service in the "mission field"—primarily Asia and Africa—with the goal of saving the world. Their mission was to heal body, mind, and soul through medicine, education, and spiritual growth.

With unwavering resolve—sometimes seemingly recklessly so—missionaries ventured into the unknown, living lives of adventure, danger, and an overpowering sense of vocation. They felt "called" and accepted high risks in order to respond to their calling. Sadly, most of their stories have either gone untold or been forgotten; many missionaries believed writing about their careers was akin to bragging and did not express the assumed humility of their roles. Fortunately, some of their stories have been told, despite the humble reticence of the storytellers.

Most missionaries were married and had families. In fact, it is likely there were more missionary kids (MKs) than there were adult missionaries. Surprisingly few books have been written about us kids, who were, in our own right, also part of the missionary effort. We had not left our homelands and decided to dedicate our lives to the mission field, but we lived as our parents did, and we often knew the lifestyle of the missionary more personally than our parents, for they always had a very different "home" in mind.

Most MKs are on a quest to find and understand their roots. We lived complex lives. We grew up in what our parents considered foreign cultures, speaking foreign languages; yet this was the environment we kids took for granted, planted in our hearts and minds. Life "on the mission field" was completely natural to us—it's all we knew. Then, at some point later in life, we were pulled out of our familiar "foreign" environments and thrust into a Western culture that we did not understand, where we had to make significant adjustments to our routines. It was often difficult to reshape our lives and transition into a new, unfamiliar way of life.

There are problems attendant to our quest to know who we are in this between-cultures world. The quest is extremely complex, challenging, and confusing; it can be overwhelming, and there are few easy answers to the questions that arise along the way.

We grew up immersed in the culture of the mission field, speaking the native languages. We understood the locals intimately and were naturally bilingual; our parents were often envious that we had no accent and were comfortably fluent in the local tongue.

Inherent in these missionaries was a desire for adventure, an openness to new worlds, and an acceptance of risk taking. And often this sense of adventure was passed on to their children. There was, however, a price to pay for this daring approach to life, and that price often fell to the missionaries' families, some of whom thrived in the lifestyle and some of whom did not. The life of a missionary child could be rewarding, intense, exciting, and memorable, but it could also be harsh, lonely, unpredictable, overwhelming, and so filled with the unexpected that it became disorienting. For me, it was a positive experience; for many previous Kodai kids it had both positive and negative elements. World War II and the Indian independence occurred during their tenure in the mission field and imposed additional, severe stress on their experience. Local politics in the mission field were unpredictable and played a significant role in the life of missionaries. Some families coped well with these unknowns and probably came out stronger for the experience, but some did not.

Documenting and preserving the biographies of missionaries is important. They not only recount fascinating and unique stories, they also contain bits of history not found in any other source. They provide insight into far-away cultures and bygone eras and into the "common people," information not found in more academically focused works sponsored by governments and institutions of higher learning.

There is also a more personal reason MKs like to document such stories. Often there is a vast contrast between the exotic worlds of our youth and our later, more mundane existence in America, and this weighs heavily on our souls. At some point in our lives, we must come to grips with this disparity, try to make some sense of it, and then put it into the context of our identities. It is a search to understand ourselves and to help explain to others what we have been through, lending insight into our frequently distinctive personalities.

The writings herein reflect an expansive understanding of the lives of our family and fellow missionaries, and the times we lived in. As with most MKs, we developed a broad worldview and an open mind. That flexibility was necessary in our lives—as it is for most multicultural children (or "third culture kids," as we are often called)—to cope with the seemingly conflicting realities and truths inherent in different cultures, languages, and countries among which we traveled. This flexibility enabled us to accommodate the vast changes we encountered daily.

This book is our quest into our missionary roots and our effort to come to terms with them. The endpoint of our searching, a sense of "making sense of our lives," is something everyone longs for, and for some of us, it is a difficult journey.

* * *

Who are Kodai kids?

We were just a bunch of young kids going to school on a high mountain top in Southern India—in the tropics, close to the equator, in the Palni Hills[4] of the Western Ghats, near the southern tip of India. Though we well knew the heat and humidity of most of India—down on the "plains"—our weather was cool on the mountain and we were surrounded by greenery—lush jungles and forests—and the cleanest mountain air imaginable. In that time it was an idyllic, healthy location.

We were sent to a missionary boarding school called Kodai School, which shone like an emerald in the small mountain village of Kodaikanal (7,000 feet above sea level) in Madras State (now called Tamil Nadu) in Southern India.

Originally, we came from eclectic backgrounds, coming from all corners of the world, speaking different languages, growing up in a vast array of cultures and religions and world-views, and of families from different professions—medical and evangelistic missionaries, diplomats, business people, oil people, plantation owners, academics, non-governmental organizations (NGOs), philanthropic organizations,

4 Also called the Palani Hills.

etc. But, after coming to Kodai, we soon came to have much in common. The shared exotic childhoods made for a strong bond that still unifies us and draws us together for reunions.

As children, we didn't feel our upbringing was particularly unusual—after all, all our classmates had backgrounds similar to our own. Living overseas in small villages and bustling cities is what we knew, what we were familiar with. It's all we knew and it was what we imagined to be normal—after all it was normal for the millions of Indians and other nationalities—in whose cultures we were fully immersed. Though most of us were missionary kids, a number of us came from other backgrounds. Where someone came from or what their parents did mattered little. We saw each other as equals—fellow travelers in a long, elaborate, adventurous journey.

When we entered Kodai School, we roomed together (boys and girls separately, of course), we ate together, we went to class together, we played sports together, we hiked together, we laughed and cried together, we played and fought together, we succeeded and failed together. We were like a family, becoming more like siblings than simply classmates.

We are an unusual group. Having been surrounded by incredible variety—of climates, cultures, ethnicities, languages, cuisines, spiritual practices, etc.—made a deep impression. Our world view was broad to the extreme. For most of us, that left us unusually open-minded and, having been immersed in Asia's profound diversity we were unusually sensitive and averse to any manner of discrimination—especially to feeling that any culture made one less than anyone else. We were blessed with being children of the world.

Especially for the classes of the mid-1950s, they saw India evolve through vast changes. The nation went through tumultuous times—the end of the British colonial era; the formation of a new large and highly-diverse nation; the assassination of Gandhi; the breakdown of the caste system; division of British Colonial India into India and Pakistan; the formation of political parties, and electoral system and Parliament; the new era of democracy; and, by the late 1940s, the evolution of a new India that was very different from its predecessor.

Of note, we lived in an India in transition from a British Colony to independence, forging its identity and shedding vestiges of colonialism. British influence remained evident in India's institutions: the railroads, judiciary, postal system, banks, etc. Oddly enough, in the midst of the political change and its uncertainties, nostalgia for the colonial order, which lasted over two centuries, hung on.

View of the plains from Coaker's Walk. (D. Wiebe)

From the perspective of young, wide-eyed, unbiased, impressionable observers, our stories provide insight into a past era, a state of human condition that no longer exists—a loss which limits the breadth of human awareness and the depth of our understanding. Thus, our stories also lend a flavor for a captivating part of the human experience that has irretrievably slipped away.

As a result of our unique backgrounds, we have many stories to tell, stories too valuable to be forgotten. Some are humorous, some serious, some endearing, some sad, some historic, and many insightful.

The following chapters chronicle our individual and collective stories as well as additional stories, pictures and maps of Kodai and India to provide background and setting.

These stories are insightful memoirs that bring drama, laughter, tears, and understanding, as well as being unique historical and cultural records as witnessed first-hand from the wide-eyed perspective of missionary children.

CHAPTER 2

Growing up overseas

We were children of missionaries, diplomats, and business folk.

The majority of us were missionary kids. Being one of them, I can speak best to that experience. We "mish-kids"—as we called ourselves—lived complex lives growing up in what our parents considered foreign cultures and languages, yet it was the life we kids took for granted and what was planted into our hearts and minds. Having been born into and growing up in the "mission field," that life was completely natural for us—it's all we knew. But, then, later in life, we were pulled out of our familiar environment and thrust into a Western culture that we didn't understand and where we had to make significant adjustments to our lives. It was often tough reshaping our lives and transitioning into incredible cultural changes.

There are problems attendant to our quest of reshaping our lives: it's extremely complex, it's challenging, it's confusing, it can be overwhelming, and there are few easy answers to the questions it brings up.

To understand this, some background is needed:

* * *

We missionary kids grew up in the midst of the height of the great missionary movement which had been growing for over century and was now reaching its peak. By no decision of our own, we were fully integrated into our parents' mission—what they referred to as their "calling"—of healing body, mind, and soul through medical, educational, and spiritual service in accord with with "Great Commission." as it appears in the Gospel of Matthew, chapter 28, verses 19-20, which—having heard it so often—many of us children knew by heart.

Most missionaries were married and the vast majority had children. Perhaps surprisingly—and in all likelihood—there were more of us missionary kids than there were missionary adults. Having grown up in the "mission field," we identified more closely to and felt more comfortable in the mission field than did our parents.

We missionary kids grew up knowing our missionary lands better than the lands of our parents, the lands of which we were citizens. We grew up immersed in the culture of the mission field and speaking the native languages. We understood the local culture intimately and were natively bilingual—having no accent and fluent in the local languages and dialects.

Inherent in the personalities of missionaries was a desire for adventure; thus an acceptance of risk-taking. This sense of adventure and exploring the world was passed on to most of their children.

Like all who long for adventure, driven by a vision of mission to explore the world and daring to break away from the common life, missionary families pay a price for this sense of mission. Some of those family members thrive in the missionary lifestyle, but some don't. The life of a missionary child can be rewarding, intense, exciting, and memorable; but it can also be harsh, lonely, unpredictable, overwhelming and so varied as to be disorienting. For me it was a positive experience. For many of my classmates it had elements both positive and negative. Local politics in the mission field were unpredictable and played a significant role in the life of missionaries. Some families coped well with these unknowns and may have come out stronger for the experience, but some did not.

Documenting and preserving these stories is important. Fascinating and unique, they also contain bits of history that may not be available from any other source; they provide insights into other cultures and bygone eras; they provide insights into the common people that are often not available in more academically focused works sponsored by governments and other institutions.

CHAPTER 3

Kodai School, a brief history

Jane Gibbs Cummings grew up in Kodai School and probably knows its history better than anyone. The following is an excerpt of the history of the school that she wrote for the book *In Celebration*.[5]

Jane's history of Kodai School begins July 1, 1901, when thirteen little tykes, boys in their knickers, girls in their pinafores, appeared at the Highclerc Hotel to start school. This excerpt takes up the story with Papa Phelps' arrival as principal of Kodai School in 1932. Much of the history, structure, organization, and reputation of Kodai School is credited to Papa Phelps' vision of what the school should be and to his dedication and leadership. He is the most well-known personality associated with the school.

* * *

A collective sigh of relief seems to waft through the Council Minutes of 1932 as Carl and Mary Phelps moved to Kodai and Carl took over his role as principal. Finally Kodai School had a principal with dedication, administrative leadership and sense of purpose with whom the Council could leave the daily administration of the school. Although he came originally for only one term, it was for the next twenty-six years that this "diminutive dynamo of organizational and academic energy," as he was once described, ran Highclerc School[6] with his own particularly unique brand of

---

5 The excerpt comes from pages 28 to 38 of Jane Cummings' book, *In Celebration: Kodaikanal International School Centennial,* published by KW International in 2000.

6 When it was founded in 1901, Kodai School was initially called Highclerc School.

administrative leadership. Papa's distinctive walk, brisk pace and long strides, each step a purposeful propelling forward, typified the man himself and the way he ran the school.

Papa Phelps, principal for 26 years, with the school's first car. (J. Cummings)

By 1934 the Council had adopted a new Memorandum of Association which remained effective, with minor modifications, through the 1960s. This document gave greater executive control to the principal and greater autonomy to the staff in carrying out their responsibilities but always with final decisions on the management of the school authorized by the Council. Clearer policies and procedures concerning representation on the Council by various mission boards were also drawn up. Variations on questions of mission board support and representation continued to be subjects of debate for years to come, and in fact, remain so today. This new Memo of Association of 1936, however, did not change the purpose of the school, which remained to provide an education for the children of American and European missionaries. It was school policy in the 1930s to limit the enrollment of non-mission students to ten percent of the total student population. With slight variations of percentages this was a policy which did not change much over the next thirty years.

"Papa" Phelps fully embraced the purpose of the school. As he once described it, "I am here to run an American school and create an environment which makes it as easy as possible for our American young people of missionary parents to return to their homelands and fit into life and college in America."

In spite of his formal demeanor and sometimes austere manner (particularly if you were in danger of being disciplined) Papa was a great cheerleader for his students. His reports to the Council are peppered with comments such as this one made in 1934: "The spirit of the student body has been exceptionally fine particularly since school reopened in January of this year. Individuals have had their occasional lapses of course, but the general atmosphere has been and is cheery and responsive to leadership to a degree that is very gratifying. We are proud of our student group and feel that one must look long and far to find a finer crowd of boys and girls."

For the next decade the size of the school remained about 150 students with fifteen staff members. A picture of the make-up of the student body of those days emerges from this account of Kodai kids returning to school every January written by Beatrice Witter Donavan in her priceless article "Indian Shangri-La," published in the Yale Review and in the Kodai alumni magazine:

> The convocation of one hundred and fifty Kodai School scholars, aged six to seventeen, occurred during the third week in January as trains from all over India spilled their untidy contents at the foot of the Palani mountains. Baggage masters and conductors (Indians all, loyal employees of the British India Railways) looked on in horror as rowdy little Americans leaped to the platform and yelled at compatriots wildly dodging tennis rackets and bedrolls thrown from the train windows. Additional trains kept coming, dumping the scholars in gangs: Baptists, Missouri Lutherans, Dutch Reformed, and other sects. Some notion of fair play ruled the apportionment of different denominations to different areas of India. Lucky heathen not to have to contend with Baptists and Methodists at the same time! There were also the Arabians, the Siamese and the Assamese. For these kids Kodai Road was the last stage of a long journey begun in the oilfields of Bahrain, the banks of Bangkok and the tea plantation of Kohima. To us 'Indians' they had a certain glamour because their parents were not missionaries and their clothes were better and their allowance larger. Also along with the tennis rackets and duffel bags, they brought victrolas; these did not fly out of the window. Whatever sophistication the missionary offspring achieved at Kodai School resulted from the influence of their American phonograph records, their clothes, their slang.

Silver Cascade—the bus up the ghat was the last stage to a long journey to Kodai. (J. Cummings)

Besides Papa another person who joined the Highclerc staff in 1933 and stayed —and became a Kodai legend—was a tiny American woman who, like Mrs. Eddy, came out to India for a "short" visit with her son and stayed for thirty-six years. As first grade teacher for twenty or more years, Auntie Powell launched countless Kodai students on their school careers. She was also active in administration and, in 1936, was acting principal while Papa was on furlough. Even after her retirement as an active teacher in 1951 at the age of 74, Auntie Powell lived in an apartment at the school, frequently visiting the elementary grades to tell a story or to give a helping hand. She died at Kodai School in 1965.

There were other significant developments in the '30s and '40s. One was to open up boarding to children of seven years or even six if "an older sister or ayah could help take care of them." Another innovation was that first steps were taken toward organizing a student government. A junior orchestra was started. A junior church was organized with students taking the primary role in organizing the worship. In the absence of any other church to which students could be received into membership, the junior church was reorganized in 1941 into the Kodaikanal School Church with its own constitution so that students and staff could be received into

Dedication of the school chapel, 1951. A fitting tribute to the founder, Margaret Eddy. (J. Cummings)

full communicant membership. And so it remains today, a fully independent church affiliated with the school.

The first Eucy,[7]. still the name of the school yearbook, was published in 1940, almost as an act of defiance. The class of'39 had wanted to do one but the staff rejected it. As soon as the class of' '40 became seniors, they began agitating to have a yearbook and got permission. However, their advisor, Mrs. Thompson, got sick. When she came back in April, she told the class that it was useless to think of a yearbook because there wasn't time to do a good job. With that dare, the seniors taking journalism class resolved that it could and would be done, no matter how hard they had to work. And they did it!

After years of negotiation, the Benderloch property was purchased in 1938 for Rupees 12,500. The property included a small bungalow formerly the Cecil Hotel, which became the principal's residence. The clearing and leveling of the remainder of the land into a playing field was an engineering feat of great accomplishment. Council Chairman Luther W. Slifer wrote, "The way in which this property shapes up

7 Eucy, a short version of eucalyptus, was the name of the school yearbook.

when leveled as an athletic field surprises even the most sanguine of us." Papa, who was very much in favor of having students involved in jobs around the school, had hoped that students would do the whole project. That was not possible but, much to their pride, students did build the field house. As far back as 1938, the Council requested that income from the Kennedy Schauffler Fund be designated to build a swimming pool. Perhaps the War was the deterring factor. In any event the dream of a swimming pool sixty years later remains that—a dream—or perhaps an exercise in the virtue of patience for all who would like to bring about change too quickly.

Easter Sunday service, 1939. (J. Cummings)

Shortly after Mrs. Eddy's death in 1935, the School Council decided there would be no more fitting tribute to the founder of the school than a Margaret Eddy Memorial Chapel. The Chapel Fund was started with a gift from the sale of Mrs. Eddy's diamond ring, which she had willed to be used for some special need at Kodai. The ground-breaking was in 1941 but, because of the War, the Chapel was not finally completed and dedicated until 1951.

And what of the life of a student during these years? Browsing through the school paper, "The Herald," edited and written by students, readers might indeed wonder if they have stumbled across a Shangri La. Evidence this editorial in the first issue in 1932: "This year many new people have come to Highclerc. We hope they like it and will continue to like it. We ourselves like it very much. Its beautiful buildings; its pretty flowers and trees; its mind-building studies; its fine sports; its opportunities for developing splendid qualities, such as sportsmanship, cheerfulness, optimism, courage, love of nature, and open-mindedness; its family spirit, all combine to make it one of the finest places we could go to."

Another student, Dick Goheen, who left Kodai before graduating, remembered Highclerc in this English term paper written when he was a senior at Lawrenceville

Preparatory School in New Jersey, "The beautiful, adventure-filled Palni Hills offer to me pleasures beyond number, pleasure which will never be surpassed, never equaled. Hiking in these Palni Hills, as may easily be imagined, can be one of the most pleasurable things in life. Good companions, coolies to carry our loads, invigorating air fanning your cheeks, beautiful panoramas, and perfectly situated forest cabins at which to spend the nights, all constitute powerful attractions ... even school in this fairyland is more enjoyable than elsewhere: again probably due to that almost inexplicable atmosphere of charm. So at last we summarize our vagrant emotions in the statement that everything in this land seems to be closer to perfection than anywhere else in the world, and who in all the universe could ask for more than that?" While these memories may have been rose-tinted, many alumni no doubt share them.

Every weekend there were hikes, picnics, boating on the lake or sports events. There were cookouts, marshmallow roasts followed by games such as capture-the-flag or kick-the-can. There were dances or formal dinners given at various staff homes or, during the Season (May through August), at the homes of students out of boarding. There were movies or plays and musicals especially during the Season. The relatively unpopulated town of Kodaikanal, surrounded by beautiful hills, was indeed an idyllic playground for students and staff alike.

The war clouds which had already darkened Europe spread to Asia when Japan entered the war in 1941. India was not unaffected. With the growth of nationalism, debate raged as to whether India should enter the war on the side of the British. And all the time rumors spread like wildfire that the Japanese would soon invade India ... had in fact been sighted off the coast of Madras ... were on their way up the ghat. Missionary families, uncertain of the future, tried at least to get the women and children back to the United States. Highclerc opened as usual that January of 1942, but every week the numbers dwindled as more and more families found a way to return to America. Those who remained in Kodai made preparations for a possible Japanese invasion. Papa and several boys trekked down to the plains to lay out a back door evacuation route via Vilpatti and on down to Palani in the event that the Japanese came through the front door, the ghat road. Trenches were dug on Block slope. Invasion fever reached a pitch in Kodai. The Highclerc Herald of June 1942 prepared a Chronology of Evacuation which recounts the following crisis management, Kodai style:

Monday, April 13: ... hearing alarming news. Rev. DeValois has suddenly come up and called a School Council meeting. Rumors fly. Everyone is wandering around

“Above the clouds” view from Coaker’s walk. (J. Cummings)

trying to gather news and make up their minds what to do. “Scorched earth” goes into effect with demolition of some electric light bulbs.

Tuesday, April 14: We go to bus station to ‘see off’ some of our number. We hand in books and go to our rooms to pack up. Suppressed exultation fills everyone. Bus office is jammed with people weighing luggage, asking for tickets, etc. Hallelujah!

Wednesday, April 15: Bulk of the school rolls down the ghat, leaving evidences of seasickness behind. Mr. Phelps has promised to reopen the school on June 1.

Saturday, May 1: When May rolls around we are scarcely settled down when word arrives that Mr. Phelps plans to reopen the school on May 11. Feverish repacking.

Sunday, May 10: School seems deserted, but hear of others coming up.

Monday, May 11: School reopens. Classes without teachers found to be quite a lot of fun.

May 11-20: Students gradually straggle in, until we are once more our ‘happy family’ though considerably depleted.

In her book “Sepia Prints” Mrs. Viola Wiebe, mother of Principal Paul Wiebe, vividly recalls the evacuation, or “white Exodus” from Kodai that May. The Wiebes,

Punting on the lake was a favorite pastime. (J. Cummings)

along with their six children and the John Hieberts with their six children, piled into one station wagon with a bag of shoes tied to one fender, a bag of topees[8] to the other and strapped canvas-covered cases with clothes on the top of the car. 'With the springs of the vehicles groaning' they wound their way down the ghat, stopping every fifteen minutes to allow the cramped fussy children to get out and stretch. Despite consuming a diet of sardines, beans and bread, replacing several blown tires, difficulty in finding petrol, and enduring temperatures which sometimes reached 115 degrees, they reached their mission home in Andhra Pradesh about four days later, the parents no doubt somewhat frazzled but the twelve children probably none the worse for wear.

One positive fallout of the war was that some of Highclerc's most notable teachers like Mario DiGiorgio, A. J. Musil, Elizabeth and Charles Caspari, and Fritz and Martha Kolb had found their way to Kodai. Caught in India at the outbreak of hostilities and unable to return to their homes in Europe, many of them chose to wait the war out in Kodai while others were interned here by the British and forced

[8] Pith helmets that served as sun hats.

Students leaving chapel in the late 60s. (J. Cummings)

to remain during the war. Some of them chose to stay on for many years after the war ended.

And thus Kodaikanal International School (KIS), as it was called by now, carried on through the forties and fifties, essentially an American school predominately for the children of missionaries but with a liberal sprinkling of non-missionary, European types who wandered by from time to time. Most of the students came from Kansas and Oregon, Oklahoma and New Hampshire, California and New York. Over 90% of the students were very well prepared for college in America and went on to colleges like Colby or Whittier, Princeton or Hope or Oberlin. The curriculum was not too much help for those who wanted to go to Cambridge University or the Universities of Nottingham, Berlin or Delhi. The ethos of the place exuded bubble gum and bobby socks, baseball and taffy pulls, square dances and Elvis Presley.

When Papa Phelps retired in 1958 after twenty-six years as principal, his departure marked the end of an era at Kodai School. The 1960s also marked the beginning of a period of turmoil and change that would impact the school and its future. As Bob Dylan would soon be singing to captivated audiences on the other side of the world, "The times they are a-changing."

Class of 1958 after Baccalaureate Service. (J. Cummings)

There were a number of principals who served the school through these years of transition. Nelson Hoffman, a Methodist missionary who was formerly the school bursar, was appointed principal when Papa retired. For health reasons, Hoffman, his wife, Marjorie, and their four children had to leave almost immediately, and the Council appointed Herbert L. Krause as principal, a position he held for eight-and-a half-years.

Herb and Rose Krause had been teachers and house parents at KIS since 1950. Their goal was to provide a supportive environment with clear boundaries and limits. Rose Krause remembers one parent asking her if she was the only staff member who had kids over for merits rather than demerits. "We often had homesick kids," she recalls. "They wouldn't come right out and say it, but you could tell by the way they talked about what was going on at home. Every now and then there would be a little tap on our door at night, and there would be a little fellow who wanted to come in and sleep with us because he was homesick. On the other hand, they had more brothers and sisters up there than anywhere else in the world."

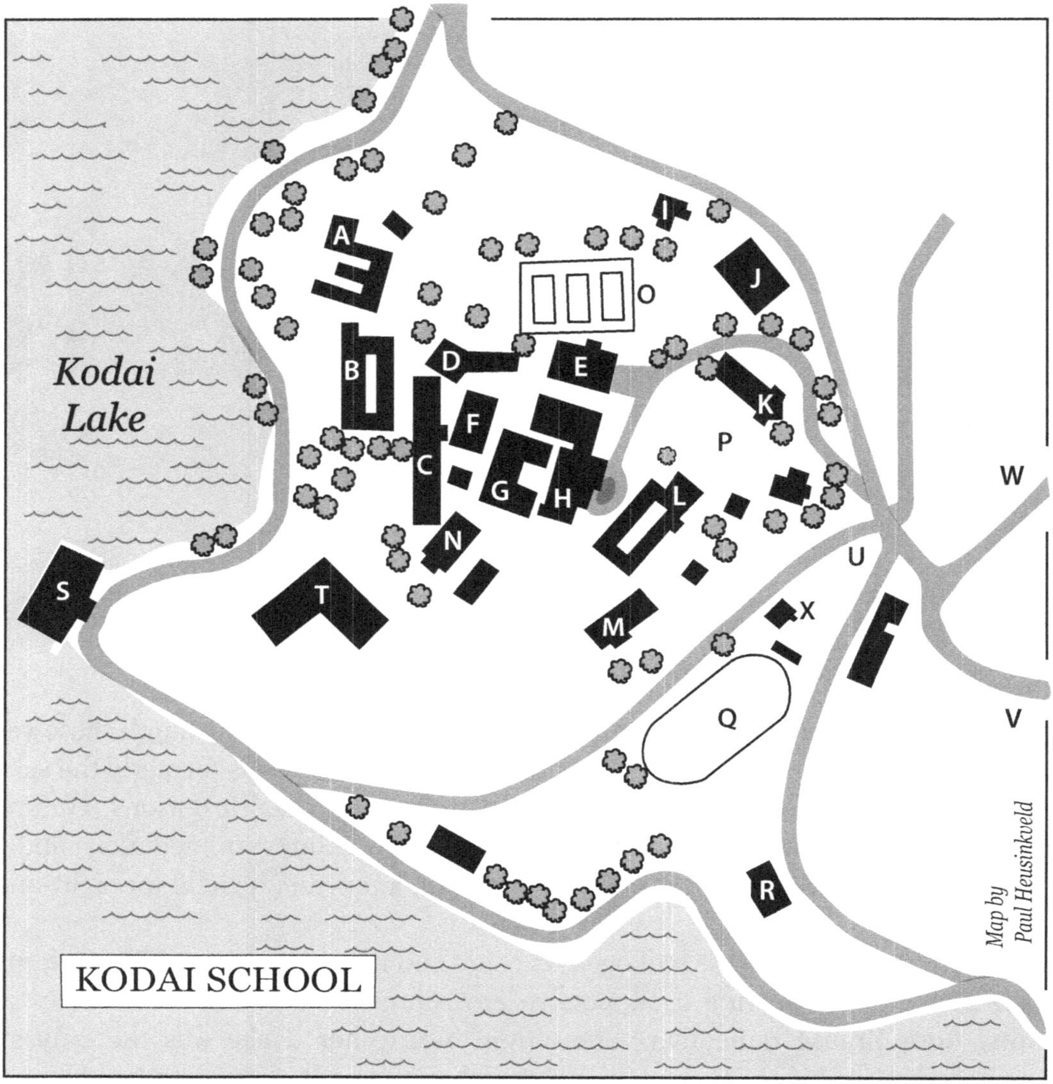

A-Wissy Dorm
B-Phelps Hall
C-Block Dorm
D-Airalee Dorm
E-Gym
F-Library
G-Class Rooms
H-Dining Hall
I-Dish Pan
J-KMU
K-Church
L-Kennedy Dorm
M-Boyer Dorm
N-Science Classes
O-Tennis Courts
P-Play Ground
Q-Bendy Field
R-Benderloch
S-Boat House
T-Carlton Hotel
U-Seven Corners
V-to Coakers
W-to Budge
X-Pereira's

Kodai School compound in the 1960s.

CHAPTER 4

Kodaikanal, a view from the mid-1900s

Kodai School is situated in Kodaikanal, Madras State (now Tamil Nadu), in Southern India. A brief historical overview of Kodaikanal helps to understand its setting:[9]

People have inhabited the Palni Hills around Kodaikanal for 7,000 years. These early inhabitants made homes of great stone slabs called dolmens, sometimes arranged in circles and sometimes with underground chambers. Their bronze and copper ornaments and great clay burial urns remain with us today. Later came the tree-dwelling Paliyans,[10] who clothed themselves with grass and leaves and subsisted on honey, roots, and leaves. They cooked the roots on fires produced by striking iron on quartz to ignite tinder from the silk-cotton trees. Even today near Kukal Cave a remnant of the Paliyans survives. Other early inhabitants included the meat-eating, Tamil-speaking Paliyans whose customs were linked to the plains, though their women's thalis[11] were distinctive white beads, and they had their own gods.

In about 1400, Vellalans from Coimbatore fled from war or famine into the Palnis, overtook Puliyan villages and subjugated the inhabitants to serfdom, and energetically cultivated the land.

---

[9] Material in this chapter was gleaned from Charlotte Wyckoff's *Kodaikanal, 1845-1945* (London Mission Press, 1945); and Dorothy Lockwood's *Kodaikanal, Gift of the Forest* (Christian Literature Society, 1964).

[10] An ethnic group mainly found in Kerala and Tamil Nadu. Also known as the Palya, Paniyar, or Paniyan.

[11] A women's necklace that symbolizes marriage and a holy bond between wives and husbands.

Between 1600 and 1800 a wave of exploited and oppressed people escaped to the hills from the Vijayanagar kings, the Mahrattas, and Tippu Sultan. Below Coaker's Walk to the south is Vellagavi, a small hamlet nestled in a hollow on a spur of the mountains, which is one of the villages they settled. Its population was later augmented by evacuees from cholera-stricken Shembaganur.

The first recorded history of this area was written by Lieutenant Ward, an Englishman who surveyed the Palni Hills in 1821. When the first map of this area appeared in 1840, the only village noted was Vellagavi.

Early days

American missionaries founded Kodaikanal in 1845. Since 1834, they had been in Madurai[12] and suffered from the constant heat, illness and death. In 1843 they built two cottages in the low hills near the present Kodai Road Station, but due to malaria, the location did not provide the anticipated health benefits. In January 1845, Rev. H. S. Taylor and Rev. Clarendon P. Muzzey explored the top of the Palni range and returned enthusiastic. At once Mr. Muzzey and Rev. J. J. Lawrence were sent back to build two houses. They were assisted by Mr. Fane, who had godowns[13] there, and Mr. Eliot, an ex-judge of Madurai, who was planting coffee in the Lower Palnis.

By June 1845 two shacks were ready, at the edge of the kanal or great forest where immense tree-ferns grew beside a stream that trickled down through mossy banks under gnarled old trees (near where the cottages of Sunnyside and Shelton stand today). Six families arrived, having crossed the plains in bullock carts and then threading the tiger-ridden mountain forests in open palanquins[14] made of blankets slung between bamboo poles. Others also ventured. Among them were Monsieur Faure de Fonclair, a coffee planter who shot bison where the lake now lies, and the Collector of Madurai; and Mr. Barker who built Pambar House. He and his successors made it the center of social life for decades. (This property has been acquired most recently by T.V.S.). Today there are bungalows in happy use that are well over a hundred years old: East House, Central House, Clavarack, Roseneath, Jaffna House, and Rock Cottage (that versatile, one-time godown, post office, clubhouse, American school, and dentist's office!).

---

[12] Also spelled Madura.
[13] An underground warehouse.
[14] Canvas chairs.

The early arrivals improved and beautified their settlement. They built seven miles of road and widened the paths through sholas[15] where big, black monkeys swung. Major Partridge of Bombay planted the first Australian blue gums (eucalyptus trees) and laid out a garden. Brother Co-adjutor Joseph Ciceron, of Savoy and Madurai introduced pear trees. Collector (later Sir) Vere Levinge formed the lake by damming the valley where three streams flowed, and he introduced fish therein. His green boat, The Lily, and another, The Duck, were the first craft on the Lake. He completed roads and paths, introduced wattle and pine trees, European fruit trees and flowers, and at Pambar House planted tea from every province in China.

The colony was thirteen years old in 1858 when the first little church was completed, roofed by flattened Huntley and Palmer biscuit tins. There were Church of England and Congregational Services in both Tamil and English. A bell from America was hardly installed before the building collapsed during heavy rains. Two years later it was rebuilt, bigger, and more beautiful for a spire erected by a visiting Swedish ship's carpenter. The site of The Church-under-the-Hill is at the Old Cemetery, where, amidst the graves of many children, stands a granite obelisk.

Coolie Ghat

In the early days, due to the fact that there were no railroads far into South India until 1875, Kodai was visited chiefly by people from nearby. A visitor had to take a bullock cart to Periyakulam and from there, if he had no horse of his own, ascend in a doolie (a roofed palanquin) or canvas chair or ride on a small pack-pony jingling with bells. Cows were driven up to supply milk, and at least one was carried off by a tiger on the way. Guns and constant song kept up the travelers' courage and scared away wild animals. The old climbing chant, "Hung-Go-gum-ha-ah-Ho" dinned itself into the ears of the dozing children in the doolies, together with the grunt and jolt when the bearers changed the poles from one shoulder to the other, and wild snatches of another song whose chorus "Yay-la—yay-la—yay-LA" was taken up as a response all down the line. The weird hoots and calls and howls in the deep forest, as they passed through, the glorious view from a summit of sunrise over the plains, the first breath of cold air from the heights above—all were woven into the

[15] Sholas are forested areas in the valleys of the mountains of South India where streams running through the valleys provide enough water for trees and thick undergrowth. The mountain sides between the valleys where the sholas occur are rolling grasslands.

children's loving memory. The only discomfort was being forced into prickly flannels while still on the hot plains. Mother was in charge of food and drink, and Father watched for wild animals and handled quarrelsome coolies.

Bullock carts in Tamil Nadu. (Peck)

From Coaker's Walk one can still see the zigzags of the trail that was finally accepted, and the town of Periyakulam, which has long forgotten its principal industry of the late 19th century—providing transportation and food for Kodai's summer visitors.

Coaker's Walk began as a path constructed by Lieutenant Coaker of the Royal Engineers. The present black and white striped surfacing was introduced on the occasion of Prime Minister Nehru's visit to Kodaikanal in 1961.

It's easy to forget how wild Kodai once was. Now there is a Township High School and three or four others, and Mahatma Gandhi's statue near the lake, where mercury vapour-lights blaze at night. Now, Kodai has piped water, hotels, rest homes, a cinema, telephones, and siren time signals. There is also the Government of India's only Astronomical Observatory, one of the foremost solar observatories of some dozen scattered over the world. The Government Hospital has an X-ray

Perumal as seen from Coaker's Walk. (Doveton)

machine and the Skippo Medical Van (the gift of the All India Women's Conference in 1949), which journeys over the hills weekly, visiting outlying villages.

The journey up

It was quite different back in 1861 when Major Douglas Hamilton was sent by the Government to spend a year in the Palnis to draw sketches of the area. His favorite spot was Berijam Lake basin, a site called Fort Hamilton ever since, although it has never been a fort. There he shot tiger and sambhur.[16] When Dr. Fairbank of the Mahrathi Mission from Bombay spent a furlough in Kodai in 1867, his camp on Prospect Point was the only house on that ridge. He collected 114 specimens of birds and discovered two new subspecies: the Kodaikanal Laughing Thrush and the White-Bellied Short-Wing. In 1874, climbing Perumal was a popular pastime; you had to leave Kodai on ponies at 6:30 a.m. and ride over rough ground to Shembaganur. There you tied your mount and climbed on foot the four remaining miles to the spring of clear water near the top. Once down again and remounted, you

[16] A large deer weighing up to 1,200 pounds.

might plunge into the deep valley between Neutral Saddle and Vilpatti and reach Kodai by 6:30 in the evening.

By 1875, trains had started running as far south as Madurai and Tuticorin, and visitors began to come to Kodai from places farther north and south. Getting down where the present Kodai Road Station stands, they traveled in "transits" (trains of bullock carts) for thirty-three miles along roads that were previously haunted by dacoits (armed bands of robbers) but were now patrolled and planted with shade trees. It took from 6 p.m. to 1 a.m. to reach the Tope (a grove of trees) at the foot of the mountains. Along the way, upon approaching certain villages, the driver of the leading cart would blow a warning on his horn, and villagers would rouse and by the flaring light of torches replace tired bullocks with fresh ones, with the least possible delay. On arrival at Tope, the leader quickly woke the sleeping coolies there and assigned each a fifty pound head-load. Large old-fashioned trunks were slung from bamboo poles, to be carried by two bearers, and small boxes were tied like panniers to pack-ponies. The long procession climbed through the dark woods to reach the half-way stop by dawn and then make the 57 zigzags to Shembaganur for a picnic breakfast. Then would come the last ascent to the top.

Kodaikanal was such a beauty spot that there would have to be a proper road from the plains to it! In 1875 Colonel Law was sent to live in Kodai in order to "trace a bridle path to the plains, of a gradient of not more than one in nineteen, the same to be widened later for wheeled traffic" and thus to provide labor for hundreds of starving people during the great famine. Law's Ghat, as it came to be known, was completed in three years. From Kodai to a point three miles below Neutral Saddle the road was wide enough for cars and carriages (brought up piece by piece on coolies' heads and put together on the hills). For the twenty miles further down, it was just a trace, following the contours of the hillsides through deep jungle. The road-approach to Kodai was to remain inadequate for thirty years more.

The settlement grows

In the early years there were few visitors to Kodai. Only seventy-five Europeans and Americans came in 1879. However, between 1880 and 1900 this number increased to four hundred during the season (May through August), of whom about one hundred—retired Army men or civilians, wives and small children —remained for the greater part of the year. During these decades Kodai expanded. Cottages were built and large estates laid out. From this period date Major-General Keays' Winsford; Merton Lodge, the property of a Madras Barrister, Mr. Eardley

Palni Hills circa 1850. (Douglas Hamilton)

Norton; Mr. J. A. D. Lloyd's Lillingstone; Bishop Caldwell's Roslyn, a gift to his newly married daughter and Mr. E. Logan's Restalrig out near Pillar Rocks. Mr. Dunnell built his 'Highclerc Hotel'. There were also Furzbank, Hillbrook, Arcotia, and the first cottages of the Swedish Settlement. Sir Subramania Tyer settled in Woodcot in Shembaganur. Judge A. S. Appasamy of Palamcottah raised his Ebenezer on a high rock site with a magnificent view, although he had to carry up tons of earth to make his flower garden.

Church properties had been developed in Kodai from the very first. As early as 1852, Father Saint Cyr of the Jesuits surveyed the hills on horseback. Eight years later, he bought the Bayne's Bungalow, renaming it La Providence, and prepared it for holiday occupation by his Community in 1861. In 1866 the Church, La Salette, was erected. Catholic churches were built in even the remotest hill villages. The Protestant Missions erected churches too. The American Madura[17] Mission built the present Union Church in 1885, primarily for the Tamil congregation, and Bishop Caldwell built St. Peter's Church for the Anglicans in 1887.

Early social life

Social life developed also: hunting and fishing, dancing and card parties, badminton tournaments, theatricals, cycling, and horseback riding—even a

[17] Also spelled Madurai.

moonlight fete on the lake. As for picnics: snowy white tablecloths spread on the ground; enormous meals served by butlers; a scrambling search for lilies or ferns; and at Pillar Rocks, by rope into dark, bat-filled caverns, to squeeze up through the "chimney" to sunlight. Mr. Tapp's pear orchard, opposite the boat house, contained a circular pavilion covered with honeysuckle and climbing roses, the scene of many a party regaled with strawberries and cream. Tennis teas were the favorite form of entertainment and every house had its tennis court. But in 1894 the only house in Kodai with two tennis courts was Tredis, the property of H.H. the Raja of Pudukottah, who, with his brother the Dorairaja, had lived in Kodai since 1890. His "At Homes" held in beautifully decorated grounds where a band played loudly were the gala events of the season. Here in 1895 was held the first of the international tennis matches, which continue to this day.

Club life had its start in the '80s. In 1887 a small Club was opened where the Kodaikanal Club now stands. Many civilian and military members, however, were unwilling to support a club which had no bar or outdoor games on Sunday, which limitations had been imposed by the American Madura Mission when it gave the site. Amicably, the Madura Mission withdrew itself and its strictures and joined the Kodaikanal Missionary Union (KMU). Gratefully, the Club made the members of the American Madura Mission honorary members in perpetua.

The Kodaikanal Missionary Union had begun most informally, with reading rooms at Arcotia, games and book teas at 'Rock Cottage,' and meetings in a dark little cottage in the pear orchard on Highclerc Hill. With the turn of the century, so many Missions were represented in Kodaikanal that it was felt a more formal organization was needed to strengthen the friendly ties between the missionaries and the civilian population. Finally, in 1923 the cornerstone of the present KMU building was laid by Mrs. Baylis Thomson, one of the oldest residents. It is now the centre for conferences, sales, tennis, rehearsals, Bible classes, Wednesday teas, and a host of other activities.

With the new century, Bryant Park was laid out by the Forest officer whose name it bears. By 1908 dense jungle was disciplined into wooded slopes, trim paths, and colorful flower beds.

In the early 1900s people still traveled from Kodai Road to the Tope by transits, now painted blue, with windows. Or they ventured in the new, clumsy, unreliable, and slow buses. They came, as always, to the difficult journey up the bridle path, but it could now be made by daylight, in an afternoon, and better days were ahead; work had started again on Law's Ghat. In 1914, Lord Pentland opened the Ghat Road, though it was not ready for traffic till 1916 or in general use till 1922.

At first, motor cycles and Model-T Fords were coaxed, pushed, watered, and cranked up the mountain, past the toll gates at Tumtumparai and Shembaganur. Within a few years everyone was going by bus all the way, through the six months of the Season. Out of Season some folks still gave the Periyakulam coolies some trade, but the motor era had begun.

Amenities and schools

This was the period when various civic improvements were introduced. The Post and Telegraph office was established in 1908. A reservoir was made in 1915 by damming the stream above Fairy Falls. The bazaar had an increasing number of shops. The new Lake View Hotel of 1919 has become the Carlton Hotel of today, the older Highclerc Hotel having already become the nucleus of Kodai School.

Since 1932, Kodai School, with its American curriculum has prepared students for higher education in the United States, and also from 1963 for the pre-university classes of the University of Madras. In 1901 thirteen English and American children formed the first classes under the kindly care of Mrs. Margaret Eddy, after whom the Memorial Chapel is named. A widow, she had come to visit her missionary son, Sherwood Eddy, and stayed to organize the new boarding school. Today's restricted accommodation limits the number to around 350. Most of these are Americans but the school also includes students of other nationalities from Arabia, Burma, Ceylon, and India.

The other large boarding school in Kodai is the Presentation Convent, started modestly at Hillside in 1916, moving to its present site in February 1917, and into its present two story building in 1920. Two smaller boarding schools are the American Lutherans (Missouri Synod) the Koehne Memorial School at Loch End; and the Swedish School above the lake, adjacent to Kodai School, recognized and aided by the Swedish Parliament.

The Jesuits who first settled at Shembaganur, producing eucalyptus oil and developing fruit orchards and market gardens, in 1895 founded the Sacred Heart College, where students from many countries study for eight years before proceeding to Poona or Kurseong for four years of Theology and a final twelve months of preparation for the priesthood.

The Kodai season then and now

Today in Kodai there are amusements.

The Kodaikanal Convention "for the deepening of the spiritual life" began in 1889. The Kodaikanal Boat Club's first minutes date from 1893. Dogs were prohibited in boats. A concert and subscription raised money to clear the lakeside of weeds. Retired astronomer Michie Smith sat on his Winsford porch and peered through his spyglass to see that rules were not broken! The Highclerc Orchestra was started by Miss Spence in 1908 with six girls playing mandolins, violins, and guitars. The Indian Club was formed in 1915. The first complete dramatic performance in the Gymnasium was probably The Mikado, given by members of both the English Club and the KMU in 1917. The Choral Union was born in 1922 when a Messiah chorus was enlisted through the efforts of Dr. J. A. Curtis. One of the tenors, Dr. Thomas Royds, an astronomer, turned out to be a gifted conductor. The first complete play was a hasty dramatization of a novel called *Patricia Brent, Spinster*; rehearsed in five days. It entertained the Club guests after the Club versus Union Match in 1924. The Community Chest Entertainments started in 1932.

The Golf Club was established near Pillar Rocks in 1880. A later Club House had its roof ripped off and blown over the nearby cliffs in the cyclone of May 7, 1930. Now an enlarged building and an eighteen-hole course, with six new holes (in 1962), caters to an international group of golf enthusiasts. Captains are elected in turn by India, Britain, and the USA.

In 1935, Mr. A. Balasubramanium Pillai was the first Municipal Commissioner. Electricity arrived in 1938, when Kodai had its own Hungarian plant with a wood-burning furnace where the present Municipal High School now stands. The Department of Health was established the following year.

A place in which to know God

Peace and harmony are ever present in Kodai, and amidst so much natural beauty, one is inclined praise God. Lady Ramanathan, an Australian, built a temple to Subramanium, as god of the hills, at the far end of Prospect Point, facing Perumal, in memory of her husband, Sir Ponambalam Ramanathan, a great Ceylonese Tamil leader. Little Hindu shrines dot the hills, and in the bazaar the Muslims have a mosque.

There are numerous churches is Kodai: St. Peter's Church (CSI),[18] the Union Church (CSI), the Margaret Eddy Memorial Chapel belonging to High Clerc[19] School, and the first Roman Catholic Church in Kodaikanal, La Salette. It is named for a shrine located 6,000 feet up in the mountains of France, where the Virgin Mary is said to have appeared in 1846 to a shepherdess, Melanie, and a younger boy, Maximin. Ever since 1866 an annual festival has been held in honor of Our Lady of La Salette. Strikingly visible from the bazaar or Coaker's Walk is the Diocesan Church of the Sacred Heart, and high on another hill is St. Mary's. There is also the American Lutheran (Missouri Synod) Mount Zion Church; and the Swedish Lutheran Jubilee Church, so named because its cornerstone was laid in 1906, two hundred years after Protestant missions started work in India after the landing of Ziegenbalg and Plutschau at Tranquebar.

During World War II Kodai served as a rest area for soldiers. The Holiday Home has been developed from the original army quarters. While war still raged, on May 26, 1945, Kodaikanal celebrated its centenary with a public meeting, an exhibition of old pictures and relics, and a pageant in which every section of the community took proud part. In May 1950, Kodai celebrated its Golden Jubilee.

Currently there are posters about Kodaikanal in the railroad stations, documentary films about its beauties, and publicity pamphlets at the information centers. Thousands of visitors climb up the ghat to see its enchantments. Many stay only a few days. They stroll along Coaker's Walk with their transistor radios, take the sightseeing bus to Pillar Rocks, crowd the lake with happy boatloads of adventurers, watch the children swing high amid the formal gardens of Bryant Park, or walk the three miles around the lake, stopping at intervals to read the notices giving historical information.

Some visitors stay on to build homes in the outlying hills and become long-term lovers of Kodai, as are the hundreds of missionaries who, like migrating birds, begin to return early each March and leave only reluctantly in June.

Kodai statistics

Area: 6.5 sq. miles (17 sq. kilometers).
Population: 12,868.
Altitude: 7,688 feet (2,343 meters) above sea level at the Solar Observatory.

---

[18] CSI is the Church of South India.
[19] Also known as Highclerc.

Climate: Summer (March-May) maximum 20°C, minimum 11.3°C. Winter (January-February) maximum 17.3°C, minimum 8.3°C. Rainfall, S.W. Monsoon (June-September) 5.79" (152 mm) N.E. Monsoon (October-December) 8.53" (216 mm).

Clothing: Tweed or flannel can be worn during the day in the summer; while warm clothing is needed for the evening and night. In the winter months heavier woolen clothing is necessary.

Languages: Tamil is the State language; English is spoken and understood by many.

Air Connections: The nearest airport is at Madurai (75 mi.).

Rail Connections: The nearest railway station is Kodaikanal Road Station which is 50 miles from Kodaikanal by road. Rail-bus tickets to Kodaikanal Out Agency are available. Buses connect with all the important trains.

Road Connections:

Kodaikanal Road, the nearest railroad station. (Kodai—Ganguvarpatty—Batlagundu—Kodaikanal Road) 50 miles.

Madurai (Kodai—Ganguvarpatty—Batlagundu—Vadipatty—Madurai) 75 miles.

Coimbatore (Kodai—Batlagundu—Tharapuram—Coimbatore) 154 miles.

Tiruchirapalli (Kodai—Batlagundu—Dindigul—Tiruchirapalli) 122 miles.

Madras(Kodai—Batlagundu—Dindigul—Tiruchirapalli—Ulundurpet—Villipuram—Chingleput—Madras) 319 miles.

Frequent buses run between Kodai and Kodaikanal Road, Kodai and Madurai, and Kodai and Dindigul. Additional buses ply during the hill season.

Public Transport: A few taxis are available in Kodai. A ferry plies across the lake from the boathouse to Taps Landing.

Places of interest in Kodai

ASHRAM: The Ashram near Pillar Rocks offers hospitality and inspiration to all during the summer months.

BEAR SHOLA: Cross the Bund and take the road down on the left. Bears once used to drink above the falls.

BERIJAM LAKE: Seventeen miles from Kodai out on the hills, this lake supplies water to Periyakulam Town.

BLACKBURNE SHOLA: A shola over the big Shembaganur ridge, where in 1837 Collector Blackburne built a small house at the head of the pass. It was soon burned down.

BOMBAY SHOLA: The area from Central House towards Lushington Corner so named after a Major Partridge of the Bombay Army who lived there.

BROCKEN SPECTRE: You can sometimes see your own shadow in a rainbow ring on the clouds at sunset time from Coaker's Walk.

CAVE: A cave five miles from the Kukal Forest Bungalow was made when huge slabs of rock broke from the cliff and tumbled down the mountain side. Forty people can sleep inside.

COAKER'S WALK: From the Union Church along the steep southern face of the Kodai Basin rejoining the main road just above St. Peter's Church. Wonderful views of the plains by day and of the lights of Periyakulam by night.

COOLIE GHAT: The old trail down the mountain to Periyakulam that was used before the Ghat Road was built. Dr. S. K. Bunker of Ceylon identified 108 different species of birds on this path in one day.

DOCTOR'S DELIGHT: Two miles beyond Pillar Rocks there is a bold bluff which commands an even finer view than those from Pillar Rocks.

DOLMENS: Dolmens (cromlechs) are to be found in many places over the hills. The easiest to reach are to be found just below the milestone twelve miles from Kodai going down on the Ghat Road.

DOLPHIN'S NOSE: On the trail to Vellagavi you can stand on this rock perch jutting out over space. You need steady nerves and a head for heights.

FAIRY FALLS: Within easy walking distance off the road to Pillar Rocks.

FISCHER'S SEAT: A place where there was once a summer house just over the shoulder of the ridge from Shembaganur above the last zigzags of the bridle path. Mrs. Robert Fischer is reputed to have sat here watching for her Collector husband riding up from Madurai.

FORT HAMILTON: A place name at Berijam Lake, although there is no fort.

FORTY MILE ROUND: "the forty mile round," was started on June 6, 1929 at Moir Point when Sir I. E. Moir turned the first sod. It was opened by Sir G. F. Stanley, Governor of Madras, in February 1932 and named after Lord Goschen, the then Viceroy.

GREEN HUT: The nearest forest bungalow on the way to Berijam six miles from Kodai.

KAVANJI: A hill village where there is a forest bungalow and nearby a fine pool for swimming.

KUKAL: Another forest bungalow with a spectacular view over the gulf to Coimbatore.

Kodai Lake with Perumal on the horizon. (Peck)

KODAI LAKE: The Kodaikanal Lake is Kodai's finest asset. It spreads over an area of sixty acres and is skirted by a three mile tarred road. There is boating from the Boat Club and a public ferry plies from the Boat Club to Tapp's Corner.

LEVINGE STREAM: A stream below Pambar House on the trail to Dolphin's Nose.

MANJAMPUTI: Also known as "Elephant Valley," it is a deep valley near Poombarai.

MARION SHOLA: Named after the first butler to be in charge of this forest bungalow, it is a stop on the "sixty mile round."

MOUNT NEBO: The high point on which St. Peter's Church stands.

MUSEUM: The Sacred Heart College at Shembaganur has an excellent museum devoted to the archaeological remains and the flora and fauna of the hills. The museum may be seen by appointment with the Father Rector.

NEUTRAL SADDLE: Four miles below Shembaganur, also called "Rest-a-Bit." Nearby is the starting point for the climb to Perumal.

OBSERVATORY: The Solar Physics Observatory situated at a height of 7,688 feet above sea level and two miles from the Lake bund was founded in 1899. The only one of its kind in India, it has done original work in solar physics. It has a twelve inch telescope. Visitors are allowed between 10 a.m. and noon on Fridays or by previous appointment with the director.

PALNI HILLS: The whole range of hills on which Kodaikanal is situated. The Sanskrit name means "pig mountains" because Lord Siva is reputed to have rescued twelve naughty children from the form of pigs into which they had been changed by a devout rishi.

PERUMAL: The mountain you can see when looking down the bazaar street. It is the Kodai landmark. It is a stiff climb, and it is said that "they are fools who never climb it or climb it twice!" The mountain looks like a volcano but it is not.

PILLAR ROCKS: Six-and-a-half miles from the Lake bund these imposing rocks make an ideal place for picnics. The views are excellent and below the rocks there are several caves and chasms for the adventurous.

Pillar Rocks, circa 1850. (Douglas Hamilton)

PRIESTS WALK: A steep, narrow footpath connecting Sacred Heart College with La Providence and La Salette.

PROSPECT VIEW: A point near the Golf Course from which the entire Vaigai project can be seen.

POOMBARAI: An important hill village in which there is a forest bungalow.

RAT TAIL FALLS: The falls can be seen from Tumtungsarai near the beginning of the Ghat road. A sheer, slender plunge of water 994 feet in length, it is one of the highest falls in the world.

SILVER CASCADE: The falls by the roadside on your right in Tiger Shola between Neutral Saddle and Shembaganur.

TOP STATION: The top of a rope railway on the Kerala border beyond Vandravu on the back road down to Cochin.

VAN ALLEN HOSPITAL: Named after Dr. Chester Van Allen, a pioneer missionary of the Madurai Mission who was largely responsible for the opening of this hospital in April 1915. A maternity wing was completed after his death in 1923.

VANDRAVLU: The furthest forest bungalow on the "sixty mile round."

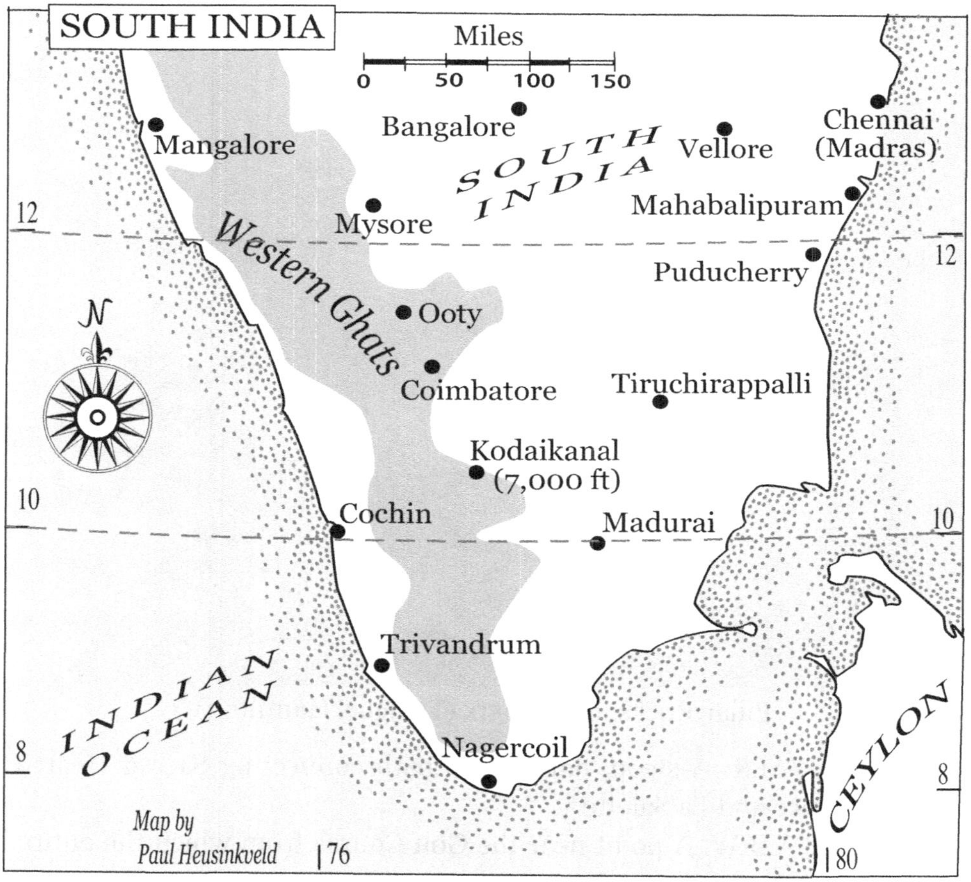

South India

CHAPTER 5

Fellow students of '55 and '56

CLASS OF 1955:
Alice Graham SILVER
Ann Bigger
Ann Gibbs
Annelena Meyer
Bernice Cawston
Carol Bond
Carol Corine Zigler
Carol LaVerne Lawton
Carolyn Enid Williams
Conrad Frank Heins
Curtis Bell
David Gordon Dickason
David William Stenger
Elizabeth Ann Gibbs
Emily Pope
Fay Ruth Voss
Frieder Hans Jungjohann
Gordon Seagrave
Harry Fredric Smith
Herman Otto Tauscher
Jean Towle REED
Jennifer Brammer
(Julia Brammer OAKSHOTT)
Jim Hatten
Joanne Hiebert SORENSEN
Joe Major
John Offering Schuring
Joyce Maxine Holleman
Julia Davis
Lois Ethel Thoms DICKASON
Margaret Little Carman
Marilyn Muir Travaille
Nancy Ann Spear
Nancy Filio
Owen Ross Thomas
Patricia Behm Hoehn
Patricia Joyce Behm
Peter Langston
Phillip Young
Robert Baker
Roy Lisker
Ruth Grace Keithahn
(Ruth Kirubai Keithahn)
Sterling Seagrave
Susie Inwood

CLASS OF 1956:
Alf Slaatten
Beth Gesler
Bruce Baxter
Bruce Carman
Burin Wongsanguan
Carla Butler
Chris Rolles
Dagmar Jungjohann
David Wiebe
Eddie Tegenfeldt
Frank Emerson
Gerald Buker
Harold Dick
Hans Kirchhof
Hubert Travaille
Jack Knoth
Jane Hatch
Keith Capen
Laura Carner
Margaret Newbigin BEETHAM
Marilyn Scudder
Mike Macc
Molly Schmitthenner
Paul Wiebe
Pat Wood
Peter Cormack
Richie Garden
Robert Mayer
Robert Lowenthal
Roger Erickson
Ronald Walker
Sanguan Zimmerman
Siem Speck
Tony Yetter
Wyva Hasselblad

The following are biographical sketches of some classmates of Kodai's graduating classes of 1955 and 1956.

Alice GRAHAM Silver

Attended Kodai 1945-1953. Graduated HS Dubuque, Iowa 1955. BA Wooster College, MA University of Michigan, Ann Arbor in British Colonial History. Married to Howard Silver from 1960 to his death in 1994. He was a professor at University of Wyoming, Laramie, where we raised three children. Teacher's certificate from University of Wyoming so I could teach 5th grade. Moved to Denver 2000 where I met and married Tom Byrnes in 2006.

Ann GIBBS Henderson

I was born in Kodai and it was my life for 17 years. I started school at the Presentation Covent but ran away from there and my mother started me at Highclerc in Grade 2 (missed Auntie Powell). Graduated in 1955. Went to Secretarial College in London (my parents were British). Met and married an Australian there, where I had 2 children. Came to Sydney in l966 where I studied to be a teacher and worked as that and as a manager in TAFE—the equivalent of your Community Colleges. Have 3 grandchildren. Have enjoyed many Kodai reunions in the US but alas no more.

Carol ZIGLER Kusserow

Carol graduated from Kodai in 1955 and then attended Thiel College in Greenville, Pennsylvania, for two years. She transferred to Wittenberg University in Springfield, Ohio, to major in music, graduating in 1959. She taught music in a public school for one year. She met Ralph Kusserow at Thiel College and they were married in 1959. She gave birth to three sons: Hans, Kurt and Timothy. She and Ralph were missionaries in Malaysia, Singapore and Tanzania.

Christopher John ROLLES

British: Class of 1956. Born in Kodai in 1939 and was there during the war and early schooling until his family left for 5 years in USA in 1946. Returned 1952-1956. B.SC Zoology Nottingham University, 1960. MB ChB Birmingham University, 1965. Worked as Pediatric Gastroenterologist in Southampton. Married Toni, a classmate, and had four children. Died January 2023. His love of India and Kodai and their influence were major factors in his and his family's lives.

Conrad HEINS

Conrad Heins, Jr. was born in Kolar, South India on April 25, 1939. He attended Kodai School from 1946 to 1955, with time away during WW II, and when his parents were on furlough in the States during his 8th grade year. He attended Randolph Macon College in Virginia from 1955-1957, and transferred to Drew University, graduating from Drew with an AB in Chemistry in 1959. He then went on to University of Illinois, Urbana, for graduate work in chemistry and received his PhD in Organic Chemistry in 1962. He was a post doctoral fellow in chemistry at Cornell University from 1962-1965. He met his wife-to-be at Cornell, (Alison Hower), and they married on June 26, 1965. Conrad worked as a bench chemist at DuPont in Wilmington from 1964 to 1968, and then took a research position at the University of Denver Research Institute. Daughters Sylvia and Katherine (Roo) were born in Denver in 1968 and 1970, respectively.

Alison and Conrad went to Scattergood Friends School in West Branch, Iowa, in 1975 as "the Science Department," he to teach chemistry and physics and she to teach biology. In 1980 the Heins family moved to Michigan, where Conrad taught a wide variety of renewable energy courses at Jordan College Energy Institute. In 1995 the family moved to Traverse City, Michigan. Conrad taught mathematics at St. Mary school in Lake Leelanau and renewable energy at Northwestern Michigan Community College. Conrad passed away at home in Traverse City on December 4, 2022.

David WIEBE

Paul and I (we are twins) were born in Hanamakonda, Andhra Pradesh, in 1937 attended by Dr. John Carman. We started school with Auntie Powell during the hill season at Kodai at age 4; at age 6 we went to boarding school there, living at Kennedy with Mr. Musil as our house parent. He read us stories from Jim Corbet's *The Man-eaters of Kumon* at bed time. At age nine we came to the US for an extended furlough, returning to India and Kodai in 1951 for the 1/2 year of 8th grade and the four of high school. I spent one semester of the junior year in complete bed rest in Kodai for TB of the spine, treated by Dr. Thomas in Madurai and Dr. Paul Brand of Vellore. Although I missed some of the adventures of my classmates at Kodai my memories are positive. Having a twin was a decided advantage.

Tabor College prepared me for medical school at the University of Kansas in spite of having a relapse of the spinal TB which was again treated with complete bed rest and meds (likely brought on by working in the potato sheds in California, sacking 100 pound bags of potatoes to earn tuition money). This time the 5-month bed treatment concluded with a spine fusion, and I've never had problems since.

I married my marvelous wife, Lorma, after the first year of med school (she taught 6th grade and made it possible). Then she roamed the world with me and our three children—first to Gorgas Hospital, a US public health facility in the Panama Canal Zone where I did an internship and general surgery training; then to Andhra Pradesh, India where I covered for two furloughed docs at two hospitals (I knew enough Telugu to manage) and of course did a lot of surgery; next a two-year readjustment to US medicine in a general practice at Pueblo, Colorado, where we added our daughter to the family; then an orthopedic residency at Gorgas Hospital in the Canal Zone; finally getting settled in Kearney, Nebraska from where we have done a number of short-term orthopedic assignments in Africa, Nepal, Bangladesh, Pakistan and of course India, where our kids all had a semester in Kodai School, and I was able to operate on kids with spinal TB in various stages of the progressive paralysis, with rewarding results.

The blessings of being a mishkid for me are multiple. It's afforded me a very interesting and rewarding life and even today some of my closest friends here in

Kearney are of the Indian community. I value my multiple entry visa to India. All of our celebratory meals always feature curry and rice.

Frank E. EMERSON

1954-56: Graduated from Kodai (earlier had been at Woodstock 1946-52). 1956-60: Randolph-Macon College, Ashland, Virginia, B.A. 1960-61: Duke University, M.A.T. (included one term junior high school teaching history and civics). 1961-64: U.S. Army (Intelligence Analyst). 1964-67: Assistant Field Director, American Red Cross (assisted, with local ARC chapters, in connecting families and soldiers; one year in Vietnam). 1967-72: University of Virginia, M.A. (history, ABD). 1968: married Mary Selden Dutrow (from Hampton, Virginia). 1973-01: Health Policy Analyst, Centers for Medicare and Medicaid Services, Baltimore. 2001-present: Retired and live in Baltimore.

Hermann TAUSCHER

Birthday 09-20-1937 in Koraput, province Orissa, now Odiya, as the fifth child of Marlene and her husband, missionaries of a German evangelical Lutheran mission. My mother had so much milk to offer me, that she decided to share it with an Indian boy of my age. So in reflecting of my life, sharing seems to have become a special characteristic of my development. I was quite unstable when I began to walk, due to one leg being longer than the other. I believe in 1938 my father was delegated to direct the seminary for oncoming Indian pastors to the plains of Kotapad. I had a very good feeling with my mother, seeing the photos that were taken between the moving to Kotapad and March 1940, the month when my natural mother died. It was a consequence of being forced by the English authorities to immediately gather with all the other German missionary families in Jeypur, then a central administrative city of the district of Koraput. It was within one or two days that everything necessary had to be packed and the families moved by police cars so there was no time to hand over the station, including a dispensary. The consequences were that anybody wishing or needing medication served him or herself. No proper supervision or control anymore. In the beginning of October 1939, my mother being pregnant, the fathers were collected by police cars and transported via police cars and train to the internment camp around Calcutta. The mothers and their children were left in Jeypur. My mother gave birth to twins on the 5th of November. That led to the permission for my father to return to his family for Christmas. Three months later my mother died together with our cook, who also had been suffering from tapeworms and took the same medicine as my mother.

Obviously that medication had been mixed up with other medicine. No time to say goodbye; within hours, death took her forever. I had, according to my sister, developed "autistic depressive" signs, barely talking and eating, and keeping whatever was served in my mouth for hours without swallowing. The twins were the center of attention and affection, and it could have been more dramatic if my older sister, Helga, wouldn't have taken the role of her mother and helped me over the years.

Two years later my father married an American nurse working for the Missouri Lutheran Mission in Vellore, south India. Alma Jungermann was very affectionate and loving to the twins, especially the younger one, Wilfried, born 11 minutes after Gerhard and nobody was prepared for this second birth. This might have led to a light cerebral damage, affecting motor coordination under which Wilfried had to suffer all his life.

In June of this year, Wilfried was, according to his will, finally released and called home.

Well, one year later all the foreigners of all countries supporting the Germans were gathered and transferred to an internment camp in Satara—close to Poona. Here at the age of six years I entered school. That was not easy for me. My brother Rolf was physically strong and fearless, jumping from the walls about 3 meters high, which gave him the advantage of not being tortured. Whereas the boys of my age, mostly children of British soldiers always designated us as "huns" and were quite aggressive.

Three years later in 1946 our family was released from the internment camp, and due to the connections my step-mother had with the American mission it was arranged that we—Helga, Rolf, and me—leave our parents and enter into the boarding school at Highclerc in Kodaikanal, South India.

In 1978, when I visited Kodai, an Indian lady confronted me with my behavior, that was characterized by getting up during the classes and walking along the windows and looking out, as if searching for our home. I couldn't remember that, because January 1947 my step-mother accompanied us to the school in Kodaikanal. I still remember how we all began to cry as we left our home in Kotapad to enter that boarding-school in Highclerc. However our stay in the boarding was only of short time, which I regretted, because the British children were all gone and we just had adapted ourselves, enjoying the pillow fights and all the other games that were offered. And then the sad news came, that all the German missionary children were to be boarded in an external boarding home: Penryn, probably due to the idea that after our parents would have terminated missionary service we would probably return to Germany, and therefore it would be better that we retain or improve our knowledge of German. That was not so successful as I conceived my knowledge of history, literature, geography of England and the USA was much better than anything concerning Germany. On returning to Germany after graduating from Highclerc school, talking, writing or traveling around in Germany was much more difficult and lacking the knowledge more embarrassing than it would have been in the USA. My older brother Rolf was not interested in going to Germany and together with the help of our new mother and her relatives in the USA found an arrangement that he could study in the vicinity of Pittsburgh after graduation in Kodai 1954.

After my graduation in 1955, I was determined to study theology and to become a pastor like my father. But that was not immediately possible as my knowledge in German was not good enough, so I had to go back to school for two years to be able to study at a German university. After ending this school, I opted to serve in the new German army. On the one hand that was a good decision, because the service was easy and I was undecided concerning where to study, and the payment was acceptable and of advantage at the time of my retirement. After one year of service, I applied to study theology in Bethel, a smaller private specialized university in the center for epileptic patients.

But I disliked theology: hours of discussion how biblical verses were to be interpreted and no possibility of verification of this or another interpretation, so in my view actually useless. What interested me more was Psychology, especially since I thought that would mean an occupation with individuals or small groups and not preaching in a church or other gathering of many people. I studied and received my diploma as a psychologist from the University in Saarbrücken in 1967. One year as an exchange student in the USA, '62 to '63, was a complete failure because the study program in Germany was completely different from the statistical and experimental Psychology in the postgraduate study program in America.

During my last years of studying in Saarbrücken I got to know my later wife, who was employed as an agent in the administrative service of the mayor of the largest village in Germany—at that time with 30,000 inhabitants. But a few years later, Dudweiler, where we got married and lived, was incorporated to the city of Saarbrücken, this against the will of most of the inhabitants of the "village."

I found employment in the labor department as a psychologist with examining and consulting of youngsters and adults concerning finding the right way to successful and meaningful work. Thirty-four years later I went into retirement, as my serving in the army and years of studying were also included in the calculation of the years needed for retirement.

My wife and I decided to end up by living in Southern France, near the Spanish border. We bought a house close to the sea, and lived there nine years, till the heart problems my wife had in the last years made us decide to give up our home and return to Germany, where consultation with doctors would be easier and more effective. But no, two weeks after our arrival in Germany my wife died due to a heart attack in the hospital. That made it clear for me, to leave that new home we had bought. The return to Germany ended with a catastrophe. I was completely undecided whether to try to live in my new house, but just as well unthinkable that I could find a new home to enjoy what we had planned and imagined. As from childhood on I was used to warm temperatures and after four years of back and forth between Spain, France and Germany, I finally decided to live in a seniors' residence in Spain, but unfortunately was cheated by a German real-estate agent—it was not a seniors' residence as promised with German residents, but just a normal vacation residence with Spanish vacationers coming and going, making good and stable contacts very difficult.

Now, 86 year old, with bad vision and other health problems, I am in the care of an English-speaking cuidadora—care taker. Without a valid driver's license and facing challenges in applying to prolong the license due to my problems of vision and age, I am grateful to have found a good friend, a stable support, an excellent driver and a good translator and finally a possibility of living a meaningful and helpful life. What more can I desire.

Jean TOWLE Reed

Attended horrible British Kimmins boarding school 1942-1943 at age five; happily attended Kodai School, 1944-1945 and 1947-1953. Graduated Northfield School, USA 1955. Graduated Earlham College Indiana, 1959. Masters at University of Chicago in Indian and Far Eastern Civilizations. Married Charles M. Reed 1963. Daughter Laura born 1970. I taught English & history, Hampton Institute 1966-68; Chinese Civilization & History at Old Dominion University 1969-70; High School English, Charlottesville, Virginia; not working in UK 1970-77 for Charles' Oxford PhD; Taught English at VPI&SU 1977-9; when in Washington, DC. at the University of Maryland 1983; librarian thereafter in Salisbury North Carolina 1988-1991 & Queens University, Charlotte, North Carolina 1992-2005. Retired Queens 1905. Got Library Masters 1905.

Jo Hiebert SORENSEN

Attended Kodai 1948-52, graduated Hillsboro High School, Kansas. Attended Tabor College, Kansas, and Wheaton College, Illinois; taught kids with special needs in Monmouth, Illinois. Married Frank Sorensen; three children, three grandchildren. Retired in Colorado. Growing up as a cross-culture kid was one of my life's greatest gifts.

Lois "Lowey" THOMS Dickason

Born 1938 in Kuwait to medical missionaries, Beth (Ethel Scudder) and Wm. Wells Thoms. Kodai School grade 1-12, except 6 & 7. Graduated Hope College, '59 and University of Michigan Physical Therapy '60. Married Kodai classmate, David Dickason '62. Dissertation and research travel to India, '64-'65, and '80-'81 (sons, John and Rob attended Kodai. Lived in childhood cottage with same caretaker cook). Practiced Physical Therapy and raised family in Kalamazoo, Michigan, while Dave taught at Western Michigan University until retirement in 2013. Moved to Penney Farms, Florida.

Molly SCHMITTHENNER Lesnick

Attended Kodai School from 1943 to 1956 (with 3 yrs off: 1945, 46 and then 1953 in States). Graduated from Kodai in 1956. Went to Thiel College, Greenville, Pennsylvania, graduated in 1960 with BA in Sociology. Attended University of Pennsylvania for two-year Certification Course in Occupational Therapy with OTR degree in 1964. Peace Corps, Venezuela 1966-68. Married Alan Franklin Lesnick in 1970. One son, William, daughter-in-law, Holly and two grandchildren. Worked 38 years as an Occupational Therapist for Dade County Public Schools. Lived in South Florida and moved to a CCRC in Orlando in 2021. Feel very grateful that I had the opportunity to grow up in the plains of India and in Kodai. For that I have to thank the Wood family for taking me on as a daughter after my parents' deaths.

Owen THOMAS

Kodai 1947–1955 (furlough 1951-2) Graduated May 1955. Oberlin College (Ohio) graduated 1959, Political Science Major. Johns Hopkins School of Advanced International Studies (SAIS), MA 1960-61, Washington D.C. Profession: International Business. Started and managed manufacturing business 1986 to 2002. Retired. Spouse for 65 years and counting, Meg Thomas, 3 children, 8 grandchildren, 1 great grandchild. Lived in Northern Virginia for 60 years. Moved to Maine 2018.

Patricia WOOD Remias

Attended Kodai from 2nd grade (1946) through graduation in 1956. Graduated from Midland Lutheran College in Fremont, Nebraska. First marriage in 1960 and had three daughters, while serving in Singapore and Malaysia as missionaries. Went back to college in 1978, where I took accounting courses in night school for ten years while working in the financial area for the Presbytery of Baltimore. Happy second marriage to John Remias in 1992.

Paul WIEBE

1956-60: via Europe from Kodai to Tabor College in Hillsboro, Kansas; soccer, hitchhiking, debate and studies, sort of in that order; two summers in California (potato sheds and a cannery), and two in Idaho (the Forest Service); Donna Beth, as in Donna Beth; BA in math in 1960.

1960-65: a year of high school teaching (math, physics and chemistry); marriage; a year in administration (an elementary school for migrant children along the Rio Grande in South Texas); twin children Cathy and Keith; pastor of two EUB country churches near Valley Falls, Kansas; graduate school (math, to sociology).

1965-87: university and college teaching (over the years in a somewhat freelance style): U. of Kansas (Lawrence), U of Illinois (Champaign/Urbana), U Sains Malaysia (Penang), U of Madras, Madras School of Social Work, Osmania U (Hyderabad), Hyderabad School of Social Work, Bethel College (St Paul), Bharathiar U (Coimbatore), Union Biblical Seminary (Pune); research (under the auspices of the East West Center (Honolulu), the Am Inst of Indian Studies, Fulbright, the Center for International Comparative Studies (Champaign/Urbana), UNESCO, the Lee Foundation (Kuala Lumpur), the Makerere Inst of Social Research (Kampala) and UNICEF; Children: five, in turn (through marriage) eight, grandchildren, Jacob, Nathan (and Hailey), Matthew (and Christine), Ryn (and Andrew) and Hannah.

1987-2001: Principal of that wonderful Kodaikanal International School of ours in its spectacular setting, Kodaikanal, Tamil Nadu.

2001-present: in retirement in and out of Coralville, Iowa. Donna Beth and I, now with four great-grandchildren (Leo, Archie, Nellie Rose and Monroe), in voluntary services of various kinds and I, over the past twenty plus years in going and coming liaison between our Mennonite Brethren conferences in North America and our MB conference in India in the work in which David's and my parents and grandparents were also engaged.

Ruth VASSAR Burgess

Born 8/6/39 in St. Margaret's Hospital, Pune, India. Parents: Rev. Ted and Rev. Estelle Vassar. Attended Kodai Highclerc School, 1947-52. Attended schools in Seminole and Levelland, Texas. Graduated from Texas Tech University in 1960 (Speech and Language major), University of Michigan 1963, University of Missouri-Columbia M.A. (1967) and Ph.D. (1979) (Speech and Language Pathology). Taught at Springfield and Strafford public schools, Evangel University (1968-76), Missouri State University (1976-2004), and Regent University (Ph.D program) 2004-2012. Married to Dr. Stan Burgess (also a Kodai student) Feb. 26, 1960, five children: John Bradley (1961), Stanley Matthew (1971), Dr. Scott Vassar (1972), Heidi Amanda and Dr. Justin David (twins 1974); ten grandchildren. Author of multiple books, articles, grants and awards.

(Faye) Ruth VOSS Harris

Attended Kodai 1953-55, graduated 1955. Attended Hope College, Holland, Michigan, Whittier College, California, '59, MS Pratt Institute, New York '88. Elementary teacher CA, VA, SC: Music Librarian, College of William and Mary, Williamsburg, Virginia 1988-2005. Married Donald B. Harris, Chaplain, US Navy in 1964, three sons. Retired in Williamsburg. Virginia. The two-year Kodai experience and fellow Kodaiites have proved very important to me in our peripatetic life.

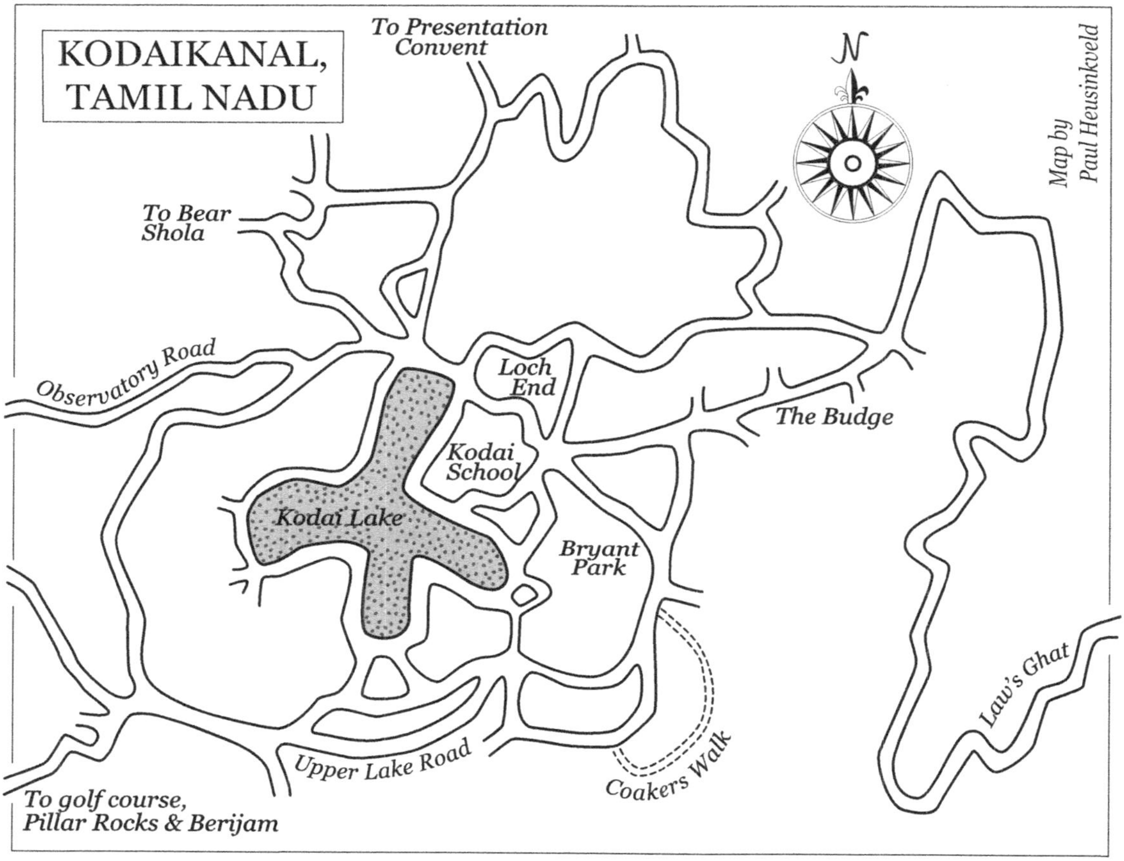

Kodaikanal and local environs.

CHAPTER 6

Kodai in the mid-1900s

Now in 2024, with the lifestyle we take for granted, it's a challenge trying to describe what everyday life was like in Kodai when we grew up there in the 1950s and 1960s. It was so vastly different that for people who have lived only in the Western world, it's hard to relate to.

We grew up in the waning twilight of the British Empire. India had only recently gained its independence, in 1948, and the vestiges of British rule, law, transport, and postage were still very evident in everyday life. India was still trying to find its identity, separating itself from its colonial past, and that wasn't an easy task; it was taking much longer than anyone anticipated. The primary challenge was forging a cohesive, common identity among a vast variety of people who spoke different languages,[20] lived in different geographical regions, ate different foods, looked and dressed differently, and had different religions and different social norms. It was a tough reality—this huge population that didn't have a whole lot in common made it tough—for the new government to work with.

In our mountain village of Kodaikanal, life was quite different from most of India. At 7,000 feet the weather was cool, nights were cold, the air was clean, and it was a fairly healthy environment.

Kodai was stunningly beautiful, as yet untouched by pollution (a word unknown to us) or overpopulation. Surrounded by grass-covered mountains and tree-lined mountain valleys called "sholas," we could not have asked for a more picturesque setting in which to spend our youth. We had our own mountain lake with its English-style boathouse and rowboats and punts. Kodai had waterfalls,

---

[20] India has 23 separate official languages; also, it is home to 122 languages which are spoken by at least 10,000 people.

Scene from Coaker's Walk. (Doveton)

cliffs, steep paths and roads, terraced farms, jungles, mountain streams, and escarpments that offered incredible views of the brown, dusty plains 6,000 feet below. On exceptionally clear days we could see the glimmering of the Indian Ocean, which was about 150 miles away. We could see the villages below lighting up at night, looking for all the world like little jewel boxes, and that's what we called them. We could see trains wending their way between rural villages and towns, leaving trails of smoke behind their coal-belching engines.

Kodai's weather was idyllic, especially in comparison to the stifling heat and humidity of India's vast plains. The cool climes of Kodai's 7,000 foot altitude had motivated the founding of our school in Kodai, and we reaped the blessing of that decision every day. We could gaze down to the plains from the nearby promontory of Coaker's Walk and sense the searing heat of the plains which were 6,000 feet below us. That view left us pondering how the sun scorches the lands below, yet we—one mile above—were comfortable in Earth's higher atmosphere.[21]

[21] Only a two-mile thick layer on Earth's surface is habitable by humankind. That's equivalent to 0.0005 of Earth's diameter. By analogy, the same proportion on a basketball would be four-thousandths of an inch.

Meandering along the edge of a mountaintop—almost precariously so—Coaker's walk offered a dramatic overlook of the broad plains below. The view etched its mark on our souls. There was something mind-expanding about that broad panorama, imparting a heightened sense of awareness. Gazing down at earth from so high a vantage point, we were above the clouds—and looking down on clouds is a rare treat for such young, impressionable minds. That looking down informed our perspective of life. The view imparted a near-omniscient perspective, as well as perhaps a level of enlightenment that was attained by realizing how very small—and how fragile—humankind's domain is. The scene enabled us to be somewhat detached from the world, and yet at the same time see it more clearly.

In Kodai it never got really hot; in fact our main concern was being too cold. Most of the year, and especially in winter, a jacket was required in the early morning and evenings. At night Kodai was always chilly. It was often cloudy and during the monsoons, we might not see the sun for days. When clouds covered us and during the all-too-common rains, a jacket was a necessity. It was strongly advisable to carry an umbrella at all times because clouds could arise from behind the mountains or from below the horizon at any time. But, of course, what young child is going to lug around a large umbrella (they were all large and cumbersome); so we didn't heed that advice.

Unless the moon was up and no clouds blanketed our town, nights were incredibly dark; pitch black with few, if any, dim street lights to guide our way outside. There was virtually no ambient light since the weak light of indoor fires or the brown glow of electric bulbs barely managed to illuminate anything outside the windows. It was not unknown to walk into a cow in the dark, scaring the daylights out of both cow and human. We all had cheap flashlights that usually didn't function, primarily because the batteries had an extremely short lifespan.

Our buildings were of the British style; the cottages were small with small rooms, brick walls, and corrugated metal roofs covered with brittle orange shingles. Any wood was painted dark green—the same color on every house. Windows were a lattice of small window panes (perhaps 6x9 inches); there were no screens. There was no heating or cooling or fans—only an occasional fire in the social room for our comfort.

Kitchens were behind the houses in their own separate small building, though somewhat attached by having a covered walkway between the two, an accommodation for keeping dry during the rainy season. This arrangement was to avoid kitchen fires bringing the whole house down.

At best, bathrooms off-campus had chamber pots—and it could get a lot worse than even that relative luxury. Only on the school compound did we actually have flushing toilets—a rare, and much appreciated luxury for performing private, embarrassing daily hygiene. Bathrooms reeked of humanity's most noxious odors or of the somewhat less offensive local cure-all disinfectant—Dettol. There were a few public bathrooms—"Water Closets," they were called—but they were simply beyond the pale, too vile to be utilized except in circumstances of extreme desperation.

Getting around Kodai was done on foot or—very occasionally—by bicycle. Very few of us owned a bike. The vast majority of the time we walked. I never rode in one of the rare cars that graced the roads within Kodai's environs. None of the teachers owned cars. Travel to and from Kodai was done by bus which took us to a train stop to board a train for long distance travel. For those traveling long distances—such as foreign travel—we traveled by ship or airplane. In our early years—up until the early 1960s—international travel was by ship; later we began using airplanes.

Other than a record player or a very rare radio or tape recorder with large reels, we had no electronic devices. For those lucky enough to have a short-wave radio, there were only two stations to listen to—Radio Ceylon or Voice of America—both of which were intermittently receivable and, even then, replete with constant static. Our typewriters were mechanical beasts that quickly exhausted our fingers; the keys got stuck and correcting mistakes was difficult, if even possible. The school had one telephone, and I never saw it used. Television was akin to science fiction. I never saw a TV in India.

Electricity was a rare, unpredictable, and expensive commodity—a luxury. If it was cloudy, stores might turn on their one light bulb when a customer entered, and they would certainly turn if off when the customer left. Light bulbs were small and gave off a weak yellow glow. Outages were common. In our dormitories, we kept candles and matches for such occasions.

There were a number of narrow, one-lane roads in Kodai that twisted around the mountains and narrow valleys. What few vehicles used them were mostly trucks carrying goods up and down the ghat.

Our allowances generally varied from 10 to 15 rupees a month.[22] There were 16 annas to a rupee and 6 pice to an anna; thus 96 pice to a rupee. However, officially there were 100 pice to a rupee. In good humor, we viewed this incongruity of the monetary system as part of the charm and mystery of life in India. Some things in life have no logical explanation.

---

22 Five rupees were equivalent to a dollar.

Tamil was the language of Madras State and Kodaikanal, but enough English was understood by shopkeepers to facilitate sales. Most of us were multi-lingual, speaking one of India's countless languages and dialects or, for those coming from Arabia, who spoke Arabic.

For entertainment we played games—tops, marbles, skating, tetherball, soccer, softball, tennis, basketball. When it rained we moved indoors and played board games such as monopoly, parcheesi, dominoes, and hearts.

The school's entertainment consisted of plays—usually very well done—and an occasional movie. Any movie that came to school was first watched by the staff to see if it was appropriate for the students' innocent minds. Occasionally, and much to our disappointment, the movie was deemed inappropriate. There was a movie house in the Budge which on rare occasions showed English-language films.

Books and comic books were the most common source of entertainment. We all had comics collections and traded them. Many of the comics became heavily worn and had missing pages, but that didn't make them unreadable. Magazines were rare. The library had subscriptions to *Time, Life, National Geographic* and two Indian newspapers that could be read only in the library.

Our health needs were looked after by a lone nurse and her assistant. They had a small dispensary—called the "Dishpan," or just "Dish"—that had three rooms for sick students. Being in the Dish was so unpleasant that one had to be very sick before succumbing to visiting there and possibly having to stay overnight. Medications were rare—even aspirin—and no one had their own personal medicine supply. I'm not aware of anyone ever having an allergy in Kodai. We did have to get shots regularly for cholera and other diseases common in the tropics. Sometimes epidemics such as whopping cough ravaged the town, and then we were forbidden to leave campus. Amazingly, we were all quite healthy. The most common ailment was diarrhea, usually the result of eating off campus.

Our clothing was limited, and, after some time we all knew each other's complete wardrobes. It was rare to have new clothing. In fact, we could recognize fellow students at great distances—such as across a valley—simply by what clothing they were wearing. For us boys, our wardrobe commonly consisted of three pants, a suit, five sets of underwear and socks, a swimsuit, a pair of shoes, and a pair of shorts and tennis shoes for sports.

Keeping our clothing clean was a challenge. We had few clothes to begin with, and then the Dhobi came only once a week to take our laundry, and then it was returned a week later. Being kids, we got dirty quickly—playing in the mud and rain. Since much of our wardrobe was at the laundry at any given time, we had to manage our wardrobe carefully—something we small kids were not skilled at. Our clothes were washed in a nearby stream by pounding them on rocks—washing machines didn't exist in South India. With the pounding of our clothes on rocks, they took a beating in more ways than one, and they wore out quickly.

In our early years, we boys gave little attention to our hair other than occasional efforts to comb it at the insistence of the housemothers. We didn't like the greasy hair oil—probably coconut oil—that was available to keep our hair in place because the oily goo would dribble down our faces. Our parents wanted our hair cut short. In retrospect, it was never clear why long hair was viewed negatively. A self-trained barber named Muhtu cut our hair with perpetually blunt scissors. Being old, suffering from a shaking hand, and constantly chewing beetle nut, left little of his attention to focus on his haircutting endeavors. There was no style to our haircuts; they were simply a way to keep our hair short and out of our eyes. Haircuts were no fun and we never got one by our own volition; we were told when to get one.

Our daily schedules were orchestrated by a series of bells that announced the time of day. If there was electricity there were electronic bells; if we were in the frequent blackouts, there was an old metal bell hanging in the school's quad that was rung manually. The metal bell's sound did not travel far in spite of how vigorously it was rung. The bells signaled when to get up, when classes started, and mealtimes.

There was no such thing as exact time in Kodai. Our times could vary considerably—probably by as much as 15 minutes—from the actual time. A few of us had watches—cheap mechanical ones that would gain or lose five minutes a day. We were constantly having to wind and readjust our watches. Real time was an illusion not even aspired to. In many respects, life in India was timeless. Time was a new and fascinating concept to the local populace who would often ask us the time and ask to see our watches which were a source of profound amazement to them.

We were perpetually hungry. The school dining room served three meals a day, and they were not to be missed since there was virtually no other source of food. One main dish was served and if you didn't eat that, you went hungry. Breakfast was usually toast and eggs, both in limited quantities and never enough to fill our ravenous appetites. Breakfast was the only meal of the day to offer bread. With respect to our nutritional needs, lunch had a main dish, a vegetable, and supper had a main dish, a vegetable and a dessert. Jokes and complaints about our cafeteria's food were legion.

CHAPTER 7

Tales from the 50th reunion

In 2005, The Kodai School class of 1955 held their 50th Reunion in Shepherd's Springs, West Virginia. As always, many Indian meals, memories, and stories were shared—here of some of those tales:

Letters Home
By Owen Thomas

Thanks to my parent's frugal nature about throwing anything away, I have a file full of letters written home from Kodai on Sunday afternoon during rest period. Hilariously entertaining to browse through them and to make an attempt to decipher some (really a lot) of the handwriting.

Here are some samples from 1947 (4th Grade), with some of the spelling and grammar improved on:

July, 1947

Dear Mother and Daddy,

How are you, I am well. I hope you are ok. I am in room 8 now because my roommate is in room 8. Please send me up some comics. Please send up the Rook cards and something to eat because I get hungry every minute of the day. I am very sorry that I didn't get a paper of the concert. I forgot.

Love,
Owen

July 13, 1947

Dear Mother and Daddy,

How are you? I am ok. I am glad that Mrs. Livinggood is gone. Please send up a package. This is what I want in it. Some jam and some Ritz and cocoamalt and a tin of Klim. The package that Aunt Irma was sending hasn't arrived yet. We have a nice teacher.

Love,
Owen

July 21, 1947

Dear Mother and Daddy,

How are you? I am ok. Just think today is the 21st. It seems that just a few days ago was the fourth of July. Today Francis Luckock (?) invited me out to lunch and Francis is my roommate. Please tell me when Lorna gets to San Francisco. Send up some books. I don't have anything to read except the Submarine Boys Trail Trip. Please send up something to eat cause I don't get enough to eat at tea.

Love,
Owen

Sept 14, 1947

Dear Mother and Dad,

How are you? I am fine. Tell Oakalal (our cook) that I liked those cookies that he made. I think that we ought to call the puppy Blackie if it's pure black or Puck the Second or something like that. Please send up one rupee one anna. That's how much a tin of condensed milk costs. Some of the boys in Kennedy are making a little place to play cars. The camping trip began on the 13th, that was yesterday. The fourth grade didn't go—horrid isn't it. I suppose next year the grade I'm in won't go.

Lots of love,
Owen

August 1, 1948 (Fifth grade)

Dear Mom and Dad,

Yesterday the twelfth grade had a carnival for all the school. They had a merry-go-round that was made by a cartwheel with a rope going up and tied to one of the rafters on the stage and had a ladder going across from one end of the wheel to the other and of course it extended out from the wheel. They had two chairs on each end of the ladder. Then they would wind up the rope and push you around. They had a fun house and you went with a partner through the place where the music rooms are and it was pitch black so you could not see a thing. You would start off and you would come to a skeleton with a flashlight shining on it—real spooky. Then you had to crawl through a tunnel made by chairs and finally you came to the other end and you had to climb a ladder and then you would whiz down a real slippery slide. I spent 8 annas. I hope that is not too much. I got four pears and got real wet while I was at it. They had a lot of refreshments for sale. They were real good. And they had a flying carpet which had a carpet tied to a pulley and the pulley was attached to a rope and then you went down in the carpet. They had a lot of other things there too.

Then after supper we saw a movie. Its name was *May Time.*

Room 1 and room 2 have got lots of tadpoles in our rooms. We have 9 and I think room 1 has 2. I am not sure. Give my love to Puck.

Lots of love,
Owen

The Taming of Mr. Musil
by Molly Schmitthenner Lesnick

As freshmen, we were all required to take Latin with Mr. Musil. Being advanced before his time, Mr. Musil divided us all into groups the first day: the high achievers, the medium students, and myself and one other student. Said student and I had to sit one on either side of Mr. Musil's desk, our profiles facing the class; very humiliating, but I got used to it.

Mr. Musil really was an excellent teacher, and a perfectionist, but he had a very short fuse and was intolerant of those who were not prepared. Phrases such as "thundering dunder blocks!" and the even more formidable "shockrfif cholera!" used to pour from his lips and he would stamp the floor at the same time.

One morning, Lowey Thoms was at the board (Lowey was in the high achievers' group), writing down some difficult declensions. She was nearing the end of the subjunctive case or something equally difficult, when Mr. Musil went into action. "No, No, you thundering idiot," he burst out. "Can't you see this is wrong, wrong!" and he stamped his foot.

Lowey, who was beginning to cry, put down her chalk, walked to the door, opened it and went out. She did not return. The class sat in stunned silence. Inside my head I was yelling "Yes, Lowey!"

Finally Mr. Musil cleared his throat, explained the mistake and went on teaching in a somewhat subdued manner. The period ended.

The next day class resumed as usual. Lowey was in her normal seat. I and my fellow sufferer continued in our normal seats by the sides of Mr. Musil's desk. But from that fateful day on, Mr. Musil seemed calmer. I don't recall him yelling out at anyone again. In fact, two years later, when I took French II, Mr. Musil's demeanor was decidedly pleasant, though he was still a rigorous instructor. Lowey, single handedly, tamed Mr. Musil.

Kukal Caves
by Hermann Tauscher

It was hot, dark, suffocatingly humid with a putrid smell of rotting leaves and branches taking your breath and droplets of moisture pearling from the branches. This was one of the sholas we had to pass through on our way to Kukal caves. Something slimy seemed to be within my socks and my feet seemed to be slipping somewhat in my shoes. I stopped to see what had happened when Rolf, my older brother, yelled at me to keep moving. Siem, a good comrade one class below us, had also stopped and was trying to remove something from the lower end of his trousers. Rolf and Frieder were accelerating the pace to get out of this damp, green jungle as fast as possible. Finally we came out into the glaring sunshine and the heat of the endless grassland—grass as far as one could see, covering the wide valleys and the gently sloped hills, with trees parsimoniously strewn out here and there.

Finding some rocks on which to sit down, we started examining our feet, our clothing. And there they were, the blood suckers, leeches—some still clinging to the jeans or shoes, others trying to get through the stockings. But some had achieved their goal and were stuck into the skin of our feet, especially mine. Others had already had enough and were lying in the shoes, thick and swollen up. Stains of blood had wettened our shoes. Rolf told us not to worry, since all we would need to do would be to cover these horrible, wormlike creatures with salt and they would immediately let loose. In fact, within 15 minutes we had gotten rid of all of them, had our shoes and socks dried, had disinfected the wounds with iodine. After eating bananas and taking some large gulps of water, we were prepared to continue our hike. "Why didn't you let us stop and get rid of these leeches immediately?" we asked Rolf. His calm response was, "Because they would have crept on you faster then you could ever have removed them."

We—Siem, Tyke, Frieder, Rolf and I—were on our way again heading for the Kukal caves after having left Kodai early this Friday morning. We were heavy laden with pots and pans, food, water and all the requirements of a camping long weekend. Arriving at a crossing of paths and no clear sign of which path to follow to Kukal caves, we discussed the situation and fixed the path we would risk. The endless chirping of the seemingly thousands of cicadas, swelling and diminishing in loudness, the lonely and somehow melancholic call of apes and all kinds of strange noises were our company as we silently, one behind the other, made our way through the grassland.

But the path became narrower and narrower. We weren't convinced we were on the right path to Kukal caves any more, but heat, thirst and fatigue smothered all discussion and turning back was out of question. After about three hours of tight walk, we discovered a small stream; it was about five yards broad with wonderful clear water gurgling down the hillside. There was no discussion now; here is where we were going to camp.

After quenching our thirst with this pure, cold water, we cleared a circle at the bank of the stream, placed rocks on which to put the pots and pans, collected grass and dried wood to do the cooking. Tyke and Siem took the responsibility for the cooking. I collected fern and grass and brought them a little higher uphill, where there was a large rock overhanging the slope. That wasn't a cave, but it offered shelter so beds were prepared. Rolf and Frieder investigated the area around our camping place to make sure we were sufficiently safe here. In the meantime the rice was cooked, and corned beef mixed with some vegetables and spiced with red chilies and curry spread its aroma all around. What a fantastic meal after such a day. We sat around the fire place, listening to all the exotic noises of birds, apes, hyenas or whatever, trying to guess what we were hearing, discussing if and how we should get to Kukal caves. When the nearly full moon made its appearance over the ranges, we stumbled up to our "cave," hung up one kerosene lamp and placed another one at the entrance to prevent animals from disturbing our sleep.

We must have slept like dead, because the sun was already standing fairly high in a clear blue sky when we finally crawled out of our sleeping bags. Some prepared breakfast while the rest were taking their morning bath in the stream. After breakfast, things were cleared up; eatables were stored in pots and cans and refrigerated in the cool stream. There was no talk any more of breaking off our camp here and trying to reach Kukal caves. We were here to discover this new area for ourselves. And so about eleven o'clock we were on our way again.

We were following an animal trail uphill and had barely made half a mile when we discovered the shedded skin of a python just a foot off the trail. Stretching it out, we found it to measure well above five yards long and with an estimated diameter of at least five inches. That wasn't something to leave us cool; we had become aware of a danger, not anticipated. So nobody had the idea of taking that skin with us as a souvenir. A cautious silence had replaced our initially excited and exuberant behavior.

Suddenly we heard a strange noise coming from somewhere downhill, getting louder fast, at first not identifiable, then sounding like a herd of deer running toward us, invisible in the grass and bush land. Four of us instinctively stepped aside of the trail; Rolf, being quite a way ahead of us, evidently hadn't taken note of that noise. In unison we yelled at Rolf to step aside, when already a huge Sambal stag, at least six feet high, stampeded past us, barely missing Rolf. It continued its stampede all the way uphill. Was that close! Why the heck was that Sambal stampeding up hill like that? Had it been frightened by us, or was some other animal chasing him, possibly a tiger? All sorts of explanations were proposed. But aside from the danger we had just encountered again, the joy of having taken a glimpse of such a wonderful animal so close prevailed and stimulated us to search for more.

We crossed several ranges and were on the point of returning to our camp when we discovered a herd of elephants grazing peacefully far down the slope. Carefully we approached the herd, looking for a good observation point. It was a herd of about 10 to 15 adults and two small ones. It was absolutely fascinating to observe these wild elephants in their natural environment. After about twenty minutes one of us whistled and immediately the herd became attentive and formed a circle around their young ones, heads turned outward. In trying to get a little bit closer, one of us stepped on a loose stone which began rolling down the steep slope. Stupid as we were, this led to letting other stones roll down the slope. With a loud trumpeting outburst the herd of elephants stampeded down hill out of our sight, leaving a cloud of dust and the sound of branches breaking behind.

What could one expect more? We climbed up the hill again and decided that we had seen and experienced enough and that it was time to return to our camp. And that is when torture began. There were so many animal trails and we had not marked ours. We really got lost, although it took us a long time to admit it. I had no idea where we were and in which direction we should go, but others were sure of the direction. The grass surrounding us was high—well, six feet high, if not more—so that you couldn't see far enough ahead. Thirst and fatigue came as we kept on walking and walking, seemingly without any sign of approaching our camp. Anxiety came up, since the daylight was rapidly diminishing, leading us to walk faster. We had to stay on animal trails. There was no alternative, since the grass was not only high, but its leaves were sharp and rough as blades. I guess some of us began praying as twilight set in.

The full moon began to make its appearance over the ranges of the surrounding hills, as we suddenly heard the gurgling sound of a stream. Yes, we had been wandering in a huge circle and had now finally, almost miraculously, found our way back to our camp. I don't remember much of anything else, whether or not we ate something. Probably I and all the others were so dead-tired that we didn't have any energy left to prepare anything.

Today I wonder what endlessly patient angel had watched over us careless youngsters.

The Kidnapping
by Jo Hiebert Sorensen

The cry woke me up. Instantly my whole body was on alert. What was it, that eerie sound that had jolted me out of my sleep?

The sound came again, a wailing cry, desperate and forlorn. It came from somewhere below the window of our upper-story room. My mind picked up the sound and tried to place it, and then I knew what it was—it was a child's cry. Someone was kidnapping a girl from this dorm where my sister Gwen and I were sleeping. Mother had left us here only hours before, and now our lives were in terrible danger.

I huddled as far down under the covers as I could, quaking. There were five girls in the room to which Gwen and I had been assigned, all 4th or 5th graders like we were. Surely if the kidnapper came back he'd go to a different room, or if he came in our room he'd grab a different child. Not Gwennie, though—she'd put up too fierce a fight. I wasn't as good a fighter; I pushed myself even farther under the blankets.

The cry came again, muffled by the covers but sounding farther away now, as though it came from down the hill behind the dorm. The kidnapper was escaping and taking the child with him. Wasn't anyone going to rescue her? I threw aside the blankets and sat up. Where was the matron? Should I wake her? But I was too frightened to get out of bed and go down the long scary hallway to her room. And it might not be a child being kidnapped and then I'd be in trouble for getting her up needlessly. Should I wake Gwen and tell her about it or, better yet, should I climb in bed with her so I would feel safe?

The cry had ceased. I lay back down, tense, waiting to hear it again but all was quiet. As I listened for any sign of the kidnapper returning, I drifted into a restless sleep, unaware that there would be many more nights of hearing the sound of a child being kidnapped—the sound of a jackal beneath the window.

And so I managed to survive my first night in Boyer Hall.

What a Day and What a Night
by Hermann Tauscher

I realize that my memories are so vague and blurry concerning details, which now seem to me to be of great importance. What was the name of the place we made this hike to? And who is we? And does any one have the answer to the "when?" Correct me, if you may, since most of you seem to have much more distinct and precise memories concerning these essential details.

It must have been quite a large group of us—15 to 20 perhaps, I suppose members of class of '55 together with several of the class below us, and strangely enough a mixed-gender group, rare enough for us boys who prided ourselves of special toughness concerning adventurous hikes.

So everything was different. The hike was well organized; we didn't miss any trails or get lost or have any dangerous encounters with wild animals or any accidents or physical breakdowns due to fatigue. It didn't even rain and the temperature was just right. So it was more of a long walk, with groupings and regroupings of the participants, almost effortless walking leisurely, relaxed, with a lot of laughter, gossiping and discussing. But it was already rapidly dimming when we finally reached our goal: a hut. This was too small to accommodate us all; so the girls disappeared into the hut, while we boys started gathering wood, pinecones or whatever suitable material for our campfire.

It had already become dark when we finally all found our places in a circle around the fireplace and began roasting meat stuck onto branches we had broken off from the mimosa trees. There we were sitting 20 miles from our school and with no humans in the vicinity, separated from civilization, hearing just our own voices or the cries of birds or other animals of the forest surrounding us. But the hours passed by so quickly in an atmosphere I might best describe as light, peaceful, in perfect harmony one with another and with the environment surrounding us; timeless, just as if we had always belonged to one another and never had any intention of going apart.

The full moon stood in the zenith of the cloudless sky as gradually fatigue overwhelmed the contentment and gaiety, letting the voices get quieter and the girls steal out of the circle to find their night's rest in the hut. But we boys stood around there suddenly realizing that we hadn't cared about preparing our night's shelter. And despite the extremely bright and clear light of the full moon, we were too tired and absolutely incapable of anything like work.

Underneath those grand pine trees there was a bed, a bed of daisies, so dense, so thick, so high, no mattress could have concurred. Here we just let ourselves fall down, one after the other, leaving enough room for each one of us to be alone with his thoughts and feelings. No worries concerning snakes or other potentially dangerous beasts came up.

Lying on my back and looking up into those silvery-blue branches high above me swaying to and fro with the gentle wind and hearing the sighing of the branches and twigs interrupted by some strange night birds call, it seemed as if I had reached a point of bliss, of closeness to all others in our group, of closeness to nature and to the eternal. What a day and what a night!

The Early Education of a Missionary Brat
by Jean Towle Reed

In my little domain I was queen. The outcaste Christian community, relegated to the outskirts of the Hindu village of Vadala, India, set the boundaries of my territory. My position as the eldest daughter of Towle-Sahib, the Massachusetts missionary, gave me power; my Indian friends were my willing subjects. Without a doubt I was a self-satisfied pre-school autocrat, indulged by playmates, cocooned by parents and nurse, exercising my unchallenged will. I was content, that is, until at five I was sent away to boarding school.

Till then Vadala for me was heavenly. When I tired of hide-and-seek I scrapped the game, whether or not my playmates agreed. I might command a search for the blood-red, speckled eggs of the weaver bird or make my followers my "family," scolding and exhorting in fluent village Marathi. Or I would abandon them to wander about the experimental farm my father ran. There I'd watch the farm boys sitting on the simplest wooden stands, perched above the ripening grain, slingshots in hand. Their job was to scare off hungry birds. And in the course of my rounds, I usually checked the cattle sheds. Among our best draft animals and milkers were the hardy water buffaloes. One day a mama buffalo rewarded my attention by giving birth and licking her calf into life.

When the Marathi Christian school pre-empted my companions, I voluntarily joined them. We sat cross-legged on the schoolroom's hard dirt floor, each child equally insignificant in the eyes of our stern Indian teacher. Every pupil had a slate and a slim slate-pencil with which to practice the strange Marathi alphabet. To chant our numbers sing-song unison was particularly satisfying. Warm winter sunlight filtered through the small, barred windows of the mud-plastered building, revealing dancing particles of dust. The room smelled comfortably of the cocoanut oil that the children used to slick their hair—altogether a friendly, yet purposeful place.

So it seemed before Mother yanked me out of the village school. I had picked up some lice with my learning. My devoted nurse or ayah, expert at finding and destroying the nits, found too many to demolish. Nor did the kerosene treatment work. Mother's desperate remedy was to sacrifice the pigtails I'd so proudly grown almost to my shoulders. To ease my humiliation at being shorn bald, Mother attached the precious pigtails to my favorite doll. Even that consolation meant little now, for during every waking hour I had to cover my naked scalp with a scarf.

Soon thereafter Mother, who had long worried over the effects on my character of my unchallenged status, broke the news. I must go to school—an English school, far from family and friends. She and Dad wholeheartedly wished that our village had an English school or that I could attend one in the nearest city, where American colleagues lived.

Since neither place had Protestant elementary schools conducted in English, the alternative was to send me to a British-run boarding school in the nearest hill station. Farewells delayed us. There were so many to leave behind—my Indian teacher; my Indian friends; Sambhaji the cook; my ayah; Alice, my baby sister; and Snowwhite, my Persian cat. Clutching my pigtailed doll, I waved goodbye.

In time we left the dusty plains of central India behind us, slowly negotiating the winding roads up the Western Ghats, the hilly region separating the Bombay coast from the inland Deccan Plateau. Instead of small, spiny cacti, scrubby thorn trees, feathery neem trees, and spreading banyans, we now saw a tangled profusion of jungle-like trees, shrubs, and vines. Monkeys fighting over berries raised the alarm as we drove by. Brilliant emerald bee-eating birds darted to and fro. Minahs and parrots raucously added to the tireless caucassing of the birds. And where they left off , the cicadas, crickets, grasshoppers, and many more took up to swell the din. The higher we climbed into the hills, the cooler the air and quieter the countryside. Mile after miles we wound around frequent hairpin turns along narrow roads without guardrails. Our destination was Mahableshwar, the vacation spot favored by the governing British or the proselytizing missionary, both desperate for relief from the oppressive heat of the plains.

As much as I hated leaving home, I noted fascinating sights on the way to the school I dreaded. The lush green rainforest dressed the red Mahableshwar earth with ferns and flowers. One could spot tiger lilies, jack-in-the-pulpits, or the aromatic jasmine so seductive to the jewel-like, tiny hummingbirds or to the elegant Indian counterpart of the bluejay, the hoopoe. One could also watch the Highland Scots Regiments whose bagpipes now and again drowned out nature's noises: they kept the English king's peace where humans lived. Here, too, I later would observe Gandhi leading his prayer meetings. But, once inside the dismal walls of the Kimmins Boarding School, I could only see my parents leaving. With their departure the color leached out of my life.

Suddenly I found myself surrounded by curious British children, pointing at my stubby hair, awkward-looking even under my wretched scarf. To them I looked like a "DP"—a displaced person. Certainly, my American speech sounded harsh amid the soft, clipped English accents. Giggles, groans, poking fingers, grabbing hands probed me. When I bridled and flinched, the English tormentors encircled me, stripped away my doll, and left us both shattered.

In the stark barracks that served as a communal dormitory, however, misery united all the children. We were young—from five to seven years old—abjectly homesick, desperately unhappy. But no paroxysm of sobs sufficed to alter our invariable regimen. Up with the dawn, each child feverishly tidied her space, smoothing the drab army blankets on her narrow iron bed frame into creaseless hospital form. The bed and its bedside cubicle for personal belongings defined each child's private preserve. Each morning we stood for inspection. The skinny, severe Anglo-Indian we called Matron could see at a glance if the identical rows of bed and girls lining the room on both sides met her immaculate standards. Any offending child suffered demerits: her free time might be curtailed, her "care package" from home confiscated.

From bedchamber to breakfast hall we marched. And woe to the child so foolish as to wet her bed. Inspection revealed the culprit, whom the baleful Matron draped with the soiled sheet, seating her in dunce-like fashion to be pilloried. Even without punishment, meals were a trial. The food was execrable—tasteless, leaden, cooked to a pulp. Porridge looked like congealed slugs. Yet we had to eat everything put on our plates. As often as I could I forced down the unaccustomed runny eggs. They insistently came back up. Many times I went hungry to the classroom.

Schooling, of course, dominated our day. Our teachers brooked no nonsense, made no concessions. Any child who dared to wiggle or speak out of turn felt the sharp rap of a ruler on knuckles or shins. One always stood up to politely answer when questioned. As soon as a child mastered the alphabet, she proceeded to reading and writing according to strictly prescribed rules. It was difficult enough to form one's printed letters with the proper penmanship: it was the more painful for me who, though left-handed, had to write only with my right hand. Stubbornly I resisted. To teach me obedience the teacher would send me to the infirmary where the nurse forced fishy-smelling cod liver oil down my throat. However good for my health, this remedy and all others failed to correct my left-handedness. Among the battles in my prolonged war with the authorities at Kimmins, it proved to be my sole victory.

In conflicts with Matron, I always lost. The most memorable occurred the afternoon of a friend's birthday party. Since Monica was a day student, I received special permission to attend her party, and thus gleefully missed the daily "constitutional" or required walk that the boarding children had to take after classes each day, whatever the weather. The party was glorious. Because it finished early, I found myself, balloon and birthday treasures in hand, back in an empty dormitory. Out of impulsive high spirits, I hid.

Failing to locate me for an hour after the walkers returned, the Matron exacted her revenge. She locked me in a pitch-dark storeroom adjoining our barracks. There she left me, terrified, while everyone else ate supper. All the rumors I had ever heard about the local panthers' penchant for naughty children crowded my mind. When finally released from my dark prison, I could not sleep for fear of the devils beneath my bed. Matron said they stoked their fires high, the better to torment wicked children like me.

Nor would I ever forget being framed for a crime I never committed. A child who could not find her precious store of candy accused me of stealing it. So hounded was I by the housemother and her assistant that after several days of badgering I capitulated to the brainwashing and "confessed." Though the candy surfaced later, no one bothered to apologize. Incidents like these haunted me in nightmares for years thereafter.

By the end of the school year my classmates and I could read and write with the facility of American second or third graders. Our teachers expected complete attention, unstinting application, and good retention. They punished far more frequently than they praised, and we learned fast: we had little alternative.

One of the few tasks we welcomed was writing our required weekly letter to our parents.

In a round, neat hand we would declare our unhappiness, plead to be taken home. These letters we turned in, ostensibly to be mailed by the teacher or Matron. Few reached their destination: all were censored. Our preceptors either destroyed the unmitigated cries of anguish, or they doctored the less damning letters.

This heartless practice was fiendishly clever, because when during vacation I described my experiences or bitterly complained of mistreatment, Mother and Dad discounted my recital as evidence of an over-active imagination. My letters, after all, showed no confirmation. Uncomprehending, my parents tried to convince me that attending boarding school worked to my long term advantage. Look, they said, at what I had so quickly learned. I would need that and more in order to qualify for an American college.

So, against my will I was returned to the English school for one more year. At Kimmins I learned many lessons, some of them unintended, but all at a price.

The Ringleader
by Ann Gibbs Henderson

I shared a room in Boyer with Pat Wood, Lowey Thoms, and Miggie Carman (maiden names). We had the room with an outside door as we were to be "trusted." Alas, we were not and on more than one occasion we left the dorm to go on the lake. On one of these occasions, we were sighted by a staff member, and subsequently I was hauled into Papa Phelps' office and accused of being the ringleader and leading my friends astray. Why I was selected as the ringleader I don't know, but I often thought it was because I was not the child of a missionary? Anyhow, I am pleased my long term friends were not led astray by me and are upstanding citizens of the US.

Another note: Lowey used to have shipped from Muscat kerosene tins of dates which we ate in this room in Boyer. These we devoured with peanut butter. What a treat. Alas it was the beginning of my fatness!

Rain, Rain, Go Away
by Jean Towle Reed

We couldn't ignore the rainy season at Kodai; it captured our senses. There was the sound. Tin roofs abounded, especially over the walkways. Monsoon rains beat a rat-a-tat-tat on those roofs that brought raining bullets to mind. The force of sheets of impenetrable rain loosed a barrage of sound over which we had to yell to make ourselves heard. An enterprising musician could have composed a tympanic tattoo to echo the rains variable rhythms.

There was the sight. I would stand in awe of the wall of water, safe in the corridor of walkways, save for the spatter of ricocheting drops. When the power-rain let up, a gentle drill of drops persisted until it seemed we'd never see the sun again. Grey was the dominant color of our monsoon season lives—grey, threatening skies; grey, damp army blankets on our beds, grey emotions. It was as if the external world made physical our inner physic wail of homesickness. As the days dragged on, it was hard not to be dejected or depressed.

The rains brought their own smells—the heavy, earthy smell of mud; the intensification of other odors, whether of cooking or rotting vegetation; the pervasive reek of mold emanating from our closets or piles of clothes. When the clouds and mists lifted, letting the sun shine, the world smelled and felt fresh, rejuvenated.

To avoid the oppression of the monsoon air, we would resort to indoor sports and activities. Some, lacking religious prohibitions, played cards. Many of us headed for the gym, where we worked off our excessive energy in basketball games or rollerskating. I went to the States with a chipped front tooth as the result of a game of "Crack the Whip."

Monsoon rains intensified everything. To counter its dominion over our lives, we would chant "rain, rain, go away; come back on another day." When the watery curtain lifted, Kodai rang with our laughter and glee.

Some Thoughts
by Joyce Holleman

I have somehow been resistant to delve into my Kodai experience and complete my questionnaire, despite the urging of several of you. I finally completed it today and then read everyone's profiles. I'm glad I did it in that order or I'd never have gotten it done. Each of you brought up so many memories for me—of you, personally, of school activities, of teachers, of places and of the experience we all have in common.

One of the most impressive things is how much we've accomplished! As doctors, educators, therapists, businesspeople, ministers, missionaries, thinkers, philosophers, parents and grandparents, our contributions to this rather crazy world have not been negligible or niggardly. We've given with whole hearts, minds and spirits as we were taught to in Kodai. Papa has to be very proud of us, wherever he's hanging out!

I've felt a little out of place since I've had a couple of divorces and no children, but we've covered lots of territory amongst us, and that area needed covering too, I guess. Along with Hermann, I had to do most of my learning about India after I got back to the states, and I'm so glad to know that's no longer the status quo in Kodai. I'm also happy, again with Hermann, that Kodai school now has a much broader approach to religious philosophy and practice. Despite the limitations to spiritual inquiry while there, Kodai offered so much more than I'd previously known, it probably gave me all my sheltered self could handle. Had it been any more liberal or inclusive in its religious teachings, I'd never have been sent to Highclerc and would have ended up in Conoor at the British girls' boarding school there!

From our profiles I was made aware again of the cliques we formed and how we excluded others we hadn't really gotten to know. The pain of not belonging is especially acute when a child is put into boarding or made to live in a different hostel than most others and finds acceptance unavailable and doesn't understand why or how to rectify the situation. I know I refused to go to the separate boarding facility established by the fundamentalist churches in the last few years I was at Kodai. Now children of my parents' denomination are sent to Penang, Malaysia to school, lest Kodai's inclusive religious policy pollute their minds. (Yes, there's still some self-righteous bitterness there! I too hated having to be different and I fought it all the way.) But I didn't feel left out of the "in crowd," and I see again how I perpetuated the cruelty of that crowd. For that I seek forgiveness from those who felt excluded—we each know whom I'm asking to forgive me.

I was always amazed by Harry Smith. He'd had to have an emergency appendectomy—I think, during our junior—year and was recuperating in the Dish while I was there for back problems, probably. We talked a lot—got in big trouble with Annie Putz for talking into the night when we were supposed to be resting, and there I was in Harry's room—and I was fascinated that he was unafraid to die, when he'd been so very ill it had been a possibility. He didn't even claim to be a Christian—how could he not fear death? Made me do a lot of thinking.

I'd had a crisis of faith that year, before or after this incident, I don't know, but Marty Heinz was on the hilltop, so I went to see her to talk about it. She was teaching us RE at that time and I knew she'd listen to me and treat my need with respect. I told her I was "up a tree" and "stumped," and she noted that it wasn't a very tall tree if that was the case. Lightened me up, to say the least, without belittling my concerns. Though I fluctuated in my adherence to my parents' teachings after that—returning to the States and their home church brought me into wanting to be accepted there—I finally found I couldn't embrace their doctrines and have since come to terms with my own spiritual awareness and practices.

Kodai, India, our teachers and our parents combined to create us responsible adults who have done our best to make a difference in our worlds. In teaching high school and working with my peers and the hundreds of students who filled my classes, I was able to give freely of myself and my experiences, all the while treating all others with much respect and dignity. It's amazing how students respond to such treatment. I often said of teaching English to immigrant students, that the only other language I was fluent in was "Smile." I'd make the student welcome and, if possible, find someone else who spoke their language in my classes or in the school, and all would go well from there.

All the Kodai influences were equally present in the "regular" classes I taught from Shakespeare to English Workshop. The most fun for me was teaching Mythology and Comparative Religion (masquerading as a religious lit course in the English department). I was so delighted when Bill Moyers did the programs with Joseph Campbell—my hero! What fun! The students caught the enthusiasm from me and crammed the classroom, with even a waiting list. Very flattering!

The practice of respect and dignity for myself and my students generated being asked to lead or participate in special programs for students with needs of various kinds. We experimented in many ways and formed deep friendships among the teachers involved as well as the students. And I truly believe I have Kodai to thank for taking my innate skills and teaching me how to use them successfully.

Unfortunately Kodai didn't have much to say to us about intimate interpersonal relationships, or about how to get our deepest needs for love and acceptance met. Apparently most of you didn't experience the same lack of those skills that I knew, and it could have been unique to my family or children of our denomination, as I wasn't alone in this disability or lack. It took us a long time to learn to love ourselves and realize no one else could love us enough to fill the needs inside. I have, as an adult, great sensitivity to the needs of others and will do all I can to support them. I was aware of others' needs as a teen, but not so intent on being kind. I knew who was being excluded and did nothing about it. I was so very glad I was included, I didn't worry much about who wasn't. Not a happy memory, though true.

It was great to be a big fish in a little pond, and I was very shocked to return to Oklahoma and a small private university where I was unknown and none cared. If I'd gone to any of the big universities away from home, I'd have quickly drowned and been totally unsuccessful, possibly not even alive. I had the sense to know I needed my family around me for the first couple of years back in the States, though their return to India when I was a sophomore was extremely difficult. The choir at Tulsa University gave me a place to belong and close friendships formed there pulled me through.

Did any others of you feel really sad that your parents weren't around for your graduations from college or your weddings? Of course, I seem to be the only one of us who's had more than one of the latter! I guess I heard that Frieder, bless his soul, had also known the pain of divorce. He and I were among the ones who were foolish enough or rebellious enough to smoke, as well! Sadly it took his life, and I've been spared any major consequences.

It was rebellion and a huge imperative to get as far out of Oklahoma as possible, as soon as possible, that led me to California, where More is acceptable and less is condemned. Both the Los Angeles area in the early 60's, and especially the San Francisco Bay area a few years later have allowed me to find who I truly am and accepted me for it. Very freeing.

I'm so proud to be a member of the Kodai Class of 1955. We're a great group and bring honor to all the other students of Kodai, before and after us.

Bahote Salaam! Namaste!

More Thoughts
by Jean Towle Reed

The profiles and memories of my Kodai classmates move me. I feel special kinship with Hermann and Joyce because they are brave enough to admit to pain and difficulties in finding their way. More often than not I felt like an outsider looking in to the close-knit friendships around me. It was years before I gained a solid, realistic sense of self—not till after my sophomore year in college. That was the period in which I lost faith in a personal God. I also lost the sense of superiority I had over those superficial Americans I boarded with at Northfield Mt. Hermon. It was humbling to learn how little I knew.

Yet as Joyce so compelling tells us, we carried away from Kodai certain truths and habits that have sustained us in the bumpy course of life. We learned a kind of communal sense, a purpose in service, and a depth of friendship I have seldom found equaled in these United States. Most of us discovered that we are hardy creatures, well-schooled in adversity, so have lived to construct new meaning. I feel more zest for life now that I ever did as a youngster and a teenager.

I think it telling that while I enjoyed re-connecting with two or three people at my Northfield Mt. Hermon 50th reunion in June, I gravitate most readily to my Kodai classmates and friends. Cheers for our common Kodai experience!

The Wisdom of Solomon
by Jo Hiebert Sorensen

"Yes, it is sin," I said heatedly.

"No, it isn't," Molly retorted.

"Yes, it is," I insisted even louder.

"It is not."

I gave an exasperated sigh. Molly was being so stubborn. I knew I was right—I knew it was sin to put something on top of a Bible. My Sunday School teacher in California had told us so. But Molly wouldn't believe me.

"We'll go ask your mom. She'll tell you it's a sin."

"Okay, let's go ask her." Molly headed across the Boyer playground toward the younger boys' dorm at Kennedy.

Suddenly I wasn't quite as sure as I had been that putting something—like Molly's notebook—on top of a Bible was quite as deadly a sin as I'd been thinking it was. Maybe if you didn't notice the Bible when you put something down on it, or if it was dark and you didn't see the Bible underneath, or if you had to clean up the room really fast before the matron checked your room, or.... Slowly I trailed after my friend.

Mrs. Schmitthenner was in her room having a cup of tea. There were fresh flowers in the vases, bright cushions were scattered around the chairs and sofa, and the room had a cheerful air. She smiled at us when we came in. I really liked Molly's mom. I wished she could have been our housemother. I looked around for a cozy spot. It would be nice to sit and chat for a bit, but Molly was getting straight to business.

"Mom, is it sin to put something on top of a Bible? Why should God be mad if I just put my notebook on my Bible? It doesn't hurt it."

Her mother put down her cup and looked from Molly to me. Her face looked serious but there seemed to be a twinkle in her eye.

"And you believe it is a sin, Joanne?" she asked.

"It is a sin. Mrs. Weins, our Sunday School teacher in America, told us it was. And she said God sees us all the time and He gets really mad if we sin." I couldn't tell if my argument was convincing enough." ... And I don't want Molly to sin and get into trouble," I added self-righteously. That should do it. Mrs. Schmitthenner would never want Molly to get in trouble with God. Now she'd tell Molly I was right.

Mrs. Schmitthenner took a sip of tea and looked at us thoughtfully for a minute. We waited. Finally she spoke.

"I think it's this way," she said. "I think God wants us to respect the Bible because it's his message to us." I looked triumphantly at Molly. She scowled. "But I don't think God is going to be angry at little girls if they put something on a Bible." Molly smirked at me; I looked down, carefully studying the pattern on the rug.

"If you can keep things off of your Bibles, that would be good," Mrs. Schmitthenner continued, "but you don't need to worry about something like that. It's much more important to remember that God loves you, not that God's going to be mad at you for every small thing you might do wrong." She put down her cup, stood up and went over to the table. "Now how about a cookie?"

The storm was over and the matter resolved. Molly wouldn't go to hell for putting her notebook on her Bible. And as for me, maybe—just maybe—God wasn't always checking up on everything I was doing, ready to vent His anger if I sinned. Somehow that made me feel a lot better. I reached for a cookie, settled back into the cushions and began to munch.

Lice!
by Owen Thomas

I don't recall what specific grade we were in when there was an epidemic of measles that overloaded the facilities of the Dishpan. As I recall, we were rotated through the beds at the Dishpan depending on the stage of measles that we were in and were then discharged to finish recuperation at Maratha House (on the road to the Budge).

My mother came down to Kodai to help with this overflow from the Dishpan. To her horror she discovered that we all had lice in our hair, presumably from one contaminated bed at the Dishpan! The "cure" was a shampoo with kerosene, or multiple shampoos, until the lice comb came out clean.

There was a board game of "Pirates and Travelers" at Maratha House that we played for hours on end and from which I probably learned more about geography than in all my educational courses combined. The most difficult destinations and highest scores were at Timbuktu and Valparaiso. Since then I have always wanted to visit Timbuktu and have managed to get to Valparaiso. Those names reverberate in my mind to this day!

Kodai recollections and the effect of World War II on our lives by Lowey Thoms Dickason

My oldest two siblings, Nancy and Pete, were in boarding school from the early 40's. My brother, Norm, joined them around 1942. That was the year of the big "scare" when the school was evacuated because it was believed that the Japanese were about to invade. All the Arabian Mission kids were taken in for several weeks by Presbyterian missionaries in the Mirage area of the West Ghats. Just before they left Kodai, Norm broke his arm while retrieving a ball off the roof between Boyer and Kennedy (his wide-bottomed British style shorts caught on the metal as he jumped and he landed on his head and an arm). It was set crooked and needed to be re-fractured and set again at the Mirage Hospital. When the Japanese turned away from India, thinking that the British-India Army would put up too great a resistance, the kids all returned to Kodai to carry on with their studies.

Kodai felt like home to us kids because Mom and Dad owned Dar-es-Salaam, a beautiful little cottage off the ghat on Fern Hill Road with a lovely English style garden. We had lived there when not in boarding without returning to the Persian Gulf for over two years because World War II made getting a ship to Muscat difficult. During the winter of '43/'44 my grandmother stayed in Kodai with us over the winter break so that Mom could go back to be with Dad in Oman. (She had just retired as founder and principal of a girls' school in Baghdad, Iraq, and came to India before returning to the US.) Mom then came up to Kodai in the spring of '44 and stayed through the winter with us.

I entered Upper Boyer in January 1945 at the age of six. Mom was housemother until I turned seven in February. Soon after that she returned to Oman. Because my siblings Nancy, Peter and Norman were already in boarding and I had several friends, I was not very homesick. My first roommate was Alice Graham. Judy Gass was another early roommate. Our room was right across from Ercky's front door. We would get in trouble because she heard every sound we made.

At the end of the school year in '45, we Thomses went to Bombay to catch a ship to Muscat; however since all the ships were taken up with returning soldiers, we were stuck in India again. This time our parents asked a woman doctor colleague of theirs who was on loan to the Church of the Brethren hospital at Dahanu Road, a bit north of Bombay, if we could stay there until they were able to get passage for us on a British-India Line ship in December. We finally got home to Muscat on Christmas Day. In a couple of weeks my siblings had to return to Kodai, and I stayed in Muscat where Mom tried to teach me. I remember that she felt sorry for me because it was hot. Consequently, when I did join my classmates—Owen, Pat, Alice, David Swan, Molly, Conrad and others, I was pitifully behind and very self-conscious of being so. I think Annalena was with us in that class. I remember that she was bright and a kind child, but also never really well. She had problems with adenoids and constant colds that apparently plagued her all her life. Her older siblings were in my sister's and brother's classes.

Harry Mondel's older brother was a pilot in the Indian force and would occasionally buzz the campus in his Spitfire plane. We would get out of our seats and run to the windows. I remember Grandma trying to get the news on a radio and thinking that the static I heard was the sound of the war. The day that the end of the war was announced in assembly we were excited, but it seemed so remote.

Miss Liddle's Book Reports
by Beverly England Williams

I was a freshman at Mars Hill College in western North Carolina and meeting Frances, a classmate from my 8th grade year when we lived in Mars Hill right after returning from Kodai. "I'm so glad to see you after four years," she said as she hugged me. "Do you remember your famous three-day book report?" I responded with a blank, puzzled look. Then she explained.

Mr. Higgins, our feared 8th grade teacher, had called on me—the new kid who had as usual entered school late, this time six weeks late. Not having heard any other kids give their book reports, evidently I began as Miss Liddle had instructed: author, title, publisher, date, main characters... Mr. Higgins had stopped me and asked me to continue the following day. I must have picked up where I left off: the synopsis, remembering Miss Liddle's instructions: "Give your audience enough of the sense of the book but do not give away the plot. Make them eager to read the book." So I began again, in my British/Scottish accent so foreign to the classmates who had never been farther than Asheville, if that far. A sentence or two, and evidently Mr. Higgins had, once again, asked me to finish the next day.

Only after I had finished my report—a totally routine one as far as I knew—did I learn that the standard in Mr. Higgins' room was about 30 seconds, after which the hapless victim fled back to her or his seat.

I think these experiences are the reason Kodai kids stick together after all these years; we understand when people ask us where we went to elementary school and we shrug and say, "All over." We understand when we were surprised that kids in the States only wanted to know "what do you think of America" and not our experiences of travel and other cultures. These memories may explain why I look forward to the reunion, and passed up my "real" high school 50th, even though I only attended Kodai for a short time.

Fruitcake
by Molly Schmitthenner Lesnick

Around Christmas time in India, our parents would get presents from local merchants and many Indian families; often these gifts were special food items. A favorite in our part of India (Andhra Pradesh) was fruitcakes. These were not the pecan-filled "Harry and David" delights so familiar to us in the States. Rather they were very heavy cakes, completely encrusted in a hard marzipan almond-flavored shell of thick icing. Inside they were flavored with rose water, ginger and other spices and a few dried fruits, and were quite sweet. Our parents would occasionally serve some slices up at tea, but we children would only half-heartedly nibble at them, much preferring cookies or the finger sandwiches.

When we would leave on our journeys back up to Kodai, our parents would always pack away goodies with us: Christmas cookies, cinnamon rolls, etc. and...a fruitcake! We would consume everything on the long trip up to Kodai except the fruitcake. Usually at some midnight feast in February, we would bring out the fruitcake, and out of desperation, among all the kids there, most of it would get eaten!

Now, skip forward to Thiel College, Greenville, Pennsylvania, where Carol (Kid) Zigler was a sophomore and Beth Gesler and I were freshmen. One day in late April or May, Carol invited Beth and me to her room after classes. "I got a package from home," she said. "Come help me open it!" We gathered around Carol's bed as she opened the package. As I recall, there were some bracelets and some pretty clothes her mom had made, and then there was a box with something inside, all wrapped around with newspaper. Carol unwrapped layer after layer, and there, pungent in all its marzipan glory, was an Indian fruitcake! We all exclaimed with delight, and Carol said, "It has come from India by sea mail and taken 3 ½ months, and yet here it sits, all in one piece!" We couldn't cut through the icing with a regular knife, but our cries of delight had by now attracted a crowd and someone had a regular long bread knife in her room, so we borrowed that and sawed into the cake. A piece was cut and there it was, fresh as if made yesterday. Carol sliced up a piece for everyone and the 3 of us ate ours with great reverence ... so far away from home it tasted so good!

My Trunk
Jo Hiebert Sorensen

My trunk: a large army-green trunk with my name and Kodaikanal printed on it in big white letters.

Everything I'd need at school went into this trunk.

All the dresses Mom made, sewing into the early hours of the morning.

All my nighties, underwear, socks, jackets, Sunday shoes.

My worn-out mitt that somehow I'd gotten somewhere, I'm not sure where.

My jacks (several missing) and two small balls.

My doll Connie, with an extra dress and the sweater Phyl had made for her...

... Along with instructions to finish sewing the sleeve on, which never happened ...

My Bible, given to me when I was baptized in the King's River at Reedley.

Everything that was mine and only mine, not belonging to any of my siblings.

Now it stands in our basement, too precious to throw away,

Holding clothes our sons wore and toys they played with when they were young,

Also too special to discard.

My trunk.

A "Drowning" in Kodai Lake
by Beverly England Williams

The Englands—Mother, John ('54), Beverly, Jeanette ('57), and 3 year-old Florence—stayed in Kodai over the winter vacation of 1949-50. While we had hoped to return Burma, political unrest in our town of Bhamo made it impossible. Dad was able to passage to India, and we had a great time showing him around and introducing our friends living in town—Ann and Jane Gibbs.

As a treat, and to keep us occupied over the holidays, our parents bought John a short-term Junior Membership in the boat club. He was allowed to take Jeanette and me on rides provided we obeyed him and never stood up in the boat.

One afternoon the three of us were enjoying the lake when an argument erupted, the usual sibling trivialities. I ordered John to let me out and stormed home. Before long I was calm and absorbed in a favorite book when I heard whispers. "Jeanette's soaked. Get towels and dry clothes and don't let Mother and Dad see her." Enemies no longer, siblings putting up a united front.

As I helped Jeanette dry off, with chattering teeth she explained, "I wanted to row. John wouldn't let me so I started to yell. To shut me up we stood up to change places. I fell overboard facing the middle of the lake. Somehow John leaned over and dragged me back into the boat. No one saw us." Knowing that my 10 year-old sister could not swim and amazed that John had had the strength to pull her out of the water, we were both relieved that she was safe and pleased that we had outwitted our parents. We could return to the lake by ourselves!

Just as we were hiding the wet clothes, someone knocked on the front door. Mother greeted an Indian man who bowed and solemnly called on his most formal English: "Memsahib, we are so sorry for the tragedy that has befallen your family ..."

Maisie Overboard
by Lowey Thoms Dickason

Because of WWII and Nancy's imminent graduation from Kodai, our first furlough since returning from the U.S. in 1939 was in 1948. Our family booked passage on an Italian freighter, the *SS Turinia*, with Uncle Jack and Aunt Bernie, Margaret (Nancy's classmate), and Francine De Valois. Other Kodai folks on our ship were the Casparis (Head of maintenance and piano teacher at Kodai) and recent grads—Bob Carman, Hal Klamen, and Maisie Korteling. There were several other passengers too, and a menagerie of wild animals in and out of cages, which were going to the Milan Zoo since it had been destroyed during the war. They were attended by an Italian caretaker who allowed us to hold a tiny tiger cub, visit the large ones in cages and watch the baby elephant drink milk from a bucket. There were also snakes, a deer, and assorted other creatures.

The trip took 42 days from Madras to Naples. Soon after leaving Colombo and before arriving at Aden, near the island of Socotra, we hit a bad storm with very large waves. Since we children had been allowed to roam all over the ship, Maisie, another ten-year-old girl and I had been walking up on the top deck to get some fresh air. Soon after two of us had come back to the whist game in the lounge, the ship lurched and we heard a shout of "Man overboard!" Mom and a few other adults had been sitting out on the deck bracing themselves by a railing along the cabin wall and singing when they suddenly saw Maisie's colored skirt flash past them and into the water. They threw red life preservers over the side and alerted the captain and first mate. Because the waves were so high, it was risky to turn the ship around, but the captain did in order to save her life. The med life preservers were helpful in locating her. It took only 15 minutes to return to where Maisie was. The crew could not put a lifeboat down because the sea was too rough. The first mate descended the gangplank and grabbed onto her as the waves rose along side of the ship. Later we learned that she had slipped when a very large wave crested over the boat. She slid between the bars, hitting her head and losing her glasses. She had a bleeding gash on her head that Dad repaired with the ship's medical supplies.

Because Mom had me in the cabin with her praying, I did not see the actual rescue but we were aware that there was a lot to be thankful for. High waves hitting the ship broadside did not capsize it. Maisie's life was spared in spite of her bleeding head in those shark-infested waters. She was a calm person and simply tread water the whole time even though she was not a good swimmer and couldn't see the life preservers without her glasses, and she did not get caught in the ship's propeller. The captain and first mate handled the ship skillfully and made a courageous decision.

The animals also took a beating, but survived. The elephant was found wedged in a passageway. The python was missing for a couple days which sufficiently scared a couple of single ladies so that they would not leave their cabins. It was eventually located curled up in a coil of rope. The deer broke a leg but Dad fixed it with a plaster cast, which was nibbled off by the end of the trip. The deer had an extra large callus of calcium deposited from his cast diet, giving Dad the idea for telling U.S. doctors later that year that edible casts might speed healing!

Mrs. Johnson
by John Heins (Kodai Class of 1954)

John felt like such a loser. Last year, in the ninth grade, he had failed Latin, so he was not allowed to move into Spanish or French along with his classmates. John didn't think he was really capable of learning a foreign language, anyway, so he might as well forget college. And then there was math ... his brother was three years younger than he and was taking calculus with the upperclassmen, while John, having barely passed Algebra I, was now struggling to get through Algebra II, even with the help of a tutor. He still didn't have the faintest notion as to why flip-flopping the divisor and canceling out stuff on each side of the equation would give the value of "x." Now, after having taken "typing" the first semester to fill-in for the missing language course, they were suggesting an elective that "would build on his strength," English, the one subject in which he did fairly well. Though God knows, his grades in Spelling were awful, and when he had to identify parts of speech and diagram sentences he felt like a moron. Heck, it wasn't as if he couldn't use grammatically correct English—that came naturally—he just couldn't seem to figure out what "the complete predicate" was, or to be able to memorize the rules of grammar and punctuation. Grammar had been his big problem in Latin last year, too.

However, he had been pretty good at guessing what the Latin vocabulary words meant because he knew so many words in English that were related, but memorizing those lists of vocabulary and the genders ... aargh! But John did love reading. In books he found a refuge from that feeling of being stupid. What on earth was a "conjunctive adverb" anyway? It sounded like an eye disease!

He sure hoped that Mrs. Johnson, the person who had volunteered to teach Creative Writing, wasn't one of those sentence-parsing fanatics! She had looked kind of weird when he was introduced to her in the principal's office last week. She had looked quite old, at least in her forties, with her yellowish hair pulled back in a bun. Her dress and shoes were kind of frumpy, too, not unlike the clothes of many of the missionary wives one saw around Kodai School, his mom included. Mrs. Johnson had crooked front teeth with a corner chipped off of one of them, but her eyes had a bright blue sparkle behind the wire-rimmed glasses, and her skin was smooth and tightly stretched over her cheekbones. Her smile, John thought, seemed rather nervous and tight. Her hand was cold when they were introduced. Mr. Phelps was the Headmaster of "Kodai School," a boarding school in the Palni Hills of South India, established for the children of missionaries and others seeking a preparatory curriculum for entry into American Colleges. He explained to John that Mrs. Johnson had been teaching English in a Christian College in China when the Communists had forced her to leave. While waiting for her husband who was still detained in China, Mrs. Johnson would be joining some of the other "refugee" teachers who lived and taught at the school.

Now John waited in the empty classroom. The other "loser" in the class, an eleventh-grade girl who read words backwards, had come down with some kind of disease, so John was by himself, reading over the "scene" she had requested he write for the first class. It was a short piece, sort of corny, about a girl who had turned down a guy's marriage proposal, then changed her mind and rushed to the railway station just in time to see his train leaving. Mrs. Johnson sat down next to John and started reading aloud. She didn't exclaim or make fun of his phonetic spelling, but read with expression that made the writing sound better than it looked on paper. John noticed that she paused in some places where he probably should have put commas. She interrupted her reading to say, "John, you really have a gift." John felt his heart begin to beat faster. "This really flows," she added.

She read on, stopping now and then, to comment on his good choice of a word, or to compliment him on a simile ... "whatever that is," wondered John. By the time she reached the last line, which she read with a tight, tremulous voice, John was feeling a strange excitement. He only half heard the words, "creative ... talented ... promising." It was as if a door was opening into a new world ... a world in which he seemed to stand taller, and felt able to take long strides with his head held high. He heard her saying, "the imagery in your last sentence is especially creative and fresh." John looked down at the line, "She stood tightly gripping the iron bars of the closed platform gate, and watched the train pull out of the station with all her hopes aboard." She held his story on the table in front of her; he saw a teardrop splash onto the paper, which she quickly blotted with a small embroidered handkerchief. John didn't dare look up.

Revised, expanded, and with the spelling cleaned up, John's short story appeared in the school newspaper about a month later. By then, John was writing with a confidence that was reflected in many other areas of his life. His homeroom chose him to be their representative on the school council. He got the lead role in the spring play, and miracle of miracles, the prettiest girl in the freshmen class kept showing up in places he would be, smiling at him. She seemed like she wouldn't mind being asked out.

Mrs. Johnson had a way of teaching that John found hard to describe until one day when they were talking about diction and connotations, she mentioned the Latin origin of the word, educator, "one who leads-out." Mrs. Johnson embodied this word...she had been leading him out of a miasma of self-doubt and despair. It was amazing, he and this older person shared a trust and respect for each other that John had never experienced before. He never asked about the teardrop that fell on that first writing, but when she told him later, he knew that he would always remember that phrase," ... the train pulled out of the station with all her hopes aboard."

Mrs. Johnson was moved, she explained, because six months earlier, in a small city in southern China, she had rushed to the railway station when she got word that her husband and other political prisoners unexpectedly were being taken from the local jail and loaded onto a train for transfer to a prison in the interior. She had arrived only in time to see the train pull out of the station ... and since that day she had received no word of him. But she would never stop hoping and praying.

Shortly after the term was over, Mrs. Johnson received the news she had been dreading:

Her husband had died in prison ... no details. Her family needed her back in Kansas. She carried in her suitcase the small portfolio of writing that John had given her, with his picture on the cover, so she would remember him. He knew that he would never forget her.

Kodai Kids Kill Sacred Cow!
by John Heins (Kodai Class of 1954)

Kodai Kids Kill Sacred Cow! Headlines in a missionary parent's nightmare.

Look, the cow didn't die, ok? Thanks be to penicillin, a trained veterinarian, and fervent prayer. Furthermore, this was not a case of premeditated bovicide—there was no "malice aforethought"; it was, as our barrister in the courtroom put it, "a case of just boys being boys." It was also fortunate that the cow's owner was not an orthodox Hindu extremist, so the issue of religious desecration did not become a factor. However, religious controversy did, in a way, contribute to the incident.

At a boarding school for missionary children in the Palni Hills of South India, it was only to be expected that Religious Education would be a required course in the curriculum. Our class in previous years had received R. E. instruction from teachers who were doctrinally "in the middle of the road." But the teacher we had that year in the seventh grade was a hidebound fundamentalist for whom the "word of God" literally meant the words of God. She would get furious at any smart-alecky seventh grader who pointed out scriptural contradictions or who smugly asked just which one of the two versions of the creation story in the Bible we were supposed believe. Since we were starting our study with the book of Genesis, the conflicts began early on.

On the day before the cow incident, Dave and I were kicked out of class for proclaiming our belief that a "just and loving God" would not deny a place in heaven to all the really good people who had not professed a belief in Christianity; Mahatma Gandhi, who had been assassinated only a short time before, was a case in point.

The teacher stated categorically that since Gandhi had been exposed to Christ's teachings but "had not accepted Him as his Personal Lord and Savior," he was doomed to eternal hellfire and damnation;" then she added, looking pointedly at us, "just as you will be if you continue to be the servants of Satan in this class!" She wasn't kidding, because when we started laughing, she sent us out to the hallway, not to return until we repented our evil ways and apologized for our insolence.

So it was that the next day, Dave and I agreed that we could save the teacher the trouble of kicking us out again by finding something else to do during the last period of a beautiful day. We made a quick exit from the school compound in search of the IJ wallah—a street vendor specializing in spicy snacks wrapped in a cone of old newspaper. We were at the top of the Bazaar hill when we met up with Delmar, an eighth grader who suggested that we all head over to Coaker's Walk, a cliff-top promenade with a magnificent view of the plains some six thousand feet below.

It started out as a contest to see who could throw a rock the farthest out over the shrub-filled slope to the eucalyptus forest about five or six hundred feet below. We found larger and larger stones to use, and the rumble and crash of basketball-sized rocks bounding down the steep hillside created an ever-increasing delight. We were in the process of trying to pry free a really large boulder when we were interrupted by the shouting of a man pushing a bicycle over the rim of a path from below about fifty yards along the walkway. He had a policeman with him.

"You have killed my cow with your stones." he cried. "You will come with us now to see Mr. Phelps!"

Mr. Phelps, affectionately called "Papa," was the principal of Kodai School, and was a well-known and respected man in the community, despite his diminutive stature. He had the reputation of being firm but fair, and invariably addressed the students as "little people," although by the seventh grade, some of the girls were as tall as he was. At least two of the three "little people" who were ignominiously being herded through the streets of town toward Benderloch Cottage, the principal's house, had on the occasion of a previous visit been disciplined by Papa Phelps for "thoughtless and destructive behavior," ie. shooting out streetlights with a sling shot, or a "catty" as we called it.

Mr. Phelps was not at home when we arrived in the front yard, but a messenger was dispatched immediately to fetch him from the school office, as it was obvious from the demeanor of our escorts that a very serious situation was at hand. It wasn't long before Papa Phelps appeared crossing the athletic field as fast as his short legs could carry him.

After our accuser had made his complaint against the three "young hooligans," Mr. Davidassen, who had accompanied Papa Phelps in case he needed an interpreter, (Papa's New England accent sometimes posed a problem for English-speaking Tamilians), then began to ask for details: exactly when and where had the cow been struck, and who had witnessed a stone hitting the cow? It turned out that the cow's injuries were too severe, almost to the point of death, to have been caused by a stone alone, but rather, the cow had been startled by the stones, had lost its footing, and fallen down the steep slope upon which it had been grazing. As to the time of the event, the noon siren had sounded only shortly before the injured cow was discovered. At that news Mr. Davidassen smiled and announced triumphantly, "Well then, it could not have been done by these young chaps, because school was still in session at that time!" That alibi was short-lived, however, as our religious education teacher reported our absences as well as our "incorrigible behavior and lack of respect for authority."

We were busted!

It is strange that more than fifty years later, the myth of the killing the sacred cow persists. It was a close call, but the cow lived. We were found by the court to be guilty as juveniles of behavior that was reckless and dangerous to the public and which contributed to the wounding of the cow. The plaintive was awarded damages: recompense for the medical bill, the cost of medicines, the loss of income from milk production during the time of recovery, as well as compensation for the potential damage to the cow's reproductive system and her ability to produce calves. By the time the court case ended some four months later, the cow had rejoined the herd, albeit with a discernible limp and a missing left horn.

From the viewpoint of an adult, I shudder to think of the distress we caused our parents and the anxiety they must have felt about the possible consequences for their missionary work if the cow had died at a time when India was just beginning to flex its newly acquired nationalistic muscles. Foreign Christians involved in the killing of a sacred cow could have become a cause célèbre. We never learned exactly how much our parents had to pay, but we three "young hooligans" got off relatively easy: loss of weekly allowance and privileges for the rest of the year, restriction to campus, and strictly monitored attendance in Religious Education. That last one turned out to be ok because our first teacher decided she could not continue teaching in the face of the growing "heathen opposition" in the class. She was confronted with just too many seventh grade "servants of Satan"!

The Power of Bubble Gum
by Gwen Hiebert Schroth (Kodai Class of 1954)

I hate boarding school! Most nights I slip into Joanne's narrow, single bed for comfort to ease the homesickness that invariably falls over me like a shroud after lights out. Then there are the rules that confine us along with the high stone walls surrounding the compound. No trips to the bazaar without a chaperone; no journeys to the bathroom after lights out; communal showers three times a week, get up to the bell, go to breakfast to the bell, change classes to the bell, 4 o'clock tea at the bell, supper at the bell, and then study hall until 9:30 every night including Friday. Eat what they serve like oatmeal with dead worms in it. Sunday night is toast, topped with scrambled eggs, and spinach globed on top. So I make sure to wear a dress with pockets into which I slip the spinach and hope the teachers won't notice the drip down my legs that end in green puddles on the floor.

We have a song in honor of the food:

There is a boarding school five miles away
Where they serve rotten eggs five times a day.
Oh, how the children yell when the hear the dinner bell;
Oh, how the eggs do smell, five times a day.

I love boarding school! Day and night I get to be with my friends; no "You can't have a friend over," or "Clean your room before you go out." Every night has slumber party potential and studies are endurable only because the tall Eucalyptus and pines promise relief in the form of hikes and camping trips. Our class votes to camp at 12-miles away Poombari where a leopard was spotted recently—we thrill at the risk. At Sunday night vespers we sit on the floor and sing hymns that choke us up with homesickness; however, we promptly forget our parents during the 3-mile walk around the lake that follows, where cow patties are strewn like land mines lying in wait for couples too engrossed to watch their step. The yearly competition between the Blue and the Gold on Field Day engenders fierce, year-long loyalty to one's team. Twice a month movies come from America sometimes starring Jeanette McDonald and Nelson Eddie who keep me awake at night, dreaming of the day when I too shall fall gloriously in love. On Tuesdays our class votes for a Saturday event—a 10 mile hike before breakfast, an evening roller skating party in the gym, a taffy pull, or a buffalo steak roast over an open fire.

But most important are my friends. All abandoned by parents who zealously toil to save souls on the hot Indian plains, we must comfort, nurture, and love one another lest that emptiness in the pit of our stomachs grow to an unmanageable size.

By instinct we take care of each other. Once Mom and Dad remember my birthday and send money for me to invite six friends to a birthday party at tea time. But there are 12 girls in my class! Sitting cross-legged on the grass beneath the Giant Stride, we solemnly solve the problem. All will attend, but each will take half a portion of cake, IJ (that's "Indian junk," like cereal peppered with hot spices), and strong tea turned muddy-white with boiled milk and brown sugar.

Our friendships remain strong even if one finds a package from America on her bed—which, by the way, never, ever, happens to me. When one of these Fortunate Girls in my five-bed room receives a package, we crowd onto her bed, ooh and ahh, sniff, feel, and exclaim over every treasure pulled from the box sent by a relative or family friend and costs more money to mail than we can imagine anyone spending on us. Even a postage stamp for a letter sent regular mail to the States—which takes three months to arrive—is more than I am willing to humble myself and beg for from Dad. So I don't write, and my former friends in America probably think I drowned on the ship coming over, was eaten by tigers, or died of snake-bite.

So, on the rare occasion when a fortunate girl receives a package from America its arrival causes considerable excitement and we begin to view her in a new light. Up to this point she has been just one of us with the usual flaws and occasional talent, but nothing of which to take particular notice. But now she seems somehow different and we feel something akin to what one would feel in the presence of a movie star like Jeanette McDonald. I search for that quality in the Fortunate Girl that is so special that someone in America would remember her, know her name, spend the money to purchase gifts, package them, and pay the enormous postage it takes to send it. I am astonished that this could happen but finally conclude that Methodists and Presbyterians can allow themselves to care more because they have smaller families. They also must have more money than Mennonites who are poor, they say, but seem to have plenty of money to send to relief.

On one of these rare package receiving days, we, the Fortunate Girl's roommates and her best friends from across the hall, all push and shove ourselves onto her bed. Anticipation runs high. First we examine the myriad stamps pasted all over the top, then, unable to delay the pleasure, we cry, "Open it!" Out comes the usual candy, a blouse, underwear, and even comic books which I am not supposed to read but do because Mom and Dad are too far away to find out and anyway Joanne won't tell. But scattered in the bottom of this package are little yellow and blue squarish shaped bits with bold lettering—Bubble Gum. What is this? We have never ever in our lives seen bubble gum. Chewing gum is precious stuff that comes in sticks, is gray, and costs lots of money, even a nickel sometimes, but we can't buy it in India because they don't have it, except maybe at Spencer's but that is about five blocks away in the bazaar, off the compound, and persuading a teacher to chaperone such an excursion is as likely as me saving a whole rupee to spend on gum, my allowance being only two annas a week. In America Joanne, with whom I share a bed, wakes up in the morning yelling, "Mom, she did it again!" Mom sends Phyllis to cut my chewing gum out of Joanne's hair. Joanne is mad at me, I am mad at losing my treasured gum; who knows when Dad or a church lady will give me another nickel even if I do my best imitation of Little Orphan Annie.

Now, when this first shipment of bubble gum arrives, we pass one of the pink globules around to be squeezed, examined, and sniffed, puzzled that these pieces of gum seem so much larger than one small stick of Spearmint or Juicy Fruit. When the Fortunate Girl pops one in her mouth and slowly chews, her cheeks puff out like she has the mumps. Encircling her, our heads touch as we lean forward, intent on her every chew. Our jaws vicariously move with hers. She moves the wad around in her mouth and then slowly and carefully works the gum over her front teeth and blows; must be instinctive, like burping. A bubble forms on her lips. Our empty mouths produce nothing. She blows harder, but the bubble pops. "Oooo," we sigh and then cry, "Let me try," already certain we can do it better. So, magnanimously, the Fortunate Girl allows each of us a turn with that first piece of gum, passing it around until everyone is satisfied that they too can blow bubbles. The flavor disappears, but the gum's elasticity doesn't.

We solemnly eye the remaining pieces of gum and look questioningly at the Fortunate Girl as we face the truest test of our friendships. Who will get to chew them all? Will she share? She will. Together we make what is deemed a fair decision, one that stands for years to come. The Fortunate Girl will make a list of all her friends in the order of her fondness for them, her best friend being first and least favorite being last. After the Fortunate Girl has chewed each piece it will be passed to the girl who is first on the list. When she has chewed the gum sufficiently, she is to pass it to the girl whose name is next on the list. When that girl has chewed it for an appropriate amount of time, she will pass it on to girl whose name is next, and so on. Separate lists are constructed for each piece of gum with names slightly rearranged so that our names appear higher or lower depending on the wad. I am never first in line but occasionally make it to third or fourth which translates to week three or four of the gum's life.

The care and keeping of each piece of gum weighs heavily on our minds. If we leave the wads on a dresser top, the servants or a girl not on The List might steal it. If we take it to class, we risk the cruelty of having to spit it into the waste basket. John Heins keeps his behind his ear but that is repugnant; anyway, it will get caught in our long hair. We finally conclude that the only safe hiding place is beneath the current user's pillow and any thief will be ostracized by all of us—the very worst possible thing that can happen to you in boarding school. The plan works as do our letters of thanks—sowing the seeds as the Bible commands—that reap a harvest of bubble gum. From then on precious pink gum arrives in almost every package from across the sea.

Relationships among us begin to take on new meaning with the advent of bubble gum. We never know who the next Fortunate Girl will be, so staying on good terms becomes essential to one's relative standing on the bubble gum list. I try passing wicked gossip around about those whose names most frequently appear at the top of the lists, but it takes considerable effort to keep the fires turned away from myself and only serves to move me up a notch or two on the lists. Staying on good terms is by far the wisest route to take, I discover.

So, that is the story. Over the years, in that dreadful but wonderful boarding school, it turns out that it is from bubble gum, not from what our fathers preach from their pulpits, that we learn the value of being kind and good. Strife and anger only serve to bump us down on the list, but sharing, compassion, and praise is in our own best interests. On the other hand, neither we nor our unsuspecting parents ever figure out that bubble gum was the number one contributor to the rapid spreading of mumps that spring—and maybe the lice too.

Thus, despite all the ups and downs of dormitory life in India, in the end, it is the bubble gum, together with our desperate need for affection, that cements our relationships. One should never, ever, underestimate the power of bubble gum.

The Silver Queen
by John Heins (Kodai Class of 1954)

I stood in the ticket line with the other tourists. The sign announced, "Take a trip back history. Experience the sights and sounds of Riverboat Travel in the mid-Nineteenth Century aboard the paddle steamers, Natchez Belle and Silver Queen."

I smiled inwardly as the name, "Silver Queen," brought back a memory from the mid-Twentieth Century, when as an eleven-year-old missionary kid at a boarding school in South India, the name "Silver Queen" held a special enchantment. I could almost hear again my fourth-grade classmate, David Swan, reverently exclaim, "That's the Silver Queen! It's reserved for Officers," as the semitrailer truck with the blue cab and streamlined aluminum trailer disappeared around a curve.

"They say it's really posh inside," nodded Ritchie Garden. "Like a fancy club. They have a pukah[23] bar with whiskey and soda and everything!"

Images of luxuriant decadence formed in my childhood mind. The Silver Queen was a

"will 'o the wisp" seen so rarely on the tortuous, steep roads of Kodaikanal in 1946 that even a glimpse of it was almost as big a thrill to us in the elementary school as hearing an airplane fly overhead.

Kodaikanal was a "hill station" located 7,000 feet above sea level, that provided a cool retreat from the torrid heat of the South Indian plains. During World War II it served as rest and recuperation center for British military forces. Quite a few of us who lived at the local school for missionary children got to know some of the "lower ranks" who were posted to the army cantonment out near the golf links. Hitchhiking, or "Lorry[24] stopping," was one of our recreational pursuits. To a diminutive school boy wearing baggy khaki shorts and a woolen sweater vest, nothing could match the sense of power derived from stopping one of the many army trucks that careened along the roads surrounding Kodaikanal. Imagine the thrill of standing on verge of the asphalt, hand held up imperiously in the "halt" gesture, to have a two-ton lorry squeal to a stop in the driver's mistaken belief that the small American white boy was a fellow Britisher.

Ritchie and I had developed some fairly effective "stopping techniques," so that many were the times we would run up to the back of a stopped lorry to be swung up over the tailgate by the reaching arms of "tommy" privates and set down amid the sacks, baskets, and bales of provisions, there to stagger for balance as one of the chaps would rap on the side of the truck calling out, "right," to the driver, and we would lurch off with a groaning of gears and a cloud of black exhaust smoke.

The English soldiers were usually delighted to learn that the youngsters they had picked up were "Yanks." With the war over the year before, and India's independence under negotiation, these soldiers looked forward to going home to England soon. Their jokes on each other and their rough humor always left me in awe. One soldier takes a light blue package of Player's Navy Cut cigarettes out of his

---

23 Means genuine in Hindi, a common word used throughout India.
24 Lorry is a truck.

shirt pocket, puts one between his lips, and asks his companion, "Got any matches, Mate?"

His buddy fishes out a small box of Cheetah Hunt brand wooden matches and hands them over. With a sputtering sulfurous flare the smoker lights his "cig," then tosses the box of matches out the back of the lorry.

"I say, Ian, that was a new bloody box of matches you chucked just now!"

"Right," grins Ian. "Lucky, wasn't I, to get to one good match on the first go!" Indian-made matches were notoriously undependable in 1946.

On the day it happened, I was on the main road below the Government Hospital, ready to take the steep shortcut up to the school compound. Suddenly the Silver Queen rounded the corner on its way up the ghat. I raised my hand in an awed salute, my heart pounding. Guilty terror washed over me as the big rig pulled over and stopped just beyond me. The back door swung open, and a man in uniform beckoned. "Well, come along, lad. Be quick about it."

My feet felt glued to the ground. It finally sank in that they had stopped and let down the steps to give me a ride. It wasn't that long a trip ... it seemed I had barely unwrapped the toffee I was offered from the Cadbury's tin when they made their shopping stop at Spencer's Emporium just above the "bund" of the lake ... but the thrill of that ten-minute ride was unforgettable. Compared to the back of a truck riding with the baskets of redolent cabbages and lumpy sacks of potatoes, it was "posh," though hardly the seraglio I had envisioned. The floor was covered with a Persian carpet; six or seven round wicker chairs with bicycle tire-rimmed bases and plush cushions were distributed about the interior. The one I occupied was too high for me to sit in and brace my feet on turns, so I half sat and half stood, barely believing my good fortune. An electric light glowed in the ceiling, and additional illumination came through "portholes" along the sides and two large windows on the front corners which afforded a view of the road and the passing scene. The only decoration on the walls was between the two front windows: a framed picture of His Royal Highness, King George VI in uniform, looking sternly at us from amid the partially furled flags of his dominions. I remember feeling dazed and tongue-tied; I don't remember seeing a bar.

I ran all the way to the dormitory and breathlessly announced that I had ridden in the Silver Queen. My proud news was greeted by disbelieving laughter and hoots of derision. "I suppose Lord Mountbatten, himself, invited you aboard!" scoffed the housemother's son from his lordly height as a high schooler.

"How many tickets, sir?" The girl's voice startled me out of my reverie.

"Um, two adults and two children," I responded. "And could you make it for the Silver Queen, please?"

With tickets in hand, I walked to where my family waited. I reflected that it had been less than a year after my Silver Queen experience that the British Raj in India had ended, and that symbol of the British Army class system no longer roamed the Palni Hills, glinting in the sun as it moved through clearings between Eucalyptus groves on the Upper Lake Road. As far as I know, I am the only Kodai School kid to have caught a ride on the Silver Queen, although there may have been others.

Several years later I was told by a long-time Kodaikanal resident that, for a while during the war, there had been two "Silver Queens" when the Officers Transport from Ootacamund, a neighboring hill station, had made a run to Kodaikanal. He had heard that on its return trip it had gone over a cliff near Pillar Rocks...and there were rumors, he said, that on certain moon-lit nights, the forester of that region would be awakened by the sound of a truck out of control on a steep downgrade, desperately clashing gears in a futile attempt to down-shift, the brakes gone and tires spraying dirt and gravel as it fishtails wildly on each curve...a flash of silver would appear momentarily in the moonlight and then...silence.

"Passengers holding tickets for the afternoon cruise aboard the Silver Queen may now begin embarkation from pier number two," squawked a loudspeaker. "All aboard, please."

The Yatomic Bhamp
by John Heins (Kodai Class of 1954)

"Have you still got it, Heins?" asked Lyle, squinting at me anxiously through the thick lenses of his wire-rimmed glasses.

"Got what?" I asked as I turned to face the fidgety eleventh grader. A greasy hank of dark hair perennially hung over his pimply forehead. The never-shaven, brown peach fuzz on his upper lip trembled as he gave his high-pitched nervous giggle.

"The Atomic Bomb!" he exclaimed. "They said you bought two and still have one left."

"Well, I do," I replied, "but I'm saving it for something really special."

Lyle started his little prance again, tugged at my sleeve, and whinnied eagerly, "Come see, behind the dorm. It's perfect."

My first "atomic bomb" had blown an empty #10 can, still smelling of U.S. Army K-ration peanut butter, into a ragged piece of shrapnel soaring in a fifty-foot arc over the precipice in front of "Boy's Block," the dormitory for high school boys attending the school for missionary children in Kodaikanal, South India. Impressive as that detonation had been, I felt my second atomic bomb should be employed in a manner less prosaic. After all, the two firecrackers had set me back my week's entire allowance. My roommate insisted that setting it off in a lift-top school desk would be "keen," but that had been done before, and, besides, the culprit had been charged for the costs of repair for both the desk and the classroom windows that had shattered.

In 1951, the Atomic Bomb was still very much a topic of conversation, even in a remote "Hill station" in southern India. It was only to be expected that V. T. Pillai, proprietor of The Kodai Warehouse, whose sign proclaimed him "Purveyor of Wholesale Goods and Sundries," should name his most powerful firecracker after the formidable weapon.

"Yes, master," Shri Pillai had intoned, seated cross-legged on the floor in his loin-cloth dhoti, and bare-chested, except for the sacred thread of a Brahmin crossing from shoulder to waist, "this is most definitely the finest of my pyrotechnic wares." He set the four-inch tube on the foot-high glass topped counter that faced the entrance to his shop located halfway down the steeply sloped bazaar hill. "With this cracker you are getting first little sparkles and then one beauteous fountain rising higher and higher each moment...then is coming one grand explosion—BOOM!" He waggled his head from side to side approvingly, "Truly one yatomic bhamp!" He smiled as he removed his Congress Party cap, vigorously rubbed his stubble of gray hair, and delicately spat a stream of red beetle nut juice into an empty cup that he kept at hand for the purpose.

V.T. Pillai's shop was a source of many hard-to-obtain items. When I had entered the shop to purchase the fireworks, V.T. was striking a match to demonstrate the high alcoholic content of a small bottle of "Vanilla Essence" to a couple of men seeking to slake their craving in a province that strictly enforced prohibition. The small puddle of liquid on the glass counter-top burned with a low, blue flame that glittered in the eyes of his eager customers.

Lyle's eyes were also glowing with excitement as he hurried me along to see his discovery. Like an anxious puppy, he scampered ahead, then ran back to tug my sleeve. "You'll see; it's really perfect. C'mon!"

I was skeptical. Lyle was one of those eccentric geniuses who often have strange tastes—mathematics, for instance. While most of us read novels, (a practically worn-out copy of Forever Amber was a favorite that year), Lyle preferred "reading" advanced calculus books, and giggling hysterically when he found a mistake or a printing error. In those days, before electronic calculators and computers, Lyle had used almost a whole roll of toilet paper in writing out the solution to some esoteric problem in physics. He was definitely a very weird fellow. Nevertheless, I allowed myself to be led to a ten-foot square grassy area behind the dorm, enclosed on three sides by the laundry room, the back bedroom of the housemother's cottage (in which were temporarily housed two seventh grade boys), and, on the third side, a wall of the housemother's kitchen with its two small windows high up to let out the leaking wood smoke from the cast iron cook stove.

And there it lay in pristine glory, exactly in the geometrical center of the square. The cow must have been a contented one to have stood there in the early dawn patiently plopping this classic specimen of "The Kodai Rose." Cows in India are permitted to roam, undisturbed, where they will because they are considered to be sacred creatures. This cow's "holy" contribution was impressive in its bulk. The cow pie[25] was least a foot and a half in diameter and a good four inches high. In texture and color it appeared somewhat like spinach soufflé. A light crust had formed to give it a gloss; it was unblemished by hoof print and had hardly yet been discovered by flies. Lyle had seen it and his scientific mind had immediately grasped its potential.

There was no question about it: this impressive pile of excrement offered a worthy employment for that last hoarded explosive! I hurried to my room and reverently extracted the treasured firework from the trunk under my bed. Meanwhile, Lyle exuberantly bounded about gathering spectators, all of whom, when they saw the target and heard I was getting my atomic bomb, bobbed their heads appreciatively and hovered nearby in anticipation.

"Omigosh," "Neat," "Keen," and the cynical, "I'll laugh if that thing's a dud," were among the comments by the onlookers as I tore the top paper to expose the fuse. A chorus of appreciative "Ooo's" greeted my insertion of the firecracker almost all the way into the squishy green center of the enormous cow pie.

By the time I was ready to light the fuse, the crowd had grown to some thirty boys, a few still in their pajamas on this early Saturday morning in August. On the third try, I got a match to light and touched it to the fuse paper. The fuse sputtered and seemed to go out; then, magically, it sputtered again, gaining force as sparks shot from the top. With a hiss, a full-bodied jet of sparks began to spray into the air with increasing intensity.

The walls enclosing the sound magnified it, but the visual effect was even more spectacular...the three white-washed walls were suddenly transformed! The spray

---

25 Cow pattie, a pile of cow droppings.

nearly reached the ecstatic spectators crouched in doorways, but Lyle could not contain himself and went rushing out into the combat zone to survey the results even as the "fallout" came raining down from above. He danced about gleefully, oblivious to the splattering in his hair and on his shoulders. Those of us more cautious were still able to watch the gray, green slime ooze down the walls and drip from the festooned chicken-wire screening of the bedroom window.

The next day, as I used a scrub brush and a bucket to clean, or at least to lighten the color of the walls, I smiled to myself at the memory of "every boy's dream come true." Having to wash down the walls and being restricted for a week to the school compound was worth it. One of my roommates, Freddy Swart, came over and reported to me, in all seriousness, that my atomic bomb had created a "ghost image."

"Waddya mean?" I asked, dipping my brush into the pail. "You mean like the ghost images in the rubble at Hiroshima?"

"Well, sort of," he replied. He pointed behind me. "You know that bedroom window there was open yesterday, and the guy's bed was right under it. They say you could see the hexagonal pattern of that chicken wire outlined on the white bedspread, but, you know, sort of elongated."

Another classmate, perhaps in condolence for my being punished, conspiratorially informed me that someone had overheard Mrs. Gibbs, the housemother, complain to the cook the previous day that her breakfast porridge had "tasted unusual."

Before I had finished the first wall, I was joined by a few volunteer helpers who appreciated having been treated to such a stupendous spectacle, and who seemed to feel a moral obligation to pitch in. But it really was not I who deserved the credit. After all, it had been Lyle who had discovered the perfect use for the "yatomic bhamp."

Trip to India
By Ruth Keithahn McCurdy

Needless to say, we had an incredible trip back to India and Kodai. I had been expecting a lot of changes so as not to be disappointed. The cities, large and small, were changed in regard to the mode of transportation; but that was the only noticeable change. Other than minimal bargaining is now done in stores. However, I could still do it, and I think reasonably well. You ask why I bargain—there's always the challenge; and the first quoted price is elevated when a non-dark face is presented, usually more than double. I was expecting huge changes in the hill station where I went to school, and that was definitely true, but it wasn't such a shock as it might have been during the tourist season (summer).

Indian stamps from the 1940s

One thing I had forgotten was the huge hospitality. We were provided with everything and I quickly learned not to admire anything as we either ended up with the article or a similar one. If we asked to see something and it couldn't be found, there were lengthy apologies as if the host was at fault. Specifically, we were trying to see the bust done of my father. But I have a German friend visiting India who has said she will do some searching, as she had seen it in 1996, on my father's centenary. Also our plates were always filled at all times. Halfway thru the trip I figured how to get around this or I would have come back looking like a blimp. And the food was all delicious. As Kim is vegetarian, many extra vegetable dishes were made even though plenty were already on the table.

It was also incredible to see old childhood friends again; and even though there was a 50-year gap, it was as if we had never parted and were still children (rather that 60-70 year olds).

And even though all our parents are gone, we had many fond as well as somber discussions about them.

We landed in Chennai (Madras) at 10 pm. but the heat and humidity still hit me when exiting the air conditioning of the airport. We had traveled by Singapore Air, which was exceptional, except for the return leg from Japan ... the crew then became mostly Japanese. But, by the next day the humidity didn't phase me (much to the surprise of the drivers) although one certainly didn't move fast in the heat of the afternoon. However, an occasional air-conditioned car ride helped when we were driving in the heat! In Chennai we shopped and shopped, but we were also taken to dance performances and the large museum. One day was spent going to Mammalapuram (Mahabalipuram) where many of the huge granite rocks have large intricate carvings as well as a very ancient temple by the sea. But now they have excavated several smaller temples and animal figures each of a single rock, although several may be of one rock—one couldn't tell. Kim was amazed at the intricacy of the carvings compared to those of the Mayans and Incas in Mexico. And I too must say they are amazing. This new area, however, may well have been flooded, but hopefully nothing was damaged or swept out to sea—including the ancient temple now protected from the waves by a large sea wall.

From Chennai we traveled overnight (south) to a hospital that my father helped get started. At first, the doctor saw patients in sheds, huts, etc. all along the highway where this rural town was located. Dad brought the multi-religious community together to build a small hospital and it is now a regional hospital—much enlarged—serving not only a large area, but people travel there for consultations. Also, the doctors travel to other needy hospitals in India, and doctors, nurses and health care workers are trained at this center. Our special treat there was the annual carol service. These were in Tamil—original Tamil "carols"—with only two "western" carols. There was a lovely musical presentation by the hospital staff and conducted by one of the doctors who has had no formal musical training.

Dad is buried in a lovely garden away from the bustle of the hospital and a memorial cottage for guests is close by. What amazed me about this valley (and actually this whole area on the plains near the hill station) was this area was so verdant! You couldn't have convinced me there had been a three-year drought. When we lived in this area, it was dry, sandy, and rocky, and had only thorn trees and thorn bushes, which only goats thrived on—goodness knows how they do so..

We were then picked up by van and taken to an institute that Dad helped start. In the 50's it was involved in training village workers who could help the people attain a better level of living. Now it contains a hospital, elementary and secondary schools, orphanage as well as a home for the elderly staff now retired, training area for women without families to learn a trade, Ayurvedic processing plant, colleges in different fields (science agriculture, etc.) and a shop where items made in their training area are sold—just to name a few. The total area was huge and totally unrecognizable, except for the original orphanage, which had an unusual arched entry. The founders are all now deceased, but many able leaders continue on. For me, the highlight of the day was when an older gentleman (I'll have to be careful how I use the term "older") came to the van as we were leaving and humbly gave his greetings, saying he remembered me—he had been raised in the boys' home and I had to go there for our cooking water (a mile from our house). For Kim, the surprise was that she was asked to talk to a class of older students and then the English teachers regarding how to conduct an English class in English. For the English teachers, I think it was an eye opener! They all showed great enthusiasm after their initial shyness!

We were given a van with two drivers for our next leg, as we wanted to find the person who had cared for my father in his last years. This took about 2 hours as the one thing that hasn't changed is that we were given the direction nar-a-po (phonetically). This means straight ahead despite the winding road and is usually given when the destination is unknown. We did finally found our destination, had a quick cup of tea and headed for the hills.

The ghat road is now almost continuously lined with houses, farms, small towns, etc, whereas 50 years ago there was only one small town just below Kodai. And the monkey population was also much bigger. There were even some hardy monkey colonies just below Kodai, whereas years ago they only lived at the lower elevations. As we approached Kodai many of the hillsides had been terraced and cultivated, and this was true of all the areas we saw around Kodai. We arrived "in the clouds" literally, so there was no view of the plains and even further than 20 feet in some areas. But we persisted and I finally found the ashram my father had started—knowing it was by the golf course—the entrance of which was totally unrecognized as the area was surrounded by small "shops" selling everything and anything. In the 50's this area was far from town. The rock where morning and evening worship was held in good weather was very much smaller than I remembered! I had no desire to approach the nearby cliff's edge—as a child I would climb down to lower rocks that were hidden from the top, despite the 1,000 foot drop.

By this time the mist had increased to a drizzle, so we headed back into town and did some more shopping as the dense fog prohibited views of anything, including the lake's edge. Since we had the van and drivers till the next town, I decided we couldn't stay for the three nights planned. Fortunately, the next morning the sun was out in full and we made the same route plus a few more sights, including a huge rock area that rises from the forest floor about 1,000 feet below. We used to wander in the caves behind it, but this was closed when a tourist fell thru the cave floor and was never recovered. How we missed this spot is beyond me. We must have had good guardian angels. The clouds and mists were already diapating as we headed back to town to take a short drive around the closest part of the lake and then head for the plains.

Finding our destination was a bit lengthy as the town had grown out and around the home of our friends. Again, we were received with incredible hospitality. The main "to see" place was the very famous and large Meenakshi Temple. They have been cleaned up considerably and we saw paintings I didn't remember from the

1950's. The paintings covered the ceilings as well as the walls. Also the columns had extensive carvings and some had figures—not just a carved column. The four entrances have huge goparums—carved towers—over each one as well as about 8 more goparams over other entrances and temples within the main one. Another area of the temple is called the hall of 1,000 pillars (I didn't count them) which had a large collection of brass and metal figures of gods and goddesses. Although only Hindus are allowed in the "inner sanctum," there are many other shrines within the "outer" temple area. Once again, Kim was amazed at the details of the figurines, literally thousands of them covering the goparums and many of the pillars. Of course, shopping and eating out was included, much to my delight, as some South Indian dishes are not made in the homes anymore.

In Chennai as well as Madurai (the town mentioned above) we had unusual "wake-up" calls in the morning. In Chennai it was the morning prayers over the loud-speaker before school began ... this was at 9 o'clock, but the children start gathering at 7:00, so the murmurings of their chatting gradually swelled to a "din." In Madurai, however, the morning "call to awakening" was the sounding of a horn and then a drumroll lasting for a few minutes. This came from the shrine located right next to our house and the natural area as well as a small goparum or entry way was visible from our second story window. So you can guess the volume. Despite this (it was quite bearable after the initial shock) our stay there was very enjoyable. This was a childhood friend who had had a twin sister, and being the oldest I thought up all the mischief. Pari also became a doctor (attending the same medical school as my sister)—as did her sister, although at a different medical school. Unfortunately, Hima passed away from an unidentifiable kidney problem which led them to not do a transplant from Pari. But as in Chennai we had many fond memories of our childhood.

We were then placed back on the overnight express train to Chennai and it was hard to say goodbye one more time. Perhaps that's one of the reasons I haven't returned sooner—the first goodbye almost 50 years ago was too hard.

One thing that was surprising was how dingy the first class carriages were—but I think these were recommended to us as we could lock ourselves in. But adjoining English-speaking Indians made sure we were awake for our trip southward, when we had to disembark. (Going north, Chennai was the last stop.) Also, the busses appeared to be much more crowded and not as nice as the ones in the 50's.

Traffic in city, as well as rurally, could be most interesting. In Chennai, the horse-drawn, human-drawn, as well as bicycle rickshaws were nonexistent. In their place were thousands of motorcycle taxis, thousands of motorcycles, hundreds of

Cattle on the plains of Tamil Nadu. (D. Wiebe)

small cars—taxis and personal, a few vans, plus lorries and buses. The latter take their half straddling the lane line or down the middle. The rest of the traffic "smerges" around these larger vehicles, not necessarily jostling for space but immediately flowing into any space that becomes empty. Needless to say the trip into town from the airport was most fascinating, as the night traffic is much heavier than the morning as a lot of the shopping is done well into the evening. And one never proceeds without the "Horn!" There are different "beeps" or a series of "beeps" for the situation involved: I'm here, I'm passing, and get over, I'm passing (the longest sequence of beeps)—just to name a few. But in the whole time there we never saw an accident and only one mild altercation! Kim marveled at the patience of the Indians, not only in queues, but driving. There seemed to be a sense of calm acceptance that eventually all would pass in time. What was amazing to me is that there were women on the motorcycles, and some were even in saris. Most of the "city" women (younger) were in "salwar chemises"—trousers and a long tunic. In Madurai, there were more bicycles, but I truly prayed for the few in Chennai. I did so want Kim to ride in a horse rickshaw—none were seen. So I wonder what happened to the horses and the pooper scoopers? But I really held my breath when driving was done in the dark (in southern India) on narrow rural roads where the bus headlights blinded you and the buses didn't get over to their side of the road. This left only a small amount of pavement for our oncoming van. But our driver seemed to know every pothole—I'm sure from the practice of getting people from the train at 4:30 in the morning in the dark. I had to smile as we were met with our name on a large placard—despite the fact that we were the only non-dark-haired folk on the platform. But my kudos go to that driver. The road was much easier in the light of day; especially around the barricades that are placed in the road—and which we had to swerve around—to slow the traffic around towns.

The other uniqueness for Kim was the eastern toilets. And with my old joints, squatting was a challenge. Only in Chennai and Kodai did the western toilets work on their own. Otherwise we had to fill a bucket (with water) to flush. But this beat the thatch outhouse that sat under the thorn tree on which a very large lizard perched. I could never convince myself that the lizard was more wary of me than I was scared of him! He never propagated! The eastern (or western) toilets on the train were the most challenging due to the lurching of the trains—they go much faster than they did in the 50's. The trains now have diesel engines, so one's hair and eyes are not in danger from the "soot." The old trains were coal-stoked and their smoke brought plenty of soot into the passenger cabins.

Even though the "home-cooked" food was all one could desire, we were taken out to eat, and if what we wanted was too "small," our meal was chosen. I had to smile as Kim and I wanted only Indian food, and in Madurai our hosts had spaghetti and Chinese food!

So even though seeing places and sites and shopping were interesting and fun, the sole factor that will remain with me is uniting with childhood friends again and their incredible hospitality. It was not just done in the name of my parents, but because we were "family"—an experience I will treasure always.

CHAPTER 8

Our Parents

During 26-29 September 2010, the Kodai School classes of '55 and '56 held a joint reunion at the YMCA of the Rockies in Estes Park, Colorado. Amazingly, almost 40 showed up, including Carol (Ziegler) and Ralph Kusserow, Ed and Miggie (Carman) Tegenfeldt, Alf and Sally-Jane Slaaten, Roger and Ruth Erickson, Chris and Toni Rolles, Bev (England) and Wally Williams, Frank and Jo (Hiebert) Sorensen, Bruce and Donna Carman, Conrad Heins, Jean (Towle) Reed, Joyce Holleman, Dave and Lowey (Thoms) Dickason, Richard Garden, Beth (Gesler) and David Caldwell, Ann (Gibbs) Henderson, Alice (Graham) Silver and Tom Byrnes, Molly (Schmitthenner) Lesnick, Owen and Meg Thomas, Stan and Ruth (Vassar) Burgess, Ruth (Voss) and Don Harris, Pat (Wood) and John Remias, Ruth Keithan McCurdy, and Laura Carner Scribner.

The theme for the reunion was "Our Parents" and the he following are what some of the students wrote about their parents:

Keith Capen
Rev. Carl M. and Louise (Newland) Capen

My father was born in 1911 of American Baptist missionaries to Swatow (now Shantou), China, a seaport about 400 miles up the coast from Hong Kong. My mother was born in Kwangju, Korea where her parents were Southern Presbyterian missionaries. My dad was a boarder at the Shanghai American School and my mother a boarder at Pyongyang Foreign School.

Even though on the surface my father was the quintessential reserved Bostonian and my mother the quintessential outgoing 'southern belle,' it was clearly like meeting while in seminary together in New York City. In 1935, they went as married American Baptist missionaries to Swatow.

First they spent a year of Mandarin study in Peking (now Beijing). Once in Swatow they spent another eight months of Tie'chiu language study. Of course, my father had spoken the language as a child and my mother had grown up speaking Korean. Nevertheless, my father had known only a 'child's' vocabulary, so he also had much to learn.

My sister Connie ('58) and I were born in the same Swatow mission hospital as my father. In July 1942, about five years after the Japanese invasion (I was born during a Japanese air raid) and subsequent occupation, my grandparents retired, taking my mother, Connie and me back to the States with them.

It was only a few months later when it became apparent that the political situation was untenable that my father was ordered home. After a very circuitous sea route back, he arrived in San Francisco around December 1, on the last passenger ship across the Pacific before Pearl Harbor.

My father returned to China in late 1943 after a seven month journey via South America, Africa, India, over the Hump to Kunming, and hitch-hiking back to a town just north of Swatow. There he remained until the Japanese moved inland. He and others quickly left for Chungking where he stayed until the end of the war when once again he hitch-hiked to Swatow.

We finally joined him in July 1946. My father was put in charge of the mission, including the missionaries, hospital, school, evangelical work, training of Chinese ministers and lay workers. My brother was born in 1948.

Soon, China was torn apart again, this time by the civil war between the communists and the Kuomingtang. Again, war reached Swatow. In October 1949, the communist army marched into Swatow as the Kuomingtang left after blowing up the airport, shipping and rail infrastructure.

We lived under increasingly tight restrictions toward foreigners and under daily bombing by Kuomingtang from Formosa (now Taiwan). My father applied for an exit permit because he had been in China for seven years and was due a furlough. After months of determining whether or not my father had been an American spy, we were given permission to leave in late May 1950.

Just in time, as it turned out because all allied foreigners were put under house arrest, many for two years, when the Korean War broke out a few weeks later. The timing was especially fortunate because my youngest sister was born in July 1950. She's the odd one—the only one born in the States!

We lived in New Jersey for two years while my father worked at the mission headquarters in NYC. Then, in August 1952 we returned to Asia, this time to Bangkok where my parents re-opened the American Baptist mission work there among the ethic Swatow Chinese in Bangkok.

The mission's choice of my parents made perfect sense. The majority of Bangkok's population is ethic Chinese, primarily Tie'chiu-speaking Chinese. However, we were now living in Thailand so my patents returned to language school and became proficient in the spoken and written Thai.

My brother speaks fluent Thai, my youngest sister and Connie some, but I never learned more than a few phrases because I left for Kodai after only seven months. I got along just fine in Tie'chiu.

When we arrived in Bangkok the International Children's Center was just being formed. Grades 1-8 were held on a large thatch-roofed platform on stilts with active cobras living underneath. I was in 9th grade, which was held at the Alliance Francaise building with nothing as exciting as poisonous snakes.

Thanks to the Zimmerman and Cummings YMCA families, my parents learned about Kodai and I flew to Calcutta in May 1953 where I was met and taken to Kodai by a former Swatow missionary I'd know as a child who'd been reassigned to India.

In 1964, my parents were again assigned to re-open work among the Tie'chiu-speaking Chinese, this time in Penang. For the fourth time they entered language school, to learn Malay. However, several years later they moved to Singapore for ten years. My father was pastor of a church for the first time instead of head of mission and it was an extraordinarily fulfilling period in his life.

In 1976, they spent a year in Hong Kong and another in Bangkok where my father was sent as a calming, diplomatic influence on squabbling Swatow church factions before they returned to the States in 1978.

Over the next years they were sent back for lengthy periods to Hong Kong, Bangkok and Singapore but the one closest to their hearts was their trip to Swatow in 1985. It was a return to where their lives and my grandparents' lives of service together had begun.

Margaret "Maggie" Carman TEGENFELDT
The Carmens

My parents, Dr. Jack and Naomi Carman, originally planned to go to China as missionaries. However, when the American Baptist Mission Board asked them to go to South India they agreed. They were assigned to the mission hospital in

Hanamkonda, near Hyderabad in what is now Andhra Pradesh but which then was part of the Nizam's territory. Almost all of the American Baptist missionary kids in South India of school age were going to Kodai School so it was natural for my parents to choose to send us there as well.

They had vacationed in Ooty as well as Kodai before sending any kids to boarding school and preferred Kodai to Ooty. Before the war both my older brothers, John and Bob, attended Kodai School. It was furlough time for our family in 1942 and we went to the U.S., a long and difficult ship journey around the tip of South Africa to avoid the war zone of the Mediterranean.

My father returned to work in India during the war but my mother and we kids were not allowed to return until 1945. By that time my father had been asked to join the staff at Christian Medical College and Hospital at Vellore, Tamil Nadu.

In January 1946 at the age of six and a half, Bruce and I joined my brother Bob and sister Elbe at Kodai School. It seems to me now a very young age to go off to boarding school but at the time it just seemed the normal way of going to school. My first friend and roommate was Pat Wood and I think it is wonderful that 64 years later we are still friends and will be at the reunion together along with many other friends made during those very special Kodai School years. I feel so blessed by God to have grown up in Kodai, to have married my Kodai School sweetheart, and that all our children attended and graduated from Kodai school as well! One grandchild is planning to spend her 9th grade year at Kodai School in 2011-2012!

Dave Dickason
How I Came to be at Kodai School

Under normal circumstances I would never have attended Kodai. Except for an unfortunate family occurrence I would probably not have met most of you nor would I have serendipitously discovered Lowey, the love of my life.

Like the majority of Burma Baptist missionary families up to, and soon after World War II, their children attended Woodstock School in north India's Lesser Himalayas—on a shoulder of the Greater Himalayan "foothills" (peaks up to 15,000 ft.), (http://www.woodstock.ac.in) When we became refugees from the Japanese invasion of Burma during WWII (we caught the last ship to leave Rangoon/Yangon before the Japanese took control), my mother enrolled my siblings and me in Woodstock School. So I am one of a few Kodai-ites (or Woodstock-ites) who has attended both schools.

Being the youngest sibling, I was hauled each day—rain or shine—in a kundi (basket) on the back of a porter from Edgehill Villa to Woodstock School to be subjected to the rigors of the formal 'Lower Kindergarten' curriculum. (I don't remember much of LK except rote-learning the alphabet, successfully tying my shoes maybe three times out of five, and trying not to pee in my pants.) I was delighted when my father arrived in north India and we went to Rawalpindi (now Pakistan) where he taught at Gordon College during the later war years. (He had taught at Judson College in Rangoon since 1931.) I was a 'free agent' again and had many hours to play (and learn Panjabi dialect) from Pyaara, the *mali*'s son.

We returned to the U.S. in 1945, having left Bombay one day before the Great Bombay Explosion (when an ammunition ship blew up and leveled the port area and central business district). My father returned to Burma in 1946, and our family followed him there when law and order were 'restored' in 1947. This was a relative term, since each night we literally locked ourselves into the second story of our house, with the things we valued taken upstairs, lest the house be broken into during the night hours.

I was home-schooled as were my sisters, thanks to Calvert School materials.

Before a family decision could be made to send us all back to Woodstock my sister Jean contracted polio (myelitis)—the disease that affected so many worldwide, Burma being afflicted lightly. The best place to treat Jean was deemed to be Vellore, since Dr. Brand was already well known for innovatively treating various central nervous system diseases. Off we went—my mother, sisters, and I—via the smoky old, B.I. coal-burner *S.S. Karo*a on a 5-day voyage to Madras, and then on to Katpadi Junction by train and, finally, to Vellore by jutka (a light horse-drawn cart).

Vellore seemed a sleepy place to a 4th grader, perhaps because it was the hot season and many were "out of station"—i.e., in Kodai. Mostly we waited for medical results and consultations with Dr. Brand, and Jean's recovery from surgery. We moved from guest housing at the hospital out to the C.M.C. campus. It wasn't Rangoon, but it was nice. I fit into a regimen of indolence easily (Calvert mostly having been left on the upstairs verandah at home in Rangoon).

Then out of nowhere this "missionary momma" materialized—Mrs. Fishman, I think. She exploded at my mother, "There is a perfectly good school not far away in the hills where this boy should be enrolled!" End of story. I was soon in-boarding at Kodai School. The semester had ended and it was the "May vacation" season. I had no roommate. Kennedy Hall was cram-full of stillness—not even a breeze. The jackals howled nightly, and were "just outside." Could they squeeze through the glassless window? How hungry were they? Where had I come? School began. I was plopped in (the second half of) 5th grade, to avoid doing 4th again. New kids. Incomprehensible fractions. Wet tomato sandwiches at tea time. "Siberia 101."

Then enculturation and assimilation—even learning—and friend-making began again.

Beverly England WILLIAMS (class of '55)
My Parents

Martin England grew up the eldest child of a South Carolina mill worker and a homemaker. When he was about ten years old, his mother scraped up enough money to buy the children a book about Africa. While the others read about wild animals, the story of David Livingstone captivated Martin. From that time on, he dreamed of becoming a missionary to Africa.

Halting his seminary training to raise funds by teaching, one summer Martin worked at the western North Carolina Blue Ridge YMCA conference center. There he met Mabel Orr, a college student and fellow staffer from Birmingham, Alabama. Courting by mail, the young couple decided to apply for appointments to Africa. The Southern Baptists, however, had a moratorium on new appointments and by this time Martin was studying at Crozer American Baptist Seminary in Chester, Pennsylvania.

Recently I read Martin's letters to Mabel, which she kept, from move to move, to the end of her life. His frustration at trying to get a mission appointment, or even a small pastorate, during the Depression is palpable. One letter ended: "Africa is off. We are being sent to Burma."

The couple married on October 21, 1933. In the next nine days they said farewell to loved ones, Martin was ordained in Philadelphia, the Methodist Mabel joined the Baptist church there, and they sailed for Burma. Leaving as newlyweds, they returned six years later with John (4), Beverly (2) and Jeanette (8 months).

Like many of you, we were in the States during the Second World War. Martin studied agriculture in Florida and Pennsylvania at Cornell. My parents—along with Clarence and Florence Jordan—founded the interracial Koinonia Farm in southwest Georgia, birthplace of the more well-known Habitat for Humanity.

We were among the first civilians returning to India in 1946.[26] Since Dad was the only family member allowed into Burma, Mother enrolled us in Woodstock

---

[26] Owen Thomas and I, as we discovered at the last reunion, were on the *SS Marine Raven* from Norfolk to Calcutta.

School and sewed on name tapes one the wardrobes of three children. While she had hoped to accompany us to Mussourie, she was granted permission to enter Burma and left India to join Dad in Bhamo.

After a difficult year in boarding as young children, we were reunited with our parents shortly before Christmas of 1948. That winter Florence arrived, the first "European" child born after the War. Refusing to send her children away again, Mother and others taught us Calvert Home Course. Later Kingswood School in Kalaw re-opened and we attended for a year.

Not yet recovered from the devastation of World War II, Burma was soon embroiled in a civil war in the south and threats of Mao Tse-Tung overtaking the north. Either Kingswood closed again or we couldn't get down country; I don't remember.

Since we lived thirty miles from the China border, I do know that the political situation was unstable. Happily for us, we had six months off from school when our parents decided that Mother would take us to Kodai and return home with Florence if it were safe.

We waited a week for our first airplane ride which took us from Bhamo down country to Rangoon. We stayed a few days at the mission guest house, hosted by David Dickason's mother, and sailed for India along with Ed Tegenfeldt. We arrived at the end of summer vacation. I especially remember a friendly girl with long brown braids, Alice Graham, whom I met before school began again.

Since Mother was not able to return to upper Burma, she became a housemother and Florence, our lovable and sometimes "pesky mascot." Dad joined us over Christmas vacation, when we shared good times with Ann and Jane Gibbs.

August 1950–with Communists in China, a Cold War threatening to turn hot, elderly grandparents in the States, and most of all, a separated family—our parents decided to return home, first to North Carolina and, after a year, to New Jersey. While we understood the reasons, John and I were particularly reluctant to leave Kodai. A letter from one of us even begs Dad to accept a position teaching math at the high school. Although my time at Kodai and Miss Little's sixth grade was short, the good memories with all of you have buoyed me for sixty years.

In some deep way, Mother never got over leaving Burma without saying farewell to her friends there. Dad worked for many years as a pension board representative, and they both served bravely in the South during the Civil Rights Era. Mother died in Greenville, South Carolina in May of 1988, and we brought Dad to New Jersey where he passed away in January of 1989.

Roger Erickson
Edwin and Ethel Erickson go to India from 1928 to 61

As I write this, in two days it will be Mother's Day: the day given to honor her name. It will also be a day to reflect on the qualities she and my Dad possessed not only to raise their four children in a country and culture not her own, but also to do it willingly. While reflecting on the motives that brought them to South India in 1928, perhaps in the process it will also add to a better understanding of myself. It's an important question: why did they choose to embrace a totally new life and environment? Thinking about it, why would any sane person choose the blazing temperatures of South India, and stay sane for as long as thirty-three years? It's like: "mad dogs and Englishmen come out in the midday sun," (Gilbert and Sullivan); and my folks weren't even British. Interestingly, as a third-culture kid, I don't remember the heat being a concern either to them or to me—though vacationing in the Tamil Nadu hill stations during the month of May was definitely the interval of respite they needed. And for us, hot climate wasn't a concern since we were absent from home for some eight months of the year while attending resident boarding school in Kodaikanal at the cool heights of seven thousand plus feet, away from the hot plains. More importantly, what really mattered was the knowledge that our parents loved their work. If they had had regrets, I am sure we children most certainly would have recognized it.

Of course I know there are many people from different walks of life who accept difficult challenges which require dedication or a sense a calling. Nothing seems to be an obstacle or barrier when they are on a mission. Was it that way with my parents? What gave them their equilibrium; what influenced their life choices early on? Knowing something about my Dad's early life, I recollect that shortly after becoming a Christian he deliberately turned his back on a promising career in the clothier retail business. Why hadn't he remained in a business he enjoyed? He spoke of a higher calling into "the ministry" and of wanting to be an "ambassador" (a calling found in 2 Corinthians 5:17-21). This required biblical knowledge so Dad entered and graduated from Moody Bible Institute in Chicago. Following that he was coached into continuing his preparation at Northern Baptist Seminary, also in Chicago. Having also felt the nudge to prepare for overseas service, he was counseled to add to his credentials a university degree which he did at Colgate University in New York State. In order to accomplish all this, he and mom delayed their marriage for five years. Finally, they felt ready and prepared to go to the "field" as it was called.

Did he really need all this added effort? It wasn't for the remuneration, that's certain. Could it have been for recognition, or call it the "sacrifice"—whatever? Hardly so, though later in their calling, some constituents on the home side seemed insistent on putting them on "a pedestal." Did adventure have anything to do with it? I doubt it, though I recall, when I was thirteen years of age, going to Cairo, Egypt to see the pyramids. That was a chance diversion as our freighter, the *S.S. Steel King*, unexpectedly took on additional cargo in the port of Alexandria on the North Africa coast. We were en route to the USA at that time for our periodic home-leave furlough.

Having observed my parents throughout their working and retirement years, I had always sensed in them the stellar and humble calling to service. It came from the desire to follow Jesus. It was the commands found in the Great Commandments of Matthew 22:37-39, and the Great Commission of Matthew 28:19-20, that motivated them to be missional in all they did.

Secondarily, from among the character qualities I observed in their lives, one in particular that stood out. That is the quality of resilience. Resilience as defined in Webster's (1973) is 1: "the capability of a strained body to recover its size and shape after deformation caused especially by compressive stress; 2: an ability to recover from or adjust easily to misfortune or change." Let's go with #2. Though I have eulogized them in almost superhuman terms, my intent is to say that it is this trait in the midst of difficult circumstances that successfully stabilizes cross-cultural workers such as missionaries. The process is biblically documented as found in Romans 5:3-5.

I admired this in my parents. Bring cultures together, at whatever level and there will be strain and stress. Resilience is an individual's or couple's capacity to both recover from and adjust to changes caused by the second culture without imposing one's own cultural traits on the host culture. Simple and humble, and yet refreshing was the illustration that comes to my mind about my Dad. He always refused the invitation—or insistence, to be ushered as a "white" person to the head of a long queue of waiting people (normally done in British-India). This was exemplary to me of appropriate rather than inappropriate status leverage.

I also learned that obedience to God's calling does lead His followers to the cross. That also requires resilience. There were some heart-wrenching experiences toward the end of my parent's thirty-three years in India that led them to "Calvary," so to speak. These were times of anguish. To sit with two opposing Church party representatives trying to arbitrate conflict based on or induced by worldview differences hurt all of them deeply. And so when a host culture suffers, the guest culture also suffers. But eventually in this case it led to a constitutional change and to a new church association name, giving the local Church leaders considerably more power than the missionaries who were there. Resilience, you see, enables individuals to mature and grow. In this process the cross-cultural missionaries become increasingly more Christ-like. When they rejoiced we too can rejoice with them, as their generational offspring.

Considering the anomalies my parents faced as they raised third culture kids, I believe it required many honed skills of discernment and wisdom that qualified them better for their overseas assignments. A truly "compressed stress" test for my parents was the loss by death of their eldest son, Gordon, to an inner ear infection at the age of seven. Their willingness to move on was one thing, but to entrust the three remaining siblings to a boarding school environment was another. Is resilience enough? Probably not, unless it is attached to three essential truths, as witnessed in their lives, both for us and for the people they had come to serve: faith, hope, and love.

" ...Faith, hope, and love—and the greatest of these is love" (1 Cor. 13:13).

More from Roger Erickson—revised May 11,2010:

My father was born in India of missionary parents. At the age of 8, he and his older brother (10) and two sisters (6 and 4) were left in Canada with two Aunts when his folks went back to India.

When Dad got ready to go to college he went to Ohio Wesleyan University in Delaware, Ohio—a good Methodist school. There he met my Mother. After fighting in the First World War—in the Canadian Army—he came back to finish college. From the very beginning he wanted to go back to India. He hoped to become a Doctor but did not have enough money after finishing college. He then went to Ohio State to get his masters. He married my Mother in June of 1924 and in September 1924 they went to India. Mom always said that they went to India on their honeymoon. They spent 42 years on the mission field. My Mother was born in China of Missionary parents. She knew she wanted to go to the mission field so had no problem with my Father's wish to go to India.

My father always worked at a high school in Hyderabad until 1947 when he was transferred to Zaheerabad—an agriculture school. The school there is called The Garden Nugar High School in honor of my parents.

I started school in Hyderabad in an English school but since I could not "obey" the strict school system my parents sent me to Kodai. I think it was 1943.

My Mother passed away in 1980 and my father passed away in 1993 at the age of 95.

Beth Gesler
George and Margaret Gesler go to India, 1936-67

Inspirational speakers seem to have been the key in bringing both my father and mother to missionary service in India. It was not an easy road.

As an active student in Luther League, my father was privileged to hear a missionary from China speak about his experiences. Dad was inspired and there began his dream of serving overseas. His father was very opposed to him going into a Christian vocation, so Dad went on a fast track to becoming a chemist and following a career path that would bring in a high salary. He enrolled in the University of Pittsburgh and a scientific course of instruction.

At about this time, Dad's father passed away. Dad transferred to a Lutheran college and a pre-ministerial course. After graduating from Thiel, he went straight to seminary, graduating three years later and marrying Anna, who he had known since Luther League days. She was attending medical school. They were planning on going to the mission field in Liberia. While waiting for Anna to finish medical school, Dad was persuaded to attend dental school, as a good friend and fellow missionary to Liberia suggested "Good dentists were needed in Liberia."

After serving six years in Liberia, Dad and Anna had a disagreement with the Mission Board over serving in a certain location in Liberia and consequently were sent to India. Shortly after coming to India, Anna died. Dad married a single missionary, Frances, also drawn to the India field, and my brother and I were born to this union. Then, tragically, two weeks after my brother was born, our mother died of typhoid fever.

Margaret Zundel, who truly raised us, came into our lives. She was also a single missionary who may have been inspired in her teens by Christie Zimmerman, another of our missionaries. We do know that by the age of 16 or 17 she had already decided to become a missionary. After graduation from college she attended Union Theological in New York. Dad and Margaret were married in 1945 (my brother and I attended their wedding), and the next year our sister, Sara, joined the family. In 1946, after ten straight years in India, Dad came back to the States for a furlough, with his third wife and a family. Passage before that had been impossible due to WWII.

After that first furlough, we returned to India, and I began my tenure at Kodai School. My parents wanted all of us to get a good education, and most of our other missionary children attended Kodai. My brother, sister, and I all graduated from Kodai.

After serving thirty-one and twenty-eight years, respectively, in the India Mission Field, George and Margaret retired. Both our parents loved their work and life in India. Dad believed in doing practical things for the Indians and became the mission builder—using his hands and ingenuity to build churches, schools, and homes, as well as preaching and evangelizing. Mom had her Bible women and loved teaching and sharing her faith. They were strong role models and taught us an appreciation for our way of life in India.

Ann Gibbs HENDERSON
The Hendersons

My parents met on the golf course in Devon, England. My mother went out to India alone to be married to my father, a businessman. They were both 35 and lived first in Dacca and then moved to Madras.

Mother must have heard about the cooler climate of Kodai and the Van Allen Hospital so that is where I was born in September 1937. Jane was born in April 1940 in the same hospital.

Of course the war was on when Jane was born and my father (who had started his career in the navy) left business and re-enlisted in the navy and was posted to Bombay where we spent some time. He was at sea a lot as a Commander of a ship which was eventually mined in Tobruk harbor. He and others escaped but he had a stroke not long after his return to Bombay and after initial hospitalization they returned to Kodai. My father went to Britain to obtain a certain type of treatment for his stroke from which he died in 1947. My mother remained in Kodai.

I started school at the Presentation Convent but was not happy there whilst Jane was very happy at Highclerc so I was transferred to Highclerc in Grade 2; hence I never had Auntie Powell.

We lived in various rented houses on Coaker's Walk and went as day students to school. Mother got a job in the school in 1953 as Boyer housemother and that is when I started to share a room with "The Georges" until I graduated in 1955.

Therefore Kodaikanal—both the place and the school—was a big part of my early life. I have returned there three times since graduating.

Alice Graham SILVER
Helen and Reid Graham go to India

My mother, Helen Campbell Graham, was born and grew up in Peoria Illinois, living with her mother, sister and grandmother. Her grandmother, Abbey Hunter, was one of the first women to be a school principal in the state of Illinois. Her mother, Bertha Campbell, taught at that school after divorcing a philandering husband, and the two girls were raised in a loving but strict home. After graduating from Knox College in 1929, Helen found there were no teaching jobs available. Her uncle, James Hunter, an agricultural missionary in north China, wrote to offer her a chance to teach math and science in the North China American School. Helen jumped at the chance and spent four years there. During the summers she and other young teachers traveled around sightseeing. During the summer of 1933, the tourists went to Japan and were visiting near Mt. Fuji.

My father, James Reid Graham, grew up in Hamlet, North Carolina, the son of a grocer. After graduating from Davidson College in 1929, he decided to go to India as a short-term missionary, teaching English and Bible in Rawalpindi. Summers he and a companion went hiking in the foothills of the Himalayas, often in remotes areas like Ladakh and the Swat valley. In the summer of 1933, his term was over and he sailed back to the USA to enroll in Yale Divinity School. On the way, he had a short stay in Japan, where he decided to climb Mt. Fuji.

You can see where this is leading. A group of American young people met one evening and agreed that together they would climb Mt Fuji, but later the rest of the group decided against it. Only Helen and Reid went. In the process, they got to know each other and when Reid left, he wrote many long letters to Helen. She returned to teach one more year in China, then returned to the US. The romance blossomed and they were married during Reid's last year of seminary. Shortly thereafter they were commissioned as missionaries with the Presbyterian Church USA to go to India.

Reid's assignment, after learning Marathi, was to establish a seminary (with the cooperation of other denominations in that language area) for Indian Christians who wished to become pastors. The curriculum was in Marathi, rather than requiring them to first learn English. It was located in Poona (now called Pune). This may sound fairly straight forward; however, there were no books written in that language except the Bible and one or two tracts.

Helen taught classes for the wives of the seminarians.

Meanwhile World War II was in progress and contact with the outside world, except through the British Raj, was very limited.

Helen and Reid had three children during those years. When time came to go to school, I attended a British Kindergarten and 1st grade within a couple of miles of the seminary.

By 2nd grade they decided to send me to Kodai because other area missionaries sent their children there and recommended it.

Each of my brothers and sisters (a 4th child was born later) followed me to Kodai. Also, after returning to the US for a long overdue leave in 1946, my grandmother Bertha Campbell came as well. "Auntie Campbell" had retired from teaching in Illinois and came to see what it was like to live overseas and also to keep an eye on her grandchildren—something we did not always appreciate.

Adventure and a desire to serve their Lord were the initial motivators for Helen and Reid. It was a lifelong passion of my father's to see Indian pastors receive as good an education as he could arrange. I think my mother tired of life in India by the mid 1950's, but she stayed on.

That's how I came to be at Kodai; however, I did not graduate from high school there. During our next leave I was close enough to finishing high school that Mother stayed an extra year (we were in Dubuque, Iowa) so that I could graduate there and choose a college to attend. She and my siblings returned to India immediately after graduation and I stayed on in Dubuque with family friends.

In 1998 I went on a KWI (Kodai Woodstock International) alumni tour led by Jane Cummings to visit Woodstock and Kodai and various sightseeing highlights as well. That's the only time I returned to India since leaving in 1953.

By Wyva Hasselblad
Norma and Oliver Hasselblad go to India

In 1933, with the Great Depression in full swing, Oliver Hasselblad and Norma Bornschlegel concluded that two people could live as inexpensively as one, so there was no reason to put off their long-planned wedding. Besides, Oliver needed Norma's help in shoveling coal to fire up the furnaces of the small country churches he was pastoring in Nebraska. The meager income from these churches was putting him through medical school, and the nickels, dimes and quarters slipped into his pockets by kindly church members helped. Instead of hiring a janitor, Norma and Oliver arrived at the churches early on Sundays and Wednesdays to shovel that coal and light those furnaces.

Norma, the youngest of seven, was a musician and budding photographer. She loved literature and Spanish, and everything musical. Her own father, when barely out of his teens, had packed a little suitcase and come to the US from Germany by steerage. His dream was to study theology and become a pastor. Admission to Rochester Divinity School set him on the way, and his friendships with students and professors were lifelong. Highly influenced by the radical interpretation of the gospel that Dr. Walter Rauschenbusch had taught, they plunged into the church's mission to end exploitation, poverty, greed, racial pride, and war. Norma grew up in the midst of those passionate debates of how the church could be faithful to a practical ministry, meeting the needs of the weak politically, spiritually, and physically.

Oliver was the surprise tail end of a family of eleven, a Swedish Baptist household, his father being a missionary to immigrant Swedes primarily in the coal mining business. Oliver's father's family, active in the Pietist movement in Sweden, were committed to religious liberty and the separation of Church and State. Because they were often beaten, imprisoned for their faith and challenged in their beliefs, they were formidable debaters, defending the Bible and its teaching about being born again, being baptized by immersion upon confession of faith and forming separatist congregations. Believing they were led by the Holy Spirit, they were a missional Christian community with an intense commitment to evangelism and socio-economic outreach. Oliver's father continued to travel back and forth to Sweden, being also deeply involved with the World Christian Student Movement. Debates in the home among leaders in mission and education as well as pioneer pastors of the early Baptist General Conference, often ended with "Vad sager odert?" (What does the Word say?")

Norma and Oliver literally ran into each other at a Christian Youth Conference (actually, Norma ran into Oliver's big feet), and soon Norma was frequenting the animated Hasselblad clan, which by this time included many spouses and in-laws as well.

One of the visitors was Rev. John Firth, a long-time missionary in Assam, India with the American Baptist Foreign Mission Society. Originally a back-door way to Burma and China. Assam was a growing mission field and Rev. Firth talked for hours about the many different people groups among whom churches were springing up. Most of these conversations ended with Rev. Firth making an urgent argument of the need for medical missionaries and urging Oliver and Norma to apply. Much prayer and seeking advice from friends and family confirmed for Oliver and Norma that this was God's claim on their lives which they could not ignore.

Meanwhile, they were pastoring a larger Baptist church in Omaha; Oliver had completed his internship and was looking for a surgical residence. The American

Baptist Foreign Mission Society (ABFMS) was struggling to keep its head above water, recalling missionaries amidst a shrinking budget. Norma and Oliver moved to Washington University Hospital, St. Louis, Missouri where Oliver had been offered the residency he needed to complete his qualifications. For a number of years only Norma, Oliver and Rev. Firth seemed to believe that the Hasselblad's would be appointed as missionaries and specifically in the Assam field. Oliver was very willing to go wherever he was sent; John Firth held out for Assam.

The residency drew to a close, and there was no call from the ABFMS. They still believed in their call, but thought perhaps their timing was a bit off. They read everything they could find on India: Verrier Elwin's earliest publications, F. Kingdon-Ward, books about Gandhi and the independence movement in India. Considering other options as a temporary stopgap, Oliver was ready to accept a position as a company doctor with the Missouri Pacific Railway. The idea of having an income was quite appealing, and Norma began looking for a piano to buy.

And then, a telegram arrived saying that the ABFMS, responding to many pleas to send a doctor to Jorhat, Assam, had scraped together the necessary funds. Oliver and Norma were to drop every other plan and hasten through the confirmation process. On 3 September 1938, with war looming over the horizon in Europe, they sailed on the *R.M.S. Empress of Asia* from Vancouver to Hong Kong, cabin #336; and from there to Calcutta on the *SS Santhia,* passing by Singapore and Penang. Arriving in Calcutta on October 11, they left for Assam by train on October 12, arriving soon after in Jorhat after a change in Gauhati.

As they arrived in Jorhat, Assam the winds of war were stirring in that part of the world. By 1942 Oliver had painted a white cross on the red tin roof of the hospital hoping to deflect any stray Japanese bombers. In June of that year began the long tragic trek out of Burma of nearly 500,000 war refugees, many thousands of whom died along the mountainous trails into Assam and Manipur—that whole story still being researched as so many died unnamed. Beginning in April 1942 relief flights of supplies, and then search and rescue operations across the "Hump" of the Himalayas to the Allied armies in Burma were taking place, flying out of Jorhat, Chabua, Mohanbari, and other hastily built air fields. Until the field hospital was built, Oliver operated with military surgeons extending the facilities of the Jorhat Christian Hospital which by then he had built about 5 miles from the airfield. Early in 1943, Norma and the children (by then 3) started the long reverse journey back to the US. The US State Department had ordered all women and children to leave Assam as the Japanese were pushing ever further into India from Burma. Oliver remained, but that is another story. Two and a half years later the war was over and the family reunited in Jorhat.

My Mom and Dad never got over their love for India. What started with a call turned into a passion, and they never stopped thanking God for the long and winding road that led them to the place He had prepared for them.

"in essentials unity; in non-essentials liberty, in all things love." usually attributed to Rupertus Meldenius

Conrad Heins
The Heins

My parents were India missionaries with the United Methodist Church. They moved to India in 1935, where my dad was the pastor of a church in Bangalore. Within a year my brother John was born. I came along three years later, delivered in the same mission hospital in Kolar where John was born. In 1941 we came to the U.S. on a small freighter, going around South Africa because the war in Europe had started. A year later my dad returned to India, leaving us in America for the rest of World War II.

A week after VE (Victory Europe) day, in May, 1945, we got a call from the mission board saying a boat was leaving in a few days from New York to Bombay and that a stateroom had been reserved for us. The boat was the Swedish passenger ship "*SS Gripsholm*." It turned out to be the first passenger ship to sail the Mediterranean after the allied victory in Europe. Most of the passengers seemed to be Arabian-American oil people who, at least in my 6-year old eyes, spent the entire time gambling, or missionary families returning to India and the far east. What I remember most about the trip was, when we were in Athens visiting the Parthenon, picking up, after it had just been run over by a donkey cart, a now worthless five million drachma note from the German occupation; playing Monopoly in all my spare time with another India missionary kid named Lyle Thoburn, who ended up going to Woodstock, and who was equally fanatical about the game; and the free chocolate that became available because some lady's case of Hershey bars completely melted in the Red Sea.

We arrived in India in July, and within a couple of weeks John was on his way to Kodai. Because we were South India folks, there was never any question about whether we would go to Kodai or Woodstock.

I started in Kodai the next January. Because I could read, I started in 2nd grade with Auntie Powell. My memory of those early days is a little foggy, but I clearly remember being in class with Bruce and Miggie Carmen, and I think Pat Wood and Molly Schmitthenner. Within a couple of months, Miggie and I got moved to 3rd grade. I remember that first year at Kodai as being very exciting but also filled with homesickness.

Jo Hiebert SORENSEN
John and Anna Hiebert

My father, John Hiebert, was one of 12 children born in a strict Mennonite home in Mt. Lake, Minnesota.

His parents had been missionaries in central India but had returned because of his father's recurring malaria. My grandfather became the pastor of the Mt. Lake Mennonite Brethren Church, head of the German Mennonite school, and, in order to make ends meet, a dairy farmer. Rules in the home were stern, and money was scarce. John was serious, studious and spent his free hours helping with younger siblings and working on the farm. "Fun" was suspect in his home.

My mother, Anna Jungas, grew up the light-hearted, much-loved daughter in the home of a quiet, well-to-do, Mt. Lake businessman and his cheerful, hard-working wife. Her parents had three children of their own and took in six others. When Anna was 12, their hardware store and home burned down and the whole family worked hard to get things going again, but through these times there was time for family, love and laughter. Later Anna would say that this attitude toward life helped prepare her for the rigors of missionary life.

John and Anna met in a church youth group, and soon fell in love. John felt called to become a missionary (we children believe the call was strongly motivated by a love for travel, history, and desire to not stay in the restrictive confines of small-town America). Anna felt called to serve God and to go wherever her much loved John went. They married, were sent by the Mennonite Brethren Conference to an area near Hyderabad, India, and eventually had nine of us children: Phyllis, Grace, Helen (died with high fevers as a baby), Paul, Betty, Gwen, me, Margy and Loey.

During the years they lived in India John and Anna came to dearly love this land and its people. Dad spent his time touring out in the villages, preaching and building schools. Mom was busy dispensing medicines (including the new sulfa drugs) from our front veranda, working with ladies' Bible studies, and trying to keep up with family and household.

Although Dad always seemed to be busy saving the world and Mom with worrying about all of us, they made sure there was time for family: devotions, music, traveling and learning the history of places we visited. At first we resented being sent off to boarding school, wearing clothes remade from ones in the missionary barrels, and always being the Poor Cousins when we visited Mom's relatives in the States. However, we learned to love Kodai School and our friends there, valued our amazing educational opportunities, and developed a life-long love of travel and interest in other cultures.

Some years later after Dad died, Mom decided to return to India with Loey, our youngest sister, and became Kodai school secretary. In Kodai she found purpose again—being with students, hiking down the ghat, exploring India by way of third class accommodations, carrying her bunsen burner and bedroll.

As we look back, it has been interesting to see the progression of our family's ties to India. As missionaries in India, our grandparents' work was to evangelize and bring Christianity to the people. Our parents went to India to teach, build schools and to develop leadership among the Indian Christians, many of whom were "outcastes." My brother Paul returned to India with his family as a colleague in the Indian college and seminary that our dad helped develop. And in recent years my niece Priya has been to India numerous times with the Gates Foundation to help women by working on micro-finance projects in some of the same villages that her grandfather built schools. My nephew Nikhil is living in New Delhi where he is engineering a solar-powered micro-grid for village lighting. Nikhil's daughter Eva is now the fifth generation of the Hiebert family in India, and like the rest of us is hooked on Indian food, markets and a colorful lifestyle.

Joyce Holloman
Carl and Margaret Holleman's Route to Kodai

Pretty little Margaret's face was entranced by the stories the missionary from India was telling during Sunday dinner. Eyes shining, she hung on every word just as she had in church that morning. Her heart was filled with great desire to do this work when she was grown. Nothing could be more wonderful than going to India and taking the glorious word of God to those who had never heard the story of Jesus and the salvation He brought to all people of the world.

As she grew up, it seemed Margaret Welker's dreams were not to be realized. Her family decided she, the true scholar, had to quit school and go to work after 8th grade, so her older brother, who didn't find school that important, could finish high school. Margaret was able to earn her way into secretarial school and went to work full-time as soon as she could. When the Depression took her job, she was most happy to use her meager savings and go to Enid, Oklahoma, to the Assemblies of God Bible School there. She could work in the office and take classes to support her never fading ambition to be a missionary.

During her third and last year of Bible School, a young man, whom Margaret had met and found very attractive, came to Enid and began his studies. Carl Holleman was as handsome and charming as Margaret was lovely, and they made a beautiful couple as they soon began to spend time together. She would accompany him in his little black Model A when he went to preach in small churches in the area, or in the jail or on the street corner, both committed to winning souls to Christ.

Margaret stayed to work in the school's office after she graduated, which allowed the couple to continue to pursue their romance and the burden for service God had laid on their hearts. Carl was as on fire for God as Margaret, but his calling seemed to be that of a preacher rather than a missionary, and this troubled Margaret immensely. She had come to deeply love Carl, but the most important objective in her life was to go to India as a missionary. They struggled with this difference in their lives' purpose, and Margaret ultimately felt her devotion to missions was more important than her relationship with Carl, and she broke off the romance.

Each continued to seek God's will for their lives as they mourned the loss of being together. One night Carl had what he always termed "a vision," in which he saw the map of India filled with faces of the land's varied peoples pleading with him to come and share the Gospel with them. Now he knew India was in his future also. This led to his reunion with Margaret, and they planned a wedding after Carl's graduation ceremony in May of 1934. Within a year or so they were en route to India where they went to Marathi language school and pastored a church in Pune. From other missionaries they heard of the girls' school in Conoor, and assumed any youngsters they might have would go to school there. A daughter, Joyce, was born in 1937, much to their delight, and things were going well.

World War II sent them home to Oklahoma after a six year term. They took a church in Enid, OK, and had a successful pastorate in a growing church. Two sons, David and John Paul (JP) joined the family while there.

After the war ended the lure of India again became uppermost in the Hollemans' hearts, so they resigned their church and once again prepared to return to their beloved India. Joyce wasn't at all happy about this turn of events, for she had enjoyed the years in Enid as the pastor's daughter, singing in the choir and feeling rather special. Her brothers, David and JP were enough younger and very close to each other, so they didn't much care where they went. The final straw for Joyce was when she learned that the school in Conoor was a girls' school and required uniforms including navy blue cotton underwear. UUGGHHH! But she didn't really have a vote in the families' affairs, and in 1949 they boarded the *RMS Queen Mary* for Southampton, England. That huge ship brought a whole new world to Joyce's awareness. Tourist class was filled, so the family was traveling Cabin class. The food on board was a revelation, for she had never seen such a variety or the elegant displays she found in the dining room. What was one to do with all the pieces of silverware? Fortunately Margaret knew about all these strange things and, being a quick study, Joyce caught on soon. Carl took her to see her first movie, a film about Scott and Amundson's struggles to reach the North Pole. The fate of the explorers was traumatic to her, as she had no awareness of acting and thought it was an actual depiction of the adventure. She dissolved in tears and had to return to the cabin. The kindly elevator operator comforted her and assured her the actors hadn't really died in the filming of the story.

In England the Holleman's boarded the *RMS Maloja*, a P&O single class steamer, where they met other families, who had children of school age, headed to various missions in India. Carl and Margaret discussed schooling with the Longs, the Schwartzes and possibly others on the ship. They learned their children all attended Kodaikanal School, and assured the Holleman's that other Assemblies of God families had their children in Kodai also. Joyce became friends with Dorothea Schwartz, who told her all about Kodai—there were boys there and you didn't have to wear uniforms. Joyce was thrilled. She'd had a reprieve and the future looked bright for the first time. Traveling to India had taught her much about her own country as well as the port cities they visited en route. But the dread of school which had hung heavily over her head was now lifted.

They arrived in India in February, but didn't get to Kodai until April. Margaret had to stay on the hilltop with the children, as JP wasn't old enough to enter boarding. As soon as he turned seven, Joyce went into boarding at Bruton with the Heiberts and Margaret Smith, among others, and the boys entered Kennedy Hall. Having other kids around who were their good friends by now made boarding a great adventure and no one felt homesick at all.

So thanks to a shipboard meeting with other Kodaiites, the Hollemans spent about eight or nine years in Kodai during two separate terms. Despite the growing pains of the teen years, Joyce felt Kodai included some of the happiest years of her life, opening her eyes to many thoughts and beliefs that guided her in new directions much earlier than if they had remained in Oklahoma.

Ruth Keithahn
The Keithahn Family

Mom and Dad were both in Chicago—Mom at Rush Medical School and Dad at Chicago Theological Seminary. They were both interested in working in India—don't ask me how they got returned to Iowa to farm with her sister and practice.

Dad was principal of a boys school outside of Madurai. But his ideas and suggestions were 30 years ahead of the times. He thought he should share his huge bungalow with other teachers, and also unbeknownst to the British and American Masons, he joined the Indian Mason as well. Consequently things happened that the other missionaries never understood—such as "thru" trains stopping at the town where the boys school was located, rather than going straight thru to Madurai. Leaving the reception committee for the new missionaries scratching their heads. Dad also became very interested in the nonviolent movement that Gandhi was leading. This was not too popular with the British, and definitely not with the other missionaries. But Dad had made friends with the local British "governor" who assured his superiors that my father had no intention in joining in the movement. One of the things Dad did in Kodai was lead a boy scout troop as well as participate in the May "productions." Dad returned after his five year "term" and married my Mom in the church where he first preached—just outside of Chicago. Both were in Indian dress. They applied to return to India, but current missionaries said, "Don't send "him" back." My parents went out to South Dakota during the dust bowl years.

By the mid 30's they had applied to several churches in the mid-west and went out to India "on faith" supported by contributions from those churches as well as private donations. At that time Dad started an ashram just outside of Bangalore, and Mom ran a clinic. An ashram was also started outside of Kodaikanal, just below Dr. Ida Scudder's hilltop home. I was actually born at the Kodaikanal Government Hospital in the late 30's (Van Allen was too expensive). Dad had soon stepped up his participation with the Gandhian Movement for Freedom much to the concern of the British. So we were sent back to the US, via the Pacific, in the fall of 1944—a whole story in itself (the war was still on). Dad ran a Congregational Institute in Indiana as well as was minister in the town's church. But once India was assured their freedom, a telegram arrived saying our visas were in the mail and we were welcome back anytime—which we did 46' or '47. Since we had been in the American school system and we were living at the foot of the hills (½ hour from Kodai Road) the decision was made to enroll us in Kodai School. Hence our arrival at HighClerc. My Mother found a variety of work in Kodai, so we were frequently not in boarding school.

Chris Rolles
The Rolles Family

Helen Johnson, my mother, had decided to be a missionary by the age of eleven. After school she went to London University and studied classics—ancient Greek and Latin—and then went to Oxford for one year to study theology. She was one of four children from a strong non-conformist family and her other main interest was music. She was an accomplished pianist and fun loving with an ardent belief in women's rights. In 1928, she was sent to India by the London Missionary Society (LMS) and expected that she would remain single and dedicate her life to her work. After intensive Telegu training she was made headmistress of a girls' school in Anantapur and later in Jammalamadugu. She enjoyed life in spite of the heat and lack of facilities and threw herself into her schools, her work with women in the villages and into translating, including religious texts and the Girl Guide handbook. Going up to Kodai during the hot seasons in May was a highlight of her year, and it was there particularly that she started her life long friendships with many of the American missionaries.

John Rolles my father came from a more working class background. He was involved in running the family butcher's shop in Bournemouth when his father became ill, but already, with support from his local Congregational church, he had made plans to become a missionary. As soon as he was able to leave the family business he went to Nottingham University College to study theology and sociology. He was also interested in music, but of a rather different sort from my mother. He played the concertina and was interested in the current pop music. He was also an enthusiastic scout and quite a sportsman, playing tennis and cricket. In 1932 he was ordained and had been prepared by the LMS to go to Africa but at the last minute plans changed and he was sent to India. He was sent for his language training to Jammalamadugu. He was billeted there with an elderly English man and the only other British person on the scene was Helen Johnson.

They were engaged within six weeks! Photos of them at that time show a tall, slim, good looking man and an attractive, fairer, rather demure, but obviously very happy young woman. Almost immediately Helen came back to England on furlough for 12 months and had to run the gauntlet of meeting his family alone. As soon as she went back to India in 1933 they were married. In the eyes of the LMS she then stopped being a missionary in her own right and became a missionary's wife. She gave up her salary and her positions on committees and school boards. From then until England entered the war in 1939 they lived mainly in Kamalapuram, from where John undertook evangelical, social and educational work in the surrounding area. He started an important group for young men, teaching them the basics of healthy village construction, nutrition and so on. Helen continued working with women along similar lines.

My sister, Shirley was born in 1936 and I was born on my sister's birthday in 1939, both in Van Allen Hospital, delivered by Anna Ruth Kortling. In August 1939 the family returned to England on furlough, Helen to introduce her husband to her family for the first time, and to show off the children to both sets of grandparents. Almost immediately war broke out and John had the option of joining the armed forces as a chaplain or going back to India, which the family did in 1940 on a troop ship in convoy around South Africa. Back in India, John resumed his previous work but my mother took Shirley and me up to Kodai and joined the staff teaching music. My parents were aware of the Japanese threat and the separation was hard for them but they were together every May vacation in Kodai and we all returned to the plains for three months over Christmas. Letters from that time show that wartime life was difficult and my father was becoming increasingly unhappy at the appalling sickness and death, especially from typhoid and cholera, that he witnessed. His medical knowledge was rudimentary but he read as much as he could and even took a qualification in Ayurvedic medicine to try and understand the health beliefs of the villagers. In Kodai meanwhile there was a sense of solidarity between the old missionary population and the unusual collection of non-missionaries who had ended up there after being stranded in India as a result of the war: people like Mrs. Oh, Mr. Musil, Mario, Fritz Kolb and Madame Montessori.

After the war in 1946 our family returned to England and while fulfilling their deputation obligations to the LMS my father, aged 38, tried unsuccessfully to get into medical school. Finally with a providential gift of £1,000, the family set off on the *SS Aquitania* for America and after many adventures he was accepted in Des Moines Still College of Osteopathy. We spent five years in the States. During that time my mother was ordained and played a major role in running a church and supporting the family by taking all sorts of jobs. In 1953, they returned to India with the new Dr. John Rolles eager to combine his old work with proper rural health care. In America, generous donations provided funds for a vehicle and equipment to travel round the district. Sadly, over the next few years it gradually became obvious that the free and nonconformist spirits that were my parents were not acceptable to the episcopal system which had been established in their absence. My mother's ordination was not recognized since she was a woman and my father was not prepared to be re-ordained because of the implication that his first ordination was invalid. After waiting for my graduation in 1956 they returned to England. My mother took on a church in a poor inner city area of London for a few years and my father became a partner to an American osteopath, providing manipulative services. He was unable to practice the full range of medicine, the osteopathic qualification not being recognized in The United Kingdom. Eventually they retired in the South of England always having an open house for colleagues and friends from their life in India and America. They died within two months of each other in 1994 and some of their ashes were returned to the area they loved in South India.

Molly Schmitthenner LESNICK
Sam and Ruth Schmitthenner

Marian Eyster (1895-1948), from Chambersburg, Pennsylvania was called by the Lutheran Church in India to teach Bible Women. She traveled with another "single lady" on a boat to England. Then they boarded another vessel bound for India on which another young single missionary called to the same church was traveling: August Frederick Schmitthenner (1897-1946), a young pastor from New York. He was accompanied by a missionary family, returning to India. On shipboard, Augie appeared to be courting both young women equally. He and Marian were both assigned to the Rajahmundry area of India and started Telugu lessons. A year after their arrival, November 20, 1922 they were married in Rajahmundry and assigned to Tanaku. There, father took on pastoral duties, as best he could practiced a little homeopathic medicine on the side, and went to visit congregations and churches in the outlying areas, often camping out for several days and traveling by bullock cart. He loved it! And mother began raising children!

During their first term in India they had three sons: Jerry, Fritz and Sam. After furlough, their second term was spent in Peddapur-Samalkott. In their second term, when Sam was five, a little girl, Katherine Marie was born. Unfortunately she died suddenly of convulsions when she was nearly five years old. My brothers duly went to Kodai school as all the kids in our Mission did when they were in second grade.

Our parent's third and fourth terms were spent in Yelleshwaram, a remote town in the agency, which my brothers and I all remember fondly and where I spent my early childhood.

Our father was a great story teller, had a wonderful sense of humor, and was extremely outgoing. During Mission meetings when controversies arose and tempers flared, he had a great way of breaking the tension by telling an appropriate story or joke. He also did not tolerate the caste system in the churches and had all the members drinking from a common cup. Mother in contrast was very quiet and sweet and just cut out to be a mother.

I was born while our parents were on furlough in the States and we traveled back to India when I was six weeks old. I attended first grade in Kodai, when Sam was a senior. This was during the war. Sam took a troop ship back to the States and we did not hear from him for a long time. My brother, Fritz, was drafted into the army after his first year of college, and Jerry, the oldest was put in an accelerated program by the army, to become a doctor. My parents and I were passengers on the *SS Gripsholm*, the historic first passenger ship across the Atlantic after the armistice with Germany.

Shortly before we were due to return to India, my father died of smoke inhalation in the LaSalle Hotel Fire in Chicago, where he had been attending a Lutheran convention. Mother and I and my brothers spent the summer at our old country place in Pennsylvania. Then at a Kodai Reunion we had there, Papa Phelps offered my mother a job as housemother to little boys in Kennedy Dormitory at Kodai School. My brothers were all grown and in college or medical school. So mother and I returned to India the next fall and spent Christmas in Kodai, where I met Jane and Ann Cummings!

Mother loved being housemother to little boys and seemed to be happy again. Then in 1948, she fell down the steps at Kennedy and ruptured a pre-existing hernia. After a brief over night stay at Van Allen, she was stabilized and taken to Vellore, where she had surgery. An hour before her surgery, she wrote a letter to the Woods and left it by her bedside. After she died in recovery, the nurses found the note and were able to contact Mrs. Wood. The letter to the Woods asked them if they would care for me as a daughter until they returned to the States, where upon I could live with my aunts.

The Woods honored my mother's request and made me a lasting part of their family. I did not go to live with my aunts when the Woods came on furlough, but through the generosity of the mission, paying a children's allowance for me, and especially because of the kindness of the Woods, I was able to return with them to India and graduate from Kodai. My brother Sam and his wife, Ruth, also returned as young missionaries to India and gave me added support during my high school years as did my father's cousin, Aunt Hilda Kaercher, also a missionary in India. But it is to the Woods that I owe a special gratitude, and to Pat, who suddenly had another sister in her life. Selah!

Alf Slaatten
Alf and Asa Slaatten

My Father Alf Slaatten was a graduate of the Norwegian Naval Academy (I am of Norwegian birth). He oversaw the Caltex Oil Co's oil tanker fleet.

My Mother Asa died in her 30's when the Nazis occupied her family's lumber farm during WWII. Mother died of an untreated burst appendix—she was denied medical care.

My Father was fighting with the British navy. He was awarded the highest medal of honor from the King. Because my father was with the allies, my Mother was sworn to silence—her brother-in-law was in the Norwegian underground forces also and she went to live with her mother. The family had 300 German soldiers on the land—she was terrified of rape and my safety. The family was controlled with Alsatian dogs and guns. After the war the Germans begged to stay in that part of Norway because they were headed home to utter destruction. They had to build a road up into the mountains on the lumber farm and then were sent home.

After the war, my Father married an American woman. I remained with my maternal relatives until my Father came when I was ten to bring me to his new marriage, and we moved to the USA. I spoke only Norwegian until school in US.

He was then sent to Bahrain by Caltex in New York. The schools in Bahrain were not acceptable and I was sent to Kodai! After graduation the family moved to Briarcliff Manor, NY, where my Father continued to work for Caltex and I went off to college in Oklahoma. My stepmother was an author in New York.

They are all now deceased. "Requiescant in Pace."

Eddie Tegenfeldt
The Tegenfeldt Family

My parents and I traveled to Burma in 1940 where they had been appointed as educational and theological missionaries with the American Baptist Foreign Mission Society. With the Japanese invasion of Burma during the Second World War my mother and I evacuated to Calcutta by ship and then to Assam to initially stay with missionaries there and finally to Woodstock to live and wait for my father to arrive. He had the responsibility for working with refugees and pastors in upper Burma as the Japanese were advancing. He finally ended up in Myitkyina in Northern Burma, and was the last civilian to have the opportunity to evacuate from that area by plane, standing for the journey just behind the pilot in a C-47 (military version of the DC-3 plane) carrying a plane load of coffins out to Assam. Many other missionaries walked overland from Burma to India under incredibly difficult circumstances.

After getting to India he joined my mother and me in Mussorie for a short vacation and then the three of us traveled to Nellore in Andhra where Dad was the principal of a Christian high school for a year. We then moved to Kodai where Dad started studying the Kachin language in the hope of getting back into Burma and working in that northern area of Burma among the Kachin tribe as the Allies pushed the Japanese back out of the country. During part of the time in Kodai my mother was on the staff of the school teaching physical education. Dad was eventually able to get back into northern Burma working with refugees, acting as temporary chaplain for the Kachin Rifles, and helping pastors re-establish churches and schools.

In 1945 my mother and I and two sisters (Judy and Alice) who were born in Van Allen Hospital during the war years when we were in Kodai, traveled on a "troop" ship back to the US and my father joined us a year later. We eventually were sent back to Burma by the mission in 1947 and moved up to the north among the Kachins. Mother taught us at home using the Calvert course. However after a little more than a year of that, my parents decided it would be better for me to be in school with other children and so planned to send me to the mission boarding school in Kalaw, in the hills of east-central Burma. It was about that time that insurgent activity broke out in Burma and the school in Kalaw closed. So the alternative was to send me to boarding school in India and discussions pursued about possibilities where missionary kids were being sent from Burma: Woodstock, Mt. Hermon in Darjeeling, or Kodaikanal.

For various reasons, Kodai won out and I went there along with the England family in April of 1949. We traveled by ship from Rangoon to Madras (a journey of about 7 to 10 days) and then on by train and bus. However, within a couple of years ship travel became very irregular resulting in missing about three weeks of school one year so the school party which by then consisted of the Dickasons, Youngs, Nancy Spear and Seagraves and myself flew to Calcutta from Rangoon and traveled by train from Calcutta to Madras and then on to Kodai Road. This continued from 1951 onwards. It was a long journey flying from Myitkyina to Rangoon and then after a day or two from Rangoon to Calcutta and then the long train journey from Calcutta to Madras and over night to Kodai Road.

My parents and Dave Dickason's parents were the last protestant missionaries to leave Burma when they were expelled by the Junta in 1966. By that time Judy, Alice and John had all attended Kodai School as well.

So, except for some early time at Kodai School in 1944-45 when although I was too young for first grade, Auntie Powell allowed me to join the class (that would have been the class of '55) until Papa Phelps heard about it and put a stop to it, I attended Kodai School from 1949 to 1953 when we went to the US for a year and then from 1954 to graduation in 1956.

Owen Thomas
The Thomas Family

Mother and Dad went to India as missionaries for the American Board of Commissioners for Foreign Missions (ABCFM) of the Congregational Church in 1928, three months after their marriage (two years after she graduated from college and shortly after he received his MBA from Harvard). Dad had traveled to Europe either the summer after graduating from Connecticut Wesleyan or perhaps a summer during college. He worked his way across on a cattle boat helping to tend to the cattle being exported to England. A few letters from his father relating to his trip to Europe are interesting in the cautions he advises, offers of financial assistance (very limited), as well as some of the Thomas relatives he was to see in St. Blazey, Cornwall. While in London, he bought a bicycle and used it as his means of transportation in the city. So he had some experience in international travel. He had also worked one summer while in college at Yellowstone National Park.

Mother had had no significant previous domestic or international travel experience and had, by all appearances, led a sheltered life as the daughter of a Congregational minister, growing up in Lynn, Massachusetts (Boston area). Her mother died when she was 16 of thyroid problems (goiter). She became the woman of the house for her father and two younger brothers. She attended Mount Holyoke College and received training in psychology and teaching the blind at the Peabody Institute for the Blind.

Dad was also the son of a Methodist minister and had originally considered the ministry as a career but "lost his religion" while in college, so he went to Harvard for his MBA and worked initially for an insurance company in Boston.

My parents met in Boston at the home of mutual friends; became engaged and married; and at, what I have understood, the urging of Mother applied to be missionaries in order to perform some Christian service for a couple of years. She had already applied to the ABCFM to be a missionary prior to meeting Dad and had been accepted. However, when they applied as a couple, her appointment was as a "missionary's wife." Dad was to take over the business aspects of the Board's Indian and Ceylon missions on the retirement of the man who had been performing those functions. Mother's training with the blind was eventually to be used in conjunction with a blind school run by the Marathi Mission in Bombay. The recollection that they intended to go for only two or three years may be apocryphal—I have seen no indication of that in their letters and considering that language training was a year-long effort, an anticipated short stay seems rather unrealistic. Whether they planned to make it a life long career at that point, or not, I do not know.

When they went to India the only means of travel was by ship and the trip required six to eight weeks. Concurrent with that, letters and other mail also required that length of time, each way. Here was a young American couple arriving in a strange land with a very different culture, weather, language, sanitary facilities, standard of living, etc. It was also a land where servants were used for virtually all household tasks in lieu of appliances and "servant management" had to be learned as well. They could not call home on the phone, use email, Skype or jump on an airplane. It is difficult to imagine what the effects of this sudden change of location would be. The Mission and other missionaries became their family and very strong bonds of friendship developed as a result.

Despite all of this, I am surprised at how few negative comments and how little complaining comes through in their letters. One must wonder what went on that was not recorded and how much loneliness and unhappiness there must have been. From this standpoint, their letters are probably not a true reporting of events. Many of their feelings and thoughts were probably filtered from their letters so as not to be negative and give cause for concern to family in the States. This must be especially so in the time leading up to their departure from India during the Second World War.

They retired in 1968 and returned to the States eventually settling down at Pilgrim Place in Claremont, California.

Lowey Thoms DICKASON
Wells and Beth Thoms

Mom was one of many Scudders born in India. Her great grandfather, John Scudder, went to Ceylon in 1819 under the Board of Foreign Missions, and to India in 1836 when non-British missionaries were allowed into South India. (He was the first American doctor to practice in India). John Scudder's seven sons and two daughters returned to India, forming the majority of the Arcot Mission (Reformed Church in America). Other generations also returned, including my grandparents,

Dr. and Mrs. (Ethel) Lewis Scudder. Ethel and Lew sent their three eldest children (Galen, Norman and Bill) as some of the first Kodai School students—had Kodai not been operating, they would have been sent back to the U.S. for their education. Six years later Mom and her brother Lewis (Marilyn and Lew Scudder's father) were sent to Kodai too. Trips to Kodai then involved night-long rides in elegant bullock bandies from Kodai Road station to the Tope, and then being carried by coolies up the Coolie Ghat in sedan chairs. At that time Kodai School only went through 8th grade, so they lived with U.S. relatives during high school later.

Dad's parents were Reformed Church (RCA) missionaries in the Persian Gulf. Drs. Sharon and Marion Thoms opened the first hospital in the Gulf—in Bahrain, in 1903. Marion died of typhoid fever when Dad was 16 months old. His father, Sharon, married the children's governess, May DePree (whose salary was provided by Mrs, Olcott—see below). Sharon died in an accident in January 1913 in Oman, where he had opened another hospital. This was just before Dad was to join his two sisters at Kodai School. Kids from both the Arabian and Arcot Mission (both part of the Reformed Church in America (RCA)) went to Kodai, as the closest American School. Oman had such a brutally hot climate that its missionaries were allowed yearly vacations in Kodai. After Sharon's death, May DePree Thoms brought the family back to the U.S. In 1931, Dad returned to the Arabian Mission as a doctor to fulfill his dream of carrying on his parents work. He was posted "home" to Oman in 1939.

Mom and Dad originally met in Kodai when their families vacationed there. Wells and Beth connected as Kodai kids again in the US while traveling on the Hudson River Dayline—owned by the Olcott family, patrons of the Arcot and Arabian missions. Beth was on an outing with the Scudder clan and Dad had a job on-board the ship. In due course they dated, married, and were assigned to the Arabian Mission.

Besides the Scudder presence in the Arcot Mission and family and mission gatherings in Kodai, there were many other factors that made me feel Kodai was my primary home. On Sharon and May's first trip to Kodai, Sharon bought a cottage that he named "May Villa" (after his new wife) across the road from what became the American Baptist compound. Many years later, Mom and Dad bought another Kodai cottage from Dr. Paul Harrison, also of the Arabian mission. They named it "Dar-es-Salaam," ("House of Peace" in Arabic; nicknamed "Door Slam"). During WWII, we kids stayed in Kodai year-round. My siblings stayed in India from '42 to Dec. '45 (myself from '43-'45) and Kodai was home base. Mom stayed in Kodai with us and later my grandmother, May Depree Thoms, came to take care of us after she retired as principal of a girls' school in Baghdad.

Brief Epilogue: When Dave had a Fulbright to do research in India in 1980-81, we enrolled our boys (John and Rob) at Kodai International School. Since the boarding was full, the school found a cottage where we could live. It was our old cottage, "Dar-es-Salaam." Amazingly, our old cook-caretaker was still there! Our beloved, Mr. P. Soosainathan ("Soosai") and his son S. Stanislaus ("Thani"), cared for us that year.

With Soosai, it was like taking the boys home to an Indian grandpa. He doted on them, and they ate gingerly all the vegetables he cooked and relished all the pies (with pictures of the Kodai Catholic Church emblazoned in the double crust!) that he baked. Sadly, Soosai died at a ripe old age about a month after we returned to the U.S. and "Dar-Es-Salaam" has since passed into other hands.

Jean Towle REED
How the Towles Came to India and Chose Kodai

The evangelist Dwight L. Moody, founder of the Mount Hermon School for Boys and the Northfield School for Girls, played a part in my father becoming a missionary. Moody wanted to provide good Christian education for the working class children in western Massachusetts. The schools were set in lovely, rolling countryside, ideally located for his educational experiment of combining the training of head, heart, and hand. These schools were probably the only American prepatory schools built around such a work-study program. Gifford Towle mostly earned his way through high school at Mt. Hermon, honing his mechanical skills while repairing furniture, doors, windows, roofs, and working in the dairy. He got academic credit for the dairy work.

Marjorie Blossom lived in Northfield. Her father worked in the creamery at Mt. Hermon, Massachusetts. The Hermonite of 1928 noted that Giff Towle was seldom at school for Sunday dinner because of a young lady, a townie attending Northfield Schools for Girls. The Hermon and Northfield years, however, yielded much more than a lifelong love match. Lasting friendships resulted. Religious life formed an integral part of the experience. If stories can be credited, meetings of Giff and close friends under a haystack at Mt. Hermon sealed their conviction that they should enter the Christian ministry. Giff, who came from a working class Quaker family in Holden, Massachusetts, had another formative influence in Alice Gifford, his mother's sister, serving in Japan as a missionary.

While Giff headed off to Massachusetts Aggie, the state university in Amherst, Marjorie went for a year to the Moody Bible Institute and to Wheaton College for two years. They wed on September 1, 1932, and thereafter Giff studied at Hartford Theological Seminary in Connecticut, graduating in 1936. He preached at Southampton Congregational Church for the next 3 years. Jean was born in Northampton, Massachusetts , in April, 1937; Alice came along in 1939.

The call to missionary work came from the Secretary to the American Marathi Mission of the American Board of Commissioners for Foreign Missions. The Towles set sail for India in 1939. After two years of language study in Ahmednagar, a small city about 200 miles inland from Bombay, Giff and Marjorie headed 27 miles north to rural Vadala, a Hindu village with a small Christian community. Giff oversaw its schools, ran the demonstration farm, supervised ministers, and shot cobras and mad dogs for Hindu villagers whose religion forbade such remedies. Eventually, when joined by a second American Board family, he concentrated on agricultural work, teaching better methods, starting a co-op for destitute farmers, and training young men in mechanical skills, including drilling wells. Maijorie worked primarily with women, but also began a social club at the behest of teenage boys, all the while helping Giff in innumerable ways.

Though an ayah watched over them, Jean and Alice had free run. Jean loved playing with her Indian friends. Maijorie and Giff decided five-year old Jean needed to go away to a British boarding school in the western ghats to be among less pliable peers, because no closer Protestant schools were available. Jean attended Kimmins for two disastrous years. In 1944, learning from the example of the Longs and Moultons in Ahmednagar, Reid Graham in Poona, and the Thomases in Bombay, Giff and Maij decided to send seven-year old Jean to Kodai School. We were halfway between Kodai and Woodstock, but friendships made the difference.

Ruth Vassar Burgess
The Calling: Not to Macedonia, but to India

Revival fires spread across the United States in the early years of the twentieth century. Camp meetings, brush arbors, storefront meeting places, tent meetings, and home Bible studies challenged the validity of many existing denominations. From these sincere enthusiasts came an urgency that the end of time was at hand. Jesus Christ was returning soon to take the chosen faithful to heaven. Their duty was to evangelize the world. “Go ye into all the world and preach the gospel to every creature. Lo, I am with you even unto the end of the world.” From these beliefs and integrating many of those from existing denominations arose a practice known as Pentecostalism.

Wednesday evening Bible Study was closing in the tan and brown rock church in Electra, Texas. Mrs. Crump, the pastor's wife of the Assembly of God, called on Estelle Barnett, 16 years of age, to close the meeting with a prayer. As the congregation bowed their heads reverently, Estelle started to pray. No audible words could be uttered. Shortly the gift of tears began flowing down her rosy cheeks. Rev. Towle, the visiting lady evangelist, said, "God is dealing with Estelle, let's pray that she will know His voice." Then it happened.

Within her head, Estelle heard the words over and over again. "India. India. India."

"But Lord, I barely know where India is. Why are you calling me to this country?"

"India. India. India," the voice continued.

"Why would you choose me? I'm just a girl from this oil-field town," continued Estelle bargaining with the insistent voice.

"Lo, I will be with you."

The believers gathered around the petite Estelle. Soon their prayers and her sobs ceased. Mrs. Crump asked, "What happened Estelle? Tell us about your experience."

Brushing her brown waves back and with a wide smile Estelle said, "I've been called to be a missionary to India." From then on everywhere there was an opportunity to proclaim the gospel and to share her calling.

Estelle met Ted Vassar, an upper classman, at Southwest Bible College in Enid, Oklahoma and enduring love grasped the couple. When Ted proposed to Estelle, she responded, "I love you dearly, but I can't marry you because I have God's call to be a missionary to India. You have never appeared interested in becoming a missionary."

"Estelle, if you will marry me, I will become a missionary. I have not received an audible call like you. I will go in obedience to the Biblical mandate to go into all the world and preach the gospel." The couple married and had a son, Bobby Jo while they pastored at Pawhuska, Oklahoma and then did itinerary work to raise financial support for their work in India.

Ted, Estelle, and their son Bobby Jo, age 2 years, arrived in Bombay, India in August 1936. They were in Poona for three months and one day when Bobby Jo died. He had appendicitis, but was treated for malaria. "Bobby passed away about 10:00 in the morning. We had to bury him on the same day at 4:00 p.m. in the Scottish Presbyterian section of the cemetery. Sure the devil tried to give us a hard time. Why would God call us to India, and then take your only son after three months? Why would He leave all those other children here who were starving and had little hope for the future?"

"Brother Vassar said, 'Estelle, we have to talk this over. We know God loves us. We know God called us to India. He brought us here. That is settled in our minds, so what we will do is to never ask God why He took Bobby Jo. If He wants us to know, that's all right, but if He doesn't, that's all right. We know God knows best.' That is how we kept the peace of God in our souls and minds. One thing both here and in India, we loved the people God called us to serve."

Question 1: How was it you came to be at Highclerc in Kodaikanal, South India?

1. My parents wanted me to experience an American educational curriculum, so that I would "fit in" when the family returned to the United States.

Question 2: Did your parents talk about their struggle sending you to a boarding school about 1,000 miles away from the village of Junnar in Bombay Presidency?

1. In later years my mother said she felt I had died, since Bobby Jo had died shortly after they arrived during their first missionary term. I was taken to boarding school two months after arriving in India at the age of seven.
2. Many years later after my father died, mother encouraged me to complete my Ph.D. She offered to come to Missouri and stay with my family while I completed the residency. Mother said she had suffered guilt many times for sending me away. Interestingly, I held no ill feelings against my parents. My father instilled in me that I was part of God's purpose for our lives. He would take care of us regardless if we were near or apart or on the plains or in the Palni Hills.

Question 3: Were there any highlights concerning your family and boarding school?

Yes, I never felt that I had been abandoned. My mother or father wrote me five or six postcards per week for 5 years while I was in boarding school. They sent me a parcel of "goodies" once per month during that time. Mother gave "Geegee bai" (an Indian maid) a sweater each year and asked her to take special care of me. Four evening prayers were installed in my mind that my mother or father prayed, which I continued to say. Before my family left after the hill season, my father bought a large tin of hard, egg candy from the shop across the street with instructions with Erky that I could have one per week.

Fay Ruth Voss
Bernard and Mae Voss

My father, Dr. Bernard J. Voss, had been in China from 1941-43 as a flight surgeon with the 14th Air Force, successors to the famous Flying Tigers. After his return and discharge from the Army Air Corps, he applied and was accepted by the mission board of the Reformed Church in America (RCA) to go back to China as a missionary. After the communist takeover, visas were no longer issued, and my parents' desire to serve on the mission field was put on hold. Then, in 1951, my aunt, Christine Voss, wrote from Iraq where she was a missionary nurse with the Arabian Mission of the RCA, that a mission doctor had contracted TB, necessitating a return to the US. She asked whether Dad would consider going out for a year to take his place. My parents contacted the mission board, decided to go, and arranged to leave my sister Bobbie and me with our grandmother in Grand Rapids, Michigan, taking only our younger siblings (Dave 6, and Esther 1) along.

Another doctor of the Arabian Mission contracted TB during that initial year, which they spent in Kuwait, so the mission board asked my parents whether they would fill out his term of an additional six years. Dad and Mother agreed, returned to dispose of property, collect us and we all left 6 days before Christmas on a Dutch freighter out of New York. After two months aboard, calling at Beirut, Bahrain, and Kuwait, we finally disembarked at Basrah, Iraq. It was the policy of the Arabian Mission to support Kodaikanal and send all the missionaries' children there. Bobbie and I had three months with the family in Amarah before going by British packet ship to Bombay, accompanied by our Aunt Christine. We traveled by train to Madras and Madurai, eventually taking the bus up the ghat to Kodai. We arrived to find all the students and faculty assembled on a veranda listening to the coronation of Queen Elizabeth II, June 3, 1953. Since I was then 16, my time at Kodai was relatively brief, but Bobbie attended all of high school, and our brother David came for the 4th, 5th and 6th grades. Even Esther enjoyed the Kodai experience as a high school senior, because after some years back in the US, my father became a company physician for the Raytheon Corporation in Jeddah, Arabia.

Paul and David Wiebe

Grandpa Bergthold was born in Piatagorsk, Russia. He immigrated with his family to North America in the 1870s. He married his first wife Katrina, whose family had immigrated from Russia (Ukraine), also in the 1870s, and had settled in Canada, in 1901.

Grandpa and "Tina" first traveled to India with their infant daughter, David's and my mother, in 1904. Tina died two months later of "Black Fever" contracted during a yeddula bundy trip to Suriapet, where she is buried. Grandpa's second wife, Anna, directly from the Ukraine, died in childbirth in 1915, in Nagarkurnool, where she is buried. He and his third wife, another Anna, are buried in southern California.

Like our grandparents Bergthold, David's and my grandparents Wiebe were also born in "Russia" and immigrated with their families to North America in the 1870s. Here they were farmers and grandfather was also a lay minister for more than twenty-five years in the Carson Township Mennonite Brethren Church in southwestern Minnesota.

Dad and mom met in our Conference school, Tabor College (where David and I, and Lorma and Donna Beth, also studied). They traveled to India first as Mennonite Brethren missionaries in 1927. All seven of us, their children, were born in India.

Dad drowned in the Bay of Bengal near Ramapatnam while swimming in 1963, and is buried in Ramapatnam. Mom, continuing in her work in India for another two decades, and finally settled in Kansas, where she is buried in Ebenfeld.

David's and my grandparents and parents were Anabaptist missionaries in a Mennonite Brethren variation. Their work was concentrated almost exclusively among Dalits (the "untouchables") in one of the most backward areas in pre-Independence India, in the Mahbubnagar District area south of Hyderabad in what were then The Nizam's Dominions. The consequences of this work has been, and remains, for David and Lorma and Donna Beth and me, and ours, an ongoing source of much curiosity and interest, and an ongoing center of attention. During college in Fremont, Nebraska, my dad, Ted Wood, was very active in a group called SVM (Student Volunteers for Mission), and as a result became convinced that he wanted to go to India as a missionary. At some point in his college or seminary career, he must have gotten in touch with the Board of Foreign Missions of the Lutheran Church, and they together began to make the arrangements to make this happen after his graduation from seminary.

Dad had been dating a young woman who was a divorcee, but the Board let him know in no uncertain terms that a divorcee was not an acceptable wife for a missionary. So he had to choose between the woman and the calling. India won, and in September 1929 he set off for New York, along with his mother, who was going to accompany him as far as England so the two of them could visit her English relatives. On the way, they stopped in Springfield, Ohio to visit my mom, Dorothea Krueger, who he had dated off and on in college. Things must have clicked for them, because this time when he proposed to her, she accepted. And then all hell broke loose!

Dad had to go on to New York to convince the Board that two would be better than one, and that it would be in their best interests to change the ship reservations and all the plans that had been in place. This took some convincing, but the fact that mom was the daughter of Dr. J. F. Krueger, who had just the previous year returned from three years in Ching Dao, China helping in the transfer of the Lutheran church work from the German Lutheran Church to the American Lutheran church helped a whole lot. Granddaddy was well respected and very convincing, and I suspect that he had something to do with my Dad's receiving the approval to marry and bring his new bride to India a month later than originally planned.

Meanwhile, Mom had to pull together a wedding in three weeks, get to know her soon-to-be mother-in-law who was now about to accompany them on their honeymoon—at least as far as England, and wrap her head around the fact that she was about to become a married woman, leave her family for seven years at a time, and embark upon the adventure of her lifetime. She also had to go big-time shopping for clothing and household items to last her through those coming seven years. The fact that she had quite recently spent a year in China with her parents probably helped prepare her for foreign travel to an exotic and unknown place. Anyway, the wedding took place and the newly married couple had a one-day real honeymoon before they took off for New York and the ship that would carry them to England and then on to India.

Mom and Dad served in Andhra Pradesh for 30 years, Dad as pastor and treasurer of the church. After Dad died shoveling snow in a snowy Nebraska winter while on furlough, Mom went back to India for another 10 years as a housemother for the teenage girls at Kodai School.

Carol Ziegler
How I Came to Kodai

My father, Virgil Zigler, lost both his father and mother before he was eighteen. His mother died of cancer, which saddened him very much and made him wish he could have been a doctor to save her. His father died of pneumonia and typhoid when Dad was only eight years old. Somehow the relatives raised him and his brother and sister and even saw that he went to Wittenberg College to get his education. There he met Jeanne Mumma who was studying to be a teacher.

Dad longed to be a doctor, but where would he get the money to go to medical school? He learned barbering and earned a bit of money. He prayed to God pleading, "Lord if you make it possible for me to go to medical school, and I become a doctor, I'll be a missionary for you and heal people in far off lands and preach the gospel of Jesus Christ to them.

My mother, Jeanne Mumma, was a pastor's kid. She also loved God and wanted to serve Him. When she and Dad met at Wittenberg, where her brother Levi was already studying, they talked together about Dad's plans to go to medical school. She told him, "I could study to be a nurse and work to get you through medical school." And that is what happened! After graduating from Wittenberg, Jeanne took nurse's training and earned money as a nurse while Virgil began his medical studies at Cincinnati. They married in 1924. Being members of the United Lutheran Church in America, they signed up to go to India under the Lutheran mission board and were commissioned in Gelnwood Lutheran Church in Toledo, Ohio, in December 1928. They arrived in India in early 1929 and were assigned to the hospital in Rentachintala and later to Rajahmundry in Andra Pradesh. There were other Lutheran missionaries with children going to Highclerc School in Kodai, so that is where they decided to send us four girls—Lucy, Bev, Carol and Sylvia—when we were old enough to go into boarding.

The Kodai "Budge" with Perumal Mountain on the horizon. (B. Peck)

CHAPTER 9

World War II Stories

In April 2016, The Kodai School classes of '55 and '56 held a joint reunion at the San Pedro Center in Winter Park, Florida. The theme for the reunion was: Our Family Experiences During World War II. Here are their stories:

Ed Tegenfeldt[27]
Our Family's Experiences During WW II

My parents along with me at age 19 months arrived in Burma (now Myanmar) in January of 1941 and were located in Rangoon with Dad (Herman) being the principal of two high schools. The war began to affect Burma in late 1941 and by January of 1942 regular air raid warnings and bombings occurred in Rangoon. At that time many women and children were evacuated by ship to India. My mother (Ruth) and I, along with Dave Dickason's mother and children left Rangoon on the steam ship Kutsang from Rangoon to Calcutta on January 1, 1942 and arrived in Calcutta on January 7.

By this time many of the schools in Rangoon had closed. However there was considerable uncertainty as to how the war would progress and if the schools could reopen. The concern was greatest for the 10th class (last year of high school) students and plans were made to invite those students back to try and prepare them for their high school graduation exams. Perhaps it was fortunate that very few students showed up on the day classes were to resume because the bombing raids from the south increased considerably, raising the issue of evacuation for all

---

[27] Some of this information comes from family conversations, but I have gleaned most of the details from one of my father's journals.

foreigners. Although there were a few air raids in the day time, most occurred at night. When the sirens went off everyone rushed to get into the trenches which had been dug. There were many nights when two or three air raids occurred. By January 13, the authorities began preparing Rangoon for a siege. The work of closing up all areas of mission work began and took some time, especially with uncertainty regarding the period of time that people needed to be away.

However, on Feb. 16, 1942 Singapore fell to the Japanese, and the next day all banks closed in Rangoon and on the 18th the remaining missionaries including my father and Dr. Dickason started fleeing north by road toward Mandalay. My father's main responsibility was to try and find teachers from the mission high schools in order to get their provident fund (retirement) money to them. Many of these had fled north from Rangoon going back to their home towns and villages.

Carried up the Ghat.

By the end of March, missionaries, Indians and Anglo-Burmans had moved to Mandalay and then up to Myitkyina in the far north of Burma. Evacuations going west to India overland from central Burma had taken place. But with several large towns falling to the Japanese in lower Burma this option closed.

Myitkyina, a large town in the far north at the end of the railway line and with a good airfield, was chosen as the best place for the large numbers of those wanting or needing to flee to await possible evacuation to India. The mission compound with school buildings, student dormitories and many staff houses as well as the church was requisitioned by the government for an evacuation camp. The missionaries including my Dad and Dr. Dickason were in charge of meeting those arriving on the trains and getting them to the "camp" and then helping them when flights were available to get to the airfield for their trip west. The numbers in the camp varied a great deal but at one time over 4,500 were staying there.

As the end of April approached there was considerable discussion on the part of the American missionaries about whether to stay on and eventually evacuate by walking out to India along a more northern route or fly out as the number of "residents" in the camp diminished. Adding to this uncertainty was the knowledge that the monsoon would soon begin when flying would be difficult and walking out even more difficult. This was further complicated as more of the transport planes were required by the military fighting the Japanese and therefore fewer were available to take people out to India.

By May 1st it was apparent that the Japanese were advancing north rapidly and it was decided that the missionaries should plan on leaving Myitkyina very soon. Dad, as the "treasurer" of mission funds, was urged to leave as soon as a place was available on a plane. On May 2nd word came that a plane had landed so Dad hurried out to the airport only to find that the plane was full with casualties and military evacuees. However, he was able to persuade the pilot to let him stand in the cockpit behind the pilot. Dr. Dickason and another missionary, D.O. Smith, were able to fly out the next day and then the two of them and Dad flew from Assam to New Delhi and then continue on by train and bus to Mussorie to join their families waiting for them there.

In June, when the new school year was to start Dad was asked to go to south India to be principal of a high school in Andhra. So we traveled to Nellore in southern Andhra and lived there for that school year. In April of 1943, when the school year ended in Nellore, word had come of the Allied forces beginning to push the Japanese out of Assam and so Dad traveled to Assam to try and find a Kachin (a northern end Burmese tribe with Myitkyina as its center) teacher.

In the meantime, Mom and I had moved to Kodai staying in Winsford compound where Alice and Nancy Graham were my playmates. The plan was that Dad and Mom would begin the study of Kachin in preparation to moving back to Burma after the war. And that began our family association with Kodaikanal and High Clerc School. Our family returned to Burma after the war and then, in 1949, when Burma was again embroiled in a domestic war, mission kids and many other children were sent to India to attend boarding school as mission schools in Burma that could prepare children to go to university in the West had to be closed. A few families sent their children to Darjeeling and Mussorie but many were sent to Kodaikanal.

Keith Capen Allen
War in China

World War II started earlier than Pearl Harbor for my family. Japan invaded Manchuria in 1937 and her troops continued south through China toward the port city of Swatow (Shantou) where we lived.

Swatow was one of the 19th century so-called Treaty Ports along the coast of China. The American Baptist Foreign Mission Society established the South China Mission there in the 1870's.

Young Keith.

My grandparents, the Rev. Randall T. and Mrs. Henrietta M. Capen had been missionaries with the South China Mission in Swatow since 1904. My father, the Rev. Carl M. Capen, returned to the city of his birth with my mother, Louise N. Capen in 1936 after a year of Mandarin studies in Peking (Beijing). They studied the local language of the Swatow area for six months before being assigned to Chaoyang, a small town upriver.

According to my Grandmother Capen's journal, the first Japanese bombing raid on Swatow occurred September 9, 1937.

On October 15, 1937, the first U.S. naval gunboats, the *USS Tulsa* and *USS Sacramento* arrived in Swatow to keep an eye on Japanese military activity and to make sure American interests and citizens were protected. They were among the other American naval gunboats that began regular patrols in and out of ports on the China coast; affectionately called the "Galloping Ghosts of the China Coast."

Throughout 1938, the Japanese conducted frequent bombing raids on Swatow under the watchful surveillance of the gunboats.

I was born in Swatow in October 1938, shortly after a bombing attack.

On June 20, 1939, we all left for vacation in Thaiyong, a hill station not far from Swatow. On June 21,1939, the Japanese invaded Swatow.

The U.S. patrols were stepped up after the Japanese captured Swatow and by early 1940, the destroyer, *USS Parrott* joined the gunboat patrols. The reason I know the names of these ships and their officers is that my grandmother invited the officers over for tea every day when the ships were in port.

My sister, Connie, was born in Swatow in November 1940.

On March 24, 1941, the Japanese moved upriver and occupied Chaoyang. "Keith thought machine gun racket in distance was ducks. Planes flew rather low over our house, but Carl wrote "I have a brave wife."

By that summer, conditions were becoming untenable—tense and threatening. My grandparents were due to retire, so it was decided that my mother would join them with Connie and me. In July we sailed on the *SS President Madison* for the United States. By November, the mission board began withdrawing all missionaries. My father arrived in San Francisco November 29, 1941 on the *SS President Taylor*, the last passenger ship across the Pacific before Pearl Harbor.

In March 1943, my father was sent back to South China. It took him seven months via South America, Africa, India, and over the Hump to Kunming, China and bumming rides overland 1,800 miles to reach Kityang, still in Free China. Kityang is 40 miles inland from Swatow where the South China Mission had a hospital and nursing school.

My father brought relief money, which he carried in his shoes. A few months later, the Japanese advanced to the front gate of Kityang as my father, the Chinese and American doctors and nurses escaped out the back gate, eventually reaching safety in Chungking (Chongqing) about 2,000 miles to the northwest.

My father remained there for the duration of the war. When the Japanese surrendered, he got rides on military vehicles, river barges or anything moving southeast toward Swatow. He arrived in October 1945. In his shoes again was money for the Chinese pastors and other Christians who had survived the war. There was also enough to start rebuilding and repairing mission property.

What were my mother, Connie and I doing during the 3½ years of separation from my father?

We lived in New York City for a while where my mother entered graduate school at Columbia University until the mission board decided she was such an articulate, compelling and attractive speaker that she withdrew to speak at churches and conferences around the country. During her absence, Connie and I lived in Georgia with her parents and during her presence we lived in Ohio.

Dependents were finally allowed to return to Asia in 1946. I had no personal memories of my early years in China, of course, but I did have memories of my father and I missed him.

Our arms still sore from cholera and typhoid shots, we sailed from Vancouver to Shanghai on a troop ship, the *USS General Meigs*. From there we flew on a C47 (the military version of the Douglas DC-3) to Hong Kong and took an overnight coastal steamer to Swatow. There to greet us was my father in a sampan alongside the ship waving madly. In July 1946, our family was finally reunited.

My war—the war I remember—came during the latter years we lived in Swatow after WWII. The Communists under Mao Tse-tung and the Nationalist party under Chiang Kai-shek had promptly renewed their civil war. Initially, the conflict raging elsewhere in China seemed unreal—at least to me.

My brother, Craig, was born in September 1948. Two of my mother's friends, wives of English businessmen, also had boys that month and all the women felt a special connection to Queen Elizabeth when Prince Charles was born two months later.

However, by early 1949 the political conditions were becoming so uncertain that foreign businesses began to leave again, inflation became rampart and nationalist government soldiers were deserting in droves. Every neighborhood in the city lived behind barricaded alleys to protect against looters. Anarchy reigned.

As the communist army advanced closer and closer to Swatow, the nationalist government bombed the airport and railroad facilities and abandoned China for Formosa (Taiwan). Soon, everyone was ordered out to the streets to watch the communist soldiers march into the city. October 1949 brought a huge sigh of relief as law and order returned and money actually had value; then, the bombing started.

Fighters and bombers from Formosa began regular strafing and bombing runs, often three times daily. We took shelter under the staircase—five of us and our servants. Craig thought this was great fun and wasn't bothered by fighters in their screaming dives. I sure was, especially after the time a fighter crashed into the mud flats in front of our house. Illogically, the bombers didn't frighten me as much because they were so much quieter and didn't dart around the sky as they dropped their payload of bombs around the harbor infrastructure.

Gradually, foreigners were placed under tightening travel restrictions outside of, and even within, Swatow. My father applied for exit visas for us. He had been in China nearly seven years and was due for a furlough.

In May 1950, the visas were finally approved and I can't tell you how relieved I was when we reached safety in Hong Kong and how thrilled I was when we sailed under the Golden Gate Bridge with all passengers on deck of the *SS President Wilson* singing, "California Here I Come." The Korean War broke out in June 1950 and all foreigners remaining in China were arrested.

That was my war. Well, I was caught up in an assignation attempt on the president of South Korea in January 1969, but that's another story.

Jean Towle Reed
The Towle Family's WWII and Introduction to Kodai

Gifford and Marjorie Towle began their assignment with the Congregational Mission Board by studying Marathi in Ahmednagar, Maharashtra, where the British Raj had a military station and prison. Jawaharlal Nehru, future Prime Minister of India, was imprisoned at that fort for some time. One day Dad looked out through the Ahmednagar mission school gates to see Italian prisoners being marched past. Later a few homesick British soldiers got brief leave to visit the Towles at their destination in the rural village of Vadala, just 27 miles north. The soldiers loved being with a family, playing with Alice and me, and going hunting with Dad. (Small deer were common in the scrubby plains.) Later, blackouts being enforced, we traveled by car with lights unlit. One night as we slowly made our way home along the dirt road at the bottom of a ghat, Dad spotted a large cat coming down the ghat in our direction. Being curious and unafraid, he got out to see better in the dark. The animal loped past us paying no attention to the nosy missionary. We kids huddled on the floor of the car, scared within an inch of our lives. As Dad got back in the car, he commented that it must have been a lion or tiger that had escaped from a circus.

Rationing was another mark of the war: butter, sugar, and gas were all very hard to come by. I still remember a wartime Marathi beggar's song: "Rationing, huh? Rationing, huh? My stomach needs filling but cannot be fed, rationing, ooh rationing, ooh."

World War II in 1944 dictated the way our mother, Marjorie B. Towle, my younger sister Alice, and I began our initial journey to Kodaikanal. "Petrol"[28] by then was virtually unattainable for civilian use. So Giff Towle and fellow missionary Joe Moulton, New Englanders both, used Yankee ingenuity to create the Toll Moll to enable travel. Taking the chassis of a useless old Ford Model T, they built on it a flat-roofed house with a long "tongue" so that 4 or 5 pair of oxen could pull it. The flat roof with a low railing allowed stowing of luggage and other baggage. Inside the car,

[28] Gasoline.

every inch of space counted. Backing on the driver's outside cubicle against the inner wall was a small stove, shelving, and a chemical toilet. Cabinets above contained utensils and supplies. Each side and the back of this "house-on-wheels" contained long "benches" below which were cabinets filled with all the requirements for travel and living for an extended period. Curtained windows hung above the benches. We kids slept on a mattress on the floor and loved it. The journey to Kodai began on January 20, 1944.

Overnight, crossing the ghat separating Vadala from the city, we arrived at Ahmednagar late the next day, moving, of course, at bullock speed. But it got us to the railway, where we joined Owen Thomas and others from Bombay. If I remember correctly, it took two nights and three days by train and a charcoal-fired bus trip up the ghat to reach the Kodaikanal hill station in Tamil Nadu. My first year at Kodai School was inauspicious, to say the least. Shortly before our trip south I had been bitten by a rabid dog in Vadala (which Dad subsequently shot). Our tiny rural hospital lacked the necessary serum, so as soon as we arrived in Kodai I had to undergo a long series of rabies shots—not fun. Mother, pregnant with our baby sister Nancy, settled with Alice and me in the mission's Maratha House at the head of the bazaar hill. Dad had to stay behind in Vadala due to the press of work. Ours was one of two American families there in an otherwise totally Indian Christian outcaste or low caste community at the edge of a Hindu village. His job was to run a Demonstration Farm (he had a degree in agriculture), oversee the boys' boarding school, work with a network of Indian Christian pastors in that region, and deal with unending appeals for help. He also served on local and mission committees.

Meanwhile, I began second grade in Kodai Boarding School where I had the wonderful teacher, Auntie Powell. She was a saving grace, such a kind and understanding woman! She cushioned the trials of that year and the one before. Beginning as a five-year-old in 1943 I had had a horrific experience at Kimmins, a British boarding school much closer to home. Little wonder I came to love Kodai School.

Dad arrived in Kodai on April 1st for a much-needed vacation and to support Mother. He made the most of it, playing tennis often at a Club with Reid Graham, Lloyd Lorbeer, Seamans, Peary, and other Protestant missionaries on vacation in Kodai. They played in teams against one another or against non-missionary civilians. Eventually a tournament was held. Those tennis matches, the hiking, the relaxation of being with family and friends and without hassle was a boon for Giff Towle.

When not playing tennis, he accompanied Mother shopping in the bazaar, socializing, as well as enjoying the Gilbert and Sullivan operettas and other cultural activities during the holidays. When Dad had to leave Kodai on May 28, he wrote in his diary that his 1944 vacation was the best he'd had in 10 years.

Baby sister Nancy was born in Kodai's Van Allen Hospital on May 6, 1944. The difficult birth kept Mother in the hospital for an extended period. Alice and I had a spell of vomiting and diarrhea. That experience presaged the tumultuous time that followed after Dad's return to work on the plains. Mother developed jaundice and amoebic dysentery, which landed her back in the Van Allen. With Dad gone, missionary friends came to the rescue. They became our extended family: the Swans took in baby Nancy; the Grahams added Alice to their family, and I ended up in the Dishpan[29] with a deadly case of bacillary dysentery. It took Dr. Thoms' intervention and kind application of a new drug. He saved my life. I was so weak and had lost so much weight that, once Mother was mostly better, she took all three of us children home to Vadala at the end of July. Such was my introduction to Kodai and Kodaikanal School.

After two months of slow recovery, my clueless parents decided to send me back to Kimmins School in the Bombay ghats accompanied by Alice so we would not lose a whole year of school. Once again, the Kimmins people lied through their teeth to my parents, who believed them despite the horrid experiences I related to them. They chalked my accounts up to a vivid imagination. Our letters were doctored by the school. How could they know?

We did return to Kodai in 1945, but left in May, I believe, on the *SS Gripsholm*, the Swedish neutral ship that carried missionaries, soldiers (unwisely) and assorted others to America. Several classmates and other Kodai students took the same ship. I remember playing hopscotch on the huge Swedish flag painted on the ship's deck. The voyage also gave me my first taste of chocolate. After docking in New York that June, I recall hours standing in line with our parents, still on the *SS Gripsholm*, while the authorities kept the passengers filling out long questionnaires, including retracing up to four generations of our forebears. Rampant rumors circulated claiming that the process had uncovered at least two or three spies on board. One was purported to dress as a Catholic priest. We endured the heat and shots before undergoing customs on shore in a huge drafty room of returnees and immigrants. Finally, we were free to join loved ones. Our sabbatical had begun.

---

[29] What students called the Kodai School clinic.

Such, such were the woes and joys of our WWII years, to borrow from George Orwell's essay on his days at Eton (See *Such, Such Were the Joys*).

Beth Gessler Caldwell
World War II memories

Blackout shades and soldiers are my most vivid memories of World War II. The shades, or course, were to keep the lights hidden at night for fear of enemy planes flying over and targeting us. As to the soldiers—at that time during the war, my brother and I were living with foster parents. Our own mother had died shortly after my brother's birth, and good friends had stepped in to care for us to make life easier for my father. Much of the year we spent in Kotagiri in the Nilgiri hills with our foster mother. American soldiers were stationed there, and individuals were invited to house them during their stay. Or it may have been they were on leave; it was a great climate. We got to know some of them quite well. They were fun to be around and loved teasing us young children.

As to war itself, I'm sure I really didn't understand quite what was going on. I know there were lengthy discussions among the adults which became hushed if there were children around. I do know the impact it had on our family, and I was aware that we could not travel to the States for our scheduled furlough as it was too dangerous for civilians to be traveling. That ended in 1946 when we finally were able to sail safely from Calcutta to San Francisco. My father had been in India 10 years by that time, with no furlough.

Even though the war was over, getting out of India was not easy. We left our home in Rajahmundry in April and did not sail to the States until July. We waited in Calcutta—with a short hill break to Darjeeling—all that time for passage. When we were finally able to leave, my new mother, brother, sister, foster mother, and I were in old officers' quarters, and my father and foster dad were in the hold in what had been a troop ship. They slept in the same three-tier bunkbeds the soldiers had. At least we could all be together for meals in the mess hall. What a journey that was—a month long trip to San Francisco!

An ironic note is that San Francisco was my first glimpse of the United States, and only 30 years later I would come back to the Bay Area to live.

Hermann Tauscher
Memoires of WWII

My memories of WWII are very imprecise, since I was not even two years old when the Germans began the war. But it was a complete disruption of life, which until then, I suppose, was, despite some problems of living in a rural area of Orissa, very peaceful with faithful servants helping my mother to manage and father teaching in the seminary for future pastors. I just imagine this from photos of a proud and happy mother with her children.

Tauscher family.

And then suddenly all the missionaries in our area were ordered to gather in Jeypore. Can you imagine that respected and well-loved missionary families being led off in military or police vehicles, gathered in a missionary compound in Jeypore, probably associated with restrictions concerning movement and communication with the leaders of the church? That must have been quite a shock for the adults: Indians as well as the missionary groups. Despite all of the missionaries being known or having personal contacts to the governor and other high British officials, all the male missionaries were transported by police vans via Vizianagram and by rail to Calcutta where they were kept for a month or two before being transferred to a larger camp in Dehra Dun. As far as my sister Helga, four years older than me, remembers, the missionaries were allowed to return to their families for or after Christmas that year.

In March of 1940 my mother died, which must have had a devastating impact on my development. The twins, Wilfried and Gerhard, were born in November '39, and they were naturally the center of attention and attraction. As Helga reports, I showed signs of hospitalism[30]—not swallowing for hours what I had in mouth and constantly swaying back and forth. There was no real family anymore—father could not manage five children and also lead the seminary—so we were taken care of by Ayas[31] or by other missionary families—with regard to when and for how long, I don't know. During the mid-1940s the male missionaries were again collected and transferred to an internment camp. My father received permission to stay at his mission station to take care of his five children and to continue his work in the seminary. When I read in the teachers' reports in Kodai of me "lacking consistency," I sometimes wonder how one can expect this after experiencing these chaotic conditions following the twofold disruption.

In 1942, my father married an American nurse working for a branch of the Missouri Lutheran church—stationed at Tilda and partially in Vellore. After the remarriage in May 1942 our family was transferred to an internment camp in Satara near Poona. According to Helga we were transported via police bus to Satara. I have vague memories of being in a bus that was motored by burning wood or coal,[32] forcing us to stop every now and then to keep the motor going. Maybe that was on our way back. Police will always guide you to the prison or internment camp but rarely accompany you back home! I believe due to my mother our mission society got to know about Kodaikanal and Dr. Gass, who spoke up for us concerning admission to Highclerc School[33] in Kodaikanal after the end of the war in 1946.

In Satara we were accommodated in different barracks, three rooms for the family and again according to Helga, a "kitchen" outside in the alleys separating the different barracks. Our family was allowed to have two servants to accompany us; I imagine that was true also for other missionaries. I have no memories of this.

Life was quite agreeable. From 1943 on I was a pupil in the German school. I don't remember much of classmates other than Aniline Meyer, nor do I have any

---

30 The adverse effects of a prolonged stay in a hospital. A pediatric diagnoses in the 1930s to describe infants who wasted away while in a hospital.
31 An Indian nursemaid.
32 A wartime substitute for gasoline which was scarce.
33 Highclerc School was the original name for Kodai School.

special memories of the teachers. The internment camp was under the direction of a Mr. Font—I think that was his name. We were not kept behind barbed wires, although there was another camp close by which was; it was probably intended for more potentially dangerous Germans. It seems the British government feared an uprising for independence with the support of Germans or Japanese.

In our camp movies were shown once a week, in general they were funny films with Laurel and Hardy, but once I saw the famous film—I think it was *Jane Eyre*. I was terribly shocked with the drama of a wife suffering under schizophrenia and still can recall the final scene when she, after having set the castle on fire, jumped right into the flames. After that, we children were not so easily allowed to see films any more. According to my sister, once a year all the children of the camp assembled in front of the director—probably on the occasion of his birthday. And we sang a song and were rewarded by small gifts of candies and the girls got bracelets.

In sum, we children were treated well and did not really suffer during the war. There were probably more quarrels between all the missionaries who were now assembled—rivalries even between the clergy are unavoidable or astonishingly frequent—than with the authorities. Differing positions concerning Nazis and the expected outcome of the war affected our parents more than us children.

We did encounter problems when we came to Highclerc where my older brother Rolf and I were exposed to continued aggression by children of British soldiers, punishing us as Huns. I was not used to such rude aggressiveness for something that had nothing to do with me. But by 1947 all of them had left for their home country.

WWII was for me a disruption of life, horribly intensified by the death of my mother. Life until then seemed to be going in a peaceful, secure and predictable manner. The disruption produced turmoil, excitement, despair and absolute uncertainty how missionary work would continue and how to manage with the children. And maybe Satara was after all more of a divine gift, getting us children, who until then had been growing up in a sort of "splendid isolation" to get to confront their peers within a sort of protected situation, where a school for us was available and from where contacts for Kodai were established. We all had to learn, that life's circumstances change and we must to learn to adapt ourselves to these changes. We had to learn, as probably all persons living or growing up in a foreign country, to be careful, polite and adaptive. At the verge of the end of the colonial era, we learned the fundamental lesson of equality of all human beings.

Nancy Thoms Block MD
The Big Scare of 1942

Tension was building in British India throughout the late winter into early spring of 1942 as the massive Japanese war machine swarmed over country after southeast Asian country on a seemingly unstoppable march westward, until it overran Burma and was barely contained at India's mountainous northeastern border by combined British, Indian and American forces. Supplies and critical personnel, including some British and American missionary doctors (such as our uncle, Dr. Galen Scudder) were conscripted from the south to assist in handling wounded, displaced people and military casualties streaming into India from Burma and the border states.

Meanwhile, in the usually sleepy south, the authorities began issuing some directives in a token effort to prepare civilian populations—at least where Europeans were most represented—for the seemingly remote possibility that the Japanese would attack that mainly agricultural region. In Kodaikanal, 7,000 feet elevation in the Palani Hills, a mixed residential and resort community of Indians, British civil servants and vacationing European and American missionaries, the call to prepare was taken seriously. HighClerc School, where we were "in boarding" for the year, was the epicenter of the buzz.

Following the British model, civil defense groups of local Indian merchants and working people were organized into small companies, without uniforms and carrying sticks to simulate firearms, and marched in drill formation up and down the playground next to Kennedy boys' dorm, drawing bemused interest among the students. Presumably they were being taught something about rescue operations in case of attack, though no equipment or vehicles to aid in such endeavors were in evidence.

Orders were given to dig rows of trenches, for refuge in case of bombing, on the exposed hillside below Boys' Block, a project in which some of the older high school boys were recruited to help, bestowing a certain semi-heroic status among younger fry. The entire school was subjected to air-raid drills and nighttime blackouts. A couple of our English 6th Grade classmates, Chris Windle and Kenneth Crossfield, infused with patriotism and inspired by the exploits of British Commandos, formed a private club, to learn and practice secret codes and clandestine maneuvers—all thrillingly hush-hush.

Then suddenly on a day in early April, panic struck. Word came that the Japanese fleet was sighted steaming toward the key east coast port city of Madras

(Chennai) with the apparent aim of cutting off and occupying southern India, which was virtually devoid of military defenses. School authorities who received the news, and a few parents, who happened to be in town, huddled quietly behind closed doors for several hours, frantically weighing their options. It was agreed to evacuate the school as soon as possible, beginning that evening, with or without consent of parents who were scattered over the whole of India as far north as Bombay (Mumbai), as well as Ceylon (Sri Lanka), Oman, the Persian Gulf, and Iraq, few of whom could be reached, even by cable, in a timely fashion. There was no time to lose. Classrooms were emptied, students were told to pack a few changes of clothes and toiletries in bags which we could carry, gather in groups assigned to adult leaders, and prepare to board buses for the hot, winding trip to the plains; thence hopefully to board crowded trains on the narrow-gauge railway to Madras, and from there disperse to points north and west.

The school evacuated almost overnight without students becoming alarmed, to the credit of a cadre of amazingly level-headed adults orchestrating the drama. We came from families who traveled a lot, coping with equanimity in difficult and unpredictable circumstances. (Yearly, the Thoms family traveled thousands of miles by ship, train and bus, for vacations and our return to school.) Students developed trust and independence, and expected all would be well as long as the grown-ups didn't lose their cool.

After nearly three days of travel by a rag-tag bunch of kids hailing from Arab countries, we jumped off the train, grimy with soot from the coal-burning engines, at the doorstep of some kindly folk from the American Presbyterian Mission in Miraj, in western India south of Bombay, who had been pressed into taking charge of us for an unspecified length of time. There were about ten of us ranging from third grade through high school: Dejongs, Gosselinks, Hakkens, Thomses, and Audrey Greenway. Our hosts were Dr. and Mrs. Bruce Carruthers, whose children and those of Presbyterian colleagues, they had just escorted from Kodai. The mission compound swarmed with children and assorted luggage.

After we were cleaned up and fed, the first challenge was a medical one. Our brother Norman, age 7, had broken his arm falling from the corrugated tin roof—which was off limits—of a walkway near Kennedy on Good Friday, and although in a cast, the bone had begun knitting in poor alignment. So Dr. Robert Goheen Sr. at the mission hospital undertook to re-break and reset it properly. He cheerfully allowed some of our bunch to watch. Brother Peter and others were fascinated. I got as far as the door of the operating theater, felt dizzy and beat a retreat; Dalton McClelland, who was with the group, got a close-up glimpse and fainted. No matter, we both ended up becoming physicians anyway.

A plan was made to send the "Arabs" on to sojourn for the next month or so, in a small, relatively cool retreat called Panhala, in the foothills of the Western Ghats, under the tender mercies of a senior (childless) couple, Dr. J. E. Napp and his wife recruited from Kolhapur. A few Presbyterian kids, including Martha and Dave Kincaid, were added for good measure. We were housed in a sprawling bungalow where meals were provided for us, and given strict instructions about saving water, as India's dry season did not end until summer. Beyond that we were pretty much given the run of the place.

Panhala, it turned out, was enchanting. Huge spreading banyan trees, the best kind ever invented for climbing by children and monkeys, only partially concealed extensive ruins of a Hindu temple and ancient granary, which invited endless exploring. But the monkeys drew by far the most attention. The boys, especially, gave them daily chase, which both parties seemed to enjoy.

Standard equipment for boys then, Indian and otherwise, was a catapult "catty" (a slingshot) made of a sturdy Y-shaped stick, fitted with a patch of cloth or leather attached by rubber strips (from inner-tubes usually) to the points of the Y. It could shoot pebbles quite effectively, depending on the strength and skill of the shooter. Yours truly participated in that activity by accommodating special requests for squares woven from string on my precious "Weave-It" craft kit, acquired at Macy's in New York on our family's last furlough. Also at hand were the ubiquitous pea-shooters. With the boys in pursuit Tarzan-style, the monkeys led a wild chase through the trees, chattering loudly and managing to pelt the hunters from time to time with green fruit. Miraculously, nobody was severely injured.

We also hiked, read, played games, "hung out" and learned from the staid and long-suffering Napps the song "Dunderbeck," which remains vividly in memory after other details of that time have faded. (More recently, as I recall the dust our group kicked up, I have wondered whether Dr. Napp identified a bit with Dunderbeck.) The song went something like this:

Oh, once there was a Dutchman, and his name was Dunderbeck.
He was very fond of sauerkraut and sausages and speck.
He had a great big butcher-shop, the grandest ever seen,
And one day he invented a sausage-meat machine.

Refrain:

Oh, Dunderbeck, oh Dunderbeck, how could you be so mean?
We're sorry you have invented your sausage-meat machine!
For all the cats and long-tailed rats will nevermore be seen,
'Cause they'll all be ground to sausage-meat in Dunderbeck's machine!

One day a very little boy came walking in the store.
He bought a pound of sausages and eggs a half a score.
But while he was a-waiting there, he whistled up a tune,
And the sausages began to dance and prance about the room. (Refrain)

One night there was a problem; the machine, it would not go.
So Dunderbeck, he crawled inside, the reason for to know.
His wife, she had a nightmare, and walking in her sleep,
She gave the crank an awful yank, and Dunderbeck was meat! (Refrain)

Eventually, this sweet time of un-regimented childhood pursuits came to an end, when it was clear that the Japanese were withdrawing their strike force from the western Indian Ocean. The United States was launching its operations in the Pacific, and the Japanese no longer posed a threat to the Indian subcontinent. Our group was packed back to Kodai to finish up the spring semester, however disorganized, with only a week or so to go before the regular May vacation rescued us from further work.

Meanwhile, a contingent of students from the American (Presbyterian) Marathi Mission and others remaining in that part of India, were re-organized into a group based in Miraj and home-schooled by mothers for the rest of the school year. Their further adventures are colorfully described in a chronicle titled "The Eucalyptus Branch," authored by the Carruthers, Kincaids, Thomases, Jackie Brown and Robert Swart.

Addendum by Lowey Dickason: The Kodai cottage, Dar-es-salaam, we owned, became our year around home during the war (and again in '80/'81). Ship passage was hard to get during WWII ('42-'45), so Mom, Dad and I would come from Oman by September. Dad would leave after a month's vacation and Mom and I would stay on through the winter, until Nancy, Pete and Norm would return to boarding. During the winter of '44, (when Molly, the Wiebe twins and I were all in Auntie Powell's 1st grade) our grandmother, who was retiring as principal of the girl's school she founded in Baghdad, came to spell Mom off to care for us. The first two years we visited Arcot Mission friends, and my Uncle Galen Scudder on the Plains during part of the winter, though we had Thanksgiving and Christmas at the cottage, with lots of decorating fun, including a real Christmas Pine tree cut from the Lutheran compound above us, with real candles. Mom returned briefly in January and February of '45 to be a temporary Upper Boyer housemother until I turned seven on February 10th, when she left me in boarding to return to Oman. Because of this prolonged time in our cottage, besides the usual month or so out of boarding yearly with our parents in September, it truly became home.

Imagine, then, our delight when in 1980-81 Dave and I and our two sons returned for a Fullbright year in India, to find the school chose to put us in Dar-es-salaam for the year. By then the school owned the cottage, and had retained our same old cook and caretaker, Susai Nathan, who had been there since the 1940's. It was like coming home to grandpa with our boys. John and Rob (8th and 5th grades) loved the freedom of walking to and from school and returning to be pampered by Susai. He was not well, but served us graciously, sadly dying the month we left India.

Owen Thomas
WWII[34]

The Thomas family left India on March 27, 1943. We sailed from Bombay via South Africa due to the war hazards in the Suez Canal and the Mediterranean Sea. The name of the ship we sailed on does not appear in any of the correspondence, but after a lot of "googling" I was able to find a website that listed ship arrival and departures by date from various ports (convoyweb.org.uk). The result was to find that we sailed on the *QSMV Dominion Monarch* directly to Durban and without being in a convoy. Most ships sailing in the Indian Ocean at the time were in convoys escorted by the British Navy.

From a letter of April 17, 1943 to my uncle Fred Thomas from my Grandad Owen: "The American Board has had a cable from Dr. Allen Taylor of Durban, South Africa, saying "Thomas party safe." This is the only word that we have on the matter.

The conjecture is that Ross and family have left Bombay, crossed the Indian Ocean to South Africa en route to America. It seems probable that Ross sent a cable when they were about to start. Peggy had written me that they would cable if they started. We think the censor intercepted this cable, so it was never received ... I guess all we can do is to hope and prey and wait."

---

34 This is an except from Owen Thomas's Family History.

The *QSMV Dominion Monarch* (pre-war).

From a letter from the American Board to Granddad Owen May 14, 1943, "Just received the following cable from Mr. G. Ross Thomas dated Durban, South Africa, May 11: "Patsy (Thomas) under doctor Taylor's care. Fractured arm and leg delaying us. Mix Lorbeer proceeding with large party missionaries."

From a letter from Mother to "family" May 16, 1943:

... "Patsy is, as I write, in the McCord Zulu Hospital, occupying one of the two rooms for missionaries. The rest of the hospital is for natives and Indians only.

On Wednesday afternoon, the 5th of May, she fell from a tree, fracturing her arm and her leg, both on her left side. She is getting along all right, though she has been through considerable pain with her leg. The arm was a more simple break, quite close to the wrist. It has not given her any pain. The leg has two bones broken, very close to the ankle. I think the ankle is involved somewhat. Our first accident of broken bones has come to pass.

You will realize our state of mind, when I tell you that just about one half hour after Patsy fell, a telephone message came for Ross to report the next morning for information. He reported and was told that our group could move that day! Of course, we could not. Consequently, Ross, having spent most of the night up with Patsy, spent the whole day getting the rest of the group of over 100 persons together and arrangements made, and all "in order." Everyone was very sympathetic. They sent Patsy a lovely gift of money, because they had no time to find a gift. I didn't see any of them except those of our own Board. Kay Mix didn't want to leave us, but there really wasn't anything she could do to help by staying, so we urged her to go on....

From a letter from Granddad Owen to Uncle Fred June 28, 1943:

"The American Board has just received the following cable marked from "overseas" which presumably came from Durban, South Africa and is signed by Ross: "Still waiting. Has Mix arrived? Thank my brother for his cable. Assure family Patsy recovered excellently. All well."

And I have just talked with Katherine Mix who was with the Thomas's at South Africa and has arrived in Boston. She says that the day before they were to leave South Africa Patsy was climbing a tree when she fell and broke both of her arm bones just above the wrist and both of her leg bones just above the ankle. She has been in good hands because the McCord Mission Hospital is at Durban and one of our good missionary doctors, Dr. Alan Taylor, is in charge. It is considered of a secret by what route Katherine Mix and Mrs. Lorbeer came, but we are pretty sure they came around the Pacific side of South America and then through the Panama Canal."

From a letter from the Board dated September 13, 1943:

"To the Relatives of Mr. and Mrs. G. Ross Thomas:

This morning we received the following cable from Durban dated Sept. 9th, from Mr. Ross Thomas:

THANKS FOR CABLE STOP TRAVEL BY SOUTH AMERICA NOW UNNECESSARY STOP INFORM AUBURNDALE HOUSE REQUIRED STOP

We interpret this to mean that Mr. Thomas and his family are returning by sea. This changes the possible plan that was made for them to go by way of South America and return from there to the United States.

While we waited for another ship to be available to continue our journey to the US, we spent time along the coast of South Africa, and at Inanda, a mission farm, but always within a days travel to Durban. Ship schedules were not publicized for security reasons and there were not many ships that would carry civilians. We had to be ready at a moments notice if a ship was available.

After 5 months we were finally able to leave South Africa on the *SS Nieuw Amsterdam*, a very large, luxurious Dutch passenger ship that had been converted to a troop transport with a capacity of 8,000 troops. After Holland was invaded by the Germans, the Dutch loaned their naval ships to the British Navy. Unbeknownst to my parents when we boarded the ship, we were not going across the Atlantic, but back across the Indian Ocean to Australia and from there across the Pacific to San Francisco. The ship had come from Australia to Suez then to Massawa, Eritrea and then to Durban. There were German prisoners of war on the ship, probably having been boarded in Suez. I suppose their destination was the US but it might have been Australia. They were allowed to make various items and I recollect getting a wooden tank that one of them had made. I also got a Koala Bear when we were in Australia.

From a letter from the Board dated October 8, 1943:

.... On October 6 we received a cable from New Zealand reading as follows:

"ROSS THOMAS AND FAMILY WELL. LOVE"

This cable came to us from one of our former missionaries to India who is now married and living in New Zealand. We were happy indeed to get word from the Thomas family, as it has been some time since the last cable from them was received. We presume that since they are now in New Zealand they will probably return to America by way of the Pacific. This may take anywhere from a month to six weeks.

From an "Annual Letter" of Mother and Dad's November 28, 1943:

"When we left Bombay on the bright, sunny morning of March 27th, we did not expect to be long on our way. For fun, we numbered the days in our diaries; we did not expect to number over 60 days at the most. But from the 27th of March, when we left Bombay harbor, until the 16th of October, when we landed at San Francisco, totaled 205 days. We had decided that if a good transport were available, we would proceed on our furlough on it. So, after various false alarms, strenuous packing and sorting, minute examinations of baggage and detailed censorship of papers, we did board a very fine large British transport. Unlike the trips many of our friends had taken on American transports, we had steward service at table and in the cabin. Our cabin was very comfortable, a peacetime two-berth one made into a four-berth. There were over 100 missionaries on board with us. Soon we accustomed ourselves to the routine carrying of life belts, the frequent lifeboat drills, and the blackout. Volunteers were asked for to stand watches on the anti-aircraft guns. Ross volunteered and spent two hours daily watching on the starboard, forward Orlikon 20 mm anti-aircraft gun turret.

For twelve days we saw nothing but water. Then we found we were at Durban, South Africa. It was Ross' birthday (April 7th). We went ashore and had a good time buying him some gifts, having a birthday luncheon and then visiting the McCord Zulu Hospital of our South Africa Mission where we met Dr. and Mrs. Alan Taylor. Little did we dream that day how well we would know them ere long! Or how familiar we would be with those hospital corridors and the Zulu nurses. We left

Durban the next morning, proceeding south—we could tell by the growing frigidity of the air. After two days of this, the boat turned right around and on the 12th of April we were told we would have to disembark at Durban! So we did, most reluctantly. Of the 100 missionaries, some found small hotels, some squeezed into the YMCA and YWCA. The Taylors took our family in.

The next three weeks seemed like an eternity. Many of the missionary group began to worry over financial arrangements. We met together every week to hear and discuss what ideas anyone had about getting on. Then on May the 5th, Patsy climbed a tree in the Mission yard to get a stick for Owen. She leaned over onto a dead branch, and came sailing down about 12 or 15 feet onto the driveway below. She just missed the soft earth bank and landed on the asphalt. Owen's screams brought us running. The result was a broken arm and a broken leg. The hospital was just next-door, and a stretcher was soon brought. So she began her three-weeks stay in the hospital. While we were there in the X-ray room with her, about a half hour after her fall, a phone call came for Ross to report to the Sea Transport Office the next morning. Patsy spent a very painful night. The leg gave her a lot of pain, and for the rest of us, a lot of concern, because the bone was split into the ankle joint.

Ross' call at the Sea Transport Office on the morning of the 6th proved to be the call for sailing on. We could not take Patsy. So we said goodbye to our friends, salvaged our baggage from the customs sheds, and turned to await happenings ... Patsy progressed and on May 25th, we informed the authorities that we could travel again. But they gave us very little hope of another transport. North Africa was then cleared of German forces, but we hoped that something would come along.

July was the winter holiday month for schools. We spent it at Inanda, where our children had a wonderful time in the country, walking, riding horses, and eating delicious and wholesome food. Patsy could ride one of the horses, and went everywhere with us.

Still no ship to take us on.

August came, and we moved into a tiny hotel at the seashore, with good rail and telephone connections with Durban. The leg cast came off in early July, and in August Patsy left the crutches behind. Running in the sand and swimming helped the ankle a lot. (The arm had healed without any trouble.) Still the authorities could give us no hope; so we investigated and made preparations to go to South America, and hoped to get up from there. We planned to go on an Argentine ship sailing about September 15th.

Then came our day: August 30th. The telephone call we had hoped for during all these months came. We left the sands and rocks, the swimming in the icy water, the sea anemones, octopuses, seaweeds, and marine animals, and went back to Durban. There, at the Taylor's home, we made the last minute preparations and left Durban on September 10.

Even more palatial and comfortable than our first ship, this one was huge. We boarded as passengers for the USA. Nothing was ever said about a port, but we had naturally supposed it would be New York, or an east coast port. After two days out we discovered that one of our table-mates was going to Wellington, New Zealand. Others we found were going to Australia. Then it became quite apparent that our route would be by the Pacific. We imagined a three-month's voyage with our friends assuming we were lost when they did not hear from us for so long.

But ten days took us to Fremantle, a few more and we were at Melbourne. Next was Wellington. Then, after just five weeks from Durban, we entered the Golden Gate.

San Francisco—the USA, terra firma—we were here! The first night was not easy, having to find a place to stay at 7 pm on a Saturday night. The Travelers Aid told us there were no hotel rooms. The War Housing Bureau to which we were referred said they only dealt with persons connected with the military. Finally, at about nine p.m., Congregational friends came to our rescue. After the weekend, we were able to find hotel accommodations, until we could get train reservations. That took ten days! And then the train was so late into Chicago that the reservations from there on were useless.

Philadelphia was next, and what a feeling to arrive at last into the arms of Ross' family. My father arrived there too and we had a real Thanksgiving—with turkey and other delicacies—but above all, a deep feeling of thanksgiving that at last we had reached the end of our journey.

Before arriving at San Francisco, passengers were eating breakfast in a hurry in order to be on deck to see the Golden Gate Bridge that had been completed in May of 1937. One can hardly imagine how excited the passengers, particularly our family, would be to see the bridge after traversing the Pacific Ocean without being in a convoy with the associated protection of destroyers. The ship suddenly listed severely due to an underwater current and many people fell, dishes rolled off of tables and general turmoil ensued. Dad came up from under the table with strawberry jam on his head that was initially thought to be blood! But we saw the Golden Gate Bridge as the ship sailed underneath it and finally brought us to the USA!

The biggest question that comes to my mind is how did my mother, in particular, survive a seven month, 22,000 mile trip with three kids, the youngest of which was a five-year-old boy, during war time, without means of communication other than cables that were very infrequent and contained minimum information? And how can she appear to have been so calm in her letters?

Other events of the year:

Japanese were driven off of Guadalcanal

The Pentagon was dedicated, the world's largest office building.

Allies landed in Sicily and mainland Italy; Eisenhower was named Supreme Allied Commander.

Memories by Phyllis, Paul, Betty, Gwen and Jo
Hiebert Family Voyage During WWII

KODAI:

Betty: We were in Kodai when the Japanese army crossed the border to the north. We had air raid drills often. Each class built trenches in the side of the hill. Our class decided to be especially deceptive and made a trench that zigzagged. But each time we went into it, we were the last to complete the drill because we got jammed up at the turns. We camouflaged the trenches with leaves and brush. When we heard a plane or had an air raid drill, we ran for the trenches or sought cover under windowsills and desks. We thought it was fun to get out of school and did not take it too seriously.

The Hiebert family.

Paul: In 1942, Dad and Uncle John Wiebe came up to Kodai in a black van to take us Hiebert and Wiebe kids down to the plains. There were two benches and a rug on the floor in the back of the van. There were so many of us crowded into it that we had to tie the topees and shoes outside the car. Dad and John Wiebe had taken the gas coupons for two mission cars and mixed gas half and half with kerosene, which they could buy un-rationed, to get the car to go to Kodai and back to Mahbubnagar.

LEAVING INDIA:

Paul: Our family was then ordered secretly to go to Bombay where we boarded the *SS Brazil*; the Wiebe family had decided to stay in India. The ship was a relatively new one, built as a luxury cruise ship for some 2,000 passengers but now converted to carry about 7,000 troops. It dropped the US troops in India, and about 400 missionaries (including Frykenbergs and Carmans) boarded it.

CAPE TOWN AND BERMUDA:

Paul: We sailed via Cape Town, South Africa. The freighter behind us was torpedoed; this was the time of the greatest number of German U-boat attacks. We spent a few days in Cape Town, where sailors caught a hammer-head shark, killed it, and ate it on board.

After Cape Town, we sailed to Bermuda by ourselves, zigzagging every three minutes during the day to keep subs from lining up to fire their torpedoes, and then making a straight run of it at night because we were fast—maybe near to 25 knots an hour (30 mph). We were in strict blackout, and so slept at night on deck. The kids ran around the ship in gangs and had lots of fun. At Bermuda a convoy joined us and escorted us into New York. Several times the navy destroyer with us thought it heard a sub and threw out depth charges which exploded under water.

Jo: I do remember Cape Town because we went into a gigantic modern store and it was the first time I ever rode on an escalator. I loved it!

LIFE ONBOARD THE *SS BRAZIL*:

Betty: The ship was under orders to have complete blackout at night. Enforcement of blackout became even stricter when a lighted cigarette reportedly was seen by a friendly ship several miles away. It was hot as it was summer and we were crossing the equator.

When it was particularly dangerous we had to wear lifejackets during the day, and those made us even more uncomfortable. We had unannounced drills and were told to go to the lifeboats regardless of whether or not our parents were there. The first time we had a drill, I was frantically searching for Mom and Dad and was told in no uncertain terms to head for the lifeboats and meet them there. Each family had an assigned boat. Like the *RMS Titanic*, we knew there were not enough lifeboats—someone would have to be left behind, most likely Dad in our family. We tried not think of it, but the constant release of depth charges reminded us of this possibility. I remember thinking I'd be brave and stay with Dad. I wonder if a choice like this actually came up, how brave one would be.

The nights were warm and many people slept out on the deck. There were so many people that it was hard to find space to lie down. The ship's cabins had been outfitted for troops and there were bunks, three or four high. Mom was with Joanne all day and night, trying to soothe her feverish body. She had gotten the measles and that turned into pneumonia.

It was a long trip, and as children we didn't worry constantly like the adults did. Life developed a sort of normalcy. We played on board deck and swam in the pool. The ship was an excellent place to play hide and seek games since there was a myriad of chairs and equipment on the decks. The first time we crossed the equator, a pool party was held. In accordance with tradition, those people who had never crossed the equator before could be smeared with spaghetti and thrown into the swimming pool backwards.

Phyllis: The voyage during the war was very dramatic. There were the nights we older kids didn't go below to the cabin as it was so hot, but went hunting about in the dark for an empty berth. One deck had been fitted with canvas berths four deep. I would head there, feel about until I found an open berth, climb up with my clothes on and go to sleep. I guess folks had enough other things on their minds to worry about us.

The meal lines were hopelessly long, up the stairs and halfway along the deck. One either had to shuffle along for an hour or go down an hour early and sit in front of the door. We used to play "Rock, Paper, Scissors" while we waited. We ate in the soldiers' cafeteria, which meant eating standing up with our trays at long, waist-high tables. I remember trying kidney stew once ... and never again.

Gwen: That was a difficult trip for our parents but for us children it was fun to play with all the missionary kids on board all day and with no school imposed on us. I recall standing on deck beside our lifeboat during a drill while Dad stood apart from us—there must not have been enough lifeboats to go around. I also have a picture in my head of the small cabin with the porthole tightly shut, the only light from a dim blue bulb in the hallway. It was so hot that we slept on the floor near the air vent to get what air movement we could.

Jo: I was only 4 at the time of this trip, but I remember how hot and stuffy it was in our cabin, especially after blackout was enforced and our portholes were sealed. At first we could sleep up on deck, but then because someone's cigarette had been sighted by another ship we had to go back down to the cabins. Dad and Mom would let us fall asleep on deck and then carry us down.

NEW YORK:

Betty: When the Statue of Liberty was sighted, the deck was crowded and all joined in singing "*God Bless America.*" We had tears in our eyes and nearly everyone was crying out of sheer gratitude for having made it safely. The hot, long journey was at an end. I recall sailing by the Statue of Liberty and Dad's saying to take a look because it would be something to remember, and it sure was. I still get tears when we sing that song.

Gwen: I distinctly remember standing on the deck of the ship with Dad, looking out at the New York skyline at dusk as the planes circled overhead, keeping us safe until the next morning when we could safely enter the harbor. When we disembarked, the Salvation Army women had tables set up and fed us with donuts. They tasted so good!

Paul: Getting off the ship and going through customs took a long time, so it was the middle of the night by the time we got into the city. Joanne was very ill so she was airlifted to a hospital when we reached New York. During the next days we stayed in the dorm rooms of the New York Biblical Seminary downtown. Mom found an automat that had ice cream, and she would bring this back to us.

Jo: I remember that Dad carried me up to the deck as we went past the Statue of Liberty, and everyone was singing "*God Bless America.*" Like Betty said, it still makes me emotional hearing that song.

After we got to New York I was in the hospital with pneumonia. Mom was going to give blood for my transfusions, but on the way to the lab mentioned that she was pregnant (with Margy), so they took Dad's blood instead. I would hear the creak of the blood transfusion machine coming toward my room and would start screaming. Once in awhile it went past and I'd curl up in bed, crying with relief. I was glad when that episode was done and we were all at my grandpa and grandma's house in Mt. Lake, Minnesota, safe at last.

Ann Gibbs HENDERSON
Life during WWII

Compared to some of the stories others have, our life was safe and comfortable. We were in Kodai for some of the war but we also spent some time in Bombay (now called Mumbai). Our father was a commander of a ship which was bombed in Tobruk harbor. He and I guess some of his crew fled successfully across north Africa to get back to Bombay. At that time (in his role as a commander in the British/Indian Navy) he was allocated a shore job in training cadets in Bombay. My mother, Jane and I joined him and we lived in a lovely house with a beautiful garden on the outskirts of Bombay.

While in Bombay we frequented a beach across the road and I remember one occasion when we were lying on the sand and an airplane flew ever so close to the ground; whether it was enemy or not I do not recall but it was a frightening experience for a seven-year-old.

What I remember of our house in Bombay are numerous geckos and two beautiful bathrooms. Jane's and mine was green and our parents' was black and white. One night our father got up in the night and went to the black and white bathroom and had a stroke from which he never fully recovered. We returned eventually to Kodai, where we lived in Jaffna House.

We spent the rest of the war and all our lives in Kodai till we finished school—a safe, secluded and beautiful place, as we all know.

Margaret "Miggie" Carman TEGENFELDT
Our family's experiences during World War II

My mother and dad were due for furlough in 1942, but in the middle of the war there was a lot of uncertainty as to whether or when any of the people hoping to return to the U.S. from India would be able to do so. Then came an announcement that a converted troop ship was being sent to Bombay to evacuate as many as possible on a long—and dangerous—voyage around the tip of South Africa to New York. Our family went to Bombay and waited there with many other families.

While we were waiting in Bombay my sister Ellie came down with measles. It seemed likely we would not be allowed to board the ship since she had a contagious disease. But Dad persuaded the authorities that she would be kept isolated if they had a cabin available for that purpose. Mother and Ellie and Bruce and I were in a small cabin and Dad and my brother John (almost 12) and my brother Bob (10 1/2) were assigned bunks in a large bunk area. Shortly after the ship left Bombay, other children started coming down with measles and many blamed our family for the epidemic. However, Dad was sure there were others who had been exposed earlier, like Ellie, but had not yet gotten sick and so without isolation, the virus spread quickly throughout the ship.

It was a very difficult voyage for Mother. Soon Bruce and I also came down with measles. And after we got over measles we came down with whooping cough! (I'm not sure how we were exposed to that.) Mother did not like ship travel even under the best of circumstances for she was often seasick. But in this case she was

Margaret and Ellie.

not able to get up on deck but was shut up in a small cabin with three sick kids ages 5 and almost 3. Dad was kept very busy along with a few other doctors on board taking care of all those who were ill so he wasn't able to give Mother much help with us. When we got a little better, John and Bob took turns watching us while Mother got her only break each day and was able to join a group on deck for an evening vespers sing-along. I think John and Bob actually listened rather than watched.

They usually sat outside the door to read by the dim light that was available in inside halls and stairways whereas the cabin was under "blackout."

The "blackout" needs some explanation. There were very credible threats to the ship from bombs from planes or torpedoes from submarines. The ship had to change course frequently and often go in a very zigzag pattern. The captain insisted that there be no lights in the cabins even with blackout curtains over the portholes. Not even nightlights or small flashlights. I can't imagine how Mother cared for us all those nights in the pitch dark! One night Bruce was coughing so hard and, of course, starting to vomit and she placed a basin under what she thought was his chin and it turned out to be his elbow. Another time she suddenly woke up, realizing she had dozed off and shocked that the room was so quiet. Bruce had been coughing almost non-stop. She could not bear to think he had died while she had fallen asleep from exhaustion. Without being able to see him she put her hand out to where he was lying to try to feel his breath or feel his chest moving up and down. Reassured that he was breathing, she wept with joy that he was sleeping peacefully at last. With all her difficulties with the blackout rules she was very frustrated that there were sailors who would smoke out on the open decks at night.

We spent quite a few days at Cape Town for some ship repairs and replenishing food and other supplies. Finally, we arrived at New York where relatives gave us a warm welcome at the dock.

In early 1944, Dad was asked to join the staff of the Christian Medical College and Hospital in Vellore, Tamil Nadu. It would mean he would not return to the small mission hospital in Andhra Pradesh where they had been working for about 15 years, but he felt God's guidance in accepting this invitation. They wanted him to come and be a professor of surgery with the qualifications needed to help the college be upgraded to offer the MBBS degree and they wanted him there as soon as possible. He was somehow able to get a place on one of the first small Navy ships to go through the Mediterranean and the Suez Canal instead of the usual route around South Africa.

Again it was a hard time for Mother who didn't know when she would get word of his safe arrival and didn't know when the rest of us would be allowed to join him in India. In the meantime she had the five of us kids to take care of and she had to find work to help ends meet. There were many factories which had lost their male workers to the military and were hiring women. Although her college education was in teaching languages, she accepted a factory job. The trip back to India, when we were allowed to travel after the war ended, had its share of difficulties also but that's another story. Anyway, I do have immense admiration for Mother for many reasons but certainly for how she coped during those war years.

I was too young to remember much about the war years, but I do have two special memories of the end of the war. When the end of the war was announced we were staying with my uncle and aunt. My uncle piled all of us into his convertible and we drove into town with the top down and joined the crowds of people who were shouting and clapping and waving flags in a joyful celebration. We were especially happy that this meant that their son, and our oldest cousin, who was in the Navy would now be safe and able to come home. The second memory was the excitement and joy of arriving in Bombay in 1945 and finally being reunited with Dad who came to meet us at the dock.

Dave Dickason
World War II Days

Rangoon, 1941: It wasn't “rocket science” (even though that term hadn’t been invented yet), even for a three-year-old. This tyke could tell not only were things not normal, but everybody seemed edgy. There were a few clear signs. In our back yard on the Judson College campus (the Baptist arts & sciences college of the University of Rangoon), the mali (our gardener) had dug an air raid trench with nice straight walls with real steps going down into it. It was a fun place to play, and was cool as its laterite clay dried brick-hard.

But the really loud sign that something was wrong was the air raid siren that blared each evening after dark as low-flying planes droned overhead. Being the youngest in my family, I had been trundled off to bed first. And I slept on a fully exposed veranda outside my parents bedroom. I had picked up enough to know these were Japanese planes and that our houses were to show no lights. The neighborhood, never brightly lit, was pitch black. People spoke in whispers. On these nights it seemed I was totally alone. Taiyamma, my little ayah and wife of our cook (Saarti), was no longer available to lug her big charge around. I missed the clean, distinctive aroma of coconut oil on her hair and skin. She had to be with her own children too in the cook's quarters at the back of the grounds, where I also got to play during the daytime. I squalled my own three-year-old's equivalent of the air raid siren on those evenings alone on the veranda, to no avail.

Suddenly one day pandemonium erupted. A ship—the last ship, it was said—was leaving the port of Rangoon at noon. It would take families, but it would not wait. Packing of small valises and bags proceeded furiously. The family Model T touring car (a rag top) was cranked to life, and my sisters, parents and I raced towards the city five miles away. En route it became clear that our driver-father would not accompany us on the ship. Men were to stay behind, and travel was reserved for women and children. The tension in racing to the departing ship did not allow sweet leave-takings. And even such as they were, they were totally disrupted by the discovery that the ship had already left the port and was sliding downriver towards the ocean as fast as possible. The ship's captain had no intention of losing his ship to Japanese bombers while sitting at the pier waiting for passengers to leisurely embrace loved ones.

A desperate search discovered a small tug-like launch near the pier. It was commandeered, and the would-be passengers on the ship transferred to it with their kit and husbands. The launch (not to be confused with a speed boat) proceeded at full throttle in chase of the departed ship. Had it not been such serious business, it might have seemed comical that the tug struggled to overtake the ship so painfully slowly—for the ship was going almost full throttle towards the sea. We neared the overside gangway. My mother, sisters, and other near-adults were handed over the side with reasonable ceremony. Being just a three-year-old, I was passed from one crew member to another—each one grabbing me by the most convenient appendage (arm, leg), handing me to the next, and finally onto the deck from where I could see my father waving as the launch dropped astern.

India, 1942: The ship arrived in Calcutta. Through the good offices of the Methodists of the Lee Memorial Mission, I think, we found our way north to Mussoorie and Woodstock School. (I am one of few, living or dead, ever to have attended both Woodstock and Kodai Schools.) There I attended "Lower

Kindergarten," and must have been certified by the end of the year as knowing how to tie my shoes, how to count to ten, and (mostly) knowing how (not to) pee in my pants. I also rode the Himalayan slopes in my very own kundi—a basket chair carried on the back of a coolie porter—from our house at Edgehill Villa to the school.

Later, after my father escaped the Japanese invasion of Burma by retreating northwards a day or two before the Japanese troops, rejoined us in India, we went to Rawalpindi (next to Pakistan's capital city, Islamabad) to teach at Gordon College (a Presbyterian mission college at which he had taught during the 1920s). After two years there (where I learned a good bit of Panjabi and street-Urdu), we went by train to Bombay where we embarked on the *S.S. Mariposa*—a cruise ship converted to a troop transport. With segregated male and female sleeping arrangements in cabins for nine (3 triple bunks) but designed for two, and with 200 Italian POWs onboard, our ship departed for the U.S.

Unbeknownst to us, we left Bombay just before the great Bombay explosion (a munitions ship, the *SS Fort Stikine*, exploded and leveled the harbor area and downtown, on 14 April, 1944. Forty-three days later we landed in Boston, having sailed to refuel and re-victual at Melbourne (Australia), then between the islands of New Zealand, and through the Panama Canal to Boston on two-meal-a-day rations. We were none the worse for wear.

Only later did we come to understand how fortunate we were as compared to the many who did not escape internment, or our friends in Burma who had no opportunity to escape to safe havens elsewhere. In some senses, many in Burma have never known a full return to normality since before those days. Their cultures and families have taken severe bruisings, if not outright beatings and losses, at the hands of soldiers, warlords, brigands, rebels, and corrupt officials in these intervening nearly eight decades.

Ruth Keithahn MacCurdy
World War II Memories

Although I was only four or five years old, I have a couple of vivid memories of WWII and the rest my mother and sister have filled in.

If troops were being moved, there was absolutely no room on the trains, but we were soon waved over to a carriage and arms extended to get us on the train through the window, with soldiers moving over to make room for us.

In Bangalore sirens went off for air raid practice and we were instructed to get under our seat or the table—which we learned to do very quickly.

In Kodai the news brought total panic to the missionaries, who immediately evacuated almost to a person. On hearing this later, I was amazed as Kodai seemed the farthest and almost safest place to me—as Stillwell's army was pushed back to the border area of Assam and India where they held against the Japanese with the help of an Indian army.

Most memorable was our trip back to the States on a hospital ship and I have many memories of that. For years we told the story, laughing at the lighthearted jokes my father told to keep some of the other missionaries from worrying. But in the late 1990's I was telling the story to some friends in Mexico and simply could not continue, I was so choked up with the fear and other emotions left over from that trip that had been submerged for over fifty years.

My father had been working with the Gandhian movement for freedom in the Bangalore area and this was quite concerning to the British "in charge" of Tamil Nadu (then called "Madras). Since America was a British ally in WWII, their hands were essentially "tied," but they finally sent a deportation notice (which was never found in the records after our return to the states). Our first departure date was delayed as my brother and sister came down with measles. That ship was torpedoed and no survivors were found. We were reassigned, but then I came down with the measles. My mother dressed me in long sleeves, told me not to say anything, and we boarded despite my 103-degree temperature.

We departed from Bombay in a convoy of two ships (one carried orphans from Europe to Australia and we have since learned how some of them were treated), heavily guarded by battleships, submarines, etc. Our first stop was somewhere along the southern coast of Australia, but we—being a mixture of Americans and Europeans—were only allowed to walk up and down a very long pier. After one or two trips back and forth I immediately returned to the ship as I was afraid it would go off without us, and there were no signs of a town or habitation whatsoever. I then worried that they would leave without my father who was not going to miss that exercise. The older boys and men were "housed" somewhere in the ship's lower decks and the women and younger children on the upper deck. But there were areas of the ship where we met and ate together.

I'm sure they took on water and supplies and then headed for an Island (perhaps Guam) to take on the soldiers who had been evacuated from Guadalcanal. We children were all watching from the top deck as they filled the whole ship with soldiers, and opened up access for the supplies to be loaded down the middle of the ship. We could see the men on the very lowest deck, looking like ants scurrying around. The soldiers filled the whole dock area and repeatedly kept shouting,

"Throw down the children, throw down the children." This I did not understand till it was explained to me that they hadn't seen children for two years or more.

We then headed across the Pacific Ocean, not stopping until we reached the States. There were so many soldiers that the mess had to feed all of us in shifts, and all the black soldiers volunteered to be cooks. The officers and crew ate last (women and children ate first) and I made good friends with the officer in charge of the mess, often going back to see what they were eating. One day I asked the lieutenant in charge what something was and was told it was "pie." "Do you want a taste?" he asked. I had been rigidly raised not to eat between meals so replied I'd have some for lunch. And the next day, everyone was served pie—not just the officers!

Our deck had access via stairs to the lower decks and it was soon clear that I wasn't going to stay put on just our deck and the top deck above. There were military police (MPs[35]) at all the stairways, and they assured Mom that someone would grab me should the ship be attacked (I refused to wear the lifejacket everyone was required to wear) and that I would not be harmed! At the end of the day, I would return for the night loaded down with candy bars, minus the hair ribbons from my braids. When they were all gone my mother told the MPs she had to have them back, and they slowly filtered back up the stairs, although a bit shorter.

Being a doctor, Mom was occasionally consulted regarding medical problems (they had medics, but few MD's) and was taken "below" to help. Even I remember her saying there were two decks of cages, with one man in each so they wouldn't hurt anyone, and could be monitored so they didn't hurt themselves. Needless to say, I wasn't allowed on those decks!

Two other incidents I remember clearly. A submarine was detected by our convoy and depth charges were "dropped," making our ship list way to one side and then list over to the other side. We happened to be in an area where the civilians could visit together and all the chairs and tables went "flying and sliding," with a few of the occupants falling over backwards. We thought it quite hysterical when a portly lady went over backwards, with her playing cards flying all over.

The other incident was more serious as several of us (all women and children) were sleeping on deck (with the blackout it was too stuffy and hot many nights) between two of the large guns. This was fortunate as we ran into a hurricane—no one had given us a forecast. We were "sloshing" back and forth between the two guns as the ship tipped from side to side and water poured over. Fortunately we were between the guns and couldn't slide out. Mother realized the force of the wind

---

35 MP is an acronym for "Military Police."

and made us all stay there, and fortunately someone realized, finally, that there were women and children out in the storm. A group of sailors, tied together by long lengths of rope, volunteered to come and get us. They must have tied down those ropes to anything welded to the ship, but they were short one sailor as each sailor took ahold of an adult or child. Mother said to put her in the middle between two sailors that had hold of the smallest children, as there was no way she would ever let go of the rope, and we were slowly brought down from the top deck, with none of us washed overboard. The next day the whole ship learned of our "escapade" and my father teased us all the way to San Diego.

In San Diego the soldiers were debarked first and it took till dusk for them all to get off the ship. Somehow a couple of reporters had managed to get on the ship and saw Dad up on the top deck with us. He was thoroughly questioned and we made it into the papers; so family and friends learned we had arrived intact and friends had us stay with them until we left for Iowa by train.

Alice Graham Silver
Memories from the war

My family was one of those stranded in India during World War II. My parents arrived in western India in 1937, expecting to be there five years before returning to the US on furlough. And then when their five years were up, in 1942, there was absolutely no safe civilian travel back to the US.

By 1940 my father had sufficiently mastered Marathi to start on his long-term goal of establishing a seminary for Indian Christians who wanted to become pastors to complete their studies in their own language, rather than learn enough English to go to a seminary taught in English.

The location for this new seminary was Poona (now Pune), further north in Maharashtra than the other Presbyterian mission locations. Poona was also the "West Point" of India, with a large military establishment. The new seminary was started in an older compound of buildings, formerly a school of some sort, in the southeast edge of the military cantonment. Military vehicles and people moved up and down the road outside the compound all the time.

One of my earliest memories is waking early in the mornings to the sound of a military band accompanying troops marching out to their exercise grounds along that road. Every day they played the same music and it sank into my memory.

When I saw the movie *Bridge on the River Kwai* as a college student, the same music was played. I knew it was familiar, but couldn't place it for a very long time.

Finally I remembered it as my wake-up music from the early 1940's: the Col Bogey March! Long formations of troops, tanks and trucks traveled up the road in front of our compound often. Sometimes the sound of the tanks and trucks was so loud that I was frightened to tears.

News of the war came to the seminary in rumors and bits—with no source being very reliable. One day a student came rushing in to my father saying the Japanese army was just a day's march away, and what should we all do to be safe? Fortunately, Dad was able to calm him. It turned out that the Japanese Army never got to Calcutta, much less to the neighborhood of Poona.

Many food items were strictly rationed during the war, so as to make sure there was plenty for the army. Potatoes were not available at all—they were for the army! We had rations for rice, wheat, millet and meat—all in small amounts. We arranged to take our wheat ration to the local bakery and they would make it into bread: 2 one pound loaves for 2 weeks. I learned very young how to slice bread into very thin slices! And to this day I prefer rice to potatoes.

The very strict rationing had another effect. My mother developed typhoid fever a few weeks after my brother Jim was born (July 1943), and she had to be hospitalized and nursed very carefully. Baby formula was extremely scarce. My dad had made friends with a local pharmacist shortly after we moved to Poona (1940 or 41). He asked for help from Mr. Macedo, who had contacts in the pharmacy circle. Somehow, Dad got baby formula for Jim and kept giving him a 2 AM bottle long after it was needed. When my mother finally came home from the hospital, Jim was nearly 4 months old and round as a teddy bear. Mother ended the 2 AM feedings right away!

Many of my memories are those of a young child: playing with the seminary students' children, going for walks to the nearby botanical gardens with Nancy and my ayah, and by the time I was five, attending the kindergarten at St Mary's school (an Anglican school about a mile away), riding on the back of my mother's bike. By 1944, my parents found their way to Kodaikanal and I attended 1st grade, taught by Auntie Powell.

I remember the special assembly in the gym celebrating VE Day.[36] Everyone was so relieved and felt the war with Japan would soon end. My parents talked about being able to go "home," which was a mystery to me. I felt home was in Poona! It was not until June, 1946 that passage on a troop ship, the *USS General Gordon*, was arranged. By that time I was part way through 3rd grade at Kodai.

---

[36] VE stands for "victory Europe," when World War II ended in Europe.

The voyage on the *USS General Gordon* was one long adventure. As a troop ship, there were officers' quarters and enlisted men's quarters. With a ship full of civilians who had been stranded overseas for the duration of the war, the women and young children were assigned to officers' quarters—12 to a cabin, bunks 3 deep, but with windows and doors leading onto the decks. All the men (and I suppose older teen boys) were below deck in the enlisted men's quarters (large dormitories). The decks had only two railings; not safe for young children. Mom was very nervous keeping track of three-year-old Jim. We met at meals and between times.

The meals were fantastic! Especially to folks used to strict rationing. For breakfast there were cold cereals and white toast! Lunches were generous. Dinners were banquets: we had turkey twice and it wasn't even Thanksgiving! Milk as a beverage was a novelty. And Ice cream!

Our route went from Bombay (Mumbai) around the tip of India and to Singapore, which was quarantined due to some disease, through the Straits of Malacca where we could see the wrecks of a number of ships. Next was Manila, where we went ashore. I had ice cream from a street vendor. What a treat. We also saw many bombed out shells of buildings, bringing reality to the destruction war had wrought. Next stop was Hong Kong, where we were allowed to disembark. I had a touch of the flu and had to stay in bed, to my disappointment. From there we went straight across the Pacific to Honolulu and then on to San Francisco. Two of Mother's cousins had come from Portland to see us and welcome us "home." Then we went by train across the US to Denver, where we changed trains. Our connection there was 2 hours late, which was disillusioning. For years Dad had grumbled about Indian trains, which were frequently late. And here we were, in "paradise" and the trains were still late.

Finally, we reached Peoria Illinois, where Mother's mother and sister and our cousins lived.

After 9 years, Mother, with three children, reunited with her family and we became "American."

David Wiebe
Growing up in India during WWII

Our parents had returned to India in 1936 with our 3 older siblings. Paul and I were born the next year with Dr. John Carman in attendance and at his residence in Hanaraakonda. I, being more mature was birthed first, Paul followed in 15 minutes.

My early recollections were living in a bungalow, wearing pith helmets and playing with our Indian friends who taught us how to fly captured flying beetles like miniature airplanes controlled by a suitable length of thread. They also introduced us to the precursor to tinker toys and legos. This was a seasonal activity at the maize harvest. The stalks have a flexible covering over a pithy center, which can be peeled off in strips, bent into various configurations and joined with pieces of the pith. An ox "bundy" was one I labored over.

The Wiebe family.

Catching “blue bottle" flies was a competition our older brother John devised When the "yappa chettu” (Neem) trees bore their non-edible fruit this was very attractive to hoards of these flies. The competition was to see who could catch the most flies with a swipe of the hand. To count them accurately you had to squish them in your hand I think our parents put a stop to this for health reasons.

Our parents decided to stay in India during the war years. It was certainly a lot harder on them than it was onus kids. There was scarcity of course but I don't remember going hungry. Paul and I did sneak into the pantry which was usually locked and where there was a big pot of lard and taking a finger full, dipping it into the sugar bag and eating it. I remember that but I don't remember the first Babe Ruth! The Japanese invasion scare while we were in Kochi had us practicing air raids and finding the nearest bomb shelters—pits dug in the woods, and the adults discussed evacuation plans. Back on the plains, Paul and I would sit on the compound gateposts as the British troop convoys passed in endless procession Occasionally they would toss some biscuits to us. What a scramble!

It was during the war years that all of us kids (six at the time) had a strange craving for dust! This was the fine dust that would collect on the rims of the Model A wheels whenever we would drive somewhere—on dirt roads of course. Arriving at the compound we would all pile out and race to the nearest wheel and take pinches of this dust and eat it. Even as I recount this with abhorrence I can remember the delicious smoothness of the texture. I don't know of any lasting ill effects of this addiction except the periodic treatment for worms. It was only many years later with an MD after my name that I understood the dust craving—a condition called PICA, which is often the result of iron deficiency anemia. Fortunately that was cured and I have had no such craving ever again! One very likely positive effect may have been the development of a very marvelous immune system. Just one of the benefits of growing up in India!

Bev England Williams
World War II memories

My parents were married on October 21, 1933 and shortly thereafter were on their way to Burma. In 1939, with two toddlers and an infant, they began the long journey back home to the American South.

We stopped in Singapore and stayed with a missionary acquaintance. I was an already thin two-year-old, recovering from dysentery. The doctor in Bhamo, no doubt a bit afraid of treating a Caucasian child, had ordered a daily diet of a small portion of plain rice and water. This toddler was starving! Our host was a single woman who doted on her little dog and cooked fresh rice for him each day. Bev, spying the rice and helping herself to it, caused a furor. The woman, fearful that Doggie would contact dysentery, rushed him off to the vet. My mother, no animal lover, was worried about me.

Fortunately it was time to embark on our ocean journey. All of our boxes, from wedding gifts to baby books to Kachin weaving and silver, were on one ship. At the last minute, Dad heard that there was a dock strike in San Francisco and changed the booking to a ship headed for Los Angeles. The first ship was captained by an old Brit who ignored the warnings that the British had recently laid mines in Singapore harbor. The ship hit a mine and went down in the harbor. Passengers were saved, but what would have been the chances for a family with three little ones? "It got sunk," was a refrain of our childhoods. But Mother always followed with, "Remember, we are all alive and grateful."

Dad's sister, a librarian, read in the library copy of the New York Times that our ship had been sunk. She couldn't tell the family, and she had to wait until Monday to call the Mission Board and learn that we were safely on another vessel. And that ship had a waiter, homesick for his own child, who took me to dine and fed me anything I wanted.

We moved often during the War, from Florida to Philadelphia to Kentucky to Koinonia Farm in Georgia, to Ithaca, New York, where my parents studied at Cornell University and the England kids played in their first snow.

Our family returned, first to India, on the *SS Marine Raven*. I learned at a Kodai reunion that Owen Thomas was one of the many kids on that voyage.

Chris Rolles
The Effects of War on Our Family

The experiences of WWII for Britain and the United States were very different. For Britain, the war started in September 1939 and she fought alone with commonwealth forces, Poles and free French, until Japan and Germany declared war on America almost exactly two years later. By that stage Britain had suffered the Blitz and the Battle of Britain. Many cities had been virtually destroyed, the country had lived constantly with the fear of invasion and the economy was on its knees.

I was born in Kodai in June, 1939 and with my parents and sister returned to England six weeks later. Britain declared war on Germany in September. Fears of war had been building but to the very end there were hopes that it could be avoided. Very quickly my family experienced the prevailing sense of siege, blackout was imposed, sirens sounded, the Germans started bombing ports and industrial sites and there was a widespread evacuation of children from the major cities.

My father, who was traveling round on deputation with Eric Liddel,[37] saw Southampton, the major trans-Atlantic port, where we now live, in flames. He was given the option to stay on serving as an army chaplain or to return immediately to India. My parents decided to go back to India. They travelled with a military convoy around South Africa since the Mediterranean was considered too dangerous. At about the same time Eric Liddel went back to China, where he was subsequently

37 Eric Liddel was Scotland's most popular sporting hero. The son of Scottish missionaries to China, his story is immortalized in the movie *Chariots of Fire*.

captured by the Japanese and died in a POW camp. Back in India my father resumed his work and my mother went back to Kodai with Shirley and me and joined the teaching staff, teaching music and sometimes being a housemother.

Back in the UK, by the end of 1940, the Germans were attacking both industrial and population centers. On December 27th 1940 in a bombing raid on North London, Toni's grandparents' house, where the family were gathered for Christmas, took a direct hit, killing her father, grandfather, aunt and cousin and burying several other family members in the debris for some hours. These included her mother who was seven months pregnant with her first child. Toni was born six weeks later, small but kicking, in a country town to which her mother and her sisters had hastily evacuated with their children.

In India the war immediately resulted in the internment of people from Germany, Austria and Italy. It also resulted in many people being stranded and unable to return to their own countries until the end of the war. Thus Mr Musil, Mario, Madame Caspari and her husband, Fritz Kolb, Madame Montessori, Helen Oh, Miss Skovhus, all turned up by some means in Kodai. As the war progressed, there were fewer Americans on the school staff and there may have been a time when the polyglot assortment outnumbered them. None of this crowd probably had teaching qualifications but they had a wide range of talents and contributed greatly to the school and remain as major figures in our memories.

I remember having a sense of foreboding, even as a three or four year old. And I now know that was a reflection of the general fear that Japan would invade India. It was a justified fear, since the British could not have defended India given they were already struggling on so many other fronts. For whatever reason, the Japanese invasion never came.

My only clear recollections of the war are the scenes of jubilation when it ended. I remember people running around, laughing, crying and hugging each other when the news arrived. A few weeks later I remember Helen Oh breaking down with tears of joy when she heard that her husband, of whom she had had no news during the war, was alive. He had been captured in Singapore by the Japanese after she had managed to escape.

Coming back to England in 1946, traveling on the *SS Stratheden* with troops and refugees, we were confronted with the coldest winter on record. There was very little fuel, coal and all essential food stuffs were rationed (and went on being rationed into the 1950s). I remember a general sense of greyness. That may have simply been a contrast with what I remembered from India. At a personal level, I was happy and too young to really understand the impact the war had made.

Farmers plowing fields. (B. Peck)

CHAPTER 10

Third Culture Kids

Kodai School's classes of 1955 and 1956 held a reunion in Williamsburg, Virginia in October, 2018. The theme was "Third Culture Kids." A number of other Kodai kids also attended the reunion.

A Third Culture Kid (TCK) is a person who has spent a significant part of his or her developmental years outside the parents' culture. The TCK frequently builds relationships to all of the cultures, while not having full ownership in any. Although elements from each culture may be assimilated into the TCK's life experience, the sense of belonging is (often) in relationship to others of similar background." (David Pollock, 1989)

The following are what some of the classmates—and other Kodai kids who attended—wrote about their being a third culture kid:

John Lutz
Up & Down the Ghat Road

The first thing that I recall is the stirring joy within as we near the approach, whether to ascend or descend.

"Going up"—the long bumpy slog from Kodai Road station ends as our bus begins the first gradual ascent, leaving the hot dusty plains behind—and marked by some halfhearted cheering.

Weaving the hairpin turns with increasing gear grinding downshifts and swaying passengers, we eagerly spy out Rattail Falls and await the first upward glimpses of Perumal.

After several water stops to cool the boiling engine radiator and driver, we are "crossing the hump" at Neutral Saddle and getting the first taste of the deliciously cool mountain weather of Kodaikanal.

We're not doing the hike up Perumal to the right today, but pressing straight onwards and upwards, through the tightening curves and narrowing roads, passing Shembug, Silver Cascades and lusher greenery as we head up into the clouds.

The sight of the plains and Periyakulam thousands of feet below is fading.

The final turns under Coaker's Walk brings the lower "budge" into sight, then the first compounds, the Bund, Kodai Lake and final turns past Annie Putz infirmary, Loch End and Highclerc—we're here!

"Going home."

When will classes be dun, dun, dun—we count the days.

Down to the Plains, Mom, Dad, baby Brothers and sister, my own, room, bike and stuff, Christmas—school's over!

Pack the bags, put on the shorts and tees, load the busses and—Oh, don't forget the pinwheel propellers we stick out the sides on descent! We're outta here!

Leaving the Lake, Bund and Budge ... Say bye bye.

Can't go too fast for the 25 miles of curves, swerves and then welcome heat.

And just like before we weave the corners and hairpin turns with increasing gear grinding downshifts and swaying passengers.

Loud cheers come from all of us as we roll through the last incline meeting the Plains. It's another fifty miles to Kodai Road, where we'll bid fond farewells to our buds and say "see you in January" or "have a great trip back to the States."

Ann Biggar Prewitt
Third Culture Kid

"Where did you go to high school?" asked a fellow freshman at Middlebury College. "In India," I replied.

A perplexed look, a pause, and a smile of relief, as the translation came to her, "Oh Indiana."

If only she had known.

I went to four different high schools from my home base in Bahrain: happy days in Kodai, India; confused days in Roswell, New Mexico for three months while a family member was ill; a girl's school in Switzerland where I learned to sew a not-so-fine seam and recite French poetry with little thought to math or science; and a good senior year in Beirut, Lebanon. At college I soon learned it was easiest to skip my past and adjust to the present as another foreign post. It was a pleasant posting but I saw it more as a stepping-stone to get back to a life in yet another culture.

And after I had earned a masters degree in California, I did. I bought a one-way ticket to Europe and was fortunate enough to find a teaching job in Germany for two years. Marriage, children, and time spent in living in Thailand and Africa followed. In Kenya, museum work became my passion and it continues to this day, this time from New York.

Of interest to me is that I wasn't the only family member who continued a life overseas. My sister and her family ended up living in Bangladesh, Jordan, Egypt, Kenya and Romania. My brother, an epidemiologist, lived and researched in Ghana, Denmark, India and Australia. And each one of us has produced Third Culture Kids too. One to Thailand with the State Department, one to Indonesia with the World Bank, and one to Palestine with the United Nations. Their kids are the newest generation of TCKs.

I'd like to hope that the generations of our family have made contributions to the foreign cultures we were, or are, living in. I can say we gained as much or more in return. A year ago my sister and brother and their children went to a ceremony in Sumatra celebrating a medical clinic my father had established over 60 years ago. It has been a circle of enrichment and I will be eternally grateful that I grew up as a Third Culture Kid.

David Wiebe
Benefits of Being a Cross-Cultural Kid

Last night I was reminded of the benefits of being a cross-cultural kid. I was once again invited to be part of an Indian Celebration—a wedding reception with all that entails. We have been a part of the international community here since we moved to Kearney in 1973. At first it was just a handful of international students, now there are hundreds. The Indian community is largely composed of professionals at the hospital and University and we have been an integral part of them primarily because of our India connections. Since Lorma died two years ago they have made sure that I am okay. I have been invited to their places many more times than anywhere else. This close association may be due to the area where I live and my profession but I'm sure being a cross cultural kid with a little foreign language skill makes a big difference. It is a joy!

In addition:

A broad worldview

Being able to share this with my kids and grandkids with trips.

The development of immunities: being able to travel the world without a lot of trouble and avoiding all the antibiotics and immunizations recommended by the CDC.

Being comfortable doing short term medical work internationally, and building lifelong friendships.

Understanding perhaps better what my own country is and also is not. Appreciation of Indian Art and Culture Indian Food—hands down the best—etc.

My biggest regret is not learning one or two of the local languages. Telugu and Hindi would have been far more worthwhile than Latin but then there wouldn't be any of those stories about Mr. Musil.

Molly Schmitthenner LESNICK
Third Culture Kid Experiences

My first gaffe was Halloweening with bigger neighborhood kids when I was in second grade in Chambersburg, Pennsylvania with my mom and dad. The kids would knock and yell "Trick or Treat," and then if no one came to the door, they gave me some kind of soap and a sponge and told me to rub soap all over the front windows of the house. I did this cheerfully, glad to be included and eventually they took me home. The next day I was really scolded by my mom and I didn't understand why till she told me what a bad thing that was to do to people's windows and I was never to do it again.

Then again in Fremont, Nebraska when I came to the States with the Woods. Pat and I were Sophomores and everyone knew each other except Pat and me and another girl we met at assembly. That first week was rough, but at least Pat and I knew each other, and we walked to high school with some other kids who lived along the way, and came home for lunch. So gradually we got to know more kids. We both joined the Y, which met after school, and Pat got into band and I joined the GAA (girls athletic association), so gradually we made friends. By the end of the year, I felt like I could stay there if I had to, but then they said we were going back to India and to Kodai and I was so happy.

Then in 1956 we came to the States and I went to my aunts in Pennsylvania, and Pat went out to her family in Nebraska. I had a childhood friend who still lived in Chambersburg and she was nice and unsophisticated and I could talk to her about things. Then at college, everyone seemed so sophisticated. I met my roommates and they were both nice and then we met our suite mates who offered us cigarettes. At that time practically everyone smoked (except me) and when you met new people, you offered them cigarettes or vice versa. They had a social mixer the first week, and everyone seemed to be talking a strange language to each other somehow. I was glad when classes started in earnest. I hated being asked where I was from. I never knew what to answer. I usually said that I grew up in India but I lived in Chambersburg with my aunts now. In any case, India was a real turn off and people didn't know what to say to me. I was very lucky because Carol Zigler (Kid) and Beth Gessler were both at Thiel with me, and we could get together when sad or depressed.

When all the trees lost their leaves, I got very depressed and I hated winter unless it was snowing or there was snow on the ground. Conversely I was delighted with spring. Once as a freshman, a guy asked me out on a date. When we got back, he asked me out on another date, but I couldn't go as I had choir practice or something, so he said, "How about a rain check?" I had no idea what he was talking about and said, "what?" and he said, "well that's okay" or something and later my roommate explained what a "rain check" meant. As I recall, there were a lot of words and phrases like that that I didn't know. I also hated the idea of sororities and did not want to join one, but eventually knuckled in as all my best friends started a new sorority my junior year and I didn't want to be left out.

I was also very naive. I took Greyhound buses a lot during my college years: to get to college, to get to Chambersburg, to visit my brothers in Ohio and Philadelphia, etc. Once, during the late fall, I think, I found a bus had been cancelled and had to wait two hours or so in a big city depot for another bus. There was this grandfatherly man there and we got to talking. Mostly he asked me questions and we chatted about this and that.

I think we maybe even got a quick lunch together. Anyway, the bus finally came and he said I should sit with him and I did, and then after the bus took off, he started telling me how he had other young girls like me living with him and he would love to have me join them too and then he asked me for a nice kiss on the lips. I was astounded and said no I had a home thank you, and no, I did not want to kiss him and then he started to put his arm around me and I panicked ... there was an empty seat up real near the driver, so I just jumped up and moved up there next to this lady who was sleeping. I said to myself that if he came up after me I would talk to the bus driver, but he didn't come up and he got off at the next town. I was mad at myself for trusting this man—he had seemed so friendly and nice and I thought all adults were to be trusted, as I trusted all the missionaries I had ever known in India. It was a good lesson for me but kind of sad too, that in society in general I just couldn't trust adults blindly.

I gradually assimilated into US culture, but I never really felt like a genuine "American" until I got older and lived in a community with my son and husband. Before that I was always happiest in a group endeavor, like "Interns in Community Service" (a Quaker work study/living program), the Peace Corps, Vista (volunteers in service to America), etc.

I also had big gaps of knowledge regarding US culture: the McCarthy era, for one, the roaring twenties, the war years here (we were in India), etc. My one regret is that as a college student, I did not participate more in helping with integration efforts in this country. I think I was a little scared and not my own person enough to get really involved. I am also sorry that my third cultureness, or perhaps just my own shyness and goody two-shoesness kept me from fully participating in and enjoying college life.

Alice Graham SILVER
Third Culture Kids

Like many of our classmates, I found the transition from our Kodai school experiences and my high school experiences in Iowa from 1953-55 very difficult. I did not get to graduate from Kodai like most of our classmates because the church board would not pay for me to return to India for only one more year. My parents' sabbatical fell just after my sophomore year of high school, so I had the last two years of high school at Senior High School in Dubuque, Iowa.

Not only was that in the public school in Dubuque, but the town was very strongly divided between the public high school and the larger Catholic high school, so there was an added layer of tension.

At 15, I wanted to be exactly like all other 15 year olds. At Kodai, I fitted in well, had many friends and felt well respected by teachers and staff. In Dubuque I knew no one and did not know how to fit in, how to make friends, how to dress, what the popular music was, what to watch on TV (we didn't have a TV anyway). The teachers at school were leery of what I might or might not know, what level classes to put me in, etc. Not knowing anyone, I focused on reading and studying. That won me no friends. Some of my classmates referred to me as "cheater Graham" because my grades were so high. At graduation there was an issue regarding what if I was valedictorian? ... and me not even a local student! Fortunately, I came in second. Although there was a perfectly good Presbyterian college in Dubuque, no way was I going to spend more time in Dubuque! I won a scholarship to The College of Wooster in Ohio, also Presbyterian, and went there.

I found that all the incoming students were very homesick, didn't know how to manage away from their homes, etc. I knew how to do that, so I became the one to help solve these little problems. I fitted in so much better in a setting where everyone else was also new.

Over the years when I have relocated to a new community, I used these skills to adjust, with some exceptions. When my husband and I moved to Laramie Wyoming, so he could try his hand at college teaching, I was far more cautious about sharing my missionary background and my India experience. When asked where I had come from, I would vaguely answer "here and there," until I was sure how my response would be accepted.

On the positive side, I knew how overseas students or other residents were feeling, so I would share some of my insights and reach out to them. This part of my experience has been more and more useful over the years. A book I read and found very insightful is *The Newcomers,* by Helen Thorpe. She was an observer/para in an ESL program at a high school here in Denver in 2014, and her observations are excellent. I'd recommend it.

Lowey Thoms DICKASON
TCK Adventures—Edinburgh University and trip to Jerusalem

My plan to spend my junior year abroad in Scotland started because I was desperate to touch base with the world after two years of college in the U.S. That year was the most exciting and nurturing of my young adult years. What helped me choose Edinburgh was my (Scudder) cousin, Meredith Miller (her sister, Barbara was in our second grade class and Meredith was in third grade at Kodai). Their mother was a Scudder and their father was a Scotsman working for Perry Co. in Madras. Meredith did her junior year at Edinburgh University and advised me how to do the same. Hope College's Dean of Students, John Hollenbach, who had just spent a year in Egypt, encouraged me and helped work out the details so I would get credit.

NPR[38] once asked listeners to tell their life story in six words. Mine would be: “Third Culture Kid, world as family.” Third Culture Kid (TCK) means I grew up in a country other than that of my parents’ citizenship, but didn’t belong in that country or relate to the citizenship country as "home." My early years were spent in a primitive Oman (Arabian Gulf) and Kodai School in South India’s hills with only a

[38] National Public Radio.

year and a half of school in the U.S. at age 10-11. Actually, since my parents grew up in the Arabian Gulf and India, I was also the child of TCKs. In fact, I had uncles, aunts and cousins in both India and the Arabian Gulf whom I saw yearly or with whom I attended school, camped and picnicked. My parents worked in Oman, "a hardship post because of its brutal hot summers." Since the Arabian Mission required them to vacation yearly in the hills, they bought the cottage, Dar-es-Salaam (house of peace in Arabic, which we kids nicknamed “Door Slam”). During World War II we siblings spent three winters at the cottage with either Mom or Grandma Thoms (who retired from the girl’s school she founded in Baghdad in '44) caring for us, since ship passage to the Gulf was hard to get. Thus, Kodai became “home.”

I felt like I was jumping off a cliff when I graduated from high school and headed to the U.S. Most of my friends were going to other schools or staying in India. I was not excited about meeting kids with whom I had so little in common. The U.S. freshman's excitement of leaving home for the first time was not mine, since I had mastered that relative independence since age seven. I related best to the few foreign students at Hope. I studied and mixed with classmates, but did not feel close to them, except Kodai classmate, Ruth Voss, who also went to Hope and was in the next dorm room. My deep sharing was through letters to Kodai friends, mainly my Kodai room mates, Ann Biggar, Ann Gibbs, Miggie Carman, Pat Woods, and Judy Gass. To thrive, I needed the stimulation of diversity and travel, so thus began a year of adventure and, in a sense, jumping off that cliff with a sort of spiritual trust that had been nurtured by my TCKness. Having flown from the nest at a young age, I had learned that a sustaining love remained over distance. As I read the letters written to my parents, I get a glimpse of that 19 year old self placing her trust in that Greater Love to help work out the details if it was truly what I needed.

Dave has asked me how I could afford to take that year abroad. My early letters at the end of '56 and through the summer of '57 are full of calculations. I would continue to receive the small monthly sum from the mission board and I saved up about $300 from my summer job of waiting tables and cleaning rooms at Castle Park resort on Lake Michigan. The article that came out in the Hope College Anchor that year, "Lois Thoms Accepted at University of Edinburgh," states that the costs would be "about the same as or less than attending Hope for a year." Ship travel over and back came from summer savings. I relied on my Kodai network in the UK and spent the month-long vacations at Christmas and spring with the Rolles and Gibbs families (Mrs. Gibbs and Jane had joined Ann).

I found short term jobs caring for three children in an apartment where the mother had a writing job at home and the Rolles got me a job with Chris' uncle in a barrister's office in London. I was pick-pocketed of most of that but the Rolles felt so bad they gave me 5 pounds. The Hope classmate, Carolyn Zhe, who accompanied me for her year abroad too, and I shared a room in the home of the Lyalls in Edinburgh. Mrs. Lyall took great care of us, feeding us a huge breakfast and evening dinner as well as snacks before bed included in the small monthly rent. When we both came down with flu, she kept a pitcher of hot lemonade at our bedsides. We had to find shillings to put in the one small heater in the room, but between us, managed to handle that. We did get chill blains, though, because of trying to warm our feet by it, while the rest of our bodies remained chilled. Kodai friends, the Newbegins (parents, John and Margaret) lived in Edinburgh and I went over for tea a few days before Margaret's birthday. Dr. Newbegin also signed some sort of paper Carolyn needed. Like other university students, we saved by hitch hiking in pairs, which is how I got to London and visited my parents in Jerusalem.

Hamid and hitch hiking to the Middle East—summer of '58:

In the summer of '58 my parents were in Jerusalem, attending a course taught by Kenneth Craag. I wanted to see them, so Carolyn, Veronica Howarth (another digs mate) and I discussed the possibility of hitch hiking to the Middle East. I talked to Chris Rolles about joining us. He agreed, as long as he could find another male to go with us. He advertised at Birmingham University, where he was attending, and another medical school student, Mike Herr, said he would go.

Veronica and Carolyn went ahead to see something of France and Italy, since we got out of university before Chris and Mike. I worked in London to get some extra cash. On July 4th Mike, on his own, and Chris and I together left London with nothing more than a rucksack with couple of changes of clothes, a sleeping bag, a few other necessities, and a little cash. The plan was to meet Mike to cross the channel together, and then I was to hitch alternate days with Chris and Mike until meeting Carolyn and Veronica at a youth hostel in Villach, Austria, on July 9th. My notes about the trip read, "Chris thought it would be appropriate to carry an American flag, but I didn't trust that people's pro-American feelings were very strong. We hitched to Dover—unusual rides—once a motor bike (with side car for me) and next a Bentley (most expensive car in the world)." We boarded the ferry to Europe at midnight where we found Mike waiting for us," and spent the night in deck chairs. Arrived Ostende early in the morning, did the town looking for a coffee shop, then flipped a coin to find out who was the 'lucky man' to hitch with me—Chris got it, so we went out to the highway. We waited an hour before a Belgian man picked us up—practiced my weak French. We got to Brussels at about 11:00 and had to walk several miles to the World's Fair. Two police on bikes pulled up to us and said, 'verboten.' We got the general idea—we weren't to walk on the autobahn. So we pulled off into a poppy field where Chris discovered to his great delight lots of bees and we took our time to bottle a few." We spent four hours there and, according to my notes, among other things, wrote a card to Kodaite, David Wiebe. Dead tired, we caught a tram through town, then hitched to a town a few miles down the road. There we waited for an hour and a half and were getting most discouraged when a Pakistani drew up and asked us if we could speak English. If we couldn't he wouldn't have picked us up. We discovered that he was going all the way to Pakistan by car in order to be there by August 1st. Therefore he would be passing through Yugoslavia about the same time we planned to. Later that day Hamid took us to the youth hostel where we had arranged to meet Mike and we continued on the next day with the four of us in his tiny Morris Minor car.

Driving in Hamid's small car, and having to negotiate constantly about the route so we would reach the girls on July 9th as planned, became tiresome, so we told him we better proceed on our own rather than ruin his trip. Hamid did not want to part with us, so reluctantly agreed to change his itinerary. He had a bad experience of being over charged at a hotel in Brussels, so was desperate for our protection to get safely through Europe, since we spoke English and a smattering of French and German. We agreed to give him a day or two more, so he could see something of Italy and sent the girls a post card to the youth hostel in Austria.[39] Hamid had wanted to go to Paris and Rome to check them out for his potential future "honey moon," but we had to be firm about not going to either, since we had no time or cash for that. He did take a few steps into France and said, "the smell was so much better than in Germany." We had time to go to Italy, but not Rome.

In the next few days, we drove through Switzerland and down the Alps to Milan. Then across Italy to Venice. At the border of Switzerland, in Basle, Hamid had assigned us each a role. I was to be the decider, but when I made a decision, after consulting with the others, or gave him permission as the driver to decide whether we should push on to Italy or stay in Switzerland if he was too tired, he was unhappy with me. Chris was to be in charge of entertainment, since he was pretty good at lightening up the tension between Mike and Hamid in the car. Mike was in charge of choosing where to buy things such as food and spent fruitless hours going

---

39 As TCK's, Chris and I were familiar with this sort of behavior on Hamid's part and did the bargaining, but Mike was so aggravated by the time we reached Villach on July 10th, that he happily chose to hitch hike alone through Yugoslavia and Greece to Turkey.

with Hamid to buy a camera and radio. Hamid was in charge of transportation. After all, he was a pilot in the Pakistani Air Force. He drove well, as we witnessed when he zoomed down Alps mountain roads, even though, we found out later, he did not have a driver's license. We were to keep law and order with Hamid's water pistol. Three squirts were in punishment of misbehavior and one squirt meant "full stop!" I don't remember actually using it, but the thought made us laugh.

Chris, Hamid, Lowey, and Mike in Venice.

We loved Venice with its nice youth hostel and waterways. We took a gondola ride. July 10th we drove to Villach and Carolyn and Veronica were glad to see us, having been treated roughly by a couple of male truck drivers and were ready to "swear off men, for the summer at least."

Hamid bought a rack for the car to fit all our things in with his, and we left Austria with us three girls packed in the back and Hamid and Chris in the front. Yugoslavia, as a communist country, was a challenge. We slept in a field belonging to the uncle of a friend we met in Edinburgh the first night, drove 500 miles the next day and picked up Chris' mail in Belgrade. We did not find any hotels open there, so found a field with a hay mow to sleep on. We were about to settle down when a couple of police guards came along and waved their guns at us in obvious disapproval. My notes read, "Chris, not a bit disturbed, proceeded to explain (with gestures) that we were simply trying to spend the night and marched them over to peer at Veronica in her sleeping bag to illustrate what he meant. This tickled them pink, but they kept on grunting and shaking their heads. Four of us piled back into the car and waited for Chris, while he packed his rucksack in the middle of the road. The guards were on either side snickering and playing with their guns perfectly oblivious of the nonchalant cracks Chris was directing at them." When Chris joined us, we drove back into Belgrade and parked under lights in the city square. Earlier in the day, in a game called "coffee potting," which Hamid had introduced, we had discussed the impossibility of sleeping five or six in a car. Well, that night we more or less proved it was possible. Mostly less as we hardly slept. The next day, we were stopped by border police who wanted to take our film; we acted dumb so they gave up. We cheered on entering Greece.

We treated ourselves to a restaurant meal and a night in a hotel, in Thessaloniki, since we thought we deserved it (especially Hamid) after our sleepless night. Our trip through Greece included riding in caravan with a Pakistani couple we had met in Yugoslavia. Unfortunately, they collided with a donkey and dented their radiator. We eventually had to leave them to sort things out themselves after making sure they had their car towed to the next town. Hamid was not pleased about abandoning them, but we needed to push on to Istanbul to meet up with Mike.

We arrived in Istanbul on Bastille Day, July 14th, and found the streets lined with soldiers. It turned out that there was a coup d'etat in Iraq and King Faisal and his family had been assassinated, but they only knew that he was deposed and were prepared for him to fly into Turkey. We found our way to the youth hostel, but did not find Mike there. He finally arrived a couple days later. The Greeks were convinced that Mike was a runaway British soldier and locked him up until he convinced them of his innocence.

Our plans to drive through Syria to Jordan with Hamid came to an end, since the border between Turkey and Syria was closed. We stayed in Istanbul for 11 days trying to decide what to do next. I wrote and telegrammed Mom and Dad in Jerusalem. It took three days to get through to them. Their reply by telegram got to Istanbul way after a letter and we finally found it under H ("Lost Homs")! I got four telegrams, one would say "come," another would then say "wait until the 28th."

Finally the fourth said "wire if flying," so I knew the decision was mine to make. Hamid and Chris were particularly helpful. The U.S. consul simply would not help since they were told to discourage U.S. citizens traveling in the Middle East. Hamid drove to Ankara to inquire of General Howie, in charge of the RAF, about the possibility of my flying to Jerusalem via a Cyprus RAF (Royal Air Force) plane. Hamid soon had to leave for Pakistan via Iran. He managed to find an American fellow who was on his way around the world to travel with him. Before leaving, he took me to the British Deputy Ambassador's office to work out a flight and then presented me with a gift of a scarf with places of importance in Istanbul on it. We had gotten to know him as a good friend and travel companion; in fact, we were referring to him as "Hami" by then. We were sad to say goodbye. Later we did get one letter from him and were glad he got home safely.

Jerusalem and return trip to England by way of Kodai friends in Germany:

I flew to Jerusalem and found that my parents had not received my last communication about my arrival time, so I called them and they came out to pick me up. I roomed with a couple single missionary young women who were also attending the course on Islam offered by Kenneth Craag. I had a wonderful time attending classes with Mom and Dad and seeing the sights in Jerusalem and other parts of Jordan. Then, after 12 days, I left my folks to join my hitch hiking gang in Athens. They were there after visiting Ephesus and other sites in Turkey and Greece. In my diary, I drew myself and my parents as stick figures—me with rucksack and ponytail waving at them while walking across the "no man's land" separating Israel and Jordan. I was wondering what to do if my messages had not gotten through, so was overjoyed to find Chris and Veronica waiting at the bus depot after taking the bus in from the airport. The night lights of the city were gorgeous. The Parthenon in the center of the hill was shining in all its splendor.

We were already well into August when we began our return trip to England. We booked deck passage on an overnight ferry from Greece to the tip of Italy. It was rough and rainy and several of us spent much of the night throwing up at the railing, so arriving at a delightful youth hostel, which in my memory was a bit like a convent, was paradise. From there we split up to return to England. I think all of us took trains. Carolyn, Veronica and Mike all returned pretty directly to England.

Chris and I took a train as far as Basle, Germany, from where we hitched again to find and visit Kodai classmates that mostly lived in Hamburg. My letter to Mom and Dad reads, "Chris and I got a very good ride with a German lady. She took us to Braunschweg by the next day and insisted on helping to feed us. At her parents' home we met an American woman who got a kick out of us and insisted on giving us $4 and oatmeal tablets, in case of starvation, sort of thing. From the youth hostel in Hamburg, we went in search of my classmate, Herman Tauscher's address and were surprised to discover it was a soldier's barracks.

We sat in an office as Herman was called to say that he had visitors. Chris and I almost fell off our seats at the sight of Herman, all spit and polish in full uniform, enter and click boots together and smartly salute the officer in the room. This seemed so out of character for our laid back, shy fellow TCK. My letter goes on to say, "He changed and came back to town with us. It certainly was good to see him."

He took us to the mission house where only Dagmar of the Jungjohann family was then staying. Chris and I stayed two nights before returning to England. It was wonderful to see Daggy (Chris' classmate). They appreciated our company, as it's hard to make friends in Germany because of formality of introduction and because people seem content to move in small closed circles of family friends." Their TCKness would have added to this feeling of estrangement, even more than we were experiencing, since their education at Kodai had been in English and according to an American curriculum so they had to learn or relearn so much to complete university. We enjoyed walking, talking, laughing, playing cards, making curry, and seeing the movie, *Bridge over the River Kwai*, in German.

My letter continues, "On leaving Hamburgh, we worked our way down to Solingen where other Kodaites live—Kirchoffs. We arrived quite late at night to find that Hans had taken off to camp for a spell. Consequently, Chris and I had to find a place to sleep. There was a field—and as the stars were twinkling merrily above, we thought we'd be safe sleeping there—but, early morning I was awakened by a few big rain drops. Thank goodness, the rain only lasted about 20 minutes. In the meantime, we took shelter under Chris' rain cape, but we found to our even greater misery that we had made camp in a cow pie! I managed to get (my white sleeping bag) washed off in a little wayside stream, rather to the alarm of the public (Hans apparently heard gossip about his friends sleeping in the field). We managed to raise our spirits by eating a bit of sausage and bread and then set off for Dusseldorf where I had a bit of shopping to do. We again spent the night (in the Netherlands) dodging drops, we started by sleeping under a bridge and ended up in a hut. The afternoon of the 30th we got to Ostende. That night on the ferry we got little sleep so were glad to get back to a bed and food that day in London. It all sounds like misery, but it was by no means unpleasant as an overall experience."

That night, Chris and I went to Battersea fun fare. You probably think our trip had been enough of a thrill. Well yes, but I hadn't been on a roller coaster, so we went and had a 'jolly good' time. The next day the others came for a reunion lunch before Veronica left and we left for Graychott (Rolles' country home). Shirley (Chris' sister) and David Firth were flat hunting for their wedding in just a few days." Several days later Chris and his parents saw Carolyn and me off on a ship for the U.S. Departure was bitter sweet, but by my senior year at Hope, I had a sense of purpose, which I lacked before. It helped that my room mate was from New York City, so my TCK perspectives did not seem so strange. I was excited about my chosen profession as a physical therapist, and started to look forward to helping people. My year contributed to my living with a renewed energy and faith. I had touched base with "world as family" and that will stick with me always.

Hermann Tauscher
Third culture kids

I have no idea, why one mentions third culture kids. It is more than a decade ago that the term culture shock was very often used, letting me wonder why now the term 3rd culture kids.

There are as many "cultures" in our life as we have environments to which we have to adapt to—from a small village in Orissa with just a handful of whites to an internment camp with hundreds of them from different nations, or to an American school, or to an out boarded home with missionary children, or to a destroyed Germany, or back to an independent India or to Kodai again, or to Germany—all almost uncountable different environments to which we all have had to adapt ourselves. That is the essence of life. Adapting to Germany was particularly difficult because in Kodai we had not acquired any knowledge of German history, geography, literature or the capability of talking perfectly like the native Germans in German concerning vocabulary and grammar. And the higher you got in your studies or academic achievement the more embarrassing it became not to have the knowledge as native Germans.

Naturally we had to adapt. And it also was particularly difficult because the established structure of friendships and familial closeness were not available as a support anymore, everything was strange, the climate, especially the harsh winters were very difficult to adjust to, the form of teaching in the school, what one was allowed to say and what not, what clothing acceptable—worn out jeans at that time not so, but later on were very popular. You can see that it would be a biography to describe these continual processes of adaptation.

After graduation, adapting oneself to a "new homeland," after so many years of absence thus meant a new and until then not experienced complicated process of adaptation and this in general without the guiding aid of the parents.

But a child growing up in the slums of Bombay and having received the opportunity of studying in school, high school and several years later to attend a university in Delhi has had just as many different and difficult adaptive processes to master behind him. Actually third culture kid means nothing more than the fact of having spent a part of one's life childhood and youth in a foreign country before one returns to his or her parent's country, a country which has changed to the same extent as the children themselves.

No, life is a continuous process of adaptation to ever changing environments. If the beloved partner dies or a disagreeable person moves close to your own house and bothers you, or you lose your job, or you go into retirement, or your physical or mental health have changed due to illness, accidents or whatever—the pattern of life will have changed and you have to adapt yourself to these new conditions. This applies to each one of us.

Studying the difficulties in adapting to another culture or to another environment can be of use to help foreigners, newcomers to adapt themselves without too many difficulties and conflicts—problems for themselves or for their neighbors. And in having experienced these transitions we might be more sensitive and understanding and eventually willing to help.

Jo Hiebert Sorensen
Being a Third Culture Kid

My brother Paul, a cultural anthropologist, and I often discussed the influence growing up both in India and in America had on our lives. He would talk about the differences in cultural expectations and global views. I, as a teacher, talked about the differences in educational opportunities and gender roles. I remember when Paul introduced me to the concept of Third Culture Kids—it was one of those eureka moments and my reaction was: okay, that makes sense; that's why I always felt as though I didn't quite fit in when we moved from India to Kansas during my high school years. And it made me realize even more fully how lucky I am to have had all these experiences. I'm thankful for this history and proud to be a Third Culture Kid.

My earliest memories are of life on our mission compound in Nagarkurnool, Hyderabad State. The first language my sister Gwen and I learned was Telugu since we spent much of our time in the care of our ayah. Our friends were the children of the teachers, pastors, cooks, and staff on the compound so difference in skin color was not an issue we much thought about. Our food was spicy, our feet were bare, our heads itchy, and we learned early to watch for snakes and to turn rocks over carefully in case scorpions were hiding underneath.

Then came WWII and my parents decided they should risk the dangerous ocean voyage back to America. During the war we lived out in the country in the San Joaquin Valley of California, surrounded by grape fields and peach orchards. The four-roomed elementary school some of us siblings attended was a surprising conglomeration of kids. My best friend was a Japanese-American girl who lived in an internment camp quonset hut with her parents (her father was a doctor and Peggy was the smartest kid in our class) and hundreds of other detainees. Then there were the "Okie" kids, whose parents left Oklahoma during the Dust Bowl, traveled along Route 66, and came to find subsistence jobs in the fruit fields. The Mexican migrant kids in our class would come to school when they weren't helping their parents pick grapes. And then there were the rest of us—white and mostly Mennonite farm kids. With two grades taught together and 40 kids in a classroom, we didn't pay much attention to diversity. Most of us were poor so that wasn't a big issue.

The war ended, my folks were anxious to return to India, so back we went. One of my most vivid memories of childhood occurred while we were taking the train from Bombay to Hyderabad. It was nighttime and I was sitting up late in the 2nd class compartment watching the little village campfires, seeing the silhouettes of palm trees, breathing in the smell of cow dung fires and earth when suddenly an unexpected, overwhelming feeling came over me—I was back home.

I was ten when four of us siblings went up to Kodai. At first I really missed my home and parents but Gwen had a room near me and that helped a lot. Gradually I came to love being at Kodai, developing friendships, being taught by challenging teachers, having a variety of sports and activities available at all times: baseball, basketball, track, roller skating, hiking, or camping. At Kodai School, we lived very much an American-style life rather than being integrated into Indian culture. I wish we had studied more the ways and history of the country in which we lived. During school vacation we kids had a life of relative ease, with a cook, servants to make our beds and carry water to our upstairs bathroom, a dhobi to wash our clothes and durji to sew dresses for school. Looking back, I realize we learned a sense of entitlement. A big regret I have is that I didn't get to know the high school girls at our mission school—somehow it wasn't expected. Instead I spent hours reading and playing piano. What a missed opportunity.

The sixth grade is composed of German, English, and American children. They have been busy giving programs and making toys for the Indian children besides their gym and choir activities. Fellow students were Robert Mayer Freider Jungjohann Robert Baker Sterling Seagrave Roger Erickson Curtis Bell, David Dickason, Conrad Heins, Peter Langton, Joanne Hiebert, Susie Inwood, Owen Thomas, Herman Tauscher, Ruth Keithahn, Julia Davis, Jennifer Brammer, Jean Towle, Alice Graham, Ann Gibbs, Annelene Meyer, Carol Zigler, Molly Ann Schmitthenner, Patsy Wood.

During the middle of my freshman year, my dad was asked to go to Kansas to be president of a Mennonite college there. And for the first time in my life I was hit with the toughest part of being a Third Culture Kid. Attending high school in this small rural town, I was out of my realm. I didn't know how to chit-chat, clothes styles had never been top of my list, I had no connection with the past experiences of other students and they certainly had no interest in mine, so it took awhile to have things to talk about. The other girls were socially more advanced than I was, while I was more advanced in studies and world awareness. I spent a lot of time trying not to do things that were considered inappropriate.

Three things that hit me the most in this new culture were:

- No sports for girls. Instead we were expected to attend the boys' games and cheer wildly for them. Being a cheerleader was a prized spot. There was no way I could try to gain a K,[40] like my sister Betty had.

- Whereas at Kodai working hard in studies was valued, here I quickly learned that girls weren't supposed to show they were smart or they wouldn't get asked on a date. I learned to hide my books under my jacket when I walked home.

- In Kodai we had a relatively wide range of beliefs. In this small religious town the rules were strict and I was expected not to question the teachings of the church as this was viewed as questioning God. One thing I found puzzling was that folks in this Midwest town were vocally fond of black people in Africa but not of black basketball players that came to town for tournaments.

Luckily, there were a lot of opportunities for me to be involved in music—cello in orchestra, saxophone in band, chorus and choral choir, piano and organ at church. Still I often felt like an outsider looking in and like my being different was not okay. I ended up pretty much going my own way.

My redemption came when, as a college junior, I left Kansas and went to Wheaton College in Illinois. Suddenly I was with a whole group of missionary kids from a variety of countries, as well as other Third Culture kids. I found myself fitting in for the first time since Kodai. I could talk about my earlier life and about global issues and others understood me. I had a sense of kinship, of belonging to a group. And then along came this guy who didn't think I was weird. He thought I was interesting and he liked that about me—and it made me learn to accept myself for who I was. So I married him.

Now as I look back I value this different way of growing up and of perceiving the world. Sure, there will always be the tough parts:

---

[40] The athletic letter award.

- I still often don't feel like a part of a group and have difficulty understanding what's expected of me
- Even after living in a place 30 years, I feel temporary
- I become restless if life is too much the same
- I find myself easily irritated with folks who are racist or bigoted and become prejudiced against folks who are prejudiced ...

But there are so many more strengths:

- Love for travel, curiosity about other people and their ways
- Acceptance and enjoyment of diversity
- Concern about folks who have a harder time than most. This influenced me toward working with kids with special needs.
- Interest in looking at strengths and limitations within cultures, not blindly believing one to be superior
- Love for food, books and movies from other countries
- Valuing kindness over wealth and standing
- Increased social awareness, concern for social justice. More courageous to speak up for what I believe is right, especially if I feel people are being harmed or discriminated against—like this current situation of children being taken away from their parents.

I've always appreciated the words in a song in Pufnstuf that ends with: "But I'd rather be different than be the same."

Chris Rolles
Third or Fourth Culture Kid

My culture clash was possibly even more complicated and significant than that of my American friends. I was trying to reconcile three cultures: English, American and Indian. And the problems I had must have been the same for the other non-American Kodai kids such as the Germans and the Swedes

My parents were very English and so were the other missionaries in The London Missionary Society. My parents met on the mission field and I was born in Kodai, in 1939. We returned to England on furlough almost immediately, but with the outbreak of war in Europe beat a hasty, risky, retreat back to India, where we stayed till I was six. I was in kindergarten and first and second grade in Kodai, where my mother was on the staff. During the war years, Kodai was fairly unique and cosmopolitan, sheltering many foreigners trapped by the war who were teaching in the school: Mrs. Oh from Singapore, Fritz Kolb from Austria, Madame Caspari from

Italy, Miss Skahoose (?) from Denmark and those who stayed on post war: Annie Putz, Mr. Musil from Czechoslovakia and Mario from Italy. The Jesuits say—give us a child till the age of five and we will have them for life—or something like that—so Kodai and India and internationalism were deeply engrained in me by the time I came back to the austerity of post-war England (rationing went on well into the 1950s) and the coldest UK winter on record.

Then my 38 year old father, wanting to study medicine, after what he had seen in his Indian village work, and failing to get into English medical schools which were flooded with young ex-servicemen, took the family to Iowa for five years and graduated as a Doctor of Osteopathic Medicine. During those five years, which I call my Huckleberry Finn years, I integrated into a poor Italian, Norwegian, American community. We were poor too. I only realized later just how poor. With my gang at school, swimming, messing around, doing my paper round, in scouts, going to the local flea pit to watch Hoppalong Cassidy and Bugs Bunny, I was completely American, accent and all. Once through our front door I was English again. I was acutely embarrassed when my friends came into my house or my mother came to school as a supply teacher. Who should I be? We came back to England en route for the mission field and the idea was that Shirley and I, like other English missionary kids, would stay behind in boarding school. An English public school education, after all, was what had made the men who made the Empire! The term I spent in an English boys' boarding school in 1952 was the unhappiest time of my life. Retrospectively, it was not all the school's fault! I was out of line with the English school curriculum and the shock of a rigid timetable, structured discipline that included corporal punishment, cold showers and the prospect of not seeing my parents for five years was overwhelming. I was very Americanized and nicknamed "yank" by the other boys. At the end of one term, Shirley and I were on our way back to India and Kodai. That was hard financially for our parents because the LMS declined to pay for our Kodai school fees. Rolles senior were breaking ranks. The Wightmans did the same and Eleanor also graduated from Kodai. It was interesting, looking back, to remember how the other English missionary parents, coming up to Kodai for the May Season, their children back in UK, regarded me, Shirley and Eleanor. They treated us with a mixture of antagonism, jealousy or sometimes with excessive friendliness which contrasted with the normal friendliness from the parents of my American friends.

The Kodai experience was wonderful. No need to tell you all why. But at 17, wanting desperately to follow my friends to college in America but not having available funds, I found myself back in England, with no friends of my own age and no educational qualifications that were recognized. It was cold and grey and the food was different. Patterns of socialization were completely foreign to me. There was lots of correspondence with Kodai friends and I was thrilled when any of them came through the UK. I was lucky to get into university by a devious route and after a shaky start found my feet and got a degree in Zoology. I then went on to Medical School where I met Toni and subsequently have had a successful career as a pediatrician. As a medical student I lived with the Wightmans, which was some sort of India continuation. Wightie's curry for lunch every Sunday! Kodai, the American connection and India have remained dominant elements in my life and I am very grateful for them. I think my history has made me very independent and given me a broader worldview than I might have had. But although life has been happy and fulfilled, I have never quite "fitted" in as an English man.

Ruth Voss Harris
Misfit or Chameleon

I am not an actual Third Culture Kid, having only experienced two years of life in Arabia and India. But if there is a name for the culture of kids who live in many different places, my sisters and brother and I would qualify. I remember living in thirteen different dwellings (including a travel trailer), and attending nine schools in six states before our family boarded a freighter in New York just before Christmas 1952 to go overseas.

Our upbringing had certainly given us the ability to adapt to new circumstances, but it hadn't always been much fun to be the new girl. I could please my parents and teachers by doing well in school, but after about the sixth grade, was finding it very hard to make good friends. I became extremely shy and quite lonely. It was easiest just to fade into the background in social situations, to pretend to be like everyone else.

The two month voyage on the freighter, with novel experiences of being surrounded by different people with different languages, clothing and ways of living was in many ways exhilarating. The adventure of traveling with all the unfamiliar smells, colors, sounds was amazing, and occasionally bewildering. But being a misfit in Iraq and Bombay and on an Indian train was exciting rather than disheartening.

The Kodai years for me were a time of blossoming, of truly enjoying everything about school, being in a dorm, making friends, being in plays, performing in music groups, playing basketball, hiking, dancing, walking. It was also a time of questioning spiritual realities, to feel that I was starting to know what being a

Christian meant, and talking with others about life and belief and what really matters.

Coming back to the US for college initially meant once again being the new girl, not having the right clothes, not knowing the popular music, often feeling out of sync. And, of course, I was without the backup of family until my sister Bobbie arrived my junior year. But the presence of other Kodai kids, notably Lowey Thoms, at Hope College, eased the transition, as well as the self-confidence the Kodai years had given me. I would never be like our classmates who had a hometown, grew up in one house, and had friends they had known since kindergarten.

As it happened, the necessity of being adaptive and flexible proved valuable, because I married a Navy chaplain. In twenty-six years of his career, we moved 26 times, our three sons were born in Virginia, California and Spain and I continue to have difficulty answering the question, "Where are you from?" Having a good marriage and a close family, including my sisters and brother, has been a great blessing and saving grace in my life. Now four of our grandchildren have been able to enjoy the stability we never knew. In some ways, I still don't fit, even though we have now been in Williamsburg, Virginia for thirty years. Being a chameleon, however, really doesn't work, and now I enjoy just being myself, now and then recalling some of our many adventures along the way.

Owen Thomas
Growing Up in a multi-cultural Environment

I have never felt that my growing up in India was significantly different from others who grew up in the States or other "first" cultures. They, too, had many different experiences. Perhaps the impact of India as a "third" culture for me was mitigated by having my Indian home in Bombay which was cosmopolitan as well as Indian and British. And Kodai was certainly not an "Indian" cultural experience. Yes, over-all growing up in India was a different experience but one that I have felt very comfortable with.

Separation from immediate family was probably the most negative effect I felt due to boarding school and leaving "home" to go to college. My sisters were six and eight years older so there was not a lot of time that we spent together as a close-knit family. I was very aware of this a couple weeks ago while watching our whole family, kids, grandkids and five girlfriends, 20 in all, spend a week together at our house in Maine. The interaction of all of the cousins, the bonds being formed, and the memories created that will last for their lifetimes was wonderful.

By osmosis, India certainly affected me. Acceptance of the differences in people was natural. On one side of our compound in Bombay residents were Hindus, another side were Jews, another side were Muslims and the fourth side was a police station (to keep the peace? It tried to during various riots.) Awareness of extreme wealth and extreme poverty was obvious. Dust, dirt, and smells were part of the normal as were vibrant colors and beautiful faces. The wide range of these experiences made acceptance of diversity and inclusion a normal part of my life.

After trying several different majors at Oberlin, I ended up in political science and then a major in international relations at SAIS thinking I would go into the Foreign Service. As events happened, the State Department said I would not be sent to India for several years and I ended up in international business with the opportunity to work in many different countries with different cultures and expectations, all made easier for me due to growing up in India.

Ann Gibbs HENDERSON
Third Culture Kid

My (and Jane's) experience was very different as we did not come from anywhere! We were born and brought up in Kodaikanal as my mother decided to be a "staying on" Brit and not leave with the mass exodus in 1947. She was British and we did meet her family on a short visit to the UK in 1951.

I then left on my own to go "back home" after I graduated in 1955. Firstly, we had a great trip through Europe with Owen and Conrad and Kay Unruh—my chaperone. Becky Biggar had come from Bahrain to see me in Bombay before we sailed. We've met in several different parts of the world since then.

On arrival in England I went to a hostel connected to the secretarial college I went to. I was very lost. The English girls my age were so different to my close group of friends—the Georges. Fortunately, my first friend Sarah was there and I spent weekends in the country with her and went to my mother's family in Devon for longer holidays. They were part of the English aristocracy so again different and again I didn't fit in to country races and balls.

I enjoyed visiting with various Kodai people from the classes of 1956 and 1957 who stopped by in London on their way through to the States. And was particularly pleased when Lowey did her exchange year in Edinburgh.

We hitchhiked to Edinburgh one time and met an absolutely sus driver near the border who we were both frightened of. We asked to be dropped off in the middle of nowhere but he decided to take us to a police station because it was dark.

The cops offered us a night in the cells but we refused and sat up all night. Regret that—a night in the cells would have been an experience!

I sought to find a church in that year on my own in London but preferred the Congregational. This annoyed my very conservative godmother and she got the Bishop of London's offsider to visit me and try and get me to be confirmed as an Anglican. I had joined the Church of South India in Kodai and that to me meant I belonged to a church but Violet (the godmother) said I had to become an Anglican to take communion. I never did but have taken communion in many different churches since then?

Mother and Jane came to London after Jane's graduation but that was short lived as Jane went to college in Oregon and Mother went back to India. I met and married Jim Henderson in my isolation. Not a good marriage and after the two children were born we came back to Australia, where Jim was from. That turned out to be—in time—a huge bonus because I now "belong" and live in the most beautiful country in the world and enjoy a diverse and good life.

Margie Hiebert
Reflections on Being a Cross Culture Kid

Even though I was only in India from ages 5-10, I recognize in myself habits of thoughts and actions acquired during that impressionable time of my development and with subsequent transfer to American culture:

1. First and foremost, I am always restless in some way. Always imagining myself living somewhere else than where I am. Not allowing myself to really settle in. I've lived in Florida for over 40 years but still feel temporary, yearning for something else, though I don't know what. Travel to new places is a high priority when I have time and money. I regret that I will probably never see all the continents or countries out there.
2. The restlessness carries over into my professional life. At the university where I worked for 25 years, I held five different positions, none more than 3-4 years. Uncharacteristically, I have been in my mid-life change career for 25 years, but still keep thinking "what else do I want to do?"
3. I struggle on some level with conflicting lifestyle choices: on the one hand enjoying luxuries, elegant clothes, beautiful art objects, symphony concerts, and exotic vacations; on the other hand, dismayed at the materialism of this country and its people, and experiencing almost euphoric happiness when volunteering

as the medical provider in a jungle orphanage in Guatemala, with the simplest of food, clothes, housing and activities.

4. I confess to somewhat self-righteous (possibly hypocritical) condemnation of narrow views of the world and its peoples: both angry with and sad about bigotry, racism, misogyny, sexism, inequalities, homophobia, snobbery, isolationism, close-mindedness, class systems (even the subtle ones), extreme nationalism, discrimination, intolerance and judgmental behavior of any kind. I'm sure living in another culture and seeing much of the world contribute to a more expansive world view.

5. A telling moment while teaching English at a university: in a class discussion with college freshman, there were loud complaints about the cafeteria food. In a burst of anger, I narrated what I witnessed in India with its poverty, starvation, children begging for food, fathers with tuberculosis having to drive bicycle rickshaws all day in pain in order to provide some rice for family supper. I told them never again in my presence to complain about their food. They never did, and hopefully they carried the message with them.

6. Now I am a nurse practitioner in geriatric and psychiatric long-term care facilities. It saddens me to hear many of my residents evidence their narrow view of humanity by referring to their caregivers with racial epithets and insulting remarks. Mostly it puzzles me, I'm sure because I was exposed to people of different races and cultures as a cross culture kid and came to appreciate the variety and value of all people who inhabit our earth.

All said, I wouldn't trade being a cross-culture kid and growing up in India for anything!

Ruth Vassar Burgess
Mt. Pleasant (1950)

High on the hill were roily puchie bugs and rhinoceros beetles snuggled mainly under the pungent pine needles. Cumulus clouds disintegrated slowly as they floated upward from the checkered farmlands on the Palni hills plains below. After school when children attempted a shortcut home we climbed the rocky incline trying to avoid wild, thorny red and purpose raspberry bushes. Then one saw a three-bedroom rental lodging. This was named Mt. Pleasant.

The Vassar family, who normally lived in Bombay Presidency, had rented this cottage for the 1950 hill season. Ted's duties as superintendent of a boys' orphanage, farming project and elementary school delayed his visit to Kodaikanal, while Estelle, their three children (Ruth, 10 years, Teddy, 6 years and Helen, 4 years) and Lillie bai, Helen's ayah had settled into the cream-colored stucco lodging. Two local women, Unna and Pushpah, assisted in the shopping, cooking and cleaning. Tamil was spoken in Kodaikanal, whereas Marathi was the primary language in western India. One bedroom was sublet to Miss Martha Kucera, a corpulent spinster, who had immigrated to the United States from Czechoslovakia. The children adored this auntie because she was an avid storyteller and precocious knitter of sweaters. Estelle, a Texan through and through, filled her lonely days with social sorties with other church guests. She had one forbidden trunk that was off limits to outsiders. Teddy and Helen wondered just what delicacies were kept in Mother's steamer trunk.

SPINSTERS AND TEA TIME:

Polite chitter chatter could be heard from the front room. Aunt Martha's knitting needles were clicking away. Periodically she nodded away as Auntie Ellen Esler's soft voice relayed the social calendar recently distributed by Highclerc Boarding School. Auntie Lydia Graner added comments about books she read while at Punalur. Auntie Mildred Ginn, was very tall, in fact her neck seemed as long like a giraffe. She carried much respect from the male missionaries. They remarked frequently that she "thought like a man." Auntie Mildred served as secretary for the Southern India Assemblies of God missionary conference for many years.

Beyond the curtained doorway one detected children's giggles. "Oh, I'm glad the children are having a good time," murmured Auntie Lydia. Estelle smiled slowly. Auntie Martha responded that maybe there might be more to Teddy's and Helen's laughter. Just then the curtains parted and in danced the twosome. They were blowing on long white rubber spirals with wide openings.

"What is going on? What is in their mouths?" asked the aunties.

Auntie Mildred said, "Take the prophylaxes away from them?"

"What is going on? Those aren't balloons. But there are plenty of colored balloons down at the bazaar in the English Store." exclaimed Auntie Ellen.

Auntie Lydia responded with a faint smile, "Those appear to be condoms."

Estelle curtailed her two younger children and was heard to say, "Can't I ever keep my life private?"

UNNA AND GERITOL:

Mt. Pleasant lived up to its name when Daddy Ted arrived from Junnar on the plains. He listened intently to our progress at school. Dad brought greetings and news from the friends on the mission compound. There were many communiques from the states, including Mother Estelle's women's magazines. But the most beloved actions were his singing and modified dances to our mother. Their love had withstood the death of their first-born Bobby Jo (1937), malaria, bubonic plague scares, famine times, and shortness of funds to take care of helpers on the compound. Now Ted was concerned that Dr. Rosenthal had given a diagnosis of high blood pressure, heart ailment, and diabetes for Estelle. Surely time in the hills would help her physical condition being away from the tropical heat on the plains.

We had enjoyed a Texas—Indian lunch consisting of red beans with a few shreds of canned pork in the stew. Warm chapattis were wrapped around white water buffalo cheese. Dessert consisted of fresh, orange apricots, purchased from the wallas at the bus station. Of course they had been soaked in purple disinfectant water for our safety.

Abruptly Daddy stood up, looked around and mentioned having stomach distemper. Then he saw a Geritol bottle, whose contents had been reported to keep one young. Ted opened the Geritol and began gulping. " AAHHaaaaa," Louder than an elephant's roar and bomb explosions on Hiroshima was our Dad's cry. As he ran out the side door we heard him scream, "Who is trying to kill me?"

Mother demanded we stop crying and yelling. She grabbed the Geritol bottle and put it by her nose. Then she looked at Unna, Pushbai and Lilliebai and asked, "Who put eucalyptus oil in the Geritol bottle?" A poignant hush fell at Mt. Pleasant. Softly and with a teary voice Unna confessed that she did it to save money.

Why had the Geritol bottle cause such a commotion? Well, it seems that in the Vassar DNA is a propensity of early smelling loss. Daddy Ted had lost his sense of smell when he was 27 years of age and could no longer detect olfactory variances. Ted did not tell the difference between fresh eucalyptus oil and Geritol solution.

ARRANGED MARRIAGES:

Occasionally the missionary men would plan hikes around the central 3-mile lake in Kodaikanal. Church business required thoughtfulness, integrity and cross-cultural understandings. Estelle considered this an opportune time for the women to gather at Mt. Pleasant and enjoy an afternoon high tea. All year long this Texas bluebonnet saved the chocolate cake mixes sent by her sisters Johnnie Mae and Mary Jo. Since cake mixes were unavailable in village India, her guests enjoyed tastes from the United States. They often exclaimed how white buffalo cream vied for frostings mixed in the states. Fresh vanilla beans brought a favor penchant beyond the imitation ones found in the black market variety. Of course two types of tea were available: there were those who preferred white English tea or those who preferred chai, the India variety laden with spices such as cardamom, cinnamon, nutmeg and non-granulated cane sugar.

Auntie Bernice Burgess and Auntie Doris Edwards had joined Auntie Martha Kucera and the Vassar women for a high tea. Frequently the friends discussed variances in wedding customs found in different sections of India. Auntie Martha Kucera let out a chuckle as she proposed the following. “How would you ladies enable a wedding proposal for your children? Would this be a contract?”

Ten-year-old Ruth gulped as she looked across the dining room table at Auntie Bernice and Auntie Doris. Each had a son, who was of marriageable age, according to Indian standards. Stanley Burgess was 12 years while Clarence Maloney was the elder being 14 years. Aunt Bernice jumped right in and said, "Our family both here in India as well as in the States would welcome Ruth in the family because of her quiet and caring ways. She even cries when she prays.”

Auntie Doris took on a stern countenance and said, "This is not how Indian marriage contracts are made. My son Clarence is the elder and must be married first. Stanley must wait his birth order time. He and Ruth will fit in better to the Indian way of life. The couple will be happier living in India, than with your son. You say Stanley has heart trouble and he may not carry on the Lord's work here in India.”

Ruth looked down and then her eyes pled with her mother, “Please excuse me from this table.” Mt. Pleasant had evolved into another title: Mt. Unpleasant.

Ruth realized she had experienced what it was like to be a Child of the Third Culture.

Paul Smith
Being a Third Culture Kid

Exposed to several cultures growing up—Chinese, Indian, Latin, North American—I end up happy being "just me.” What culture is that? I discovered the universe is a rich smorgasbord to discover. Chopsticks, fingers, a fork, language, friends, violin or cello, where to live is all my choice. What gives me joy is learning, exploring, and sharing. My neighbor likes jazz, a big car, and cornflakes, but I prefer Johanne Sebastian Bach, a bike, oatmeal with fruit for breakfast. I say, let's go solar, and leave the carbon in the ground, respect nature, save the world, not a popular idea. Viva la diferencia, something to celebrate.

Dave Dickason
"Difference" is the Difference

Guilty! Guilty! Guilty! As long as I can remember I have been a minority-of-one, a "fish out of water," a "hired gun," the guy who marched to a "different drummer"—i.e., a TCK. This was uncomfortable, since my missionary mom always instructed us kids to "be nice" and to fit in. But how to restrain the internal voice wanting to shout, "But the emperor isn't wearing any clothes!"?! I seem to have absorbed both family values and Burmese culture by osmosis at the same time, if that is possible. The Burmese never say "No"—they just don't say "Yes." And I've gotten very good at committing to "definite maybe's," as Lowey knows.

How I comprehended Burmese culture is a mystery because Rangoon (where I was born) was a city alien to the Burmese. Before WWII it was a metropolis, but its people came from India (mostly), and China, with a few from Europe. That is to say, they were all foreigners too. Burmans (ethnic Buddhist Burmese-speakers) hated British rule. So I was a foreigner among foreigners. You'd think I would have thought of myself as normal. But from an early age I knew I lived in a "plural society" (a term first coined in Burma) where people of different linguistic backgrounds live side by side in their own un-gated communities. There was a "plural economy" mirroring the "plural society." My plural society niche was the American Baptist Mission—which ran many schools, one college (where my father taught), a hospital, and missions (with churches and Bible schools) to specific ethnic groups (mostly hill peoples) who did not share the values or orientation of Buddhist Burmans. Other Kodaiites from this Mission were Ed Tegenfeldt (and siblings), Phil Young (and siblings) and Beverly England (and siblings).[41] Their parents served in different ethno-linguistic mission stations, so my exposure to mission life differed greatly from theirs. I was fascinated, during the year I worked in Burma after graduating from Kodai, to travel to different mission stations and to see how different they were as compared to Rangoon—the city today called Yangon.

Kodai acculturated me to the "Christian" West, as it did Phil Young and others. But I returned to Burma after graduating from Kodai. I catalogued the Mission's Divinity School library collection of approximately 10,000 books. A solitary job, I also studied Burmese. I studied Burmese Buddhism (Therevada) too. And I observed Burma's national politics. I became a tour guide for international visitors,

---

[41] Our classmate Nancy Spear was the only child of Methodist missionaries. They lived in Pegu (now called Bago), forty miles from Rangoon

and dreamed of opening my own tourist guest house in the old British "chummery" (for single men) called the Pegu Club in the British Cantonment, not far from the Shwe Dagon Pagoda.[42] There were on many days twenty people at our dining room table, since my parents ran the Mission Guest House. Lots of interesting people were sprinkled in among the already interesting Baptist missionaries who came "down country" for various purposes.

I regressed culturally after Kodai. I became more of a Burman than I realized. I learned many of the colloquialisms of Burmese, while the few American ones I had known grew rusty. My English became British-accented, and it took me years to learn to speak "American."

I never intended to work in Michigan, but I had to work somewhere, didn't I? Raised in multiple cultures I had learned how to think "outside the box." My big concern was: Could I think "inside the box"? My career took many twists and turns, and I was not aware early I was a "change maker." Over the years, I taught many courses in Asian Studies, international studies, geography, history, and environmental studies—as well as statistics and information technology. I set up three research centers and ran the University's community college in Malaysia, but it is the last research center I am most proud of—a world-class imaging center preserving historic maps for global change studies.

Lowey and I have two marvelous sons. John is a doctor, jazz saxophonist, and tennis player. Rob is a journeyman brass and woodwind repair craftsman, as well as an accomplished saxophonist and choral musician. In their own ways I suspect they have benefited from—or survived—their parents having been TCK's. We took them for a year to India where they learned about their parents through their own Kodai experience, and where we lived in Lowey's old family cottage, Dar Es Salaam, with the same family caretaker, Mr. P. Soosainathan (or 'Soosai' as we called him).

Life moves rapidly, and the day after Christmas, 2012, I looked at the snow and ice on our deck and said quite involuntarily, "I should have retired yesterday." A career that had been filled with so many interesting challenges from original vision to raising funds to innovative outcomes no longer fascinated. It had been stimulating and an outlet for creativity. I retired in mid-2013 after 50 years in higher education. Lowey retired some years before that.

---

[42] In New York City today, the Pegu Club (no relative of the original) is a trendy eating and drinking establishment. My problem, though, was I didn't have the capital to buy the building (elevated on stilts), nor did I have the money to purchase a Volkswagen microbus to ferry my hoped-for clients around Yangon. (Now you know why I am not an Asian billionaire now.) Ah, the trail of missed opportunities....

As TCK's, we decided to move to Penney Retirement Community (PRC) not far from St. Augustine, Florida, since we've never been deeply "rooted" in any place.

There were many retired missionaries and pastors there with international experience, some of whom we knew. We moved there in November 2013. PRC swept Lowey immediately into all kinds of volunteering. Great! But I soon discovered a retired college professor in such a place is close to being unskilled labor! Perhaps women are more relational.

I've pursued two projects since, and am close to finishing both. One is a biography of Lowey's dad, Wells Thoms—a legendary figure in Oman even today. The other is assembling the memoirs of Dr. Stanley Mylrea whom some of you knew after he retired in Kodai (he was a doctor in Kuwait for forty years). Both men were TCKs. I think I've found it easier to write about these two people precisely because of my TCK-ness. After all, all writing is autobiographical, or so it is said. Growing up in Asia at the end of the colonial age has given me a sense of that era many others might struggle to comprehend.

So now I am discerning whether these manuscripts top off my career as a budding author-storyteller—or whether other "out-of-the-box" challenges loom around the corner.

Bruce Carman
Third Culture Kid

Being a "Third Culture Kids" wasn't a "recognized" thing when we graduated and came back to the USA. And I had family around when I started in college: Miggie also a Freshman at the University of Rochester with me, Ellie was there as a senior, my brother Bob was there in medical school, and my folks were on furlough. So—while I did experience some problems in school—I became sort of "addicted" to television to the detriment of my studies, I'm not sure that was a "Third Culture" experience or something others coming from "No TV to unlimited TV" might also be troubled with.

I passed all my Freshman year courses and was invited to join the Freshman Orientation Team for the next class. But my TV addiction continued, and I also put time and effort into my job in the Food Service, and participation in the Chapel Choir—again neglecting my studies. So I did poorly and ultimately quit college and joined the US Air Force.

When I got out two years later I entered Bethel College in St. Paul, Minnesota and again allowed other interests to intrude on my studies; especially my job as

Business Manager of the Bethel College Choir—responsible for arranging the "Tour" in the Spring, which involved a lot of correspondence. That tour took us to the east coast and included concerts in Boston, New York, and Washington, DC. I arranged a tour of the White House through Senator Eugene McCarthy—Minnesota's junior senator at the time—and he arranged for us to meet and sing in the Rose Garden for President Kennedy! (The spring of 1963—just 7 months before his assassination.)

But—I didn't graduate because of some "incompletes"—and it was 16 years after I graduated from Kodai before I finally finished college! Not a great accomplishment—but it has certainly been an encouragement to some young people who have been struggling with college over the years since then! It makes five or six years to finish sound great.

Donna came into my life during the long college career—and she made a huge difference in my interest and ability to finally finish the degree! We lived in Minnesota during those years, and after having two natural born children (David came 10 months after our wedding—the day before Christmas in 1968, and Katie a year and a half later), we adopted two sisters from Mother Teresa's orphanage in Delhi. They joined our family in November 1976 and we've celebrated "Happy Arrival Day" ever since!

After the girls, Sarala and Leela, had been with us for 6 years we went to join the staff at Kodai School—starting in January 1983. And we were there 4 ½ years—as Dorm Parents for high school boys in Phelps Hall for 2 ½ years and then moving to LoBen for the last two years. I started as an "unqualified" general science teacher for 7th & 8th grades, and then became the "Administrative Officer" for the last two years. Donna moved from being "Housemother" at Phelps to being "Head Houseparent" for a year, and then a volunteer the last year—helping in the dispensary occasionally and also in the Under Fives clinic for the local operational staff and their children.

When David and Katie graduated in 1987 we moved back to Minnesota where I worked as a truck driver and then dispatcher, and Donna worked in "Home Health" nursing with Ramsey County. David went to Letourneau University in Texas and Katie attended Bethel College. Sarala and Leela had finished 7th grade in Kodai and attended high school in White Bear Lake, Minnesota. When they graduated, and David and Katie finished college, Donna and I moved to Cannon Beach, Oregon, where I took over the job of Business Manager of Cannon Beach Christian Conference Center. Donna again worked in Home Health nursing—for the Providence Hospital in Seaside.

We both retired in 2003—after 10 years in those jobs—and immediately began ten years of being "Retired and Re-Fired for God's Service"—which involved volunteer service with Wycliffe Associates on five construction and remodeling teams in England, France, Germany, and Cameroon (where our son, David, and his wife were serving in Aviation with Wycliffe Bible Translators.) We also went on "Eye Care" teams to China seven summers: 2005 to 2012, helping with cataract surgery performed in a Coleman "pop-up" tent trailer parked beside rural hospitals (actually small city hospitals which meant the cities could sometimes be over 100,000, but were poorly served by specialists—especially ophthalmologists.)

In 2013 we moved from the north Oregon coast to Meridian, Idaho—a suburb of Boise—where Katie and Leela and their families were living. That meant five of our seven grandchildren were there and we figured it wise to live near our grandchildren before they moved on to college and "who knows where" and visit the coast, rather than the other way around. We have really missed the coast and our friends of 20 years—but are glad we made the decision, and have made many more fine friends in Idaho, continue volunteering at church and our church's Bible Camp, but not on overseas teams now.

Jean Towle Reed
How Bridge My Worlds?

I stand at an upstairs window of Riverwood, a federal house built by slaves in the 1790s for a prosperous Scots-Irish farmer. The house is on a modest hill, a high point at the furthest southwestern edge of the city of Charlotte, North Carolina. What changes I see since the Reeds moved here in 1991. Yet beyond the development replacing the abundant woods of the former countryside, I "see" the story of my life.

CHILD'S WORLD: After all, I am a Third Culture Kid, a missionary kid who arrives with her parents and younger sister Alice in British India in 1939, at the beginning of World War II. Gifford and Marjorie Towle are assigned to a small Christian community on the outskirts of the Hindu village of Vadala. Due to Giffs agricultural expertise as well as his credentials as a minister, we end up on the scruffy plains of Maharashtra, twenty-seven miles from the nearest post of civilization, Ahmednagar. Dad oversees a Demonstration Farm, mission schools for boys, the Indian pastors of the area, and has many administrative responsibilities. Being mechanically gifted, he also creates a mechanical unit and trains local young men to repair farm machinery from the States for the co-ops he creates for poor local farmers. Eventually he teaches them how to handle explosives and drill wells when monsoons fail and famine strikes. Mother works with the women and children and helps Dad in the office.

Busy parents assign ayahs to Alice and myself, which allows us considerable freedom to play with the compounds' Indian children. I become fluent in Marathi and love to lead them in games. If memory serves me, I'm a sunny, happy child. I can explore the farm, watch the mongoose chasing a snake, and hear the creaking of the waterwheel. Then, when I become five, my parents, worried about my education, believe it necessary to send me to Kimmins, an Anglican boarding school in the ghats between Vadala and Bombay. The British students gang up on us two American intruders. Anglican nuns and Anglo-Indian dorm "mothers" make us obey using fear and deceit. They unsuccessfully try to force me to switch from writing with my left hand to my right hand. They alter our weekly letters home to prevent us reporting our unhappiness. I hide from the dorm mother. When she finds me close to supper time, she locks me in a pitch dark storage room until bedtime, warning about the prowling panthers in the vicinity. I am thoroughly traumatized.

I stand on the Boyer Hall bridge feeling queasy. I survive 16 rabies shots upon arrival in May, 1944, at Kodai School in South India's Palni Hills. Protestant Missions in India and Ceylon established the school to provide an American curriculum enabling their offspring to attend US colleges. In 1944, I face trials besides a roiling middle. My family is split up among the families of other missionary friends. Dad remains on the plains due to his work overload. Mother remains in Kodaikanal's Van Allen Hospital after giving birth to our baby sister, Nancy. Mother's subsequent jaundice keeps her there. I end up in the Dishpan—the school dispensary—with a deadly bacillary dysentery illness. A missionary doctor from Arabia, father of my classmate Lowey Thoms, saves me with some of the precious penicillin he reserves for his family.

My experience at Kimmins affects my relationships at Kodai. Now I am a very fearful, unconfident child. It is not easy to make friends with others my age who have already formed close friendships with each other. Nevertheless, I love playing outdoor games such as Capture-the-Flag, engaging in sports, and hiking many a weekend. Otherwise, I spend hours in the library browsing, reading with no guidance—mostly mysteries, animal stories, or occasional historically-based literature. My favorite reading retreat is at Maratha House, the mission bungalow at the head of the Bazaar road used by vacationing families. A tree by the gate has branches that create an ideal seat largely hidden from the public. There I can read uninterrupted or watch the traffic below. Once, observing a Hindu religious procession, I see an old woman with an iron bowl containing coal embers atop her head, only separated from her scalp by a thin, rolled cotton cloth circle. How does she bear it?

TEEN & YOUNG ADULT WORLDS: I stand next on the steps of Merrill-Keep Hall, the dorm in which I live as a junior. Furlough has taken the Towle family back to the States in 1953. My sophomore high school year is my last at Kodai School. I am full of anger, hurt, and disdain: I direct my immediate anger at Kodai School for not teaching courses about India, its history, language, literature, and culture and not preparing me for the shock of transition to the "fast" United States, especially its teen culture. I find most of my fellow students at Northfield boarding school (founded by evangelist Dwight L. Moody) using their free time to learn how to paint their faces and nails and attract boys. I never dated at Kodai, though some classmates did.

The Connecticut River near the juncture of New Hampshire, Vermont, and western Massachusetts divide Moody's school for boys, Mount Hermon, from Northfield for Girls, a five-mile hyphen. Both are designed to develop head, heart, and hand: head represents academic skills; the heart, emotions and Christian care; and hand stands for practical skills in domestic and other work. Most of the Northfield girls seem shallow. Their religious life appears conventional, not deeply felt as that of virtually all Kodai kids. They pay little heed to matters crucial in India and other countries, casually overusing water to brush teeth, shower, and the like. Some have upper class airs. I write a critique comparing Kodai and Northfield Mt. Hermon cultures. I do not truly fit at either place. Later, I have to admit that both Kodai and Northfield prepare me well for college work and provide a fine musical education.

I stand as a counselor at Camp Wapanaki on Lake Fairlee in Vermont for the summers of 1953-56. Because I have no skills in swimming, canoeing, and other standard camp activities, I become an instructor of religion. I tell updated Bible stories adapted to the age and TV world of the campers. Kids seem to enjoy them.

When the older campers produce the musical Brigadoon, I paint the scenery. It's nice to find I have appreciated skills. When the owner and director finds from my reports on the campers in my tent that I have a knack for writing biographical sketches, she keeps me after Camp closes to write parents about the progress of their kids. As a reward, thereafter she pays for me to join other counselors undertaking a long canoe trip down Maine's Rangeley Lakes. As unpracticed as I am, I have a wonderful time.

SEX: During these summers I go out with a handsome young counselor of another camp. He makes moves I resist. I know nothing of sex. How should I manage romantic relationships? My parents never explained. They suggest that it is best not to kiss the guy unless I'm serious enough to marry him. Somehow I assume that Alan and I are virtually engaged before I go off to college. That is another huge beef I have with my Kodai era. The most evangelical missions dominated the school. We get no sex education. We can't even visit famous Hindu temples in the region for fear of being titillated by the explicit sex acts of the gods sculpted on their exteriors. My solution is to avoid any genuine intimate relationship, even in college.

SEPARATION: Being separated from parents and siblings is perhaps the most devastating, long-lasting cruelty of missionary life. At Kodai dorms are populated by members of the same class or group of classes, so one seldom sees a younger sister, for instance. Old patterns of closeness break down. When my parents and sisters return to India in 1956, I feel abandoned. The Mission fathers deny me the right to go back with them for my final year with my class at Kodai. 'It's too expensive," they say. They fail to count the cost to me for the rest of my life. I do not see my parents again for five years. They attend my graduation ceremonies, but miss my serious illnesses at college—i.e., a bad case of mononucleosis that keeps me in the infirmary for three weeks, messing up my academic year and making my sense of isolation all the greater. Alan's mother comes to visit me in the infirmary to give me a New Testament from him and word that Alan and I are not engaged. In 1957 or 1958, the Asian flu sweeps the campuses and I fall victim. I end up with bronchiectasis. The hacking is hard on me and my roommate.

COLLEGE AND GRADUATE SCHOOL: I stand at the entrance of Earlham College in Richmond, Indiana. It is far from my New England, mostly Quaker relatives, but I choose it because its Quaker heritage makes me feel safe. Unfortunately, Earlham lacks counselors when I desperately need one. Freshman year is academically easy. I major in English, a choice I rue as my interest in traditional literature wains. By my junior year I wish I'd chosen history. Too late to change. I graduate with an undistinguished record. Still, I profit from experimentation. I join the Concert Choir and travel with it to various East Coast venues. I try drama and play the lead in Rider to the Sea but fail to lose myself in the character. My successes stem from drawing on my India background. I demonstrate my version of Indian dance, with mixed results. Finding I do public speaking fairly well, I use missionary remarks about a small Ganesh worship spot to illustrate how many missionaries fail to respect Hindu culture. In that speech I declare to an

Earlham audience that I have lost my Christian faith. My parents, despite not understanding, continue to show me unconditional love.

After a miserable year as Secretary to the Harvard Press editors, I get a break. Yagi Irshick, well ahead of me at Kodai, successfully pleas my case at the University of Chicago. The Powers That Be accept me in the Indian and Far Eastern programs with modest scholarship help. I live at International House along the Midway that divides the University from the heavily Black Southside. A tall, good-looking young man, also at "Int" House, attends the same class on Laboratory Course on Historical Method. He is the first Southerner I've met. His excellent manners, sense of humor, social ease, and clear intellectual heft make him attractive. We date. He writes me a poem that leads me to think he can see into me. Scary. He takes me to the Chicago Symphony and to dinner. I'm unaccustomed to the attention. We share interest in lefty politics. It is 1960: the University, like Berkeley, is a hotbed of leftist activity. Charlie helps to write the New Left magazine. Chicago is an intellectually exciting school. I use my Kodai and Northfield comparison as the basis of an anthropology paper, showing how a Margaret Mead or her equivalent would analyze them. It earns me an A in the course.

By 1961 we are serious about one another. Though I get no engagement ring, we consider ourselves engaged. Charlie takes me home in Waynesville, North Carolina, amid the Blue Ridge mountains to meet his parents. Sadie looks askance. Do I deserve her precious only child? She is the engine of the family, running a high end ladies shop that serves local folks as well as the well-to-do Asheville elites and wealthy Floridians or other tourists. She consider it her duty to dress me from Hales, her store. She puts a notice in the newspaper about our engagement.

Political change in the county results in a Republican Draft Board. To pay back the long-entrenched Democrats, the Republicans draft Charlie away from the University of Chicago for the Vietnam War. Sadie gets him entry into the Navy Officers' Candidate School.

MARRIAGE AND ADJUSTMENTS: I stand for our wedding vows. My parents are on furlough in the States. Dad agrees to marry us according to our revision of the wedding vows. Mother makes my wedding dress from a lovely white and silver sari. We are wed on September 20, 1963, at the Walker Missionary Home the day after Charlie graduates among the top five of his Officer class at Newport, Rhode Island. No time for a honeymoon. We must be at the Supply Officers' School in Athens, GA, the next day. We are horrified to learn about Kennedy's assassination there. Those six months of grinding through almost impenetrable Navy manuals absorbs almost all Charlie's time. Lonely for me. It sets a pattern for the future. Though Charlie tries to fail out, the Navy doesn't believe his record at Athens. They assign him as a Supply Officer on an admiral's ship at Norfolk. The AGC-17 never gets closer to Vietnam than the Mediterranean—and that's okay with me.

While in the Navy, Charlie decides he wants to study ancient Greek maritime business. By now I teach history at Hampton Institute in Hampton, then at Old Dominion. I can support us while Charlie uses the year to read, plan for crash courses in Latin and Greek at the University of Virginia, and help me with lesson plans. At UVA he launches his plan. An Oxford don who teaches him Greek puts him in touch with Geoffrey de Ste. Croix, one of two world class ancient historians in Oxford and Cambridge. Charlie and I debate whether he should apply to Harvard or Oxford. We choose Oxford. Our doctor finds a malignant thyroid in examining Charlie. Surgery delays his move to Oxford. Meanwhile, I join Charlie in Charlottesville, teach English for one year in Albemarle Public High School, then work in the University of Virginia's Alderman Library's Manuscripts Division. Our daughter Laura is born in 1970. In 1971, I precede Charlie to Oxford while he recovers from surgery. Borrowing a car and baby necessities, I find us housing. I have become resourceful.

We sit in Geoffrey de Ste. Croix's home, sipping tea, chatting, and marveling at marvelous gardens surrounding the house. Geoffrey is a prince. He encourages Charlie, guides him through the more rigorous language training he needs and advises him about Greek merchant shipping. Charlie works from morning to night for six years at Oxford. Our new friends provide the social relief. I spend many waking hours with Laura, who flourishes. I also take advantage of Oxford lectures, music, and French at the Polytechnic. I even try to learn Arabic for a bit. When Charlie's mother (suffering from dementia) dies, he has to spend months in Waynesville for the funeral and settling her estate. A very lonely time for me in Oxford.

CAREER YEARS: We stand at Virginia Tech after Oxford, where Charlie helps to get a large federal grant to set up a cross-discipline liberal arts program. He's anchored in the History Department, but also team teaches in the liberal arts program. I teach English Composition part-time at Virginia Tech and find what teaching or library jobs I can wherever we go. While at Tech I create and run an After School program for gifted kids, drawing on the skills of various Tech professors and departments. The transition for Laura to American public schools is considerable, but the good friends she makes help.

We spend a wonderful year at the Harvard Center for Classics in Washington, DC.

We stand next at Catawba College in Salisbury, NC. Here Charlie is in charge of the liberal arts program. Salisbury is charming town of about 40,000, where we already have a dear Davidson College friend and made more. Charlie indulges his sense of mischief to their amusement. I work as a children's librarian at the public library for most of our time is Salisbury. I love it.

Now we stand in Charlotte where Billy Wireman, president of Queens College, lures Charlie to run its more thorough liberal arts program. Tiring of administration, Charlie stays on as one of Queen's most honored and beloved professors till retirement in 2012. I work in Queens' library and write grants for the Advancement Division, retiring in 2005. By then, I earn my library and archives graduate degree from the University of South Carolina. I choose to spend time with our delightful grandson and our daughter and son-in-law rather than try to work in archives.

So what have I learned as a TCK over the years? I still have difficulties with confidence, yet I know I have coped remarkably well, considering I do not know until I'm seventy-five that I have had Attention Deficit Disorder since birth. Focus has been a problem. Nonetheless, as my doctor says, I find ways to cope. Now that I am 81, that is harder. I have long thought I'm like Leo the Slow Learner. My social and emotional development was delayed longer than most. Being a TCK is partly responsible, yet I have discovered a resiliency in myself. I have earned my mantra: Survive, Adapt, Transform.

Pat Wood Remias
Third Culture Kid Brief Thoughts

There is no doubt in my mind that my life has been shaped by my Third Culture experience. Thank goodness for that nomenclature that captures who I am and that gives me an identity that I had never quite grasped during my early years of adjustment to my parents' homeland. Thus, I am only really home when I am with my fellow Third Culture kids. For me, home is not geographical, rather a mindset.

How was I shaped by my India experiences? Let me count the ways. First, there are the easy, obvious ones: the curry addiction (is that emotional or gastronomic?); love of bright, maybe gaudy, colors; bracelets on my arms; love of travel.

There are the more subtle ones: the feeling that I am a citizen of the world, not of a specific country; the delight in the diversity of peoples; the feeling of respect for other cultures and other people who are different from me; the acceptance of less-than-perfect cleanliness; the ability to adapt to what we have to work with rather than complaining about what we don't have.

Then there are also the negatives which can be summed up as: the impatience with provincialism, narrow-mindedness, excessive patriotism.

I got to choose my second husband when I was more mature and fully aware of who I am as a Third Culture Kid, and so I chose the child of immigrants who sees himself as a part of a much larger world than this country, who welcomes diversity of cultures and points of view, and who enters joyously into the reunions of these amazing Third Culture Kids from Kodai and India.

So, so you think I was shaped by my Third Culture Kid experience?

Gwen Hiebert SCHROTH
Third Culture Kids

I find there are advantages and disadvantages to being a Third Culture Kid.

Advantages:

We see things globally; for example, when quoted the price of an expensive medication or when I buy a car, I immediately wonder how the poor of places such as India or China would view such huge amounts that we hand over as a matter of course. When I view news of far-away lands, I can place myself in those spots with little effort, imagine the sites, the odors—both good or bad, hear the multitude of sounds and feel the press of crowds.

We are able to view situations and other matters from various standpoints. I can appreciate that folks from other countries do not see things the way we do, rather viewing matters through a different lens, and I enjoy imagining what they see through that lens, especially if they are from the Indian culture.

We can enjoy books written by native authors and movies taking place in other lands, for example: *The Marigold Hotel* and books by Jhumpa Lahiri and others.

Best of all, we have an endless supply of amazing stories to tell to our children and grandchildren!

Disadvantages:

When my family returned to the U.S. and settled in a small Mennonite community in Kansas, I felt totally out of place, out of style, and so different that the gulf between me and my peers and the community was never fully breached. Neither my classmates nor teachers had an interest in finding out where I came from, what it was like in India, or where I went to school. Most simply ignored my sisters and me. That sense of being different has been difficult to shed. Maybe it never can be, as borne out by the fact that I do not feel that same difference when I am with my family, Kodai classmates, and friends from India. As with siblings, we do not have to explain much as so much is already understood. We have a special bond, hence the term, Third Culture Kids.

Conrad Heins
Encountering America as a 3rd Culture Kid

When I left Kodai to start college, I wasn't so much a third culture person as a boarding-school-in-the-remote-hills-of-South-India culture person. I was homesick not just for Kodai School, but for Kodai Lake, and the town itself as well as the scenic surrounding hills. When I came to America it was with the feeling that I was very much an American. I quickly came to realize that I was a stranger in a strange land and I wasn't ready for what I encountered. Americans were wealthy, owning lots and lots of stuff. They came from families that owned their own homes. Money was important to them. It was a car culture; all of my classmates owned their own cars, and you couldn't go anywhere without one. At the same time, I found it difficult to be anyplace where there weren't roads and cars and people. My biggest pleasure was immersing myself in coursework while listening to classical music in the record room of the library. My college was near Richmond, Virginia, only an hour from Washington. I visited the capital a number of times during my first year of college. I visited the Indian Embassy whenever I could. Folks there were very friendly; they always invited me to have lunch with them at the embassy cafeteria—Indian food, of course!

It took me about three years to adapt and feel comfortable in America. And this was the America of Eisenhower. It would have been a great deal more difficult in Trump's America. Much of this adaptation was a result of my maturing—there's a lot of growing that occurs between 16 and 19. By this time, however, I understood myself to be an American but also one who was very much a part of another, international, culture.

Ruth Vassar and Stanley Burgess
Creating a New Normal (2018)

Peace I leave with you, my peace I give unto you:
Not as the world giveth, give I unto you
Let not your heart be troubled, neither let it be afraid.
My peace I leave with you. John 14:27, Holy Bible

Children of the Third Culture birth have a different normal. Intimately they inherit the DNA, of their birth parents; however, their emerging folkways are molded by the sociocultural customs of a distant land and people. Thus a new and novel cultural phenomenal has been formed. Children of this Third Culture create their novel norms that are distinct from that of their parents, their novel associates and in the future for their children.

Is there a difference in the home-making of families where both parents are Children of the Third Culture? Stanley Burgess and Ruth Vassar Burgess carry such credentials. He was born in Nagercoil, south India in 1937 at the Salvation Army Hospital to Bernice and John Burgess. Ruth was born in Poona, west India in 1939 at St. Margaret's hospital to Estelle and Theodore Vassar. Both children attended an American based curriculum school high in the south Indian Palni hills. Ruth was in boarding 5 ½ years, whereas Stanley was a day student at Highclerc boarding school. The two main troublesome events during that childhood time were the splitting of British India and World War II. Both families returned to the United States on furloughs to the midwest. Jumping ahead, on February 26, 1960, Ruth and Stanley were married in Abilene, Texas and moved to Springfield, Missouri.

The following questions are often asked of their five children. (John Bradley—business man, Stanley Matthew—attorney, Scott Vassar—medical physician, Heidi Elizabeth—homemaker, and Justin David—Presbyterian minister) First, "In what ways was your childhood rearing similar or different than that of your peers?" Second, "Did having two parents who were Children of the Third Culture have an impact on your enculturation?" Our responses included:

Personal Expectations: ("Self Rule = Rule Over Self." (Mahatma Gandhi))

We were expected to be self-sufficient; we grew up quicker

Be trustworthy Be responsible Be loving

Life Expectations: ("A spirit filled with truth must needs direct its actions to the final goal." (Mahatma Gandhi))

We were citizens of the world

Sense of social service was expected, you can make a difference.

Cultural Open Doors: ("What we have done will not be lost to all eternity. Everything ripens at its time and becomes fruit at its hour." (Vivyavadana))

Free to visit and settle in other countries

Be friends to people from other countries

Invite others to stay at our farm while going to college

Indian artwork was celebrated in most every room

Cook and share Indian food

We wore Indian clothes for special occasions

Multiple Perspectives: ("Let us overcome the angry man with gentleness; the evil man with goodness; the miser with generosity; the liar with truth." (Maha Bharatam))

Search for realities

Don't be one sided

Question in order to see if there are multiple perspectives

Parents' Approach: ("The positive always defeats the negative, courage overcomes fear, patience overcomes anger and irritability, love overcomes hatred." (Swami Sivananda Sarasvati))

Applauded their children's achievements

Did not want children to be limited

Aware of social systems (having witnessed the caste system)

Important who were our friends

Sought sabbaticals and other types of educational leaves

Felt betrayed when children were less than global citizens

Often-used retreads or used vehicles

Known as travelers, not as vacation people

We were physically adventuresome

Children were expected to be culture bearers

Remember your grandparent's lives and homes

Leobuchhandlung, 1965. Springs of Indian Wisdom. New York: Herdes Book Center.

Margaret Essebaggers Dopirak ('54)[43]

During the process of this writing I was to learn a great deal about my parents and their work, my siblings, and about our family life and travels. But who and what I learned most about was myself, how spending my growing up years in India left me unprepared for life in the United States. I was now not just an MK (missionary kid), but a TCK (third-culture kid)! Although I considered myself to be a well-adjusted and normal teenager in India, I found that when I arrived in the United States at the age of 16, I was out of step with and ignorant of the ways and culture of my teenage

---

43 Excerpt from an article I wrote for 7 Roads, (a Kodai Alumnae magazine) to promote my book, published Feb. 2016.

American counterparts. The somewhat sheltered life I had in India left me vulnerable to feelings of inadequacy both in terms of self-confidence and self-esteem when making the adjustment to the American scene. Eventually, I overcame these feelings, but the lack of self-confidence, as well as my naiveté, impacted many decisions I have made as an adult.

I discovered I am not alone in finding it a difficult transition to make. My siblings, as well as many of our Kodai classmates from that era, have similar experiences. At that time, Kodai School did not offer the students resources for learning about contemporary American culture—the music, mores, fashion, lingo, etc. And, in my case, neither did my parents—probably because they were ignorant of these things themselves. We kids learned what we could from students who had been in the States recently, or from relatives' letters which imparted newsworthy information to be passed along.

Of course, we did not have the technology which today's students have: cell phones and computers and the internet—instant information and communication, photographs and videos. With accessibility to all this information, today's students making transitions to other cultures are, no doubt, able to learn a great deal about other cultures and countries. Despite, or perhaps because of increasing globalization, TCKs will continue to be a subset in the world's population. My experiences as both an MK and a TCK are expressed in my book *Missionary Kid: Born in India, Bound for America.*

Missionary Kid: Born in India, Bound for America, published Feb. 2016. website: www.missionarykidfromindia.com, or email me: mkfromindia.net.

Available in paperback and e-book versions from amazon.com, amazon.eu, barnes&noble.com, and for all Apple devices from the iBook app.

Joyce Holleman
Being a Third Culture Kid

When I arrived in Kodai, I was out-of-boarding, as my brothers weren't old enough to go into boarding. I was in 6th grade and quite mature, wearing hose and heels for Sunday service. My classmates were wearing bobby socks and flat shoes and were still playing jacks. I knew how to play jacks and I intended to fit in, so I too dressed down for church and joined in the jacks games. I was quite boy conscious, and all the 6th grade boys were shorter than I was and had formed a club focused on one of the girls—not very fertile ground to look for a boyfriend! I made up for the lack in later grades, having a string of boyfriends, most of whom didn't know I was attracted to them. In my Sophomore year I chased Ralph Korteling until he caught me and he was my boyfriend until he graduated a year ahead of me. A sad time.

Being used to getting good grades in all subjects, I was floored to find I didn't understand the arithmetic the 6th grade was doing. The others were all comfortable with all the equivalents and I was barely into fractions. If someone had spent some time with me and explained the concepts, I'm sure I'd have caught on rather quickly. But as it was I was swimming upstream and losing ground daily. Very frustrating.

The next round of math was Algebra I, at which I did not do well, though when Geometry came along, I excelled once again. I missed Algebra II, and took an hour of piano instead.

Meanwhile, I was in boarding, first at Bruton with Joanne, Gwen and Betty Hiebert, Margaret Smith and some other girls, and, after the Hieberts went home on furlough, I boarded in Boyer Hall. There I had quite a few roommates, most notably Elaine Shuster and Ruth Voss.

I was very involved with music, especially vocal, being in chorus, choir, the girls sextet and occasionally soloing. In 8th grade, Mario assigned me the "He Was Despised" solo in the Easter portion of *The Messiah*. I was so scared I was shaking throughout.

Kodai School's music department gave me a wonderful exposure to classical sacred music. My prior experience had been with gospel music, which, while grand in its own way, wasn't the classics. I didn't understand the Latin I was singing but the music was exquisite and I gloried in it.

My dad was chosen baccalaureate speaker for our class of 1955, and I was a commencement speaker and played a piano solo at graduation.

We left Kodai's hilltop right after graduation and went home to Pune, to prepare for returning to the States. Nancy Spears went home with us as her parents weren't due for a furlough. We left India on the *S.S.Victoria*, and found there were 27 young people on board in tourist class. Much fun was had by all. We disembarked in Naples and visited friends there, then went on to briefly tour Europe: Venice, Geneva, Paris and London. We took the *S.S. Ile de France* from Southampton to New York, and we, and Gerald Beuker, were the only young people on board. Very boring. Standing at the railing of the ship as we pulled into New York, I was struck by the many colors of the cars that sped by on the streets.

In New York, Nancy went with her family and we continued on our way to Oklahoma. I came down with a bad case of tonsillitis and we had to stay in New York a few days for me to become well enough to travel. It was extremely hot and I was miserable. My brothers got to while away the time by going to professional baseball games so they were quite happy with the layover. Finally, we were on our way to Oklahoma. My folks' home church had provided us a car to drive from New York to Tulsa. To my amazement Dad drove it on the freeways and streets of the cities just like he hadn't been driving on the "wrong" (in India, cars drive on. The left) side of the road for the past six years. Remarkable man!

My grandmother rented us a house to move into. Unfortunately, it was on a main highway through Tulsa, and the noise made it difficult for my parents to sleep. We kids were busy exclaiming over the goodness of milk, the wonderful ice cream available and all the delicious food in general.

Come Sunday, I had to borrow a dress from my cousin, as mine were too out of style, and I was always determined to fit in. Soon my girlfriend from childhood took me shopping and I was very embarrassed since I didn't know what size I wore in anything: shoes, hose, underwear, dresses, socks, slips, nothing. So much for fitting in. The dress she bought for me was sleeveless, and I knew my dad would not be happy. But since my friend from church bought it for me, there wasn't much he could say. I was torn between wanting to be up to date and pleasing my parents, but ever the rebel, I chose to be up to date and feel guilty.

I took my entrance exams for the University of Tulsa, and was promptly offered a scholarship for half tuition. I accepted and was soon enrolled as a music major. That was a mistake. The competition was far more advanced than I in both talent and skill, so by the second year I switched to being an English major, which Kodai had prepared me well for. I continued to get scholarships and major in English until I graduated in 1959. My musical involvement was as a member of the University's Concert Choir, which performed in Tulsa and went on a tour to New York each year during Christmas break. The choir was my home at the University and gave me a place to belong.

When my family returned to India in 1958, I lived with my grandmother. This was not too successful, as she and I had different agendas for me. When I graduated, I went to Houston to a job my great uncle had arranged for me. After that summer I returned to Tulsa to teach High School English. Thirty-six years later I resigned from teaching high school after what was a successful career. Despite all this I still feel like a TCK with one foot in two worlds. When I returned to India in 1976, the minute the door of the plane opened and the smells of India came pouring in, I knew I was home.

Bobbie Voss Chase
Being a Third Culture Kid

The Voss Family: Ruth Voss Harris, Alberta (Bobbie) Voss Chase, David Voss, and Esther Voss Rollen.

Ruth and I arrived at Kodai for the first time on the day of Queen Elizabeth II's coronation. Our idea of unobtrusively joining a new school was immediately frustrated. When we drove up to the flag green that day, the entire student body was gathered on the porch, listening to the BBC radio report of the coronation. So much for our plan of keeping a low profile!

Fitting in to life in Kodai as high school students wasn't all that difficult. It probably helped that growing up we had moved a lot and had changed schools almost every year. However, I do remember envying the experienced Kodai kids who seemed so secure in knowing what to do and where to go, and even some knew how to speak Tamil. Also, since our parents were working in the Arabian Mission, we were a bit different (along with the other missionary kids from the Persian Gulf area) from the kids who had lived in India most of their lives. For one thing, we were usually "in boarding" during the May holiday while most of the students were able to spend the time with their families who had come up to Kodai for the May season. That made for a few interesting adventures.

I never thought that we were very different from other college bound students, until we returned to the States. I have great admiration for Ruth who was two years ahead of me and who had made a happy and successful adjustment to being at Hope College in Holland, Michigan. She was a good student and was very involved in music, student government, drama, was in a sorority, and had even found summer jobs—all on her own. Coming in, I remember feeling very estranged from the girls in our freshman dorm—they were really into matching sweater sets and white buck shoes—and I had been assigned (as part of a missionary scholarship) to the job of cleaning the dorm bathroom. Coming from India, that was not an easy thing for me to do, and I realized for the first time the effect the caste system of India had had on me. Also, although people were kind, the atmosphere of the college felt very tight to me—in my opinion there didn't seem to be much diversity in thought or people. The next year our family moved to California and Ruth and I went to Whittier College which with its Quaker background and Southern California attitudes felt more comfortable to me.

Going to Kodai was a unique and happy experience. The close friends, the excellent teachers, the opportunities for doing music, hiking, camping, traveling, being introduced to Indian culture, as well as to British India history and its aftermath, meeting so many people who had dedicated their lives to helping others, all have influenced us profoundly. It seemed excellent to us that our younger brother, Dave, went to Kodai as a fourth and fifth grader, and that our sister Esther was able to be in Kodai as a high school senior along with Olivia Chase (my sister-in-law) when the Voss and Chase families were working in Jeddah, Saudi Arabia in the late 1960s. When my husband Ben and I were heading to Dhahran in 1982, we were happy that our son Andrew was able to spend the last four months of his high school years in Kodai so that he too could share in the special quality that Kodai School has brought to all of us.

Loey Hiebert KNAPP
Third Culture Kid for Life

Third Culture Kid? Absolutely! And wouldn't have it otherwise.

After my father died and my older siblings were off on their own, my mother and I returned to Kodai for my junior and senior high school years. I say returned as I was born in Van Allen and Kodai was integral to my family's story—all eight of us went to school there for some period of time. While I went to school, Mom worked for the school as the principal's secretary and, being an employee, she was allotted a travel allowance to use over the long winter vacation. Being an intrepid explorer, Mom used the allowance and the free months to introduce me to as much of India as possible—from Cape Comorin to Kashmir and Calcutta to Mumbai. Of course, we traveled 3rd class on the train, which meant long hours at various stations, often in the middle of the night. If lucky, we found a chaise lounge in the women's waiting room to settle into, but more than likely we just settled on the platform like everyone else—luggage for a pillow and a sheet over our heads. I can still hear the hawker cries selling "beedis,[44] cigarettes, chai, coffee ..." (you have to add the singsong intonation and chee-chee accent yourself). Recently I was stuck in the Denver airport overnight due to a cancelled flight—so what did I do? Pretended I was back with Mom on a train platform—positioned my carry-on luggage for a pillow and covered my head with a scarf and, guess what, felt quite at home remembering those trips with her. Though, this time there were no beedis.

That is a small example of how the two worlds, India and the U.S., overlap for me ... one transitions into the other, not always with ease, but always with interest. I

---

[44] A beedi is an inexpensive Indian cigarette, basically just a rolled up tobacco leaf.

have a strong affinity for India and have continued my association with the land and people until now and always will. After graduation from Kodai, I went to a small Quaker school in Indiana, Earlham College, which was about as different from India as one could get. I found it bland, flat, and homogenous where India had been colorful, adventurous, and diverse. I worked hard to find a way back to India and found it through the University of Wisconsin junior year abroad program—I spent the year in Benares (now Varanasi) where I worked as an apprentice weaver in a factory during the day and studied history and art in the evenings. I also met my first husband, Rajan, and returned to the States with a ring on my finger. The marriage didn't work out but the two children, Nikhil and Priya, are fabulous. Nikhil married a Caucasian and has one biological daughter and one adopted from Madhya Pradesh. Priya married an Indian American and has a son and daughter. So, my small family ranges from all Caucasian, ¼ Caucasian; 3/4 Indian, ½ Caucasian, ½ Indian; 3/4 Caucasian, ¼ Indian; and all Indian. What fun!

I married again, to Gary, and returned to work at Kodai for four years after a long career at IBM. That return to the mountains and the adventure of India brought back my love of life—and it also started a new career in textiles. I now live in Montana but return to India for three months each year to explore villages where the textile arts are still thriving. I love meeting the textile artisans and working with them to figure out what would sell in the U.S. I am now working with a silk yarn factory in Bangalore to design silk and wool yarns—let's see where that will go.

A important aspect of India for me is the Ayurvedic medical system. I have had chronic fatigue, cancer, hip replacements, and other issues—and, while the surgeries were successful, the aftermath of the drugs was debilitating. I began experimenting with the Ayurvedic approach to health and am now an impassioned advocate—I spend three weeks a year at a center in Goa, India and feel it has changed my life with the after effects of the drugs a distant memory.

I love the duality of being a third culture kid. During the day in Montana I meet local friends while at night I have Whatsapp conversations with Pasha, Arjun, Aftab and others. For nine months of the year I eat my oatmeal and stir fry and then for three months I get to have dosai and biriyani, but always chai first thing in the morning! What could be better?

Paul Wiebe
Along the second street section of Coralville on the way to Emmaeus

> "And it came to pass, that; while they communed together and reasoned', Jesus himself drew near; and went with them" (Luke 24:15, KJV).
>
> "My true being is unborn and changeless. I am the Lord who dwells in every creature. Through the power of my own appearance, I manifest myself in finite forms" (Bhagavad Gita 4:5-5).

Walking into the early morning sun along Second Street in Coralville, minding my own business, thinking about thinking about something I was thinking about thinking about, thinking rather about happy and less than happy things and about breaking bread together with others and about what Donna Beth might be thinking about for supper, thinking mostly about how wretchedly things can turn when "empty vessels" come to take over control in the centers of power and about getting through the exercises I do when I walk to keep these as well as those parts in what at least resembles working order.

I, in my sandals and khaki trousers and an old white t-shirt and with my bald head and scruffy white beard doing what I still can to walk like a younger man, at least like a younger old man, by now knowing, indeed knowing full well through experience that even an awkward kick at a dandelion might not turn out well.

Past the entrance into our HyVee, then past the car wash, looking both ways.

When to my left in front of the Casey's at the next corner, and coming along the sidewalk to the same intersection I would reach at exactly the same time I saw a young African American no more than twenty-two-or-three with dreadlocks and a pendant around his neck and wearing a black shirt hanging loose over a black t-shirt then down over baggy jeans, he moving along with the kind of grace and resilience in his step that I could by now only at best remember.

Two very different worlds on a collision course ... and I thought about suddenly "remembering" something, something that would cause me to slow down or turn around or perhaps look into my pocket in a pause.

Thought about maybe turning left at the intersection rather than heading straight along, as I had intended, whatever to keep a little air between him and me.

All the time knowing that whatever might or might not have entered his mind along similar lines as our two worlds came together, that he could have left me in his rear view mirror in not more than a stride or two, had he so chosen.

But neither did he nor I choose as we might have.

To the result there we were in a moment, I "yesterday and today" and he "today and tomorrow," the two of us from our very different worlds, walking along side by side, first in a sideways and quizzical acknowledgement of each other, then in an exchange of pleasantries, then in genuine and most meaningful conversation.

Along the Second Street stretch on the way to Emmaeus that fine morning in the joy of the Lord.

Union Church.

The main intersection, called “Seven Roads” in Kodaikanal with the gate to Kodai School in the center.

The Budge

CHAPTER 11

More Kodai tales

The following are more stories from the Kodai classes of 1955 and 56.

Molly Schmitthenner LESNICK
Early Memories of Auntie Powell

Auntie Powell was my first grade teacher. She had also been my 3 brothers' first grade teacher 10, 12 and 14 years before me. We all loved her. Alice Graham and I and Lowey were the only girls I remember in first grade. There were lots of boys. One day, under her direction, we put on a play for our parents about the Brocken-spectre. I just remember us carrying umbrellas and looking over something that said "Cliff" and waving to our shadows in the rainbow. There was a cute song she had made up too. Half of us were the kids and half the rainbow Brocken-specters[45] so the kids waved and jumped and the Brocken-specters imitated them. It was fun and we got a lot of applause.

One day at school, just after lunch, Auntie Powell said she had a special surprise for us—imported candy, and she asked us to form a line to the left side of her desk. There was a lot of jostling and shoving and at last Auntie Powell got angry and chided us for shoving. She told us just to stop and then called out, "Lois, you are the only person in this room not pushing or shoving to get in line; why? " Lowey looked down at the floor and said, "I was just waiting." Aunty Powell seized on this and said something like this: "You see, Lois is not shoving or pushing. She is being polite and waiting her turn. Lois, come to the head of the line." And then she said,

---

[45] A magnified shadow of a person cast against a cloud opposite from the sun.

"as it says in the Bible: 'he who is first among you shall be last, and the last shall be first!'" After that whenever we lined up, we tried to be in last place.

Another day, Alice and I were arguing about something and called each other bad names, like "stupid" and were sarcastic with each other. Auntie Powell said, "young ladies, stop that and be quiet. You are staying after school!" After the dismissal bell rang, we stayed in our seats. Auntie Powell made us each go up to a blackboard and write 100 times: I will not fight. I will not fight. I will not fight. I suppose Auntie Powell sent a message home with other kids going our way, because our mothers came to pick us up, and we were in disgrace! We never argued in class again.

My last memory of first grade happened like this. I was walking home from school with the Zigler girls and I confessed to Lucy, Carol's oldest sister, that we were having a spelling test the next morning and I was very worried that I would forget how to spell some words. "Oh, that's easy," said Lucy. "Tomorrow when you wake up, look at your spelling words and write down the three or four words hard words on the back of your left hand with a pen. That way when she calls out the spelling word, if you don't remember how to spell it, just look at the back of your hand and write down the word on your paper." It sounded easy enough, so the next morning before school, I did just that...wrote down the words in pen. When it was time for the test we got out our paper, and Auntie Powell called out the words one by one, giving us time to write them down. I kept my left hand up on the desk and must have looked at my words there at least four times. Suddenly, Auntie Powell was hovering over me. "Molly what are you doing?" I responded that I was copying the hard words from the back of my hand when she called them out. Auntie Powell said, "you are cheating!" Now until that moment, I thought this was an acceptable thing to do since Lucy, an older kid, had told me about it. I had no concept either of test taking or "cheating." So I was very astonished. I think Auntie Powell must have sensed this, because I have absolutely no memory of what she said or did after that.

Perhaps she gave me an F on the test. From that moment on I never cheated again, but I remember being mad at Lucy for getting me in trouble. I didn't trust big kids as much after that.

Moving ahead about 60 years, my husband, Alan, and I discovered that Gerhard Tauscher was living in Deland, Florida. We began calling him on the phone and planning a get together. Alan and I always take the Auto Train when we travel North, so we arranged to meet Gerhard for lunch at a Cracker Barrel restaurant in Sanford. We had a great reunion, talking over old times at Kodai. Gerhard told us that all the German Lutheran kids were in internment camps with their parents in

India during the War. When WWII ended, the children were sent up to Kodai to attend school. All the grade school kids were assigned to Auntie Powell. Practically none of them knew any English. Gerhard said that Auntie Powell worked hard to remedy that: she got pictures of trees, boys, girls, water, hills, campus buildings and made books for all the children with English words for all the pictures. Then she would show them big pictures and read the words aloud and they would copy her aloud. Pretty soon they began to learn English. A lot of the older Kodai students also helped Auntie Powell in this endeavor. He especially remembered how helpful Shirley Wood was to them. By the second year that they were there, they were already talking pretty well in English, thanks to total emersion and to the hard work of Auntie Powell. They all loved and respected her totally.

Conrad Heins
Kodai People I Remember: Whitey

I remember Mrs. Wightman—Whitey—but in ways that are different from the ways I remember my other teachers, like Mr. Musil or Mario. Although I guess you could call her one of my teachers, it didn't have anything to do with school.

I best remember Whitey as an indefatigable hiker. She was our chaperone not just for the shorter hikes—the 10 mile round, Berijam, climbing Perumal. She also was one of the trip leaders to Rat Tail Falls and, the one that brings back the most memories, the hike to Palni, where the last 7 of the 30 mile-trip were on the plains in the hot sun. Whitey kept trudging along, encouraging those of us who were starting to droop. That was the hike where I ended up so exhausted that I fell asleep on the floor of the Palni train station and then on the floor of the 3rd class carriage that took us to Kodai Road.

I remember her as a very good Bridge player. There were wonderful Sunday afternoons when Whitey would invite Ann Gibbs, Harry Smith and me over for a few hours of Contract Bridge. Whitey was gracious, funny and played with a skill that made you want her as a partner and not an opponent.

I also remember encountering Whitey's wrath. I think it was for the Senior trip to Cochin, when I needed to get money for the trip but had forgotten to do it during the school week. So on the Saturday before the trip, I came rather sheepishly to Whitey, who was the school bursar, asking for 30 rupees, which in those days, at least for me, was a fair amount of money. Harry Smith was with me for the same reason; there were days when he was almost as absent-minded as I was. Well, Whitey was furious with both of us, and let us know her feelings in no uncertain terms. She did get us the money, however, which was received by two grateful, very humbled students.

Pat Wood Remias
Jeezubai

It's hard to explain. The conditions have to be just right. It has to be January cold. The shower water has to be comfortingly warm and welcoming, with steam pouring out when the warm water hits the cold air.

We second and third grade girls are led down from Upper Bowyer into the Lower Bowyer shower room where Jeezubai awaits us in her sari covered with a huge rubber apron. I just remember feelings, not events. It is so comforting and so warm as she helps us get soaped up and then rinsed off, going from one girl to the next. I feel so cared for and I never want to leave that shower.

Now I'm 77. Under the exact right conditions, I can hardly force myself to get out of the shower. Where is Jeezubai when I need her?

Bev England Williams
Kodai People

May 26,1948, 'Euretta," Kodai

Dear Daddy (still in Burma),

On Sunday I met a girl, Alice Graham, who lives down at the bottom of the hill from us. Her parents are missionaries in Poona. Yesterday, Jeanette (my younger sister) and I went to a tea party at her house and met some of the other girls my age.

School starts on Monday. I will do the last half of 6th grade, because they are in the second part of the year. There are beautiful flowers here. I'm going to see Alice now so I'll stop for this time.

Much love, Beverly

(No doubt other Kodai kids landed in a new school in a new country in the middle of a school year. If you had an Alice to shepherd you, you were fortunate!)

Another welcomer was Ann Gibbs, especially during the long Christmas holiday. The Englands stayed in Kodai and our dad came over from Burma. I believe that Ann and her family attended the Anglican chapel on the other side of town from the school. Our dad, who came from generations of country Baptists, was both honored and nervous when asked to help with the Sunday vesper service. As ordered, we were dressed in our best and on our good behavior. But Florence, only three, looked back as the rector and Dad were beginning the processional, and called out in horror, "Mom! Daddy has on his bathrobe!"

Several of you, who attended Kodai much longer than I did, recall Agnes Liddle as an exceptional teacher. Do you remember the oral book reports? They were really book reviews; we learned well.

After doing part of 7th grade, we left Kodai to return to the USA as a family. I attended 8th grade in the small town of Mars Hill, in Western North Carolina and returned there, after high school in New Jersey, for the first two years of college. At freshman orientation, I met several of my 8th grade classmates who greeted me with, "Oh, Bev, we remember you and your three-day book report!" What?

Evidently Mr. Higgins had called on me before I had had a chance to hear the standard one-minute, or 30-second, report. I began as Miss Liddle had taught us when he interrupted, "You may continue tomorrow." Next day, describing the characters, "You may continue tomorrow." Who knew what a splash a Kodai Kid with a British accent would make in a rural North Carolina school?

Owen Thomas
The Boatman

There are memories of numerous people and activities associated with Kodai, many of which could be described as "unforgettable," proof of which is that I can still remember them! This recollection is, however, more in line with miscellaneous than unforgettable although it crosses both topics.

One local Kodai resident that many people probably never noticed or had occasion to meet was the boatman who rowed the ferry between Tapps Landing and the Boathouse. As my folks lived in Shelton or Sunnyside on the far side of the lake when they were in Kodai, I frequently used the ferry and got to know this man.

As I recall, he was about five feet tall, thin, very dark, appeared to be old (but I doubt that he was) and quite gregarious in Tamil with his normal customers. After several trips, I asked him—mainly in sign language—if I could try to row the boat for him. I think he was in disbelief when it dawned on him what I was trying to say. However, he agreed and we changed seats.

Now this ferry boat was not like the normal rowboats of the Boat Club. This was an old, heavy, high-sided boat with benches on the sides and stern. The oarlocks were two pieces of wood and the oars were not very long. Being rather small myself at the time, it was not easy to get the oars into the water or to stay in the oarlocks. It was necessary to have your arms above your shoulders, which made rowing rather difficult and jerky. The first time I attempted to propel the boat was something of a disaster for me but a very humorous occasion for the boatman. But he was tolerant of my poor performance and allowed me to continue and further develop my skills in using short, choppy strokes rather than smooth, long strokes typical of a normal rowboat.

After that initial trial he would allow me to row anytime I appeared. Of course, the normal customers thought it was quite a show and rather strange for a little white boy to want to row the boat!

I wish I could say that I got to know this man in more ways than just as a boatman, however, his good humor, his hard work and our friendly association primarily through hand gestures has made him a memorable character for me.

Ed Tegenfeldt
Unforgettable "Characters" in Kodai

Here are very brief stories of two Indian men who many of us in the classes of '55 and '56 had some encounters with or at least knowledge of during our student days in Kodai.

During those wonderful years many of us had some contact with these two men who had establishments across the road from the KMU.

Mr. Bandy, who I believe was originally from Kashmir, owned the Bandy Brothers store where he sold varieties of Kashmiri handicrafts such as rugs, brass and paper mache objects and exquisite wood carvings. He stayed on with his family in Kodaikanal even after Bandy Bros closed.

But as a Kashmiri Muslim family I believe they felt quite isolated.

When we returned to Kodai as adults as part of the school community as well as working at Van Allen Hospital I had occasion to visit with Mr. Bandy and later take care of him with his congestive heart failure. One night he was admitted to the hospital and obviously was not going to survive but was still fairly alert—at least to the point where he understood that his end was near. But contrary to what most Indian families desired when near death, he did not want to be taken home and furthermore although his wife was there, he wanted me to stay by his side, which of course I agreed to. A short time later he died with my arm cradling his head.

Right next to Bandy Bros was the Cure House ("The Cure House is your Care House") where among various kinds of "remedies" we could also purchase ice cream. This was owned by Dr. Ghose, who sometime after we all graduated closed the Cure House and purchased land out beyond the Convent and just above Vilpatti where he had a small farm and also started a bakery. But his main work included a blending of alternative medicine with spiritual healing. He and I had many interesting conversations after I returned as an adult. His son, Prasanna Ghose, was a student at Kodai School and graduated in 1980. Prasanna still runs the bakery and has a store in the shopping complex on the way to the "budge" selling bread and pastries as well as ice cream.

Jo Sorensen
My Unforgettable Person: Miss Liddle

I loved having Miss Liddle for a teacher. She expected a lot of hard work from us but then commended us when we did well. I remember putting a lot of effort into my assignments since she was an exacting teacher.

There was one time, though, that I got by without her noticing—a least I think so. I was sitting in the back of the classroom, absent-mindedly getting my books out, when I heard her announce the student who would be the first to give his book report that day. Book report? I'd forgotten all about that. Frantically, I tried to think of a book I'd read recently but couldn't think of one. So my mind went into full gear: I'd make one up. By the time it got around to my turn, I had a title, an author, a storyline. I got up, gave the report, and sat down. Then a double miracle happened. No rebuke or question from Miss Liddle. No sudden death from the wrath of God.

Sitting in the back of the room does have its advantages.

Beth Thoms Dickason (with a little editing by Lowey Thoms Dickason)
The Taurinia trip to Italy, when Maisie Korteling fell overboard

In 1948, right after our daughter, Nancy, graduated from Kodai School, it was not easy to get ship's passage from India to the United States. There was a backup of people wanting sailings after World War II. There was no air service yet. Some families had to split up, sailing on different ships, so our family was happy to hear, from Jack DeValois, that he secured passage for their family and ours and several of Nancy's classmates, on an Italian freighter, the *SS Taurinia*.[46]

There were fifteen in our party: Jack and Bernadine DeValois; Margaret and Francine; Madame and Mr. Caspari; Wells, Beth, Nancy, Peter, Norman and Lois

---

[46] Also knows as the *MV Taurinia* (MV means merchant vessel). "SS" is an acronym for steamship.

Thoms; Maisie Korteling; Hal Closson; and Bob Carman. About 10 other passengers were on the list. Among them was an English couple with a little girl about Lois' age. There was a gentleman hairdresser from Singapore, and an Italian adventurer and entrepreneur who owned part of the *SS Taurinia's* cargo, which consisted of animals for the Milan Zoo, which was being opened again after its closure during WWII. Of our party, five were just graduated from high school at Kodai and were enrolled in colleges in the U.S., for the coming fall. They were Margaret, Maisie, Nancy, Hal and Bob.

We were told the *SS Taurinia* would sail from Madras for Naples, Italy, some time during the first week in May. So we took rooms at the Madras YWCA and awaited boarding advice. Bob and Hal discovered a place near the YWCA where they could get ice cream sodas. There were also the unavoidable hawkers who peddled their wares from house to house. Several came to the YWCA, sat cross-legged on the spacious, plant-lined verandah and spread out their vessels in brass and silver, ivory elephants, embroidery, silk tie-dyed scarves, jewelry, etc. One produced a stuffed mongoose encircled by a stuffed cobra, its head in the mouth of the mongoose. Bob picked it up to look and the hawker said, "Very nice piece that for only 100 rupees." "100 rupees!" said Bob, "I'll give you five." He did not want the mongoose and thought his offer safe. "No, sahib, that's too little, 50 rupees." As we came and went that day, the hawker kept coming down. Finally, at the end of the day, with a resigned tilt of his head and wave of his hands, he said, "Take it!" Bob was now stuck with his "bargain." He put the mongoose in a bureau drawer till we packed up to leave and then the tail, stiff with wire, got caught so that he couldn't open the drawer. Concerted effort finally extricated the prize. Later at the customs in New York, Bob carried his mongoose under his arm since it did not fit in his suitcase, but the agent let it through. Eventually, the wire poked through releasing saw dust and Bob had to toss it.

We boarded the *SS Taurinia*, after several days of waiting, and set sail for Colombo, Ceylon. A British P&O liner with the Australian water polo team aboard put into the Colombo harbor the same time we did. During the two days our ship was delayed in Colombo (because we arrived at the outset of the Festival of the Tooth, when nobody worked) our party took a trip to Kandy. There they saw the great Buddhist "Shrine of the Tooth," as well as rubber and tea processing factories and beautiful views. Norman and I didn't go as Norm came down with mumps. He and I went instead to a country club and, from a safe distance, watched the water polo team practice. Years later, Richard Pengelley, Janet Storm (Kodai class '48) Pengelley's son, captained that Australian team in the Olympics.

After we resumed passage and were a couple of days into the Indian Ocean we were all at dinner, at the dessert course. There was an air of anticipation and all eyes turned toward the Chief Steward as he approached carrying a cake. He placed it in front of me. I knew then the kids had remembered my birthday. It remained for me to cut the cake. At the pressure of the knife a liquid oozed out. The cake was doused with brandy—an Italian nicety we did not fully appreciate! Though one wished to be polite, when the next of several on-board birthdays was imminent, we tactfully requested that a pie be provided instead of a cake. Little did we appreciate that American-style pies did not exist in Italy. The next time, the chef proudly produced a heavy, rich almond torte, soaked in brandy. We gave up; however, the spaghetti on the *SS Taurinia* was a delicious daily entree and a favorite of the young people.

Our next episode could have been a tragedy but turned into a miracle. Already running behind schedule, our captain was steering a more southerly course than usual across the Indian Ocean to avoid the path of the oncoming westerly monsoon. Eventually, however, to reach the entrance to the Red Sea we had to veer sharply northwest up the African coast and were caught in a rough sea. Many of the passengers were in their bunks, seasick. A few of us were on deck, sitting on the lee side of the ship. The waves were huge and coming at us broadside. The ship was rolling and we were holding onto the cabin wall railing to keep our deck chairs from sliding. Someone started singing, "My Bonnie lies over the ocean," and we all joined in.

Maisie, Lois and the little English girl had gone to the Bridge deck to walk in the fresh air. The two little girls had come down but Maisie stayed up to watch the waves. Then suddenly, the *SS Taurinia*, in an exaggerated roll, shipped a wave right over the top deck, which cascaded over and down the lee side like Niagara, encaving us. We were dry, but not Maisie. She was in the wave washed overboard. We caught the flash of her green blouse in the wave as it poured off the upper deck and down into the ocean in front of our eyes. We gave the alarm to the Bridge, "Girl overboard!"

We rushed to the railing and sure enough, there was Maisie in the Indian Ocean! We quickly released the life saver rings from the railing and threw them overboard. Most were white but one was red and easier to see. Sailors tried to launch a lifeboat but without success. The Bridge was our only hope. Little by little the *SS Taurinia* slowed down, made a precarious turn about, in the middle of which the ship canted dangerously, hanging leeward at a sharp angle for a few interminable seconds, and then righted herself and was on her way back. Now where was Maisie?

In a few minutes, the captain and first mate on the Bridge sighted the red life saver, pulled up near it, and there was Maisie, about thirty feet away, treading water. A rope ladder was let down and a sailor descended. Maisie swam to it, was helped onto the first rung and climbed onto the deck. The whole operation of 18 minutes, seemed like hours. What a miracle to have Maisie back! Spontaneously, all who spoke English, broke out with the Doxology, "Praise God for Whom All Blessings Flow!"

There were hazards we did not know about until after Maisie's rescue. The ship's 1st mate told us that we were in a shark-infested area. Maisie was bleeding from a cut on the back of her head, and because she was very near-sighted and had lost her glasses when the wave knocked her down, she hadn't seen the rings. We also knew that the 1st mate was very sweet on "Ze Maisie," and that he risked the safety of the ship, passengers and cargo to save her (Maisie agreed with this upon visiting Dave and Lowey Dickason in 2015).

Wells Thoms sewed up the cut in Maisie's scalp, and she rested the remainder of the day; she was up next morning, her usual self. "What did you think about when you were out there in those huge waves all by yourself?" someone asked. She said, "I hoped the ship would come back and gradually it did. I'm a poor swimmer, so I just tread water. Then I thought, 'I'll have a good story to tell my children'."

Wells and Jack DeValois were both fun loving, and decided that we should celebrate Maisie's rescue with some merriment. We made up a song about the event and held a tournament of games.

The animals bound for the Milan Zoo were kept near the forward hatch, most of them in cages, though a baby elephant was allowed room to roam. When we came into rough seas, some cages broke open. The animals were badly shaken up and undoubtedly terrified. In the wake of the storm, the boa constrictor was reported missing. The lower cabins were located on a hallway, which opened onto the forward hatch. Could the snake be in the passenger area? We kept our cabin doors shut. A couple of single English ladies who shared a cabin refused to come out, and had their meals delivered to their room. After a suspenseful day and night the huge snake was found where it had taken refuge, in the center of a large coil of anchor rope near the prow. The poor thing was seasick.

The baby elephant, looking for relief from his discomfort, fled into the hallway and into the first cabin he came to, which happened to be the one Peter and Norman shared. He wedged himself in between the two bunks for a nice safe feeling. The problem now was how to get him out. His keeper came with a watering can of milk and a bunch of alfalfa, which, with coaxing, finally got the baby to back out.

The male Sambur needed attention. In the ship's rolling he had fallen and broken his right front leg below the knee. His keeper came to Wells in great distress. Could Wells splint the leg? Wells found some bandages and plaster of paris in the ship's infirmary cupboard, and set the leg. A month later, before reaching Naples, Wells, with the keeper's help, went to remove the cast. They found it had already disappeared. The Sambur had chewed on it until it was all eaten up, but the bone had knitted with unusual speed, thanks to the extra minerals ingested. Wells was delighted, but the keeper was upset. He wrung his hands in despair. "My beautiful animal is deformed. There's an unsightly bulge on his leg!" Wells tried to console him. "Cheer up," he said, "Your Sambur is alive and well, and has four good legs. With his antlers held high he can still lead his herd!" Wells suggested there was a precedent here for healing fractures—eat your cast for rapid results. Try it next time!

In May, the Indian Ocean and Red Sea weather was exceptionally hot and humid. The children found their cabins stuffy so they carried their mattresses up to the top deck and slept in the open. This deck was directly adjacent to the ship's smokestack, so come morning they were a sooty lot from the greasy diesel smoke, but they slept well.

The *SS Taurinia's* ports of call were Eritrea, Djibouti, Port Said, and Beirut en route to Naples. At Djibouti there was a dance going on near the pier, to which some of our party went. Others of us ventured to the bazaar to get a lemon squeezer for Madame Caspari, who was seasick, and wanted lime juice to counteract it. Unfortunately, we forgot to ask her the French term for "lemon squeezer." We came back empty-handed, as we hadn't seen one anywhere and our pidgen-French didn't work. It turns out the term is "Presse-citron," or something similar.

In Port Said, some of us dickered with the boys in the fleet of small boats that flocked to the sides of ships in the harbor, selling their wares. Decorative leather ottoman covers were a popular item. Other young boys had made a flourishing business of begging for coins to be thrown their way, for which they dove into the clear water. When we docked in Beirut with a couple of days to spare, we took a most interesting tour of the Greco-Roman ruins at Baalbek. The cool, dry air of the green Lebanese mountains was a refreshing change.

When we finally disembarked, in Naples, after 48 days' sojourn on the *SS Taurinia*, we were glad to be on land again. We traveled through Italy and Switzerland. There, we toured a Nestle factory, ate all the chocolate we could and were each given a box full. When we returned to Genoa to board a ship to the U.S., there was a sudden strike. All businesses closed and our ship was unable to dock. Togliatti, the Communist leader, had been shot. We had nothing to eat but our chocolates, until Wells found a few shop back doors open and we could buy a little bread and a few other things. Fortunately, Togliatti recovered and everything went back to normal. We were able to board our ship and all was well.

Pat Wood Remias
Changing Tables in the Dining Room

Oh, the anticipation! Oh, the excitement! Is today the day that the new table lists will go up? Let's go up and just casually look on the dining room door. Nope. Not yet. But when? It's so important to the next four (or six or eight) weeks to find out who our table mates will be. Will they bring their mom's homemade jam and share it with the table, so that we can have good jam on our toast under the cream? Will any of those boys that we would like to hang out with be assigned to our table? Will the conversations be interesting or scary? Will we be with the Burma people who tell tales of the Japanese soldiers capturing and torturing missionaries?

Who makes up those table lists anyway? How does Tex always get to be at Mario's table? That's it! It must be Tex who made up the table arrangements. That's how he honed his skills that he later used to plan Nixon's trip to China! You're welcome, Tex, for using us as guinea pigs.

Hal's WWII and Kodai Experiences
By Bernice Dueck

Recently I was able to chat with Helen Friesen, Hal's sister, about Kodai times, and also recalled things myself from his sharing with me through the years. Here are a few of the memories:

Hal's family, the J. J. Dicks, were in route to India via the Pacific in 1941. Sister Helen Friesen recalls their traveling in the darkness, attempting to see something out of their portholes. Their ship zigzagged through the ocean waters seeking to avoid any Japanese submarines. They actually embarked at Pearl Harbor, off of Oahu, only a month before the bombing!

Hal told me about the artistry of music teacher Mr. Digorgio, a former concert violinist from Italy. He also shared stories about the fearsome language teacher, Mr. Musil, who hailed from the Czech Republic, who was known to terrorize some of the students, especially a few girls.

Hal and friends.

Hal loved his life experiences at Bruton. Fellow roommates, Dave and Paul Wiebe, brothers Paul and Bill, and I think Don Unruh as well, made up a dicey and adventurous mix! Hal spoke well of their house parents, the Ewerts.

Kodai Lake was a beautiful and romantic focal point, as well as the scene for plenty of mischief! Hal talked a lot about the Pear Wars. (I'm sure his friends can fill in the details here.) Hiking in the Palni Hills and in the Pumbar Valley formed some of his fondest memories. He told me a funny story about one of their hikes, and how Dave managed to catch poison oak.

A great adventure was had by Dave and Paul Wiebe, Roger Erickson and Hal the summer of 1956 after graduation from Kodai. The lively four boarded the ship, *MS Asia*, from Bombay to Naples, going through the Suez Canal. The handsome but poor MK's took 3rd class, but it wasn't long before they met some gals from 1st class whose parents were from the diplomatic corps. In Naples they picked up a small VW rental. Apparently they stayed in available hostels and sometimes slept on the ground like the first hippies, living on huge loaves of bread and deli cheeses. Hal made mention of the beautiful young Italian gals with their buxom mamas. They headed north touring Europe, and landed in Amsterdam where they dropped off their little 'bug.'

Ruth Vassar Burgess
Memories of the Middling Years. 1947 to 1952

Highclerc Boarding School

Father's complexion was pink and he looked feverish on the day as he escorted me down to my room in Boyer Hall. He showed me which dresser drawers were mine and those belonging to my roommate. There were two closets. Soon Miss Erickson, whom the girls called "Erkey," would store my blue trunk and sleeping roll down in the storage room. As a parting gift my dad gave me a large tin of hard candies. Highclerc allowed the residents to have two pieces of candy per week, if their parents purchased the tin of sweets. But the tin of sweets did not make up for the sorrow and loneliness as I heard his steps becoming fainter and fainter when he walked down the hall of shadows. Tears flowed out of my eyes and hick-ups of stress caused my chest to heave.

Because of the transom window between some rooms, I heard two girls talking. Later I learned they were just second graders. I had been placed in third grade.

"Did you know there is a new girl next door?"

"Yes. I bet she is crying because her daddy just left."

"Yeah. She is crying for sure." Giggle. Giggle.

Anger flooded the new girl's mind. No, I will not let them make fun of me. They will not see me cry. For the next five and a half years, tears would only be let out during prayers.

Highclerc brought different and changing expectations. You sought a trusting, peer group within the larger student population. Friendships were tenuous and best friends could shift, though lifelong friendships also a distinct possibility. Out of necessity we learned how to advocate for peers. Occasionally, there were teachers who favored some students over others. So one managed different sets of expectations, while being true to one's self. I learned it was advantageous to find who were the classy and kindest classmates? You ask, "How did the under classmates stay in the good graces of older boarders? How did one meet the expectations of parents who lived a thousand miles away?" Being alone forced me to think, be determined, and exhibit courage when in unusual circumstances.

By grade five, Ruth's class, which was considered a small one, became aware the older kids sounded strange when they talked. We learned they were speaking Pig Latin. Soon we learned how to take off final consonants and stick them in front of the first letter of each word. But learning Pig Latin did not make us distinctive. We wanted our own language. Walla! We invented Donkey Language. Now, have you heard of or learned our distinct language? "Leafet uhlafus hearlafear youlafoo speelafit elafit." Yes, Donkey Language is spoken only by a small elite group of international polyglots.

In 1947, early in my time at Highclerc, Mahatma Mohandas Gandhi was assassinated. Cautions were taken on the night of his death. As an act of precaution, the children in Boyer Dormitory picked up their pillows, put on their robes and sat on the center hallway floor. No one knew what the aftermath would entail. Oil lamps flickered down by the wooden entrance gates to the Highclerc compound. The following dirge was written about Ruth's hero.

They were young and far away from their parents. As one of youngest children, she heard the staccato and rising volume of the radio; Tamil words filled the dining room. Mahatma Gandhi had been shot. The great savior, the Mahatma, was in undetermined condition. Sorrow and pity filled her heart. Who would have done such a deed?

The cooks shook their heads. "Who was responsible? But who could hate the Mahatma? For what reason would they desire the death of the great one?"

Static noises permeated the airwaves as the announcer curtly spat, "It has been reported a white man has murdered India's savior. Once again the colonial curse has struck Mother India."

She looked at her friend's hazel eyes and noticed fear for the first time. The principal rushed to call the police for protection. The teachers began clearing their throats, fiddling with their serviettes, and nervous laughs could be heard. The black eyes of the waiters turned from water to coal fires as they looked from her to him; from him to him, and at each other.

"Mahatma, oh, Mister Gandhi, I'm sorry. I was sorry for you that hot afternoon in Poona when the crowd was carrying you on a howdah and people were everywhere. You looked small and your slender hands moved slowly as they moved into a "namasthay." Those around you looked like an ocean with many colors—each blending and moving. Human wails, drums bonging, animals braying, stringed instruments plucking, but you were quiet and serene. You had a calm and a peace. Truly, Mister Gandhi, I am sorry.

The day after Mahatma Mohandas Gandhi died, the seven-year-old girl felt her whiteness. She felt relief to hear that a white person had not shot her hero.

New Assembly of God mission folk arrived in Kodaikanal during January of 1948. Mrs. Bernice and her son Stanley Burgess took up residence in Arcotia Lodge.

It was rumored that Stanley had a heart condition and the rest of us children must not get him too excited. When May rolled around, Bernice's husband John invited the Pentecostal families in for an afternoon prayer meeting. It was loud and tears ran down cheeks. Then it was announced that there were two accomplished piano players in their midst—Stanley Burgess and Clarence Maloney. Of course, requests were made to please play something. The black, upright piano resounded with classical music selections. Then Teddy Vassar sang his "ABCs" song. As we walked out the door, Helen was squatting in the flower garden relieving herself—just like the hill folk at Junnar. On the way back to their cottage on Noyes Road, Estelle asked Ted to assess the two musicians. He thought Clarence played with heavy hands, but Stanley played with emotion. Acceptance of Stanley began on that cloudy and rainy afternoon. Ruth blushed and hoped no one saw her flushed cheeks.

On Sunday afternoons, the borders were confined to their bedrooms and told to write a letter to their parents. Ruth wrote the following letter in 1950:

Dear Mother & Daddy,

How are you? Mother we changed rooms yesterday. I room in the end room with Marquita (Smith) and Beth (Gesler). They ignore me as if I wasn't there at all. They eat and play in front of me and don't even ask me to join. Yesterday was Marquita's birthday. I gave her a balloon and some candy. She didn't invite me or Margaret (Newbigin) or Dagmar (Junyahan). She said she would invite me. But I don't care because Margaret had invited me to her house for tea. At her house we played Heads and Tails. Also, we put a puzzle together.

Last night there was a play tunnel. It was fun. On my spelling test I got 92 or 90. I don't quite remember. Esther isn't taking music lessons now. She got three lessons. I am trying hard. Teddy is o.k.

Love, Ruth Vassar

We boarders bonded with nature and her many wonders. Wild raspberries and sour rhubarb brought tasty delights. Wonder and creative images crept through one's mind while watching the white, cumulus clouds float over the plains far below. The green moss and unusual shaped rocks opened up the possibility of creating fairy lands. Hunting rare bugs, such as the rhinoceros beetles, and discarded match box tops taught careful observation skills. Chameleons became delightful pets, but difficult to feed and keep.

Stealing pears for the upper classmen's pear wine brought commendations. Sharing one's weekly boiled egg meant protection by an upperclassman. Then we realized redemption during Holy Week as we scattered across the mountains picking white canna lilies for the Easter Cross.

By the sixth grade, we decided that things were getting too dull. We sixth grade and two fifth grade girls were housed in the larger end room in Boyer Hall. Beside the bay window was a large rope ladder in the window box. Telling our male classmates about the rope ladder, we hatched up a plan where the boys could come and visit us. That night as the light faded, we saw Eddie, Bruce, Richard, and a couple of other boys creep out of Kennedy Hall. Silently and slowly we dropped the rope ladder down to the ground. Eddie and Richard were to hold the ladder steady while Bruce, who was smaller in height, climbed upward.

Things were going well until we heard Erkey's red goose shoes walking down the wooden planks towards our room. Suddenly, she turned on our lights. All of the guys ran back to Kennedy Hall, except Bruce. Erkey saw his startled face outside above the windowsill. Bruce was left hanging and swaying in the breeze. Where were we girls? We were trying to pretend sleep with our sheets covering our faces.

Then there were the weekend events. Hikes were planned according to the students' ages. It was a pleasure to exit the compound, but we were never allowed to leave by ourselves. On the weekend adventures, even with blisters on our heels, we enjoyed being in the cool, crisp air. On one of these adventures we spent the night in pup tents at the Pillar of Rocks. Early the next morning we were awakened to hear the maharaja's hunting party down by the creek. There were tiger paws in the mud. This indicated the great jungle beast had stopped for water during the night. Were we frightened? No, we only wished we had seen him.

Positive anticipation rocked the Highclerc Compound as the student body was divided into the orange and blue teams. This was for spring “field day” where everyone from grade 1 to grade 12 participated in track and field events. Although we whispered our color preferences, our unsaid hopes were that you would be on the same team as Marilyn Scudder or the athletic German students who lived in a separate boarding compound down the hill. So we practiced our jumping, running, catching and dodging during recess and after school. After the evening meal we were expected to be in study hall or reading in our dorm rooms.

Half of the girls took showers on Monday and Wednesday. The other half had a Tuesday and Thursday schedule. Everyone took a shower on Saturday. We dried our long hair with towels or crouched close to the wood stove in the big room. Our usual fun games were planned for the weekends, such as checkers, Chinese checkers, charades, and making up stories using the costume trunk. A special fun game was "Murder in the Dark, Speak Murderer Speak.”

My classmates and I shared our childhoods at Highclerc School. For five and a half years my classmates and I became bonded. Fading away were our blood cousins in the United States, Great Britain and Germany. We realized there were multiple perspectives and each one deserved understanding. We were becoming children of the third culture. Certainly, we felt our futures were uncertain, and clearly we knew no one would provide for our destinies. We had to be strong and make our own destinies.

Roadside stall on the plains of India. (Peck)

CHAPTER 12

Kodai before us

The following recollection by Charles "Chuck" Gosselink also captures the ambiance of the Kodai School we knew.[47] Chuck graduated from Kodai in 1953, when some of our older siblings were already attending Kodai School. Chuck's descriptions are close to those that the boys of '55 and '56 experienced.

Plain Tales from the Hills

I know them, love them, see them once again.
Their cloudy summit veiled in misty rain ...
I'm homesick for you, mountains that I know,
Oh, hills of home, the hills of home.

Oscar J. Fox

Sam and Ruth[48] were the only ones to see me off at the bus stand. My twenty classmates and I had graduated more than a week ago and most of them had already left Kodai, headed for their homes on the plains or directly to the US to be ready to start college in the fall. I had lingered a while, to spend a little more time with my

---

47 "Plain Tales from the Hills" is a chapter from Charles Gosselink's book, *Ashar Creek*, which describes his childhood as a missionary kid. Born in Busrah in 1935, he attended first grade in Kodai School in 1942 with Aunty Powell as his teacher. After furlough in the US in 1945-46, he returned to Kodai for sixth to twelfth grade, 1947-1953.

48 Sam Schmitthenner and Ruth Gosselink Schmitthenner (Chuck's sister) were also graduates of Kodai School.

sister Ruth and Sam and their two children, enjoy a picnic on the lake, have one more meal at the Brahmin Hotel, and amble one more time around Coaker's Walk. I was reluctant to leave. And so now I was traveling alone.

We said our final good-byes as the bus pulled away from its station on Post Office Loop. The bus went up the road past Woodville Compound, Furzbank and Maratta House, and down to the junction at Seven Roads, with the halva man's stand just across from the main gateway to the school. We drove on past the KMU and Kashmir Emporium, past Lockend, the Dish, Wissahickon, and Little Wissie, to Spencer's and the Bund, and then down the winding thirty-mile Ghat[49] Road to the plains. I tried to hide my tears, though there was no one there to see them. I was leaving the place on earth that I knew better than any other, my "home from home," where, counting up the months, I had spent more of my life than even at my real home in Basrah. While I might have hoped, I did not expect to return.

I have earlier suggested that the rewards of missionary life outweighed any sacrifices my parents might have experienced when they made the commitment to leave their homes and families in Iowa and spend their lives in faraway Arabia. But one sacrifice they made must have been very difficult, and that was to have to send their children off to boarding school in India at a very young age and not have us at home with them during those important years when we were growing up. Yes, they had us in Basrah during our long school vacations and we were all together when they, in turn, vacationed in Kodaikanal. Perhaps it is time to describe the school which we attended and our lives there when we were not with them. I do not know what my parents thought, but I believe that their close acquaintance with the school and friendship with many of the staff members and teachers must have made their sacrifice a little more bearable.

I had first visited Kodai when I was only three months old. As missionaries of the Arabian Mission, my parents ordinarily expected to have a vacation only every other year, though mothers who had children at school might get away for a shorter time every year. But in 1935, both of my parents were scheduled for a vacation, and so in June, three months after I was born, they, with my older brother Jim and me, left Basrah for the ten-day, 2,500-mile trip by ship, train and bus, to Kodaikanal. It might seem strange that they would go to India for vacation rather than the nearer hills of Lebanon or the even closer resort areas in Iran. However, in those days, the Persian Gulf was seen almost as a British lake, an extension of British India, and even southern Iraq looked east toward India for its economic and cultural

[49] An Indian term of several meanings, but in this case simply a road through the mountains.

connections. Missionaries of the Arabian Mission, from Iraq and the Gulf, traditionally spent their vacations in India and sent their children to Kodaikanal School, which my sister Ruth was already attending. The Reformed Church in America, which supported the Arcot Mission in South India as well as the Arabian Mission in the Gulf, subsidized the school, and so it was the normal thing for our family to vacation in India and natural for Ruth to attend Kodai School and also Jim and me as we came of age.

I have already written about my early experiences of traveling to Kodai, especially during the war years, and of my first exposure to the school itself. Those events, along with an understanding of what my older siblings had done, laid a strong foundation in my mind for what was to come. Even though I had just spent a year in the US, where I lived at home with my parents and attended the local public school like any normal American kid, when we returned to Basrah in the fall of 1946, I knew what was expected of me and I was ready. By the time my brother and I left Basrah for Kodai in January 1947, I was excited. Going off without my parents was a rite of passage. After my one unhappy experience in second grade, when Mother had left me in boarding at Kodai School for five months, I was never again troubled with homesickness. I loved Kodai, the beauty of the hills, the familiarity of place, the companionship of friends, the feeling of independence. I was happy when my parents came to Kodai for vacation and I could leave the school boarding department and live with them for a few months, and I looked forward to traveling back to Basrah to spend the Christmas vacation at home. But being away from home and parents for months at a time seemed be the most normal thing, and I never questioned it.

Kodaikanal is located at 7,000 feet elevation in the Palani Hills of Tamil Nadu State in South India, seventy miles from Madurai, the closest major city. Though the area was visited by British officers and civil servants early in the nineteenth century, some of whom built small houses or hunting camps there, it was American missionaries working in the Madurai area who popularized the site as a hill station, a retreat from the heat and the ravages of malaria and other diseases they suffered every summer in their places of work on the plains below. Indeed, it was known to them as the Sanitarium before the name Kodaikanal (*"Gift of the Forest"* in Tamil) was adopted sometime late in the century.[50]

The Palani Hills seem to rise straight up from the flat plains surrounding them. At about seven thousand feet, the hills flatten out into a plateau of rolling grass covered hills and forested valleys, with gentle streams and pleasing waterfalls. The highest hill, Vandaravu Peak, rises to only a little over eight thousand feet. From Kodai, at the edge of the plateau, one can look almost straight down to the plains, six thousand feet below. One of those early British visitors, the Collector of Madura, Sir Vere Levinge, had dammed a small wetlands area and created a four fingered lake where several valleys came together. It was a lovely spot and soon attracted American missionaries from all over South India seeking rest and recuperation. A town grew up to support the growing summer population and eventually took on a life of its own, with a local agricultural industry, bazaar, schools, temples and churches. Still, even into the middle of the twentieth century, most of the prime real estate, the area around the lake and overlooking the plains, was owned by American missionary organizations.

Kodaikanal School was established in 1901 in response to the concern of the growing number of American missionaries in South India for the safety, health and educational needs of their children. Up in the hills, in a protective environment, Kodai offered a perfect location for a school. Started as a small boarding facility for younger children, it grew and expanded until by 1930 it offered a full curriculum and boarding option for students from kindergarten to twelfth grade. It remained a small school, never exceeding 150-200 students until about 1970, when it began to change. Until that time, it was primarily an American school, offering a standard American course of study, with the expectation that most of its graduates would go on to college in the United States. Most of the students were the children of American missionaries, though in later years it also drew the children of American diplomats and of families involved in business or commerce. There were some British students, usually the children of missionaries, and there were always a number of students from the German mission school nearby, which offered elementary classes but sent its older students to the American school. One of my classmates was a German girl whose father was in business. British and German students who graduated from

---

[50] My wife Char's great grandfather Thornton Bigelow Penfield, was a missionary of the American Madura Mission from 1868 to 1871. He suffered from ill health for much of those three years before his untimely death and was sent to Kodai to recuperate from his illnesses several times. In his letters (see Only for Jesus, The Penfield Correspondence, 2018, edited by Charlotte Mertz) he refers to the site only as the Sanitarium, never Kodaikanal.

Kodai School usually had to take an additional year of study before they could qualify for admission to British or German universities.

If the student body was mostly American, the faculty was much more cosmopolitan. The principal, Carl Phelps, and most of the teachers were American, but the school enjoyed the service of others who were not. My third-grade teacher was Danish, my Latin and French teacher was Czechoslovakian, our choir and orchestra director was Italian, a history teacher was Austrian, my piano teacher was Swiss, the school nurse was German, and our housemother for a time was English. Some of these teachers had been caught up in India during the War, held by the British government as "enemy" internees, but were allowed to spend their time of detention at Kodai. Several stayed on at Kodai even after the War. The school was often short of faculty and staff and Mr. Phelps would then try to recruit parents to fill in, sometimes to good effect, sometimes not. My mother, who was well qualified to teach math and history, was persuaded to help out several times, and I believe Mr. Phelps, or Papa as we knew him, would have been happy to hire her for a longer period if she had been available.

What is missing here are Indian students and teaching staff. There were always a few Indian students, whose parents either planned to send them to the US for college or merely wanted them to be fluent in English so that they could be more useful in the family businesses. The major drawback for Indian students was that Kodai would not have prepared them for the exams they would have to take to enter Indian universities. I would think that Kodai might have been able to hire more Indian teachers, especially for math or science, but I remember only three on the faculty during my time there, our biology teacher, the librarian, and our long-term instructor in manual training. Of course the serving staff—the clerks, cooks, gardeners, maintenance workers, cleaners, and so on—were all Indian, and what would we have done without the ayahs who helped take care of the little kids and made sure the big kids made their beds, kept their rooms tidy, and took care of laundry on dhobi day? On the whole, we had limited contact with Indian people of a more educated or professional class.

In truth, Kodai School was a little island of America in an Indian ocean. We thought we knew something of India, and loved what we knew, but our knowledge was really quite superficial. Our curriculum included nothing of Indian history and culture. We were offered no instruction in Indian languages. While the school emphasized training in Western classical music, we learned not a note from the Indian tradition. It would have been argued, I suppose, that the primary purpose of Kodai was to prepare American students for higher education in America, and for that purpose these Indian subjects were not relevant. Yet I think there was more to it than that. We were still in a colonial frame of mind in those days, more interested in what we might bring to India than what we might learn.[51]

Fortunately, the school has changed over time. It is now an International School, offering an enhanced curriculum, including Indian history and culture, while maintaining some of the unique features that made it such an exceptional school before. The student body is truly diverse, Americans making up only a fraction of the total. Most of the students are Indian, coming from all over the country and the Indian diaspora, but many other countries are represented as well. It is a better school now, though very different from the place I knew.

At that time, in spite of some shortcomings, the old Kodai School met my educational and social needs and was exactly the sort of place I needed to be. When I graduated from Kodai, I was well prepared academically to meet the high standards of the college I attended in the US, though I had had no electives, Advanced Placement, or International Baccalaureate classes considered so essential today. More important, perhaps was the social support the school and my fellow students gave me. We shared a common background. Most of us considered ourselves Americans and owned the cultural heritage of our parents, but we had grown up in other places, spoke other languages, and felt comfortable in those surroundings as well. At the same time, we were always considered foreigners in those places we called home, while not feeling completely at home in the country of our heritage. We were, in short, Third Culture Kids.

David Pollock defines a Third Culture Kid as an individual who, having spent a significant part of his or her developmental years in a culture or cultures other than the parents' culture, develops a sense of relationship to all of the cultures while not having full ownership in any. Elements from each culture are incorporated into the life experience, but the sense of belonging is in relationship to others of similar experience.[52] That experience is illustrated in BJ Elder's description of growing up of missionary parents in China and eventually entering the Shanghai American School:

---

[51] There were a few teachers who felt it important that we should know more about the country and the people around us, who might assign essay topics that forced us to do research on some aspect of Indian life, but they were the exception, and I don't think they got much support from the principal. My band director, Mr. Thompson made sure we could play the Indian national anthem, and thereafter we were asked to play "Jana Gana Mana" at every official function in town.

[52] David C. Pollock and Ruth E. Van Reken, *Third Culture Kids*, p. 13.

The students were mostly the offspring of American missionaries, businessmen, and diplomats, but there was a sprinkling of pupils of other nationalities as well, including Chinese whose parents could afford to send them to SAS. Here, for the first time, I was with others my age who, like me, had lived in more than one language and inhabited more than one world and knew, without speaking of it, what it was like to be home at not-home.[53]

Students at Kodai came from all over. Most came from places in southern India but may have grown up speaking Hindi, Marathi, Telegu, Tamil, or Malayalam. We had students who came from Burma and Thailand, and from Muscat and the Persian Gulf countries, and they often spoke the languages of those areas. The missionary kids tended to have some semi-permanent home, while the children of businessmen and diplomats had often lived in several countries. Our varied backgrounds were not strange to us—it was the ordinary thing. Rita, my German classmate, likes to tell of the anxiety she felt when she arrived at the school in 1948, shortly after the War. She feared we Americans would treat her as "the enemy" and was surprised when she was welcomed into the fold. I don't think the rest of us gave it a thought. Kodai School was a comfortable place, as the record of my correspondence shows.

I wrote home to my parents every Sunday, following a habit drilled into me by my father and reinforced by the practice of my siblings. My mother kept all those letters, which, taken as a whole, provide a good picture of my life at school. Considering that she often sent them on to Ruth and Jim, who were in the US, it is remarkable that they survived and that I now have an almost complete collection from the time I entered sixth grade until I graduated from high school seven years later.[54] Over the years my handwriting improved; my spelling did not. I find the letters surprisingly chatty, as if I were sitting across from my parents at the dinner table, describing the events of the day. I wrote about classes and teachers, tests and scores, the terrible food, the games we played, the hikes we took, the special events and the mundane. The letters are peppered with the names of classmates and friends. My parents knew them all and were acquainted with most of their families as well. If someone new showed up, it was worth a comment. "Two new guys moved in, John and Sterling Seagrave. I think they may be the sons of that Burma surgeon

---

[53] BJ Elder, *The Oriole's Song*, p. 88.

[54] With airmail available after the War, it took only a week for my letters to reach Basrah. Mother's letters to me took five or six days, usually arriving on Saturday, so that I could comment on them or answer her questions when I wrote back the following day.

guy."[55] It was like attending a local public school in a small town, close and intimate, where everyone knew everyone else despite, in our case, the distance separating us from our families.

When Jim and I sailed from Basrah in January 1947, we left our parents with an empty nest. It must have been especially hard on Mother, knowing that she would not be going to Kodai that year and would not be seeing us for ten months. Jim and I were too busy thinking about what was ahead to give much thought to what we were leaving behind. We arrived at school two weeks late. I went into boarding in Kennedy, rooming with an old friend John De Vries and Jim went into Boys' Block where he shared a room with his close buddy Rob Roy Storm. Though only a tenth grader, Jim took his responsibilities as older brother seriously. In a letter home he explained that he had gone to see Papa Phelps, shown him the record of my Calvert course work and persuaded him that, though I had attended only a few weeks of fifth grade in the US, I was prepared to enter sixth grade. I was happy to be reunited with my old classmates, though the first few weeks were hard. It turns out I had missed out on fractions. My teacher, a parent who was just filling in until our regular teacher arrived, was not of much help to me, but my desk-mate, Don Oberdorfer taught me what I needed to know. And then Miss Agnes Liddle arrived. She was, I believe, the best teacher I ever had. She certainly pulled me through what was for me an academically challenging year.

Jim and I settled into the routine of school life very easily. The school bell rang early to wake us up and then a little later to call us to breakfast. It would ring again at noon, for dinner, and then at six for supper, and between those calls, it would summon us to class. I can still hear the peal of that resonant bell, ringing out across the lake and surrounding hills. During the week we were busy with classes and Saturdays were given to hiking or special events, such as the annual field meet or decorating the church for Easter. On Sundays we all dressed up to attend the regular Junior Church service. After Sunday dinner, usually something special such as chicken curry and pilau, we retired to our rooms to write our letters home. And then we were free.

As young kids we were largely restricted to the school campus, allowed to venture around the lake or down to the Budge only if accompanied by a chaperone. There was plenty to do. We roamed the campus in small packs, playing in the now abandoned trenches on Block slope, left over from the World War II Japanese scare,

---

55 Dr. Gordon Seagrave was a missionary doctor in Burma and famously the author of *Burma Surgeon* and other books.

or climbing trees, particularly the "Monkey-up," a clump of several tall conifers with adjoining branches, where the brave could cross from one to another. We played tree tag until someone fell out of the tree. He was not seriously hurt but the game was banned after that. To everything there was a season, and we played through the marbles season, the top season, the kick-the-can season, and others I have forgotten. No one planned the schedule; it was as if one day we woke up, put away the marbles and began playing capture the flag. We played marbles and tops by Indian rules. Tops was particularly brutal, as we filed down the screw point of our tops so that we could hit and split our adversary's toy spinning in the circle. Marbles, or "mibs," involved playing for keeps, until the more skilled had a bagful of marbles and the losers had none.

As we grew older, our interests turned to the "American" sports of basketball, baseball and flag football, as well as soccer and tennis. Girls played basketball, softball and tennis. With little competition available locally, we usually played intramural games in various configurations. Occasionally the teachers and parents might put together a baseball or basketball team to challenge our "varsity" teams. In my letters home, I dutifully reported the scores of all those games and would only note here that we often had higher numbers in baseball than in basketball, much to the disgust of Papa Phelps, who reportedly had played minor league ball before coming out to India. We traveled to Madurai to play American College and Hindu College in basketball several times. They were good competition, though our height and fast break tactics usually won the game. Once, in my memory, we took on the local Indian high school boys in a track meet, but we were so much bigger and faster that there was little competition. It was embarrassing, for both parties, and we did not meet again. We would have lost to them if we had played *gillidanda* or *kabaddi*, popular village sports. We found good competition when we took on the school servants' soccer team. They regularly beat us, though they played in bare feet and we in flimsy Bata tennis shoes. They had a good team and always did well playing other teams in town. However, none of them wanted to play goalie, and so one year they invited my brother Jim to play that position, even in their town league games. He enjoyed an experience none of the rest of us ever had.

Once a year we had an all-school track meet, with races and other competitions for all grades, down on Benderlock Field. We were divided, I don't know how, between the orange and blue teams, and for a brief period, passions ran high in support of our particular color. The grade school classes had competitions of various kinds. In high school, we could choose our particular track and field events and competed by age groups rather than class. After the final relay races and after the final score had been announced and the winning team congratulated, we all sat down on the field and enjoyed a meal of rice and curry served up on banana leaves by our kitchen staff.

By the time we reached junior high, the boys, at least, were free to leave the school campus and wonder around the town and lake. In high school, we were allowed, with permission from our parents, to hike or ride our bikes out into the hills without a chaperone. We usually went to well-known destinations though we also explored lesser-known areas, usually in search of streams or waterfalls. Favorite, but challenging, hikes included climbing Perumal, the iconic volcano shaped mountain, a picture of which is found in every tourist brochure now, or walking down to the plains 6,000 feet below. Perumal was not much higher than Kodai, but we had to hike or take a bus several miles down the Ghat Road before we could begin our climb to the summit. The plains hike involved making our way down the steep, stony "coolie ghat" to Tope, at the base of the mountain, and then walking several miles through flat paddy fields to the town of Periyakulam, where we could catch a bus to take us back to Kodai. Both hikes left our knees feeling like putty for several days. There were more restrictions on where the girls could go off campus, though they were always included on chaperoned class hikes and camping trips.

Twice a year all of us, from fifth to twelfth grade, went camping on a three-day weekend. We went by class or combined classes, the lower grades going to closer destinations such as Green Hut or Poombarai, the high schoolers hiking further to Berijam Lake, Marian Shola, Vandaravu, or Kukal. This was a different kind of camping experience. While we were hiking on foot, the school was sending our sleeping bags, food, pots and pans, <u>and</u> and a cook out by truck, so that when we arrived at our destination, there would be a hot meal ready and waiting for us. Thereafter, we did help with preparation and clean-up, but this was trekking in the British colonial style. Each of the sites had a small three-room cabin maintained by the Forest Department. A small kitchen was housed in a separate shed, where the cook could sleep. Usually, the girls stayed on one side of the cabin, the boys on the other, and the middle room was reserved for eating, games, and storytelling. But if it was dry, we would be outside around a camp fire. When rain was expected we would line the dusty floors of the cabin with readily available bracken and sleep with the clean, fresh smell of newly cut ferns.

Each of the destinations had its own attractions. Berijam, about twelve miles from Kodai had the lake for swimming and boating, if we could locate the old dugout canoe, left on the shore somewhere. Marian Shola, eight to ten miles further on was known for its ibex cliffs, where we might spot those animals, more accurately called the Nilgiri tahr, or see wild bison. If we were lucky, and the sun and clouds were right, we might be rewarded with a Brocken spectre, the rare phenomenon when our shadows were projected on the clouds below, surrounded by a halo of colored light.

The road on from Marian Shola passed through a beautiful grassland meadow, watered by a meandering trout stream. The Vandaravu cabin, thirty miles from Kodai, was set in a pine forest just below the ridge including Vandaravu Peak. From there we could see the orderly tea plantations of Travancore[56] in the far distance. The jungle in the near valley below might reveal wild elephants, bison or deer. Kukal was not as far as Vandaravu but seemed more remote. From there we could visit Kukal Cave, a large overhanging rock that must have given shelter to animals and humans for eons. It looked out over the broad Manjampatti Valley, known for its herds of elephant, bison, and chital (spotted deer)[57] and the Adivasi[58] tribal folk who still lived there. To get to the cave and back, we had to pass through a leech forest, which we accomplished by running single file, each person with a leafy switch, brushing off the leaches which attached to the legs of the person running in front of us. At the end of the run, we checked each other and removed the leaches that managed to latch on.

The six camping sites, all connected by a passable gravel road, made up what we called the eighty-mile round, a trek accomplished by some campers during the longer May vacation. A shorter version, the forty-mile round included only three of the cabin sites and might involve tent camping. The ten-mile round was a day's hike, less interesting scenically and seldom used except for quick bike trips.

But all of this was ahead of us. When I arrived with Jim in 1947, I still had much to learn. Though I enjoyed the short hikes, especially to the streams at Wiffy and Gundar Valley, and went on at least one camping trip, I was more interested in activities at the school. Jim, following Mother's instructions, made sure that I was signed up for piano lessons with Madam Caspari. He found an upperclassman to teach me the alto horn, just as he had learned to play the flute from our future brother-in-law Sam Schmitthenner. Though music was an important part of the

---

[56] The area formerly known as the Kingdom of Travancore became part of the State of Kerala in 1956.
[57] In later years, I had the opportunity of hiking down into the valley two times and was fortunate to see those animals on each occasion. On one occasion, our math teacher Steve Root carried his rifle and was able to shoot a chital. As he was butchering the deer, two tribal men appeared. In return for helping us carry our gear back up the mountain, Steve gave them most of the carcass after he had saved a few choice pieces for himself.
[58] Indigenous people.

Kodai experience, there were never enough music teachers, so older students often took responsibility for teaching the young and earned a small stipend for doing it.

In March, Jim arranged a birthday party for me. In fact, since our birthdays were only a day apart and we had almost the same guest list, I shared the celebration with John King. We invited our classmates and a few other friends. The kitchen staff provided minimal decorations, and we all sat down at four o'clock for a big tea of sandwiches and lemonade, topped by—Oh, no! The kitchen could not provide a cake, citing shortages of flour and sugar caused by the War. We were skeptical, but accepted the jelebies, a spiraled sweet Indian confection, that the kitchen supplied instead. Jim almost missed the party because he was laid up ill in the dispensary, known as the dishpan or dish, with some now forgotten malady. He made it out for the big event. I remained remarkably healthy in that, my twelfth, year.

Easter Sunday came in early April. On Saturday we went out foraging for lilies to decorate the gym. I went off with Norm Thoms and two other people to harvest lilies from a garden, where the local owner, a friend of the school, had offered us half of what he had in bloom. Others found good pickings growing wild on the slope below Coaker's Walk. Some of the upper classmen went in the school truck to Bombay Shola, where they cut branches of large tree ferns. I cringe now at the thought of cutting those beautiful plants in that old growth forest, but we didn't know better in those days. However, the gym was certainly beautiful when we finished decorating it that afternoon. Sunday morning we had a treat for breakfast—corn flakes—a rarity in our fare, which usually consisted of *suji* or *ragi* or some other cooked grain. The kitchen staff, most of them Christian, came out to sing *Christ the Lord is Risen Today*, in Tamil, and we all joined in on the alleluias. The Easter service later that morning was mostly music, with each grade group contributing a song, culminating in a cantata presented by the high school chorus. In my letter home, I pronounced it "very good."

The next weekend, we all went camping for three days. The fifth and sixth graders, chaperoned by Mr. Musil, hiked to Poombari, by way of the swimming pools at Wiffy Stream. We held our annual field meet the following Saturday. My team, the Orange, won and it should be noted that our captain, Robby Storm, broke the school record for pole vault by half an inch, a record that had been held by my brother-in-law to be, Sam Schmitthenner. Then it was the end of the school year, at least for the high school students, with the usual concerts, recitals, and final exams, leading to graduation for the seniors and May vacation for the rest of us.

And now Kodai was invaded by American missionaries, coming from all over South India for a month of rest and rejuvenation before returning to their sometimes isolated mission stations on the plains. They packed that month with all sorts of activities—hiking, camping, picnicking, boating, tennis, baseball, coffee parties, dinners, and all the things they missed the other eleven months of the year. On Sundays they gathered at the big Union Church, that was also home to the local Tamil Protestant congregation, where they could sing familiar hymns and pray and worship together in English. There was the May Sale, where the several denominations that sponsored Kodai School sold items from their mission industries (embroidery, crochet work, furniture) or things they had imported from the US (clothing, books, games, toys) to benefit the school. The Kodai Missionary Union (KMU) sponsored four special performances: a musical variety show, a three-act play, a Gilbert and Sullivan operetta, and an oratorio. The principle performers had been chosen the previous year and had had a chance to learn their lines or music, but the chorus and extras had only a week or two of rehearsals. The missionaries exhibited an extraordinary depth of artistic talent.

Most of the children had gone to live with their parents that month in the cottages the mission boards maintained for their vacationing members[59] but some, including the Arabs, stayed in boarding. We were well taken care of there, but our classmates remembered us, too, and we were often invited out for Sunday dinner. My roommate John De Vries asked me to go on a short three-night camping trip with his family, where we actually stayed in tents, and Jim and Robby Storm were invited to hike and camp the eighty-mile round with the Carman family.

One day, our music director Mario di Giorgio, asked me to come down to the gym that afternoon, where he was rehearsing the *HMS Pinafore*. There he announced, without really giving me a choice, that I would be playing the part of the mid-shipman in the show. The ladies measured me up for a costume, and the next day I joined the cast. I had no speaking part but I did have to make a face sometimes and engage in other antics. Jim, Nancy Thoms, and Janet Storm were already in the chorus. Jim reported that the dress rehearsal was terrible, the first performance passable, and the Saturday night show a resounding success. At the cast party afterwards, we could each have a guest, so we invited Janet's brother Robby and Nancy's brothers Norm and Pete. We Arabs sat at one table and enjoyed the talents of the other cast members at the after-dinner show.

---

59 Such was the ecumenism of the Kodai School Junior Church that my only understanding of denominational differences in those days was where each denomination had its cottages—Winsford Compound was for Presbyterians, Woodville was Dutch Reformed, Furzbank was Methodist, etc.

Too soon, our vacation was over and we returned to class. Jim entered eleventh grade and I continued with sixth. Jim continued to play his role as big brother. In earlier correspondence, Mother must have asked about the state of our clothes. I replied that I had had my everyday leather shoes resoled twice but I did not ask for anything more. Jim said that he needed some socks and a good white shirt and that was all. However, he reported, I would need "quite a lot of stuff." He hoped he could pick up something for me at the May Sale. Evidently, that did not work out, because on June 2 he wrote, "Say, Chuck is getting awfully low in pants. If you know of anything that can be done, do it!" He said he thought I would prefer long pants now. Mother must have replied, suggesting that Jim buy some cloth from the bazaar and ask her old friend Peter the tailor to fix up something for me. Jim wrote back that cloth was still rationed and he did not have a ration card. Within a couple of weeks, Dr. Mylrea arrived back in Kodai from a visit to Basrah and the Gulf bringing me two pairs of short pants and one long. The whole transaction took about six weeks, but in the end it all worked out.

At least I had something decent to wear for the observance of Indian Independence Day on August 15, 1947. In describing the event, Jim wrote that 1,500 students from all the schools in Kodai showed up to join in the celebration at our flag green. Before the ceremonies began, some of the Indian kids came around distributing little, paper, card sized Indian flags, several of which I still have today. There were talks by the Mayor and Council President, by Mr. Phelps and the principal of the Indian high school and by several other important people. Our school band played the national anthem, the music to Rabindranath Tagore's poem, the "Jana Gana Mana," a paean to a united India. And then the British Flag, the Union Jack, was lowered from the flagstaff and the new Orange, White and Green flag of the Republic of India was raised. It was the beginning of a new era, though I certainly did not understand what that meant at the time.

Dr. Mylrea's return to Kodai in mid-July coincided with the arrival of Aunt Pat Storm from Bahrain, Uncle Wells and Aunt Beth Thoms from Muscat and Uncle Lew and Aunt Dorothy Scudder and their children from Kuwait. For the next two months, Jim and I were invited out almost every weekend to join in a combined Arab activity of some kind—a hike, a picnic on the lake, a steak roast, or pot-luck dinner. On one occasion Aunt Beth invited us out for the whole weekend. It was wonderful to be a part of that family and to enjoy the delicious food—American, Arab, or Indian. On Sunday afternoon, Aunt Beth asked Norm to accompany me back to school. When we were half way there, the heavens open up, soaking us thoroughly in just a few minutes. Norm took me back to his home, where Aunt Beth gave us hot baths and fixed me up with some of Pete's clothes. The next morning, she sent me to school in my own dry, pressed pants and shirt. It was a reminder of what a close-knit family the Arabian Mission was. Our parents might be absent, but we were well looked after. There was one more celebration, the combined birthday party for Robby, Nancy and Jim, held every year in mid-September. And then we began counting the days to the end of school.

Dr. Mylrea made reservations for Jim and me on the *SS Dumra*, leaving Bombay on October 21. It would mean leaving school a few days early, but the alternative was a much later ship. We would be traveling with the Storms. Our departure was still over a month away, but we were busy and the time passed quickly. We wrote home about end of the year activities, the tests and concerts and individual recitals. I wrote about hikes and a roller-skating party in the gym. Jim wrote of dances, a moon-light punting party, and Sunday evening walks around the lake. Jim and Maisie Korteling were a couple now. In letters home to our parents, my brother seemed very happy.

We stopped writing letters a week before our departure from Kodai, so I have no details about our trip home. Mother's diary notes that we arrived in Basrah on October 30, so I presume we had no problems along the way. I am sure we were happy to be back. The two months at home were filled with the usual activities: lots of tennis, basketball with the boys at the school, piano practice, reading, bellum[60] picnics. Thanksgiving and Christmas came and went, and then it was January and time to head back to Kodai.

The following years at Kodai were much like the last. India's independence did not affect us much. We raised the Indian flag every day, of course, but right next to it, on the same flag green and at the same height, flew the Stars and Stripes. We were still an American school and I suppose we felt we had some territorial claim to that piece of land. Jim graduated a year and a half later. He traveled back to Basrah and then on the US to attend college. After half a year of eight grade, I moved on to high school.[61] We followed a standard curriculum for that time: English, math, science, world and US history, Latin and French. I enjoyed geometry but struggled in algebra. I did not take the optional calculus class. I loved chemistry and considered making that my major in college.

---

[60] A small boat holding about eight people and propelled by paddles or poles.

[61] Grade school classes at Kodai ran from January to October, but high school classes ran from June to May, with two months' vacation at Christmas, so that seniors graduating in May would have time to get to the US for the start of college in the fall. The off-set was made possible by reducing eighth grade to half a year.

Music absorbed a good deal of my time. I took piano lessons every year (though without much lasting effect), played the alto horn in the school band and trumpet in the orchestra. I sang in the high school chorus, the a cappella choir, and a men's quartet. The a cappella choir sang for Junior Church services, the annual sacred music concert, and occasionally at the Union services at the American Church. The quartet, made up of Jim Schaefer, Don Oberdorfer, faculty member Julius Scott and me, sang in church and in the occasional variety show, where we liked to sing barbershop.

Kodai School was known for its music program. During my years there I was fortunate to have exceptional teachers, two of whom deserve further mention. Madam Elisabeth Caspari had a doctorate in music and pedagogy and had founded a well-known music school in Switzerland. While she was traveling with her husband in India, war broke out in Europe and she was unable to return home. Somehow, she found her way to Kodai. I well remember her group music classes and individual instruction in piano. As young kids, my classmates and I enjoyed our time with her. Her method of teaching involved assigning colors to the notes of a musical scale. I never became a strong musician, but the foundations she laid helped me in all my later endeavors with piano, instruments and vocal music. Madam Caspari went on to become a leader in the Montessori education movement in the US, and her method of piano teaching in Kodai was, I think, a foretaste of the educational approach she would advocate later.

Mario DiGiorgio was an Italian concert violinist on tour in India when Italy joined the war in Europe in 1940. He was about to be interned by the Government of India when a parent of a Kodai School student, who had heard him play in Bombay, persuaded the authorities to let him serve his internment at Kodai. Serendipitously, it turned out to be a perfect match. He served out his time in Kodai until the end of the war and then stayed on until his retirement some years later. He became a much-appreciated member of the school community. Aside from teaching violin, starting a fledgling orchestra, and directing the school choirs, he was a willing chaperone on class hikes, camping trips and school dances, and participated enthusiastically in other school and community activities. I know he was valued by his colleagues on the faculty. He was not without his foibles, one being his short temper. He was a musician, who strove toward perfection, and was impatient with students who would not try to be better. He was often irritated when directing the school chorus, when students were talking and not paying attention or could not get the music right. In exasperation, he would bring down and break his baton on his music stand (He may have bought them by the gross!), and on several occasions, he simply walked off shouting, “I am fed up!” In other situations, he could be kind and understanding and even, if called for, offer his broad shoulder to cry on. Mario was an essential member of the Kodai School community.

The War brought several other teachers to the school. Fritz Kolb was an Austrian, who was mountain climbing in the Himalayas when his country was drawn into the war. He, too, was interned, though his anti-Nazi credentials in Austria were well established. Eventually he was released to the supervision of Kodai School. He was a great hiker, of course, and friends tell me he was an excellent history teacher, but he was there only a short time, and I did not know him well.

I did know Alois Musil, our Latin and French teacher. He was from Czechoslovakia and, though not interned, decided to spend the war years in India, finding his refuge in Kodai. I studied with him for four years, taking Latin and then French in succession. His teaching style was not inspiring. He taught us grammar and assigned endless list of vocabulary to master, where nothing less than 100% was acceptable on his weekly tests. French was taught like Latin, a dead language we were never encouraged to speak. Still, I remember enough from both languages to get me through the daily crossword puzzle. Outside of class Mr. Musil was fun to be with. He joined us on hikes and camping trips and loved to tell stories around the campfire. He tried to teach us manners when we sat at his table in the dining room, without much success. He liked to put Marmite on his toast at breakfast but never shared that treat with the students sitting with him. He, too, had his foibles. He did not like the smell of young, probably unwashed bodies, and would walk into class ordering, “Open the windows! Open the windows!” even on the coldest days. Once one of my classmates brought in a bottle of hydrogen sulfide he had made in the chemistry lab below us. When he quietly removed the stopper from the bottle, the odor dispersed, and Mr. Musil, assuming that the smell came from the chem lab, shouted, “Close the windows! Close the windows!” For the next forty-five minutes we all suffered the effects of that joke.

At some point, we boys discovered the girls. Oh, we knew our classmates well. Ellie Carman and Mu Nichols were always the brains of the class, though Fred Clothey was certainly their equal or more. The girls were also more mature, as when Fred dashed off a caricature of Mahatma Gandhi on the black-board, which we boys found clever and hilarious but the they thought was disrespectful. By the time we reached high school, the number of girls in our class had grown to seven and we began to take more interest in them. Timidly, and then with more courage, we began to ask them out on dates, which meant sitting together at the movies next to everyone else in the class, attending dances where everyone danced with everyone, or going on the Sunday, after vespers, walk around the lake, where at least we might hold hands in the dark. I found a steady date in Sally Jones and spent as much time with her as I could, but we were all perhaps too close, too "family," to take these relationships too seriously.

We boys were much freer than the girls. We could go off together around town, or the lake, or into the hills in a way the girls could not. We regularly went down to the Budge to the Brahmin Hotel, where we enjoyed a snack of *puri baji*, *dosai*, *Mysore pak*, and *caffie*, or even *meals*,[62] if we had missed our lunch at school.

The Kodai "Budge" (bazaar), ca 1950. (J. Cummings)

In 1950, Mother traveled back to the US to attend my sister Ruth's wedding to Sam Schmitthenner. Dad came to India to spend the summer with me. We moved into the Thoms' house, *Dar-es-Salaam*,[63] and invited Pete and Norm to join us. Soosai, the cook and caretaker, looked after us. I have fond memories of sitting in the cozy living room around the fire place, three of us doing our homework while Dad read. When we had finished, we might play Rook or checkers or some other game until it was time for bed. Dad chaperoned our class camping trip to Kukal in September. That was the year we tried to catch frogs in the nearby wetland. I think we caught more leaches than frogs. We butchered the frogs and fried up the legs in butter. My memory is that the reward was not worth the effort. Back home in Kodai, we waited impatiently for pictures of the wedding, which we knew my Uncle Bog, who had presided over the service, had sent off to us immediately. When the battered package finally arrived, we saw that though it had been addressed to "Dar-es-Salaam," Kodaikanal, South India, the proper address to use, the US Postal Service had sent it to Dar-es-

---

[62] *Meals*, a "Tamil" term meaning a full vegetarian meal of rice, vegetables, yogurt and curry, served on a banana leaf.
[63] House of Peace, in Arabic.

Salaam, Tanganyika. The pictures were not damaged, in spite of the distance they had traveled. The wedding was an all Kodai affair: the bride and groom, maid of honor and all the groomsmen were graduates of the Class of 1944, except for Jim, who was of the Class of 1949.

In 1952, Ruth and Sam, with son Bill, came up to Kodai in late April and took me out of boarding to live with them. They had come back to India in 1951 as missionaries of the Evangelical Lutheran Church, stopping in Basrah on the way out to spend Christmas with us before going on and settling in Rajahmundry, in what would become Andhra State. In Kodai that year they lived in a Lutheran owned cottage high up on St. Mary's Road. I recall waiting for the first bell for school, which could be heard even that far way, and then racing down the hill on my bike to reach my classroom a minute before the second bell rang ten minutes later. Of course, after school I would have to pedal uphill all the way back to their house.

It was good to be with the Schmitthenners, to spend time with Ruth again and get to know my nephew, Bill. I took several hikes and camping trips with Sam, once to Manjampatti and once to Berijam. When he suggested a biking trip to Munar, in Travancore, by way of Vandaravu, I was ready to go. We invited Jim Schaffer to come with us. The trip would require us to skip school on Friday, but we were both out of boarding and thought we would not be missed. We had a wonderful trip, exploring new territory and seeing new sights. We arrived home late on Sunday. When we got to school the next morning, our classmates greeted us with knowing grins but said nothing. Soon we were called to the principal's office. Papa confronted us, and we told him the truth—which somehow, he already knew. Finally, he said in exasperation, "Was Sammy Schmitthenner with you?!" Sam and his classmates had had a reputation for exuberant tomfoolery, which Papa had had to deal with when they were students. Now it was if Papa was saying, "I sent you back to college, you went on to seminary, you became an ordained minister, and now you have come back here as a missionary, and I still have to deal with your shenanigans! Will this never end?!"

In October that year, after school had closed, four of us took a trip to see the sights of North India. I first went to Rajahmundry to see Sam and Ruth and my days-old new nephew Hans and then backtracked to Guntur Junction. There I met Don Oberdorfer, Jim Shaefer, and Ed Erickson, and we boarded our train for Agra. Their mothers had provided food for at least three trips north, so that once we entered our four-berth compartment, we had no reason to leave except to buy coffee or tea or some kind of bottled soda water. The trip took at least two days, but we were comfortable, well fed, and happy to be off on our own. In Agra we had arranged

Humayan's tomb, New Delhi. (Peck)

to stay in an unoccupied classroom of a mission school. We visited Fatehpur Sikri, the Agra Fort, and the Taj Mahal and lingered to see the Taj by moonlight. In Delhi, we found accommodations at the YMCA and were fed delicious North Indian food. We saw the Red Fort, the Qutab Minar, Humayan's Tomb, and many other sights of Moghul Delhi. I remember feeling I should have studied Indian history before starting on our excursion. While the others returned to Guntur, I traveled alone by train to Bombay, where I caught my flight to Basrah. Our journey fed my love of traveling on Indian trains, a love I have never lost, though I know I would have quite a different, and probably disappointing, experience if I tried making that trip today.

My last semester at Kodai was busy and passed quickly. I was on the staff of our senior yearbook, *The Eucalyptus*, and did a good deal of writing for it. I was also tasked with soliciting ads from local businesses to help finance the project. On my first visit to shops down in the Budge, I was singularly unsuccessful. Back at school, Mr. Hoffman, our school business manager, heard my complaint and offered to go with me. It was amazing what a difference that made! Shopkeepers immediately agreed to advertise, and when Mr. Hoffman smiled at the more prosperous shop owners, they quickly raised their offers from the minimum 25 rupees quarter page to a half or even full-page ad at 100 rupees. We raised almost the total cost of publication that afternoon. In a one company town, it was important for those merchants to maintain good relations with the business manager of the school.

Shon was the photography editor and spent a lot of time at that task. Once he invited me to accompany him on an early Saturday morning photo expedition, a bike ride on the ten-mile round. We stopped often and he got some good shots. I suffered a punctured tire, which we patched temporarily with the adhesive from a band-aid.

We got back to Kodai in time to participate in a senior-staff tennis match and then went out in the afternoon for some more photos. Shon was a good photographer with an artist's eye. Our 1953 Eucalyptus was the first, I believe, to have colored pictures, including a beautiful scene of the lake on the cover.

Shon was also an athlete, excelling in all sports, especially the individual events of track and field. At the annual field day that year he won several blue ribbons and broke my brother Jim's record in pole vault. Jim had broken Robby Storm's record in 1949 by half an inch. Shon bested Jim's record by ten inches. I was not a great athlete, but I could run. I won the 100-yard dash and the 440, though I was disappointed with my performance in the latter. I had broken the school record in practice but could not do it that day.

We celebrated Easter in the usual exuberant way. On Saturday we cut ferns and lilies and helped to decorate the gym. Ruth and Sam and the kids had come up to Kodai early and were there for the celebration on Easter Sunday morning. The high school chorus, under the baton of Mario, with Sally at the piano, sang "The Story of Easter," a cantata by Roy Ringwald based on fourteen well-known spirituals. It was different from our usual, more classical, Easter offerings but I thought it was beautiful and enjoyed singing it. There were a few solos. Del Long handled the tenor arias and a trio of girls sang the alto and soprano solos together.

Our class went to Berijam for our camping trip that year. We had been there often and were disappointed with the choice, but most of us went anyway, determined to enjoy our last camp together. In retrospect, I believe it was on camping trips that we developed our sense of unity. At school we saw each other every day but we were always with others, and at the end of the day the girls retired to Boyer and the boys to Block. On our trips we were together as a class, putting up the tents, preparing and eating the meals, planning activities, and sitting around the camp fire at night telling stories and singing. Indeed, some of our members who had decided not to come that year, biked out the following day to enjoy the camaraderie. We hiked and swam and had a good time. The weather was perfect. And then in the evening, the girls produced a cake they had somehow kept hidden, lit the candles and we celebrated my birthday.

Ruth and Sam invited me to stay with them for the few weeks before my departure. I was very busy at school, but it was wonderful to be able to go "home" at the end of the day. My nephews Bill and Hans were good company. My piano teacher, Miss Rosendaal, held a recital for her students, and with her coaching I actually enjoyed playing for the other students and guests, including my sister. Though I was never going to be a great pianist, it was gratifying to finish on a high note. We rushed to complete our corrections of the *Eucalyptus* proofs and get them back to the printer and we held one more fundraiser, a Senior Carnival, to help pay for it. I worried about making a final decision on whether to attend Hope or Oberlin College and was relieved when Oberlin offered me a two-year tuition scholarship and tipped the balance. I studied for and then took my final exams. And then it was over. I had written Mother and Dad earlier that though I liked Kodai more and more, I was ready to move on to some place new.

Ruth joined the other mothers in planning for our commencement banquet down at the KMU. I don't recall our commencement program, the speakers, or the awarding of diplomas and if I wrote to my parents about it, the letter was lost. I remember that the banquet was a gala affair, and I think Sam was one of the after-dinner speakers, bringing down the house with his stories. There were several other farewell parties. I was invited to the Arcot Mission celebration for John De Vries, and then because I was staying with Ruth and Sam, I attended the Lutheran picnic for Gordon Peery, Jim Schaefer, and Don Oberdorfer. And then we all dispersed. Many of my classmates were booked on ships leaving Bombay the following week, as was I, but I left Kodai later than most.

I caught up with John King and his family in Madras and traveled with them by train to Bombay. The mission guest houses were all full, so I got a room in a hotel at Ballard Pier, near the docks. I had a day to pick up my ticket from Mackinnon Mackenzie and a visa from the Iraqi consulate, and then had a day to find and say goodbye to friends who were in town waiting to board their ships. I mailed off my last letter, expecting that it would reach home before I did, boarded the *SS Dwarka* on the afternoon of May 13, 1953 and sailed off on what I thought would be my last trip through the Arabian Sea and up the Persian Gulf to Basrah. After a brief stay in Basrah, I traveled with my parents back to the US and the next chapter of my life.

EPILOGUE

In closing these tales of our Kodai School years, it's appropriate to ponder how they came about, how it happened that we had such unusual lives of growing up overseas and going to Kodai School in the mountains of South India.

We have our parents to thank for that exotic life. Thus, something must be said of them.

* * *

We had incredible parents. They were, in large measure, intrepid and determined characters with a strong inclination toward adventure.

The definition of an adventure—exciting, unusual, and often hazardous—fits them well. They were highly-educated; ventured from comfortable lives in Western culture into the unknown of the Orient; traveled extensively and immersed themselves in foreign cultures; learned other languages and became bilingual or multi-lingual; were personally and severely impacted by political turmoil and revolutions; witnessed major turning points in the history of our world; witnessed nations advancing from the Middle Ages into the Twentieth Century; adjusted to the daily challenges of being immersed in another culture; partook of the flavor of both the mundane day-to-day events as well as those of intense drama; lived lives of purpose and philanthropic service to humanity; in amazement, they witnessed both the good and the darkness that humankind is capable of; saw a broad scope of drama and what life is about; and saw the grim reality of suffering that many in the third world face.

It is to these incredible people—our parents—whom we have to thank for the exotic childhoods we were afforded.

Our parents were involved in missionary (medical, educational, and spiritual), diplomatic, business, higher education, and non-governmental organization (NGO) work.

Considering that my parents were missionaries, I can speak best to that parentage. From my perspective as a mish-kid, the missionary life was a good one. Being bilingual, experiencing different cultures and ways of viewing the world, and being brought up by parents committed to the well-being of others provided profound insights into the human condition. My parents lived philanthropic, purposeful, and mostly contented lives focused not on material riches but on the riches of mind and soul. For the most part, they lived the type of dedicated, purposeful lives most of us talk about but are too afraid to take the risk of living.

My experience has left me with a positive view of life. This perspective—mostly positive—is not shared by all Kodai kids, and that difference needs mentioning. There were those who thrived in Kodai and those who did not.

Our missionary parents were generally humble folk who played down the uniqueness of their lives, careers and selfless service. Nonetheless, their philanthropic lives—and hence ours also—and careers were adventuresome, meaningful, productive, inspiring, and by any standard, well-lived.

What led them to the mission field, motivating them to give up a secure life in the western world and go to strife-torn, poor, undeveloped, and sometimes dangerous countries? What made them brave physical hazards, political upheavals, disease, lack of sanitation, and all the rest?

The short answer is they wanted to make the world a better place by serving others, especially the poor—"the least of these" as the Bible puts it—and committing themselves to bringing peace and well-being to the world. Service to others is the prominent thread that runs through our parent's lives and careers.

Did our parents have an impact?

At the very least, we can say their world-view was, to a large degree, imparted to their children, to each of us.

Our mothers provided education, medical care, and spiritual fellowship to many. Their quiet, out-of-the-limelight (women's lives were more confined, less open or public) contributions were often not easily seen or quantifiable, yet they were legion. They went to the women of India—whom, in many cases, men were not allowed to see—instilling a sense of self-confidence and self-worth in addition to teaching them to read and write and sharing at a spiritual level. The local women used this new outlook and knowledge to better their lives in matters of nutrition, family planning, family health care, women's rights, and life's everyday problems. The women's new knowledge was multiplied exponentially through subsequent sharing with their families, relatives, and neighbors.

Our fathers' work and contributions provided education, medical care, spiritual understanding, and reconciliation in a more open and public manner. They taught in schools, brought western education to India, and worked in the mission hospitals—facilitating clinical visits, surgeries and other medical care. They improved the health of countless thousands of individuals, and saved many lives.

To temper these adulations, and lest one get the impression that our parents were ideal paragons of humanity, it must be made clear that they were, of course, less than perfect. Our parents were indeed good people, but—as any child can attest to concerning their parents—they were not saints. To be clear, our parents made mistakes—they were human beings after all—yet there's good reason to believe the positive impact they had far outweighed any mistakes they made.

In sum, I think it is safe to say that our parents indeed made a difference—in fact, a tremendous difference. Such certitude should instill a sense of hope and positive worldview in all Kodai Kids and encourage us to follow their example.

Kodai Lake and the boathouse. (D. Wiebe)

Perumal, Kodai's iconic mountain and skyline. (B. Peck)

APPENDIX A

Ann Margaret Gravely grew up in South India and attended Kodai School in the 1940s. She wrote "Summers in the South Indian Hill Stations."[64]

Summers in South Indian Hill Stations

I have already written about Fred Gravely's[65] meeting with Laura Balling in the divine hill station south west of Madras in 1925. Kodaikanal became a important part of my childhood and adolescence, but, to put it in context, here are brief notes on the major hill resorts which we visited at various times. Madras in the hot season was terribly hot, rising to temperatures of 110°F in July and August, and deemed unsuitable for women and children (and Governors!). So families tended to leave their menfolk to sweat it out on the plains and move to the cool and very beautiful mountains. There are two ranges, both parts of the Western Ghats: the more northerly, and, therefore nearer Madras, is the Nilgiri chain, while Kodai is in the Palani hills, somewhat south. In order to reach any of the hill stations we had to travel overnight by train, from the Central Station in Madras to the foothills of the Nilgiri Mountains (part of the Western Ghats), which was from nearby Egmore Station to the Palani range. This was, of course, enormously exciting for us children, but involved the adults in a good deal of preparation of the carriage before our mother, who had an almost pathological fear of diseases, and had, with the governess, swabbed down every surface with disinfectant.

Then beds were made up and John and I vied with each other for the top bunk. I have no proper memory of eating in the train, but, of course, remember very well the many food vendors who walked up and down the platform shouting their wares.

---

64 Charles Gosselink (Kodai class of 1953) shared the document with the author.
65 Frederic Henry Gravely (1885-1965) was a well-known scientist, as well as being director of the Government Museum in Madras (Chennai). He and Laura Balling were married in 1925.

It was wonderful to go to sleep in the outskirts of Madras and wake up as we approached either Mettupalayan for the Nilgiris, or Kodai Road Station for the Palanis.

OOTACOMUND

Ooty (or "Snooty Ooty") was developed as a hill resort by the British in the early 1800's, and became the summer capital for the Government of the Madras Presidency. Lying 7,349 ft above sea level it was always cool, even though the summer midday sun, of course, beat down hot. It was and is surrounded by tea and coffee plantations, and the hills were originally inhabited by an indigenous tribe, the Todas, who still had villages in the Nilgiri hills during my childhood. They were polyandrous, many husbands for one wife, a buffalo culture, very strong and good looking, and were studied by Prince Peter of Greece whose friendship with our father I have recounted elsewhere. Ooty had the distinction of having a small mountain train—we called it the toy train—which went up the ghat from the station in the plains to the resort, a real pleasure in which to travel. We spent the summer of 1937 there, the year King George VI was crowned. Our English grandmother sent magazines with articles, which supplemented those we got in India, and I remember poring over every picture of the Royal Family and the various exciting-sounding events. We were in Ooty because our father was deputizing for the Director of Fisheries, who was away on furlough for a year. Father didn't stay with us all through the summer, but was there for longer periods than usual, and, presumably went to the odd governmental meeting. None of the details do I remember, nor exactly why we went to Ooty that year, instead of the more usual Kodai since Father was always a Government servant, but chose not to go to Snooty Ooty. Mountain hikes were wonderful fun, and in Ooty we could see troops of monkeys jumping from tree to tree in the jungle paths, and lots of gorgeous plants and mosses growing wild. Walks with our father were always interesting, because he told us a great deal about the flora and fauna, transforming excursions into nature studies.

KOTAGIRI

Another hill station in the Nilgiri hills, Kotagiri is about 20 miles away from Ooty, but in my childhood we were not at all aware of the proximity. It was the preferred summer resort of the Danish missionaries in Southern India, and for this reason our mother asked to spend the summer of 1939 there, assuming, as we did, that we would be leaving India for good in the autumn of that year. John and I did our usual lessons under instruction by Edel Rasmussen and we had many social occasions with the various Danish families who were spending differing periods of vacation there. There were also German missionaries who had a small school in Kotagiri.

My most vivid memory was going to the Anglican church on Sunday, September 3rd, and hearing the minister telling us that Britain was at war with Germany. The German teacher ran out in tears, everyone was shocked and naturally wondering what the implications were for them individually. One important decision was quickly made: that Edel, very young for her age, and always homesick for her parents, must go back to Denmark as soon as possible. Our future took a few weeks to be decided; FG's mother wrote to say that everyone believed that the war would be over soon, so why don't we stay in the safety of India until it was over.

Our father had handed in his resignation as Director of the Museum, but his deputy wasn't really ready to assume the responsibility and was glad to keep things as they were for one more year. Our passages to England were cancelled, and our parents started to look for suitable schools for John and me, something they had never imagined they would need to do. One possibility was the English boarding school for girls in Coonoor in the Nilgiri hills, but that would not help my brother. And in any case, our mother, probably rightly, didn't think the education provided was particularly good, and she had great ambitions, at least, for me.

KODAIKANAL

Kodai was the resort in the Palani hills where our parents had originally met in 1925, where they built a summer cottage in 1928, which they sold in 1938 in preparation to leaving India, and where, in the end, John and I found our first school in the American Missionary school in the spring of 1940. Unlike the Nilgiris there was no nice small train winding up the hills from the plains, but a much less pleasant three-hour journey by bus or car, a real torture for people who were prone to travel sickness. It was such an important part of our childhood that I will start at the beginning, before John was born in 1932 in the Van Allen Nursing Home, a small hospital on the edges of Coaker's Walk, which has maybe the most beautiful view in the world, supervised by an American Dr. Otto.

The first impression upon getting out of the terrible car-journey was the strong scent of eucalyptus, and the freshness of the cool mountain air. Our cottage was called Westover after a home in Fred's family town, Wellingborough,

Northamptonshire. It was approached through a thick wood with a deep cutting beside the Lutheran settlement. One walked down beside a pear orchard, through a large white gate and, on the left was a small dwelling, while in front one saw the top of a small hill at the foot of which ran a small stream. Daddy made a wonderful terraced garden with fragrant roses, agapanthus and red hot pokers in a deep bed just in front of the house. Then there were steps down to another layer of flowering plants; I think one more giving into an uncultivated field bordering the stream. Up the other side was a similar hill, at the top of which resided Mrs. Hacker, an English missionary married to another who had two daughters. One of these, Edith was also married to an English missionary, Wilfred Scopes and they had four sons, the eldest of whom was my playmate down in the stream and later, when we were twelve, was my first boyfriend. I visited Westover in the spring of 1974, after a trip to Australia, and, amazingly, found it virtually unaltered to the roses in the garden to some of our pictures still hanging on the walls.

Inside, the house built by a Swiss architect called Schetty was very small with sparse furnishings, no electricity and no modern plumbing. Cooking was done on a wood burning Bonnybridge stove, washing-up took place on the back veranda, where the wood was stored and where there were rooms for our servants. The main house consisted of a good-sized living room with an open fireplace where we burned eucalyptus logs in the evening, plus three small bedrooms, each with an adjoining bathroom with commodes and wash basins into which hot water from the kitchen was brought to wash. There was a tin bath, again filled by hot water brought by a servant with no wheels to assist him. There was a very small stove in each bedroom, very rarely used—I have vivid memories of getting into a cold bed in a cold room every night. Early mornings and evenings were cold, (and in winters there were hard frosts) but during the day when the sun was up it became pleasantly warm. Light was given by kerosene lamps in the bedrooms, and a more powerful calor gas lamp in the living room where we ate and read.

It was a wonderful place for a lively imagination, and I peopled the stream area with fairies and brownies and a troll. Our father made up stories about all these imaginary creatures and we had many conversations about them. When John came along I had a playmate, at least when he grew a bit, and I also made friends with a neighbor's small boy, Luther, near enough for us to run into each other's houses and play in the woods together. Other young Americans joined us, and, naturally enough, I began to speak the group language, forbidden in the house, so I switched between English and American depending upon where I was.

The pear tree orchard was another excellent venue for fantasy play. I cannot remember when I first climbed a tree, but fairly early I became proficient and entirely fearless, swinging from tree to tree at the top of the canopy, while I constructed imaginary rooms in various trees. At night the orchard was occupied by jackals which howled a great deal, disturbing my sleep in the bedroom nearby.

Separation from our father was hard on our mother, although she had, of course, always the company of a Danish teacher, and also many friends among the American missionaries. Maybe Daddy, sweltering at his desk in the Museum, felt the separation more keenly. There was no telephone communication between them, but frequent letters, and the occasional treat for me in the shape of an enclosed letter from Daddy. This reserved scientist, who wrote rather dry articles and books on various academic topics, wrote lovely letters to his children, often illustrated by a line drawing. One was about a mongoose, one of a family from the garden, always welcome because they kept snakes away; this one often visited at dinnertime in the evening and was a favorite topic in letters to the children.

A most unusual event in the summer 1935[66] when I was seven deserves mention. Our governess at that time was Lydia Larsen, who was in the middle of her three-year contract with my family, and who much later on became a missionary to India. Like all of us, she was fond of hiking in the beautiful hills around us where, among other things, one could in those days find and pick armfuls of fragrant wild orchids, growing on damp rocks. One day, in her time off, Lydia went to find orchids for our house. She was several miles from home when she noticed a sharp pain in her left ankle and a green snake scuttling away in the undergrowth. She realized she had been bitten and was entirely alone on a mountain side with no way of summoning help. She trudged slowly home, her leg swelling all the time until it was three times its usual size. To add to her woes her breathing was reduced to gasps and her heart was painful; she was quite sure she was going to die. Fred, fortunately, was in Kodai at the time, and was well aware that there were no deadly snakes in the Palni Hills, but took the precaution of calling on an Indian authority on snakes, resident in the town, who confirmed his belief, and was able to tell our family something about pit vipers. None of which was any help to poor Lydia who needed an antidote serum which could not be found locally. I understand that nowadays all Government hospitals are required by law to hold stocks of snakebite antidotes, but in those days serum for a non-lethal bite was not to be found.

---

[66] Ann was born in 1928, she was probably in the Kodai School class of 1944.

Lydia shared a bedroom with me, and through a long, frightening night she lay panting in a bed beside mine, attended by two American missionary doctors, who could supply nothing more than moral support, and, I expect, a prayer or two. One of them had to leave Kodai the following day, but, by then the poison had done its work, and, although far from well, Lydia had accepted the fact that she was not going to die and was, in fact, on the mend, and wasn't too worried about his departure. In fact, the physical effects of this episode remained with Lydia forever, although she went on to have a long and useful life in India and later Denmark.

While we were very young we were not expected to go on long hikes in the hills, but often went up to the lake (never swam in by anyone) or to Bryant park, at the end of the lake where there were trees to climb and sometimes we met other English children. But they were not kind to me, teasing me mercilessly about my apparel, as usual slightly odd in that we wore hand-knitted woolen socks, in my case bright red in color. How I hated them, but these were the only socks on offer, so I wore them protesting. There were always many boats and punts on the lake, but our parents did not belong to the boat club (nor any other club in Kodai) so we didn't have that fun early, although later we did. There was a regular ferry crossing the lake, costing a few annas each trip, and we went on this when we went to see our Madras dentist, who followed his clientele during the hot weather.

I don't remember any corporate religious observance in the early years, although I feel there must have been some. Our mother, a Danish Lutheran might have been expected to enjoy one of the American Lutheran churches, but they tended to be cliquish, and the Anglican church on Coaker's Walk did not figure into my early childhood, although it became significant during my adolescence. David and Margaret Clutterbuck, who shared lessons with us in Madras also came up to Kodai when we were there, so our home school continued.

The Kodaikanal Missionary Association did figure in our lives, putting on regular operettas by Gilbert and Sullivan, open tea parties for anyone interested, had a library, and in general was a focus for adult social exchange, taking their children along. The KMU[67] had a building in the grounds of the large school for American missionaries, Highclerc, which was deemed unnecessary when we were very young, but in which we were both enrolled in 1940 when the family settled for the war years. It has prospered over time and is now the fairly well-known Kodaikanal International School, still taking pupils from all around the world, but nowadays predominantly Indian.

---

67 Kodaikanal Missionary Union.

THE WAR YEARS

The winter 1939-40 was, as always, delightful, but also strange in that we no longer had proper lessons: the Clutterbuck children had gone home to England, Edel Rasmussen had gone back to Denmark, and, as a substitute we had a very young German Jewess, Liv Liebermann, whose task was to teach me German, which she did. But I don't think there was any maths or science teaching, although I was by now eleven years old, and John approaching eight. Our mother was brought up with Rousseau's educational philosophy which underlies the free school movement, and teachers that children learn when they are ready and needy. I had read very early and read avidly anything which I could get hold of, but John who suffers a mild dyslexia was not so fortunate, and presumably nobody noticed that he needed some extra help in acquiring reading. My dearly-loved mother was very busy, taking a course on writing short stories, writing diet sheets for poor Indian children in a local nursery school, and attending lectures given by Dr. Maria Montessori[68] in the Theosophical Society's headquarters near Madras. And Liv had no idea about teaching, so she concentrated on speaking German with me. I read *Little Women*, *Anne of Green Gables*, the *Woman's Journal* and some school books sent from England such as *Our Island Story* (English history) and stories about countries like Africa, among other things. I wrote stories, learned the piano and Indian dancing. All very nice, but not a balanced educational diet.

We had cancelled our plans to go to England and to school there and instead we were destined to settle temporarily in Kodai; by now our parents no longer owned Westover, so we requested permission to live in one of the YMCA houses in a complex known as Association Hill. By this time electricity had arrived in Kodai, but in all other respects the houses were very similar to our old one. The several dwellings, of different sizes and type were designed and built by the Swiss architect who had designed Westover. He had a workshop in a small town called Katpadi,

---

68 Maria Tecla Artemisia Montessori (1870-1952), the founder of Montessori Schools, was an Italian physician and educator. She was teaching a course in India in 1940 when Italy entered WWII on the side of Germany. Thus, the British interned her in India from 1939 to 1946. She spent much of the time in Kodaikanal. She was a strong advocate for the rights of the child and was awarded the French Legion of Merit and the Dutch Order of Orange Nassau, as well as nominated for the Nobel Peace Prize. Similar to Montessori's situation was that of Dr. Elizabeth Caspari who taught music at Kodai School and later moved to the United States where she was an early promotor of the Montessori method and schools the rest of her life.

near Madras, where he made lovely furniture to order,[69] and made for us everything we might need for a large household in polished rosewood and ultimately shipped back to England in 1945 (members of our family still use some of it). Our first home was much larger than our own cottage, built on two floors, semi-detached with our neighbors an American businessman's family. There were two daughters, about the same ages as John and me, who became firm friends.

Among other families on Association Hill was one belonging to a Norwegian pianist, married to a Bengali, who, with her children, was trying to settle herself as a good Indian wife, not altogether easy in those days; her son, Dillip was a good friend of John's, who also got very pally with Chris Windle, who lived with his English mother in one of the cottages, and who was, among others, part of a gang who perpetrated minor delinquencies. A really good friend was Dalton McClelland,[70] son of an important figure in the YMCA, and his wife Maude, who spent long periods in a home on Association Hill. Dalton always seemed to be hungry and made the rounds of the friendly homes at about tea-time when he politely stood beside the table and remarked "That cookie looks good." He excelled himself at the very American outdoors wedding ceremony which took place in his parents' garden; when the bridal couple cut the cake, Dalton could be heard asking "May I have the crumbs?"

There was a properly equipped playground on Association Hill on which we and our playmates spent many hours of enjoyment, and also the extensive grounds which extended down a hill to tennis courts near the bottom, below which was a stream. Many running games went on of which my best memory was for one called Kick the Can.

Going to school for the first time at the age of eleven was a shock, although I had for years longed to be in school. First of all, the excellent Principal of Kodai School had to decide where to place us, since we had had such a peculiar educational upbringing. So far as I was concerned he gave me the Stanford Binet intelligence test, very verbally biased, which I did well and was placed in the 8th grade, while John went in at the 3rd grade. But what a trial it all was to begin with; I was the only

---

69 The wood shop and furniture factory in Katpadi were the Arcot Mission Industrial School, part of the Reformed Church in America (RCA) mission and hospital complex in Vellore, India. The Industrial school was founded by Ben Rottschaefer of the RCA and who was followed by Ben De Vries whose sons, David and John, attended Kodai School.

70 Dalton and his mother were good friends with the Gosselink family of the Arabian Mission.

English pupil[71] among 16 American boys and girl, a butt for teasing by the boys who called me Limey or sometimes Gravy, and laughed at my habit of twisting my hair. And, of course, my maths was really almost nonexistent; now I had to grapple with sums in dollars and cents, while I had only the haziest idea of what money was for, not ever having shopped alone, nor having more than the basic rudiments of Indian money, let alone English. I was taken in hand by a brilliant teacher called Agnes Liddle,[72] who quickly put me on my way and I was soon able to calculate compound interest sums in dollars and cents without having any real idea what it was all about. Meanwhile John struggled with reading and writing, and says he never liked going to school. It is perhaps surprising that with such a poor start in his educational life, which persisted, he ended up as a very distinguished consultant orthodontist in a major British University. During the war years John and I had very little to do with each other, and led separate lives within the same family.

In 1941, our father retired and joined us on Association Hill. Pearl Harbor happened on his birthday, December 7th, and America joined the war which made a big difference to the general feelings toward us, their Allies. I remember this period as the nicest year of my whole academic career. At the end of 1940, when I went into High School in 9th grade, there was an influx of English pupils, including a girl who became my bosom companion, Jenefer Westlake, and Peter Scopes[73] whom I used to play with in the stream near Westover, now clad in a smart English school suit and with an accent like mine. We fell in love and he walked me home from Saturday night dances, no kissing, of course—it was a mission school, after all—but a warm arm around my shoulders as we trudged along. We started Latin and a bit of Greek, geometry at which I excelled, biology, American history and English with another brilliant teacher. I started to be, first on the Honor Roll and then on the Special Honor Roll, becoming very competitive and hard working. But the flaw was games of any sort. I could never manage to stand up on roller skates, one of the activities which went on in our gym, nor do anything with baseball, a game which terrified me, although it was played with a soft rather than hard ball. But when teams were picked

---

[71] Later, more English students would come to Kodai School, among them David and Shirley Firth, parents of Colin (well-known British actor) and Jon Firth. The English alumni from Kodai School often hold reunions in England.

[72] A Presbyterian missionary, and one of the longest serving teachers at Kodai School.

[73] Peter was probably in the Kodai class of 1944. He was the son of Wilfred Scopes and had three brothers. When Wilfred's wife died, he married a teacher from Kodai School and, later in the 1950, he was on the National Christian Council in Nagpur.

I was always one of the last to be chosen, along with a classmate who was deaf and rather retarded. So in the end I was excused and took instead private dancing classes, which suited me much better.

There were American kids who rejoined the school after some years of education in the USA. Among these was the glamorous Elinor Potee, with Shirley Temple curls and a different pretty dress every day. She quickly set the tone for the whole of the first years of high school, and I started to use hair curlers every night, have a variety of bows to finish off my curls, and generally tried to keep up with Elinor's example. She was academically gifted, great fun, sang and danced and has remained my friend ever since, although now we are separated y the Atlantic Ocean.

There was a popular music teacher who started a glee club where we sang the latest songs from America, including many by Irving Berlin. She also conducted a good orchestra and choir, including a rousing choral piece for Easter.

Naturally enough, there were gestures of patriotism from time to time, and we saluted the American flag very solemnly at regular intervals, and I learned the text of the Gettysburg Address as part of a hymn-like song. Religious observance took place on Sunday mornings at Junior Church in the KMU building, part of the School campus, and involved excellent hymns, some prayers and usually a good sermon, sometimes preached by one of the student's fathers.

Not all the American missionaries used our school, let alone our informal church, which supplemented the American Church near Coaker's walk. Opposite the Kodai school campus, just over the road was a church with a proper steeple, and a school for younger children. This was the property of the Missouri Lutherans,[74] a very narrow, fundamentalist sect who worshipped only with their own kind and whose children were also segregated until they went to suitable high schools in America. During the war they had, of necessity, to remain in India, and several joined us for scholastic activities, but never religious instruction or worship. They, of course, abominated the theory of evolution, and Fred found all his diplomatic skills needed when he taught biology in the 10th grade, a couple of years after retirement. One day he included in a test the question: "What is the main evidence for the theory of evolution?" Back came from a Missouri Lutheran the answer: "None." Our poor father was in a dilemma, since he believed in a person's right to stand up for his church's teaching almost as strongly as be believed in evolution. In the end he gave the boy a few marks for steadfastness, a real tribute to a teacher's fair mindedness.

---

74 Known as Loch End compound.

The story was told of an English missionary surgeon, working in The Christian Medical School and Hospital, founded by the American Dr. Ida Scudder.[75] He once operated upon a Missouri Lutheran and later showed him round this famous establishment, whereupon the patient remarked "You are sure doing some wonderful work here, but you know you are damned just the same." To which the surgeon replied " I may be damned but I will not be damned by you!"

Then there was the Rev. Blanchard[76] who, with his wife, Bula Dell (nee Hagaman)[77] (1920-2017), walked painfully out of Burma and into India, ending up in Kodai in 1942, and taken on as a teacher of English. I cannot remember where he worshiped, but, as a Tennessee Baptist he too had fundamentalist leanings, and persuaded all the high school boys that dancing was evil. Otherwise he seemed nice and normal enough.

I haven't written enough about the wonderful long hikes in the mountains, which we regularly took led by our father. Not one to sit around in retirement, he made a beautiful garden around our home on Association Hill, started to keep bees, taught biology at school, started the first Scout Troop and took as walking to many hidden places as well as the more usual tourist rambles. We would think nothing of trekking for 10 miles, taking water in bottles and sandwiches in rucksacks, never minding heavy rain which might suddenly hit us out in the mountains, we just got wet! Magical places like Fairy Falls, Pillar Rocks, Dolphin's Nose and, much nearer, Bear Shola falls gave enormous pleasure to all of us, and, later the servicemen who came on holiday and rest periods. A rare treat after a long, hot tramp was to bring home some very young eucalyptus boughs with their very tender pale blue leaves which were placed in a tin tub with very hot water, making a special scented bath. Who cleared up after the mess I did not really care, I certainly did not find it part of my responsibility!

I was fully grown, in many ways old for my years, enjoying life to the full, and seemed to have grown out of adults whom I had much loved as a young child. These included several Danish missionaries whom our parents sometimes paid their

---

75 Founder of Christian Medical College Vellore and Vellore Medical Center, one of the largest hospitals in India, located in Vellore, 75 miles west of Madras (now Chennai, Tamil Nadu).

76 Probably Rev. William "Maurice" Blanchard (1912-1989), American Baptist missionary in Burma circa 1939-1942 and South India circa 1942-1966. (American Baptist Historical Society)

77 Bula Dell Hagaman Blanchard Hanes wrote the book *Remembering 25 Years of God's Faithfullness in India.*

Roadside temple.(Peck)

railway fares so they could escape from their mission fields in the hot plains. Lydia, for example, now a missionary looking after a school, was without funds from the home country. My mother used to have a dress made for her whenever she had a new one herself. I wasn't much interested in my old friends, so absorbed was I in my new.

APPENDIX B

Margaret Eddy's Story

The following is an excerpt from a talk given to Kodai School students in the chapel during Founder's Week, October 1997, by Bonnie Belle Pickard and John Chote:[78]

Margaret Eddy was born on November 14, 1848 in Ohio, and moved to Kansas in 1856. She went to school in Leavenworth, Kansas with William Cody, better known as "Buffalo Bill." At age 14 she entered Elmira College and then began a teaching career at age 16. She saved money to go to Vassar but could not graduate because of astigmatic eyes. Unfortunately, there were no corrective lenses at that time. She married George Eddy when she was about 24 and ran a drug store. They had three sons, George Sherwood, Dana, and David Brewer. Mr. Eddy died suddenly in 1894, leaving her with comfortable resources. She and the boys pledged to live economically and to contribute the rest to humanity. In 1900, Mrs. Eddy went to India to visit her missionary son, Sherwood. While there, she saw a great need for English-medium education for children of missionaries so that they could live in India (instead of boarding in US or England) and be prepared for further education abroad.

Margaret Eddy became the first principal of Kodaikanal School.

Highclerc Hotel, what is now the Administration building, rented one room to Mrs. Eddy for Rs. 15 a month. On July 1, 1901, a school opened with 13 pupils ages 8 to 14. The four staff members included Mrs. Eddy (principal), Miss Churchill (teacher), Mrs. Jeffrey (housemother), Miss Thompson (music teacher).

---

[78] This article appeared in the *Kodai Alumni Magazine*, Spring 1998.

Early each morning the pupils had to line up in the front hall at the tap of a bell and Mrs. Eddy would go down the line inspecting their necks, ears, fingernails, and shoes. On one occasion when the bell was rung, a little boy had a brief interview with her just before inspection began, and then whispered that he had been excused for the school because he had a stomach ache. By the time Mrs. Eddy had started down the line she discovered an epidemic of stomach aches had attacked the school. To the students' great astonishment she had a great sympathy that lasted to the end of the inspection line. They were all excused from school! It was hard for them to appear afflicted in the view of their delight, but the next minute their joy was slackened. She announced that everyone was to be bundled up in steamer rugs and set in easy chairs out on the large verandah. When she had all properly tucked in, she disappeared for a moment and returned with a huge twelve ounce castor oil bottle and a tablespoon. The castor oil lasted as far as her sympathy had lasted and not one was overlooked. From that day onward the school was surprisingly free from stomach ailments.

Mrs. Eddy's rigid standards of honesty are among the most vivid of all her "children's" memories of her. There was to be no beating around the bush, no hedging, and no qualifying of direct answers. Those who did try to cheat Mrs. Eddy never slept on comfortable beds until they confessed.

But that is not saying she was not the source of much fun at Highclerc. When she came to kiss her "children" good night they would crawl under the blankets and put their feet on the pillows to be kissed. She always pretended it was a huge joke on her and acted as if it were a surprise and had never happened before.

The next year, the hotel owner, a Miss Orlabar, saw the success of the school and raised the rent to Rs 150 a month. Mrs. Eddy promptly moved the school to Rock Cottage. Within the next year, Miss Orlabar decided to sell Highclerc Hotel. For one thing, business was off, and she had a spiritual awakening in which she realized that such sports as tennis were the work of the devil, and even at that time there were tennis courts at Highclerc! She was also convinced that the Second Coming of Jesus was imminent and she began selling off her property as rapidly as possible.

Mrs. Eddy took up the challenge and spent the next year traveling back and forth between Kodai and America trying to raise funds to purchase Highclerc Hotel. Once she interviewed a rich woman to ask her help in raising the money needed, some $10,000. When the woman mailed her a check for $100, she sent it back with a note saying,: "How shall I ever raise the needed sum when you, from whom I expected so much, send me only a hundred dollars?" As soon as this was in the mailbox, its writer suffered torments of doubt and misgiving, but by return mail the rich woman sent $1,000!

By 1903 the funds had been raised, and Highclerc was purchased. Most of the rooms were used as dormitory rooms with one room as an office, another for a dining room and a third for a social room. A large rose garden occupied the space where Alumni Hall now stands. As the school continued to expand, Airlee and Barton were purchased. Barton was eventually demolished and Kennedy built in its place. A little later, Wilson House was purchased. It now houses the Vice Principal, Dean, and Chaplain's offices.

Mrs. Eddy served as Principal of Highclerc without salary until she developed a neurological disorder which forced her to return to the US. There she continued to support the school through active fundraising efforts.

Mrs. Eddy was one of those petite, quick-moving persons that suggested a wren. Her interest in others was so keen that she completely forgot herself, and it fell to her relatives to insist that she have sufficient and proper clothing. She said once, "My daughter-in-law took me last week to buy a dress. I don't like the present styles. I will not have mine short or narrow, and I will have a pocket." She preferred cotton stockings to silk so that she could give the money saved to help struggling students.

The three characteristics that people remembered most were her love, her loyalty, and her enthusiasm. No one who came in contact with her ever forgot her. She could forget herself, and whatever there might have been in her life of either joy or sorrow, in giving herself to others. Full of activities, determined that the things she believed in should result in deed, she gave herself no rest until the thought was carried out in useful service. Mrs. Eddy was completely dedicated to the school. She planned for it, raised money for it, wrote about it, helped recruit for it, remained acquainted with its alumni, criticized and complimented it, and constantly donated to it.

Margaret Eddy died in September 1935 from cancer. In her will, she requested that her diamond ring be sold and the proceeds given to Kodai School for any of its needs. In May of 1936, the Council of the School reflected on the lack of a permanent place of worship on the campus, students and staff having worshipped in the social room, the classrooms, the KMU, and the gym over the years. With this in mind, the Council designated the money from the diamond ring be used to start a fund to build a chapel for "Mother Eddy's children." Her sons, Brewer and Sherwood, also pledged money to the project.

Ninety-six years later, we are all still "Mother Eddy's children." We all profit immensely from the energy and enthusiasm she put into making a dream of providing education for children in India come true. Perhaps the only way we can thank her now is to commit ourselves to looking at the needs of others—and then committing ourselves to meeting those needs. In that way, we can each contribute to the legacy of Margaret Eddy, and make the world a better place.

Saint Peter's Church on Coaker's Walk. (D. Wiebe)

APPENDIX C

A brief history of Kodaikanal

Nora Mitchell, a much-admired teacher, taught geography and history at Kodai School from the 1960s to 1980s. Her book *The Hill-Station: Kodaikanal* is a well researched and detailed overview of Kodaikanal. The following is an excerpt from her book.[79]

A brief history of Kodaikanal

A long-standing problem for Kodaikanal, was its inaccessibility. Several attempts had been made in the previous century to lay traces for a good carriage road and to connect the existing ghat trails by rail, none of which had fully materialized. At the turn of the century steam-propelled motor vehicles began to arrive in India. The Raja of Puducottai owned a French-manufactured car already in 1904, but it could not be used for Kodai as there was no road. In 1905, a resident of Kodai induced a Trichinopoly motor company to establish a bus service from Kodai Road Station to Periyakulam, with a detour to the Tope. This eliminated the slow transits and reduced the journey from the station so that the entire trip could be done in daylight hours. Work on Law's Ghat Road was also recommenced by the Public Works Department and the governor, Lord Pentland, came to open it in 1914. However, it was not yet safe for general traffic and remained closed for two further years. Several of Kodai's permanent residents drove up in cars and motor-bicycles in 1916, leading the way towards an irreversible trend. Kodaikanal Municipality

---

79 Nora Mitchell, *The Hill-Station: Kodaikanal* (The University of Chicago, Department of Geography), 1972, pp. 130-136.

became alarmed at that time at a possible automobile invasion for which Kodai roads were ill-suited. They passed a bylaw prohibiting the use of motor vehicles within the settlement. With no penalty attached, however, the by-law was seemingly disregarded. Road improvements were started as quickly as possible and the law repealed. Within two to three years the maistries[80] and coolies at Periyakulam retained almost no employment.

With each improvement in turn, Kodai became more easily accessible, and this accessibility was reflected in the growth of the hill-station. Between 1891 and 1901 the permanent population had increased by only 200. This represented the period after the results of the railroad extension had already been effected and it was still necessary to wait all day at the railway station to travel through the cooler night by transit and chair. Between 1901 and 1910 the population rose from 1,912 to 2,906, an increase of almost a thousand. The period in question was the time of the installation of bus services from Kodai Road Station to the Tope so that the journey to the hill-station could be completed before dark. Between 1910 and 1920, the decade of the construction of the motor road and of buses direct from the railway station to the hill-station, the population rose to 4,283, a further increase approaching one and a half thousand. After the 1920s, cars increasingly became more easily available to larger numbers of people, making the ride to the hill-station considerably less difficult each year for a greater proportion of visitors within driving distances. Though not the sole reason for the expansion of the hill-station during these years, greater accessibility together with sufficient space for expansion, were obviously important factors. The census figures show permanent population rose to 6,523 in 1930, 9,724 in 1940, and 10,941 in 1950.

The permanent population increases in their turn reflected the seasonal population increases. As more holiday-makers visited the hill-station, opportunities for trade and services became greater and many Indians who sought their fortunes at the hill-station remained there. The actual numbers of seasonal visitors was not regularly recorded, but where such figures, or estimates, are available, it appears

[80] A maistry is a foreman, a leader in charge of a work crew.

that the seasonal population varied from approximately one-third to one-half more people than the permanent population.[81]

The government attempted to beautify the station with a park, named Bryant Park after the pioneering officer. In 1920 the Forestry Department put the park under the control of the Curator of the Botanical Gardens in Ootacamund,[82] who soon discovered that he was unable to supervise work in both places. In 1924 responsibility for the park was transferred to the Kodaikanal Municipality, together with an annual grant for its maintenance.[83]

The municipality also made itself responsible for the improvement of the bazaar conditions of the town. Controls were set up to safeguard the prices and quality of foods, and co-operative stores were established in 1919, owned and controlled on an economically sound basis by many shareholder residents of Kodaikanal. They are still a flourishing concern. A municipal market was opened two years later and the municipality established through the years several travelers' bungalows and rest houses for the convenience of government officials and tourists.

Still after the completion of Law's Ghat, the dhobies (washermen) for Kodaikanal continued to live down in their Periyakulam homes. Early Saturday mornings they drove their donkeys up the deserted Coolie Ghat loaded with clean laundry which was distributed to its owners in Kodai while the dirty wash for the next week was collected and taken down. The dhobies preferred to live and work in the warmth of the plains. Though the municipality built a new dhobie-khana—a laundry establishment—by the side of a stream about two miles below the bazaar, it took several years before the dhobies became acclimatized citizens of Kodaikanal.[84]

---

[81] Figures available from various sources of unknown reliability are:
1909 in season 4,025, compared to 2,906 out of season,
1920 in season 6,069, compared to 4,283 out of season,
1930 in season 9,857, compared to 6,523 out of season. (Nora Mitchell, *The Hill-Station: Kodaikanal* (The University of Chicago, Department of Geography), 1972, p 131.

[82] Another British Hill Station, also called "Ooty."

[83] Season Committee, Kodaikanal Township, Summer Festival, Kodaikanal (Madurai: Noble Press,1969), pp. 14-15.

[84] This reluctance on the part of the dhobies to settle at Kodaikanal was probably also related to earlier British attitudes, as well as to climate. Still in the first decade of the twentieth century, laundrymen were prohibited from polluting the streams around the settlement. See: E. M. M. Lloyd, *Guide to Kodaikanal and Its History* (London: Ward, Lock & Co. Ltd., 1909), p. 13.

Health services were at first established entirely on a private basis. Though officially classified as a health sanatorium in the early years, Kodai's chief health factor lay in its preservation by outdoor exercise rather than in the cure of sickness. Kodai claimed no true hospital at all in the nineteenth century. A room at the back of the post office at Hock Cottage served an apothecary until 1873 when a small building was erected for medical consultations at the site of the present P.W.D. Inspection Bungalow. Europeans, however, generally enlisted the services of civil surgeons or missionary doctors on vacation in the hills. Many are the stories of operations performed on dining-room tables, and doctors and nurses seldom received their full vacation. The Madura Mission medical personnel had so many serious cases in the early years of the century that East House was fitted up as an emergency hospital, and doctors started a subscription for an operation theater. Sufficient money was raised to construct the Van Allen Hospital in 1915, and it was expanded to include a maternity ward in 1923. Its expansion and maintenance have been entirely by private subscription and fees, various missions and some of the seasonal activity clubs being the major contributors.

In 1926, the governor of Madras laid the foundation stone for a municipal hospital. British medical doctors and Catholic missionary nurses who served the hospital for many years were replaced by Indian staff already long before Independence. Also in the 1920s, a government veterinary hospital was established to serve the growing numbers of farmers, fruit-growers, and market gardeners whose livelihood depended on their draft animals. Seasonal visitors also took pets to the vet for treatment. A Department of Health was established in 1939 with a resident officer in charge.

The astrophysical observatory expanded during the years. Though basically a central government rather than a local concern, it nevertheless became involved in affairs of the local community: its director was for many years the municipal chairman, it encouraged student visitors, and it became an additional hill-season attraction. With British equipment procured in the first two decades of the century, together with its high altitude position in close proximity of the equator, its scientists produced high-class solar research which gave the observatory an international reputation. A machine-shop was set up at Kodai which made it possible in the 1940s to build enough apparatus to keep a number of experimental research scholars busy on a variety of solar problems. In 1948, a new magnetic observatory was established at very little cost as many of the old instruments could be repaired and modernized at the local shop.

An unplanned responsibility of the municipality developed very early, rose to high peaks during the two world wars, and has seemingly become a tradition: that of using Kodaikanal for the internment of political prisoners. Already at the turn of the century the Wazir of Chitral and the Afghan princes Akram and Azam were interned at "Belleview." The ex-Maharaja of Nabha was a political prisoner in Kodai for twenty years. During World War I, "Loch End"[85] was at first used to house German nationals, while a new camp site was built two miles out from the main settlement, and used in both world wars. The camp has since been converted into the Holiday Homes tourist center. Conversely, Kodai also became the temporary sanctuary for many European refugees from both Nazi Germany and Communist Russia during and after World War II. In 1945, Kodaikanal School staff represented eleven nationalities.

In the surrounding hills the Forestry Department planted blue-gum and wattle to keep the settlement supplied in firewood for cooking and heating requirements as well as to beautify the landscape and prevent soil erosion. They also built rest houses in the early years of the century, each containing a kitchen, dining-room, and several bedrooms, so that hikers and campers could have safe lodgings for the nights. Keys to the houses were available in Kodaikanal and a party of hikers often sent coolies in advance with food and bedding. After the arrival of the motor-car, the huts were in even greater demand as non-trekkers were then also able to stay out in the hills.

The Game Association stocked local streams with rainbow trout and a fishery was opened on the northern edge of the lake. With the automobiles came the necessity for better roads outside the settlement so that these pleasures could be enjoyed by more people. Some of the previous hiking trails were widened for vehicular traffic. The first to be completed was the "Ten-mile Round" linking the Observatory on the northern side of the settlement with the golf course and Pillar Rocks on the southern rim. In 1929, the District Board turned the first sod for the Goschen Road, popularly known as the "Forty-mile Round." It extended the earlier shorter route, linking Poombarai with Mannavanur and Berijam. It was completed by 1932. A decade later a second ghat road was started from Berijam to Top Station and Munnar and eventually to Cochin, a total distance of 160 miles. It passes through beautiful countryside, but is an extraordinarily slow dirt road. Until 1970 one needed approximately eleven hours to reach Cochin this way, and the road was impassable after heavy rains.[86]

---

[85] Both Belleview and Lock End are European compounds near the lake.

[86] In 1970 the road was considerably improved. It is now an all-weather road and its 160 miles of mountainous territory can be driven in eight hours.

A great municipal concern was the construction of a power house in 1938 and then in 1940 the connection of Kodaikanal to the electrical supply at Pykara in the Nilgiris. Shortly after that, links were made to Mettur in the north and Pabanasam in the south as alternative supply systems. Gradually private homes were able to install electricity, and a private company built a cinema, the Kodaikanal Talkies, at the foot of the bazaar road, which showed English, Tamil, and Hindi films. The municipality installed a loudspeaker through which they announced season activities and instructions to holiday-makers, and a siren which whistled out the hour four times a day starting at 6:00 a.m.

The municipality thus played an important role in the development of the hill-station. It endeavored to ensure that the entire community became aware of the various functions of the hill-station. It worked on behalf of the permanent residents, wealthier European as well as poorer Indian groups; it was to some extent involved with seasonal activities of vacationers; it planned to utilize the resources of the hills to satisfy the needs of both permanent residents and seasonal clientele. An Indian was appointed municipal chairman as early as 1921, and since then Indians have alternated with British in the capacities of both chairmen and commissioners, the highest posts which were available. Thus, when Independence came and there were no more British leaders, the municipality could continue to function as it always had. It continued to welcome both Europeans and Indians to share the hill-station amenities.

Expansion of Year-Round Activities

Though original thoughts regarding the possibilities of opening up the Palni Hills as English farming colonies did not materialize, there was, nevertheless, a definite year-round European enclave in Kodaikanal which developed steadily through the first half of the twentieth century before Independence. The numbers of Europeans who sought permanent residence in Kodaikanal increased with Kodai's accessibility. As it became easier to travel up from Madras or Madurai, it also became possible to live in Kodai and yet remain involved in certain former activities on the plains. Retirement could be partial at first and even when complete there was no decisive break from former friends such as a return to England would have necessitated.

Other factors combined with those of easier accessibility to assist the expansion process. During the era between the two world wars and from then on with ever-increasing acceleration, the cost of living in England rose at a far higher rate than old age pensions. In England it became more and more difficult to manage on a pension, whereas with the same financial allowances it was still possible in India to pay servants' salaries. Furthermore, the warmer, sunnier weather was a great inducement for Madras Presidency civil servants to retire in Kodai, especially as social ties were often closer to fellow Kodai pensioners than to strangers in the British Isles. The British remaining in India after the start of both world wars were physically unable to return to the British Isles for several years and their numbers also helped to swell the permanent population at the hill-station.

Though the Indian population in Kodai also expanded during these years, the hill-station was basically a foreign exclave. The way of life of the permanent residents in their attractive, large compounds inside the basin was enhanced by the support of the Indian residents out of sight in their crowded Indian quarters outside. Europeans had no cause to enter the Indian sector, as daily shopping was done by personal servants and work contracts were arranged with the chief contractor whether he were British or Indian. The leaders of the municipality were Englishmen in the early years. They organized the township according to their British training and set traditions which Indian leaders later followed.

As the number of permanent European residents increased, so a large Indian population was needed and could be supported in order to serve this clientele, and generally it seemed that amenities which benefitted the Europeans also, if indirectly, benefitted the Indians. For example, the municipality was organized primarily for the welfare of the Europeans, but it became the means whereby better sanitation and fairer prices were available in the Indian quarter. Schools and medical services were rarely created only for one stratum of inhabitants, even though such institutions were organized by private concerns rather than by the municipality. As already noted, those Indians of wealth and high social standing, who lived inside the basin, were accepted as part of the European enclave.

The Educational System

An indirect role in the expansion of the hill-station was played by Kodai's educational institutions. In the early centuries of British colonialism in India there was no question but that children were sent to England when they were old enough to be educated. This spirit predated to the hill-station era when the feasibility of using the hill-stations for schools, at least for younger children, was considered, so that long-term parting from parents might be delayed until more advanced specialized education began. The British did not, however, establish schools for their children in Kodaikanal, as such schools had already been set up in the Nilgiris.

The first school to be established in Kodaikanal was a Jesuit seminary. With sanction from Rome the construction of a novitiate was commenced in 1894 and a course of philosophy started the following year at the Sacred Heart College in Shembaganur. Students remained there approximately eight years and then completed training for the priesthood in Poona or Kurseong. The school was basically organized for Indian students, though others were accepted, and one of the original considerations for its site was that Shembaganur, being approximately 1,000 feet lower than the La Providence Jesuit property, would be less cold for Indian students. The priests maintained a strong scholastic interest in the local geography of the Palni Hills as well as in more abstract philosophies. They systematically studied the flora, fauna, geology, and archeology of the hills, and they opened their rare museum collections and models to the public on request. It was largely through their efforts that many of the dolmen circles were protected as historical monuments instead of being chopped for stones in the new ghat road.

Two English-medium schools were important during the half-century: High Clerc (Kodai School) and the Presentation Convent.[87]

The American Madura missionaries had the use of a boarding school in Oberlin, Ohio, but this meant sending their children half a world away and in the early 1890s agitation started for a school in Kodaikanal. Kodaikanal School was opened in 1901 with eight very small classes and a boarding home for thirteen children.[88] Though small, the school was typical of Kodai's international early years in that the children represented both American and British families, working as missionaries and civil servants. At first efforts were made to fulfill curriculum requirements for entry into both British and American universities. As British administrators were slowly being replaced by Indians, and especially since Independence, however, the number of English children attending Kodai School has been negligible, so that the American curriculum only has been followed.

---

[87] During the course of the first half of the twentieth century the Catholics, as part of their missionary activities in the hills, set up various schools for Indian children. These schools, though basic to the welfare of the Indian population residing in and around Kodaikanal, were only of indirect concern with regard to European expansion in the hill-station.

[88] The school rented the Highclerc Hotel property at out of season rates until it could afford to buy the hotel. It is locally still referred to as Highclerc School though its official name became Kodaikanal School.

Once the school was established at Kodaikanal the parents of school-children would make plans to visit the hill-station each year. If they or their missions did not own property in Kodai, they would need to rent a home to be with the children during the holidays. Vacations were arranged so that the long school closure was in winter at a time when students could comfortably live on the plains. In the summer it was expected that parents visited their children at the hill-station.

The school attracted children from American families living in many parts of India[89] and neighboring lands. Though essentially a school for missionaries' children, it accepted any student willing to abide by the rules. Several missions used the school's residential facilities. Other groups established their own boarding homes and sent the children as day-scholars to the main campus. Whatever the arrangements, the school played its part in assuring that most Americans in South Asia chose Kodaikanal as their hill-station.

Kodai's other permanent English-language school was the Presentation Convent. In the very early 1900s, when the Rev. Mother Xavier of the Sisters of the Presentation in Madras visited Kodaikanal, recognized the advantages of having a school in the hills and made arrangements to buy property, apparently even before any funds were made available. In 1916, children were brought up from Madras and the foundation stone for a school was laid. It opened the following year with remarkably little furniture or other conveniences. Dormitories were British-style, with large rooms containing many beds and little privacy. Thus costs were minimal, but teaching was of a high caliber and the school grew steadily. Boys were accepted only in the elementary department. In the high school, girls take the Senior Cambridge examinations and, if musical, may also prepare for the Trinity College of Music certificates. The school caters primarily to English, Anglo-Indian, and Indian students.

Also of note were the non-English European schools and boarding residences. Already during the first world war when German nationals were repatriated or interned, the Swedish Mission took over the work of the Leipzig Lutherans and also their compounds in Kodai. Later they bought properties in the same general location, spreading along the Upper Lake Road. The two communities shared a church, alternating Swedish and German services during hill seasons. The German Lutherans belonged to several small mission groups from different origins in Germany, and they worked in different areas in India.

---

89 A similar institution known as Woodstock School, had been established in the Himalayan hill-station at Mussoorie.

The Germans suffered political hardships during both wars and at least two missions disintegrated. The Breklum Mission bought the Penryn property—a compound adjacent to Loch End, near the lake—which was converted into a boarding home for all German-speaking children.

In the 1920s, the Swedes opened a Swedish elementary school at their Solvik property, located on the Highclerc hill. Tenth-grade students either returned to Sweden for further education, or in an ever-growing tradition, first graduated from Kodaikanal High School.[90] Because of these school and boarding establishments almost all German and Swedish workers in India visited Kodaikanal hill-station regularly to be with their children, to use mission bungalow facilities, or to visit with fellow countrymen.

There were other European schools of temporary duration which were influential in their day. One such was the Montessori School, Maria Montessori opened while she was interned in Kodai for two years during World War II. During this time she ran a school for young children of all nationalities, and also organized a training course for teachers to which two successive groups of students from all parts of India were able to take the opportunity to study under her guidance.

---

[90] In 1970 the Swedes sold the Solvik property to Kodaikanal School and moved to their completed new school and boarding at the Swedish Settlement on the Upper Lake Road.

APPENDIX D

Reunions

The Kodai classes of '55 and '56 have held a number of reunions:

2021: September 19 to 24 in Sedona, Arizona:

1st row: Molly (Schmitthenner) Lesnick; Ruth (Vassar) Burgess, Bonnie King, Jane (Gibbs) Cummings, Alice (Graham) Silver, Pat (Wood) Remias, Ruth (Voss) Harris, Miggie (Carman) Tegenfeldt, Bobbie (Voss) Chase, Meg Thomas. 2nd row: Stan Burgess, Stan King, Mark Garrison, Nancy Garrison, Paul Heusinkveld, Donna Beth Wiebe, Gwen (Hiebert) Schroth, Jo (Hiebert) Sorensen. 3rd row: David Wiebe, Tom Byrnes, John Remias, Richard Garden, Paul Wiebe, Ed Tegenfeldt, Owen Thomas.

Not pictured: Bernice Dueck, Loey (Hiebert) Knapp, Margie Graham, Michelle Heusinkveld, Steve Sorensen.

The reunion was held in spite of taking place during the ongoing Covid pandemic; nonetheless, it was a wonderful reunion, enjoyed by all and a welcome break from the loneliness of the pandemic's isolation.

2023: January 15 to 20 in Jacksonville and St. Augustine, Florida

The reunion was a Road Scholar tour, "Amelia Island and St. Augustine: Coastal Treasures in Florida," wholly dedicated to Kodai alumni.

Left to right: Ben Chase, Bobbie Voss Chase, Ruth Voss Harris, John Remias, Lowey Thoms Dickason, Owen Thomas, Molly Schmitthenner Lesnick, Alan Lesnick, Ed Tegenfeldt, Jo Hiebert Sorensen, Pat Wood Remias, Margie Hiebert, Miggie Carman Tegenfeldt, David Wiebe, Jean Towle Reed, Gwen Hiebert Schroth, Paul Heusinkveld.
Not pictured: David Dickason.

2024: September 8 to 14 in Quebec City, Quebec, Canada

The reunion was another Road Scholar tour, "Whales, Fjords and French Canada: Saguenay and the St. Lawrence," wholly dedicated to Kodai alumni. It began and ended in Quebec City, with a four-day trip to Tadoussac, Quebec which included whale-watching as well as touring the local fjord of the Saguenay River and a number of museums along the coast of the Saint Lawerence Seaway. The reunion also included Kodai School kids and graduates from classes other than '55 and '56.

Attendees of the 2024 reunion in Quebec (left to right): Frank Emerson, Ed Tegenfeldt, Mary Emerson, Ruth Voss Harris, Don Fletcher, Gwen Hiebert Schroth, Carla Fletcher, Jo Hiebert Sorenson, Paul Zorn, Janet Petri Zorn, Pat Remias, Meg Thomas, Frank Remias, Miggie Tegenfeldt, Owen Thomas, Toni Rolles, Paul Heusinkveld, Michelle Heusinkveld. Note that Don Fletcher, Paul Zorn and Paul Heusinkveld are from the Kodai School class of 1968.

Of note, during our time in Tadoussac, we saw dozens of whales, including beluga whales, minke whales, humpback whales, and even a blue whale.

The above mentioned reunions are just a few of the many reunions that the Kodai classes of '55 and '56 have held to celebrate the extraordinary and exotic childhoods they share in common and the strong life-long friendships that developed by boarding at Kodai School. Those years as missionary—and diplomatic, business, etc.—kids were in a different era that is hard to relate to in modern day times and society. These Kodai Kids experienced history and everyday life in a way that cannot be realized anymore.

The reunions serve as a time reaffirm friendships; to recount stories of their exotic childhoods in India, Kodai School, and life since graduation; to share in eating Indian cuisine; to share our stories of adjusting to the western world; to try to make sense of how different the world has become from that we knew in our youth; and to just have a lot of fun.

Thankfully, the classes of 1955 and 1956 have invited other Kodai Kids—and their spouses and friends—from other graduating classes of Kodai School to join them in their reunions. For those of us who were not part of the classes of '55 and '56, it has been an honor to have been so invited and to share in such fun and memorable occasions. Such times put the world in a better light that is too beneficial to be missed.

There's discussion among the Kodai School graduates of '55 and '56—and their spouses and friends—of holding another Road Scholar reunion in 2025. So, we need to stay tuned.

BIBLIOGRAPHY

Addleton, Jonathan S. *Some Far and Distant Place: Muslim-Christian Encounters Through the Eyes of a Child*. University of Georgia Press, 2002.

Alter, Stephen. *All the Way to Heaven*. Henry Holt and Company, 1998.

Barss, Marcia E. *Far from Home.*, Victoria, BC, Friesen Press, 2021.

Chamberlain, Mary. *Fifty Years in Foreign Fields*. NY, Abbott Press, 1925.

Chenoweth, John. *Sent: Reflections on Mission, Boarding School and Childhood.* Monroe, IL, 2020.

Cordell, Ruth Lightfoot. *A Missionary's Daughter in India*. 2008

Crossette, Barbara. T*he Great Hill Stations of Asia*. Westview Press, a Division of HaperCollins Publishers, Inc., 1998.

Cummings, Jane Gibbs. *In Celebration: Kodaikanal International School Centennial,* KW International, Color Press, Walla Walla, WA, KW International, Color Press, 2000.

DeLong, Gordon and Alma. *Letters from India, 1945-1967*. Mission Press, 2021.

Dickason, David G., *Faith, Hope, and Love, The Hakeem's Journey*. Holland, MI, Van Raalte Press, 2022.

Dopirak, Margaret H. Essebagger. *Missionary Kid, Born in India, Bound for America*. 2016.

Harrison, Timothy S. *Before Oil: Memories of an American Missionary Family in the Persian Gulf, 1920–1939*. Rumford, RI, Rumford Books, 2008.

Heusinkveld, Paul A. *Elephant Baseball: A Missionary Kid's Tale*. Grand Rapids, MI, Eerdmans, 2017.

Heusinkveld, Paul A. *Margaret's Mission: To Arabia, Africa, and India*. Grand Rapids, MI, Van Raalte Press, 2021.

Heusinkveld, Paul A. *Returning to Kodai School,* Mindscapes Press, 2024.

Kraft, George C., III. *A Place to Call Home: A Missionary Kid's Tale*. Holland, MI, Van Raalte Press, 2022.

Luidens, Donald, *Seeds of Hope, Hate, and Change*. Holland, MI: Van Raalte Press, 2020.

Miedema, Virgil, *Murree, a Glimpse Through the Forest*. Amur Maple Books, New Delhi and Washington DC: Amur Maple Books, 2002.

Miedema, Virgil, and Stephanie Spaid Miedema. *Mussoorie and Landour*, New Delhi, India, Rupa Publications, 2014.

Mills, Andrew. *Home in India: A Pilgrimage with People and Poverty in South India*, Eugene, Oregon: Resource Publications, 2021.

Mitchell, Nora. *The Hill-Station: Kodaikanal*, Chicago, IL, The University of Chicago, Department of Geography, 1972.

Mondol, Harold Ananta Kuma., *Passage from India*, East Lansing, MI, Michigan State University, 2021.

Murray, Elaine Delong, and Marcia Barss. *The Elephant Ride*, Hemming Hill Publishing House, 2021.

Poffenberger Mark. *Grassroots Forest Protection: Eastern Indian Experiences*, Asia Forest Network, 1996.

Poffenberger, Mark. *Village Voices, Forest Choices; Joint Forest Management*, Oxford University Press, 1998.

Ralston, Ruth Stevens. *Maharajahs, Monkeys and Mangoes*, 2010.

Schmitthenner, Sam. *Ramblings with Ruth*, Quiet Waters Publications, 2003.

Schroth, Gwendolyn Hiebert, *Curry Corduroy and the Call*, Denver, CO, Outskirts Press Inc., 2011.

Scudder, Lewis R. *The Arabian Mission Story*. Grand Rapids, MI: Eerdmans, 1998.

Unrau, Ruth. *Hill Station Teacher, A Life with India in it*. North Newton, Kansas: Kidron Creek Publishers, 1997.

Vandrick, Stephanie. *Growing up withe God and Empire, A Postcolonial Analysis of 'Missionary Kid' Memoirs*. Thompson-Shore, Inc, 2019.

Van Ess, Dorothy. *Pioneers in the Arab World*. Grand Rapids, MI, Eerdmans, 1974.

INDEX

Made in the USA
Las Vegas, NV
04 October 2024

96284875R00184